BYRON AND ROMANTICISM

This collection of essays represents twenty-five years of work by one of the most important critics of Romanticism and Byron studies, Jerome McGann. The collection demonstrates McGann's evolution as a scholar, editor, critic, theorist, and historian. His "General analytic and historical introduction" to the collection presents a meditation on the history of his own research on Byron, in particular how scholarly editing interacted with the theoretical innovations in literary criticism over the last quarter of the twentieth century. McGann's receptiveness to dialogic forms of criticism is also illustrated in this collection, which contains an interview and concludes with a dialogue between McGann and the editor. Many of these essays have previously been available only in specialized scholarly journals. Now McGann's influential work on Byron can be appreciated by new generations of students and scholars.

JEROME McGANN is the John Stewart Bryan University Professor, University of Virginia, and the Thomas Holloway Professor of Victorian Media and Culture, Royal Holloway, University of London. He is the author of *Byron, Fiery Dust* (1962) and *Don Juan In Context* (1972) and the editor of *Lord Byron: The Complete Poetical Works* (1980–1992).

JAMES SODERHOLM is Fulbright Scholar and Associate Professor of English and American Literature at Charles University in Prague. He is the author of *Fantasy, Forgery, and the Byron Legend* (1996) and *Beauty and the Critic: Aesthetics in an Age of Cultural Studies* (1997).

CAMBRIDGE STUDIES IN ROMANTICISM 50

BYRON AND ROMANTICISM

CAMBRIDGE STUDIES IN ROMANTICISM

This series aims to foster the best new work in one of the most challenging fields within English literary studies. From the early 1780s to the early 1830s a formidable array of talented men and women took to literary composition, not just in poetry, which some of them famously transformed, but in many modes of writing. The expansion of publishing created new opportunities for writers, and the political stakes of what they wrote were raised again by what Wordsworth called those "great national events" that were "almost daily taking place": the French Revolution, the Napoleonic and American wars, urbanisation, industrialisation, religious revival, an expanded empire abroad, and the reform movement at home. This was an enormous ambition, even when it pretended otherwise. The relations between science, philosophy, religion, and literature were reworked in texts such as *Frankenstein* and *Biographia Literaria*; gender relations in *A Vindication of the Rights of Woman* and *Don Juan*; journalism by Cobbett and Hazlitt; poetic form, content, and style by the Lake School and the Cockney School. Outside Shakespeare studies, probably no body of writing has produced such a wealth of response or done so much to shape the responses of modern criticism. This indeed is the period that saw the emergence of those notions of "literature" and of literary history, especially national literary history, on which modern scholarship in English has been founded.

The categories produced by Romanticism have also been challenged by recent historicist arguments. The task of the series is to engage both with a challenging corpus of Romantic writings and with the changing field of criticism they have helped to shape. As with other literary series published by Cambridge, this one will represent the work of both younger and more established scholars, on either side of the Atlantic and elsewhere.

For a complete list of titles published see end of book.

BYRON AND ROMANTICISM

JEROME McGANN
The John Stewart Bryan University Professor, University of Virginia

EDITED BY
JAMES SODERHOLM
Associate Professor, Charles University, Prague

PUBLISHED BY THE PRESS SYNDICATE OF THE UNIVERSITY OF CAMBRIDGE
The Pitt Building, Trumpington Street, Cambridge, United Kingdom

CAMBRIDGE UNIVERSITY PRESS
The Edinburgh Building, Cambridge CB2 2RU, UK
40 West 20th Street, New York, NY 10011-4211, USA
477 Williamstown Road, Port Melbourne, VIC 3207, Australia
Ruiz de Alarcón 13, 28014 Madrid, Spain
Dock House, The Waterfront, Cape Town 8001, South Africa

http://www.cambridge.org

First published 2002

Printed in the United Kingdom at the University Press, Cambridge

Typeface Baskerville Monotype 11/12.5 pt. *System* LaTeX 2ε [TB]

A catalogue record for this book is available from the British Library

ISBN 0 521 80958 4 hardback
ISBN 0 521 00722 4 paperback

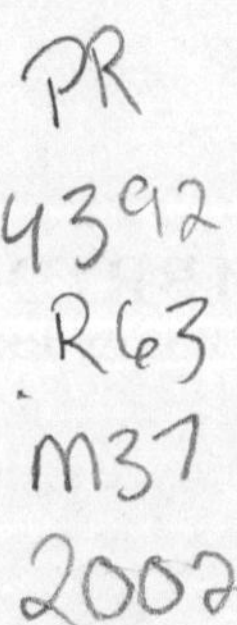

Contents

Acknowledgments

This book would not have appeared but for the insistence and persistence of two dear friends, James Chandler and James Soderholm. I hope it meets some of their standards and expectations.

Because the material has been culled from various essays published over the years in different venues, I have revised the original texts, often somewhat heavily. I thank the editors for giving their permission to reprint pieces from the following books and journals.

"A point of reference," in *Historical Studies and Literary Criticism*. © 1985. Reprinted by permission of The University of Wisconsin Press.

"Byron and Romanticism: an interview with Jerome McGann," in *New Literary History*, 32 (2001), 47–66. Reprinted by permission of the Editor of *New Literary History*.

"Literature, meaning, and the discontinuity of fact," in *The Uses of Literary History*, ed. Marshall Brown (1995). Reprinted by permission of Duke University Press.

"Byron and the anonymous lyric," in *The Byron Journal*, ed. Bernard Beatty, (1992). Reprinted by permission of the editor.

"What difference do the circumstances of publication make to the interpretation of a literary work?" in *Literary Pragmatics*, ed. Roger D. Sell, (1991). Reprinted by permission of Routledge.

"Byron and the lyric of sensibility," in *European Romantic Review*, 4 (Summer 1993), ed. Grant Scott. Reprinted by permission of the editor.

"Poetry, 1780–1832," in *The Columbia History of Poetry*, ed. Carl Woodring. © 1994 Columbia University Press. Reprinted by permission of the publisher.

"Private poetry, public deception," in *The Politics of Poetic Form*, ed. Charles Bernstein, Segue Foundation (1990). Reprinted by permission of the publisher.

"Byron, mobility, and the politics of historical ventriloquism," in *Romanticism Past and Present* 9:1 (Winter 1985). Reprinted by permission of the former editor.

"Milton and Byron," in *The Keats–Shelley Memorial Association, Bulletin Number XXV* (1974), ed. Dorothy Hewlett, pp. 9–25.

" 'My brain is feminine': Byron and the poetics of deception," in *Byron. Augustan and Romantic*, ed. Andrew Rutherford (MacMillan, 1990).

"Hero with a thousand faces: the rhetoric of Byronism," in *Studies in Romanticism*, 31 (Fall 1992).

"History, herstory, theirstory, ourstory," in *Theoretical Issues in Literary History*, ed. David Perkins, Harvard English Studies 15, 1991.

"Rethinking Romanticism," in *English Literary History*, 59 (1992).

"An interview with Jerome McGann," in *Cambridge Quarterly* (Fall 1993), with Steven Earnshaw and Philip Shaw, recorded at Warwick University, England.

"Byron and Wordsworth," with thanks to the School of English Studies, University of Nottingham.

General analytical and historical introduction

This is a book of "double reflection," as we used to say twenty-five years ago (early 1970s), when the earliest of the writings gathered here was first published. In a moment I'll try to explain why it is, and also why I'm putting this book together now.

Double reflection, perhaps one has to recall, is a Hegelian/Marxist phrase that named the kinds of theoretical passions driving so much of everyone's work in the late 1960s and early 1970s. It seems slightly quaint now – a sort of kangaroo among the beauties of current scholarship.

"Return with me now to those thrilling days of yesteryear!" That was how the narrator introduced *The Lone Ranger* radio program, a passion of mine twenty-five years before I wrote anything in this book: "The Lone Ranger," that is to say another (mid twentieth-century) avatar of The Giaour, The Corsair, Mazeppa. Beyond Baudelaire, Berlioz, Kierkegaard, Melville, Nietzsche, etc., the Byronic generations do go on.

But in 1964, when I began my research on Byron and Romanticism, those generations had been dispersed almost entirely into popular cultural venues. A first reflexive move for me was therefore my graduate research: a doctoral thesis on Byron and the theoretical problems of "biographical criticism." I wanted to study why Byron, who for nearly a hundred years fairly defined, in the broadest international context, the "meaning" of Romanticism, had all but disappeared from the most serious forms of academic and professional attention. It seemed odd that such a glaring historical anomaly, not to say contradiction, should not be at the very center of scholarly attention. For the problem raised crucial theoretical issues.

I am writing this very sentence in January 2000, in the same room – the Rare Books Room of the British Library (erstwhile, "The North Library") – where I wrote my doctoral thesis in 1965. *Non sum qualis eram* – but more importantly, neither are Romantic studies. Byron does not loom across the European scene as he did in the nineteenth century but there has clearly been a return of the repressed. (Would that the same could be said for another figure of immensity, Walter Scott! But even as I write this "the dawn is red," so to say.)

Why this book, then? If the essential reflexive point was to rethink Byron and, through him, the history and forms of Romanticism, surely the past thirty-five years testify to an achievement of that project. And I'm uninterested in simply gathering a certain record of my written work, especially since my sense of time has grown, alas, somewhat more acute. The digital revolution has set in motion, especially in the past ten years, movements and changes that are upheaving humanities studies at every level. Making sure that scholars and educators, not technocrats and administrators, have a hand in guiding and – in Shelley's sense – "imagining" these changes has become a daily educational concern. Under those circumstances, what is the point of a book like this?

So, double reflection. The academic history that these essays entered and sought to influence has developed along various dynamic lines, many of them conflicting lines, during the past twenty-five years. Reading the essays in the context of the distinguished series of books they are now joining, I am most struck by the differences between nearly all of these books and nearly all of the essays.

Of course all exhibit a "turn to history," a turn taken in the essays and exhibited in the series' books. But the latter engage a much more various socio-cultural order of materials than the essays do. An objective reporter – myself, for instance – might say that Michel Foucault, Raymond Williams, and Pierre Bourdieu are the books' presiding deities whereas Mark Pattison, Millman Parry, and Galvano della Volpe haunt the pages of the essays. "Byron and Romanticism" orbits in a universe of textual theory, literary-critical method, and a certain history of scholarship and education.

It is this difference that interests me and makes me believe these essays have something new to say.

– But they're the same essays. Or have you made some kind of radical changes to them?

– Some changes to the texts, yes, but nothing that alters the semantic content in an appreciable way.

– What's new then?

– What's new is the way we live now. Take any literary work, preserve its semantic – even its documentary – identity as best you can, and then track its changes of meaning as it passes through the attention of different places, times, circumstances. Dante Gabriel Rossetti, taking his cue

> directly from Dante, commonly handled his works in this way. He shuffles "the same" poem into different contexts again and again, as if he knew it was not a self-identical "thing," as if he were determined to expose its many-mindedness – how it is many-minded – in concrete and determinate ways. Rossetti's works are interesting partly because, more clearly than many artists and poets, he makes a drama of artistic meaning as performative and eventual. We still often seem to think that art's multiple meanings are a function of something they possess on their own, inherently or essentially as it were. But the truth is that meanings multiply like lives, through intercourse.

The exchanges I seek are with the scholarship and educational scene around me, and that is represented in a distinguished way by the books in this series. In this respect I have two general subjects I want to raise here as a preface to the essays. One has to do with the relatively narrow methodology that characterizes these essays (as opposed to what we find in the series' books). The second concerns the stances we may take as scholars or teachers – as educators – toward our work.

THEORY AND METHOD

There is a history here that must be briefly replicated. In 1970, by a sequence of odd chances, I began the project to edit Byron's complete poetical works. To that point I had no interest in or knowledge about editing. My work had been dominated by "theoretical" and philosophical pursuits. I wrote a long MA thesis on the theoretical conflict between the Chicago Neo-Aristotelians and the New Criticism, and a doctoral thesis on the theoretical problem of biographical method (in the general context of the formalist and structural models of criticism that were dominant at the time).

Editing Byron brought a nearly complete deconstruction of my thinking about literature, art, and culture generally. The subject is too large for this place. It's sufficient to say, I think, that the editorial work threw me down to where all our literary ladders start: in the concrete circumstances of those material and ideological histories that engage the production and transmission of "texts" (in the pre-Barthesian sense of that term): texts as documents made and remade in a theoretically endless series of stochastically generated feedback loops, all very particular.

Like so much cultural criticism of recent years, the books in this series illustrate just how intricate that stochasis is – at how many levels it operates, in what remarkable ways these levels connect and interact. Placed alongside it, as these essays now are, my work seems – *is* – limited and restricted in focus. The objective reader, myself, easily sees in the essays the permanent influence of New Critical "close reading" methods.

We shall have to reconsider the current relevance of such methods for a scholarship and pedagogy that has recommitted itself to historicist models of criticism – models specifically cast off by the New Critics who promoted the practices of "close reading." Let me set that matter aside for a moment, however, in order to comment on textuality and editing. These subjects and their practices are profoundly important at this specific historical moment.

For some years now "Theory" has lapsed as a driving force in literary and cultural scholarship. The main lines of the work have been felt as complete (for the time being) and we observe a widespread process of implementation and refinement.

"Theory" remains volatile and exploratory in one area, however: in textual and editorial studies. This remarkable situation is the effect of an historical phenomenon affecting every level of society, not least of all education and the humanities: the breakthrough of Internet and digital technology into our normal practices of work and living. Digital media are ultimately forms of textuality. It is therefore unsurprising that the first practico/theoretical explorations of these technologies in the humanities should be made, as they are, at the foundational levels of literary scholarship and education: in the libraries and archives and in the work of editors, linguists, and textual scholars of all kinds. One has to return to the fifteenth century to find a situation comparable to the one we now witness and participate in.

None of the scholarly works in this series has been significantly marked by these notable events. None makes use of the technology and none engages the theories and methods being experimented with and developed out of this technology. Yet digitization and intermedia are already altering the way we perceive and understand cultural phenomena. The recent explosion of "History of the Book" studies is a direct function of the nexus of historical studies and humanities computing, for the new technology has driven our view of books and texts to a higher level of abstract perception.[1] The moment when one can make a virtual book, when you can reconstruct it according to the design protocols of computer technology, you realize that you "understand" the book in a new way and at another level of consciousness. Similarly, recent years have shown remarkable explorations into the structure and relation of image and text. The most dynamic (not to say the most volatile) developments in these areas are being driven by digital technologies. Indeed, we are beginning to realize how and why we can deal with (analyze, read, interpret) text as image and vice versa. The realizations emerge, however, not from the reflections of "Theory" in the traditional sense, but from people actually building and implementing computerized tools and instruments.

Why do I raise these matters here? Because these studies of Byron and Romanticism were all shaped in a trajectory of textual and editorial work that reached its fruition only in the hypermedia theory and electronic scholarship that has dominated my work since I went to Caltech in 1981. At that point several things began to become clear. First, that textual theory and editorial practice were and had to be the foundation of all literary studies; second, that all synthetic and interpretive operations – what used to be called "The Higher Criticism" – were implicitly shaped "in the last instance," as the Marxists would say, by these forms of so-called "Lower Criticism" (the processes of language and document transmission; or, the materials, the means, and the modes of production); and finally, that at certain critical historical moments the only theory that could serve as such would have to be some kind of particular, goal-driven practice.[2]

When I began my work as a scholar, Byron and editing were both marginal literary concerns. To work on Byron in 1965 was perforce to work on a subject of "purely/merely/largely historical interest." By 1980 the adverb in that phrase would be replaced by others. But to *edit* Byron between 1970 and 1992 was to drive the historical issues in special directions. For one thing – I will come back to this – it focused my attention on the field of the closely read text. For another, it made me aware as I had never been that the literary works descending to us have been made and remade by specific people and in particular institutional settings. Finally, I saw quite clearly that all these makings were historically relative and relevant, and that the edition I was making was of the same kind. "Romanticism" itself was objective and determinate only because (and as) it had been made, revised, and refashioned under different conditions by different people with different agendas and purposes. (A relativist perspective had of course been fairly widespread in the academy since the early 1960s at least, and it would grow more acute during the 1970s and 1980s. The perspective did not develop robust historicist forms and methods until the 1980s and 1990s.)

Those last two effects of my editorial work changed everything since they led me to execute the edition under a regular attention to its circumstantial character. Editing *Lord Byron. The Complete Poetical Works* (1981–1992) thus became a continual reflection on the limits of its own design, and on the material and historical determinants of those limits. Eventually I found myself needing, seeking after, critical and scholarly instruments that could incarnate, so to speak, those kinds of reflexive and experimental demands. History would become the lover of necessity. Editing Byron in codex form passed over to editing Rossetti in online hypermedia: from editing as a closed system to "Editing as a Theoretical Pursuit."

THINKING AND WRITING

These essays tell that history, I think, more clearly than the edition of Byron – which was constructed during the period when these essays were written and which created the conditions, if not all the conditions, that made the essays possible and even necessary. The clarity of the essays is in certain ways greater than the edition because of a difference in form and genre. Nothing appears more monumental, more *finished*, than a large scholarly edition. The volatile history I summarized in the previous section of this Introduction is latent but largely invisible in *Lord Byron. The Complete Poetical Works*. The forms of such things wear robes of authority, order, and a massive *integritas*. They lend themselves not to openness and self-reflection, least of all to change. Narrativity, even in a discursive mode, has greater flexibilities.

Under the horizon of a literary practice that has idealized the standard critical edition, however, critical commentary itself reflects that aspiration to – that apparition of – finishedness. Walter Pater, M. H. Abrams, Harold Bloom: all are pilgrims of the absolute, more or less modest, more or less imperial. Even writing in the essay form we have wanted to get things right, to say something *definitive* (the supreme quality, we used to imagine, of the critical edition). And while we can achieve this under certain limitations and conditions, we can never know that we have done it. (Alas, we often *imagine that we do know such things*.)

In certain disciplines – engineering for example, perhaps the hard sciences – aspiring to correctness is a needful thing. But in humanities I think the aspiration is misguided and finally misleading. The aspiration should rather be toward thoroughness, clarity, candor. Being clear, open, and as meticulous as possible are goals exactly as problematic as being correct and complete. They are goals, however, resting in an initial reflection on the self and its uncertainties.

As I read these essays now (objectively) I recall some of the stories they tell, some of the histories – Lilliputian, intramural – they reflect. One of these I've already told. Another interests me as well and seems worth retelling here. It's the history of the (failed) pursuit of a satisfying form of critical commentary, a form to mirror or index the editorial instruments I also grew to need. As I said earlier, when I began trying to make a critical edition of Byron I knew virtually nothing about editing. Making the edition was a passage from the utter dark. I have put "Byron and Milton" at the beginning of this book because as an essay it appears to me the least successful in the collection. It's in *fact* the earliest of the essays, but that's not why it comes where it does. I initially thought not to include it at all, it seemed so unsatisfactory. But in *truth* it did not seem unsatisfactory to me when I wrote it in 1972, it only seems so now. So now it also seems an effective, even a satisfactory way to begin a story of failure. It's also satisfying to admit that my first impulse was to exclude it. That's an important element in the story too.

Note that I still think I'm correct about many things I wrote in the essay. Certain matters of fact are beyond dispute, like the clear literary allusions. But the essay isn't satisfying because of those matters of fact. However, it seemed satisfactory in 1972 – it was written, I now think I remember, to make a show of myself at the English Institute – in January 2000 it's satisfying to put it at the head of this book and to wrap it in this commentary.

I would grow dissatisfied with that kind of essay and would try to escape it. For a while I was much taken with the style of the polemical pamphlet, and after that with the dialogue. I tried the latter early on, in 1970, and wrote a book in dialogue. It won a prize from a society of poets (!) but seems to have had no other success at all, nor any impact on scholarship.[3] When I returned to the form in the late 1980s I tried to crossbreed it with Poe's hoaxes and then stage the writing as a Wildean truth of masks. These are the critical works I get greatest pleasure from having done.[4] As Wilde wisely said, "Give a man a mask and he will tell you the truth."

– But Jerome, we're always wearing masks.

– This is true, I now see. But once upon a time I thought otherwise. Byron, that masked man and lone ranger, helped to free me from the illusion.

– Because?

– Because I'm a Romanticist and hence completely involved with a "poetry of sincerity." With ideals of the Self, and of self-discovery through a dynamics of spontaneous overflow and reflexive turns. Nor do these operations cease to interest me. But Byron, a great practitioner of such manoeuvres, was also – not always but often, and often enough – their clear-eyed student.

Reading Byron's romantic spontaneities and overflows one came to see that they were masked forms, rhetorical strategies. All gods reside in the human breast, Blake said. So do all poems. They are dictated from the eternity of embodied mind.

– So?

– "Sincerity: if you can fake that you've made it." So goes one of the most notorious proverbs of post-Modernism. It's an X Generation's version of Baudelaire's wonderful address to *his* readers: "Hypocrite lecteur, mon semblable, mon frère." The source, for Baudelaire at any rate, is Byron.

– It's grotesque, cynical – hopeless and helpless.

– If you say so, perhaps. But not necessarily. The problem lies in the ways that culture – that is to say *ideology*, that is to say *false consciousness* – enlists works of imagination to its causes. Culture is always seeking to turn poetic tales into forms of worship, "the Wastes of Moral Law" as Blake called these things.

– So the ironist Byron is good, the "sincere" Wordsworth is bad.

– *Please.* I confess I *am* tired of answering that kind of remark. It's just a way to maintain some kind of moral ground as the measure of art. Blake was perfectly right, art has no truck with morality, it's a field of revelations and imitations. Wordsworth is splendid, Byron is splendid. Byron is in fact Wordsworth's salvation, his way away from being possessed by the demons of culture. They are to each other what Blake called Corporeal Enemies – that is to say, they are Spiritual Friends.

– Each others' masks.

– Just so. Each is the other's limit state and "bounding line." But in our day – in this Blakean "State" we are passing through, Byron has been the salvific Voice of the Devil – because our Heaven and our Law have been – in the terms I've been using here – "Wordsworthian."

– At least they have been for *you*.

– Yes, that's right. What I'm saying is only objectively – it's not generally – true.

– (You keep insisting on this matter of your *objectivity*! What's all that about?)

– (Think about it. Anyhow, you're digressing.)

– OK. A key problem here surely lies in the way critical and theoretical writing – commentaries and reflections on primary acts of imagination – commit themselves to perceiving, defining, and even acquiring "general" truth. "To generalize is to be an Idiot" Blake declares. Of course it isn't at all idiotic to generalize – unless you're an artist! But from the artistic point of view, works of culture will always be regarded with suspicion. For works of culture do and must aspire to general authority, and the greatest of these works achieve some degree of that authority.

But artists and works of art occupy an equivocal position in the world of culture, as Plato saw very clearly. His view was that the poets and artists should be expelled, that they were at best charmingly unreliable.

He went on to say – it's important to recall this – that they might come back if they "or their friends" could make a case for their work *in other-than-artistic terms*.[5] It never occurred to Plato that artistic work *as such* – not art as mediated by philosophers or critics – possessed intellectual or cognitive authority – or that this authority rested exactly in the peculiar intellectual character of artistic work: that it embodied a reflexive form of unmediated knowing. For Plato – and the view remains widespread, if much less lucidly held – art is a craft, not a method of knowing the world and reflecting on the self. Building on the empiricism of Enlightenment, Romanticism installed "The Aesthetic" as a form of knowing. The institutions of culture have always resisted this claim of art, and in our own epoch, when the claim has been so powerfully advanced, the resistance took an accommodating form. So "the function of criticism at the present time" has been to translate works of art into other cultural terms – as if they could not speak on their own behalf and authority. (That "present time" isn't just Arnold's specific Victorian time, it is the period of the past 200 years *in general.*)

The clearest way to see how an Aesthetic form works is by comparing it to the operational procedures of a different form of knowing. Logic, for example. Peter Ochs has recently exposed with remarkable clarity the development of Peirce's work by tracing the history of its errors and its attempts to correct those errors. Most important, Ochs tracks the work in the context of Ochs's own self-reflexive thought. The Peirce we encounter in Ochs is a special creature developed from a kind of double helix, one strand "Peircean," the other "Ochsian," with each strand fused to the other in order to generate this new intelligent creature, this study of Peirce by Ochs. Here is Ochs's general description of what he is doing:

> My thesis is that pragmatic definition is not a discrete act of judgment or classification, but a *performance of correcting other, inadequate definitions of imprecise things*. Pragmatic reasoning is thus a different sort of reasoning than the kind employed in defining things precisely. It is a corrective activity . . . My thesis is therefore not a thesis in the usual sense. Since my claim is that to define pragmatically is to correct and that to correct is to read, my "thesis" is better named my "corrective reading." But that is not quite right, either, since my claim is that reading cannot be done "in general," or "for everyone," but only for someone: for some community of readers . . . And this is not to correct Peirce *per se* but *to correct problems in the way Peirce would be read by a given community*. The point is not that Peirce is wrong and I can see better! Not at all. Only that his pragmatism can show itself to another thinker only in the way that thinker acquires the practice of corrective reading . . . To exhibit

the meaning of pragmatism will therefore be *to perform some way of correcting the meaning of pragmatism.* For this study, I read Peirce's writings on pragmatism as his corrective performance *of* pragmatism, and I offer the following chapters as one way of pragmatically and thus correctively studying his performance.[6]

I regret having to set aside so much of this interesting work in order to attend upon one matter: the issue of intellectual generality. Ochs says his reading is not "in general," and while this is the case in the sense he means, that is no sense that would make sense to an artist. Ochs proposes to engage Peirce's work at a secondary level of generality – not "in general" (universal) but "under the horizon of generality" (for a certain "community"). To do that is to make something other than an aesthetic commitment to the work being done, it is to make a moral or social commitment. (Let it be said that artists themselves make such commitments all the time, as they should, but that in doing so they are putting their art to some social use – for better and/or for worse.)

Of course it might be objected that I am merely pointing out how we distinguish an abstract or ideal "form" in all forms of thought, and hence that Aesthetic Form is merely a way of referring to that entity (what Aristotle called the "formal cause" of anything). In this sense Logic, Theology – whatever: all forms of thought may have their formal causes distinguished.

(Who is making this argument, who is writing these sentences?)

But Aesthetic Form cannot be subsumed by formal cause. It is formal cause perceived and functioning as material cause – to stay with Aristotle's categories. And its final cause is indeterminable from any perspective available to us. In this sense Aesthetic Form is like that fabulous medieval "circle whose center is everywhere but whose circumference is nowhere" – but only *like*, because this will always be a circle with a determinate material form, what Blake called (playing with his words) a "Bounding Line." Blake and all artists *can* thus play with their words, or whatever they work with, exactly because their primary care is to operate with their ideas through their *materials* (for an artist – Shelley and Byron illustrate this unmistakably – to think is to make something, to make something concrete). Material forms, articulations like "Bounding Line" (or the artist's physical marking of some such line), are physically determinate but cognitively flooded. Underdetermined cognitively, overdetermined materially.

BYRONIC TEXTUALITY

Ochs set about to correct Peirce's errors via a pragmaticist reading of Peirce's work. It reminds one of Blake's efforts to "correct Milton's errors," which is as we know one of the main themes and "leading tendencies" of Blake's work. It *is* a leading tendency because, in Blake's view, giving a form to Milton's errors is a way to expose his own. Unlike Blake's, Ochs's writing does not turn his critique simultaneously into a self-critique. This is not to denigrate his study but only to point out a generic limitation of the critical powers of discursive form.

I have brought Peirce (and Ochs) into this discussion because their work helps clarify the contemporary critical relevance of Byron's poetic discourse. Ochs recovers for us a Peirce who gradually moved from pragmatism to pragmaticism, from a philosophic program of error-correction to a program reflecting on its own processes of error-correction. In this movement Peirce discovers the form of the existential graph, a form of philosophic commentary and reflection that clearly seeks to break free of the material limitations of discursive form.[7] Peirce's existential graphs are the equivalent of Kierkegaard's masks and, later, of the dialogical drama Wittgenstein stages in the *Philosophical Investigations*. In each case we observe a theoretical mind seeking for critical forms that will escape the limits of discursive form.

Poets do not employ language discursively and the example of Blake, just glanced at, illustrates one important result of their choice. In this respect poetry will always be the demon – that is to say, the redemptive dream – of philosophy. In our day Byron has emerged, has returned, as a demon of great consequence. We have had fifty years to look back with clarity and horror and an inevitably cynical wonderment at the spectacle of Western Civilization. We have an Imperial view of this scene, we are – as Byron knew himself to be, as Wordsworth (for example) deliberately chose *not* to be – "citizens of the world." Byron's eyes have been here before, have seen all this. Most important of all, Byron saw himself as part of the scene: a player, a participant, "doomed to inflict or bear." What a difference it makes to survey the Great Wars' bestial floors from the vantage of Vietnam, Palestine, Northern Ireland – Bosnia, Kosovo, Cambodia, Chile, Uganda . . .

How does one *live* in such a world and with such a disillusioned view of it, being in it? Byron's verse poses that question over and over again – it is one of his "leading tendencies," to pose the question *and* to keep posing it. Here is one famous posing (from *Childe Harold's Pilgrimage IV*):

But let us ponder boldly; 'tis a base
Abandonment of reason to resign
Our right of thought, our last and only place
Of refuge; this, at least, shall still be mine:
Though from our birth the faculty divine
Is chained and tortured, cabin'd, cribb'd, confined
And bred in darkness, lest the truth should shine
Too brightly for the unpreparéd mind,
The beam pours in, for time and skill will couch the blind.
(st. 127)

The truth of this text comes as the contradiction between its "what" and "how." "[R]eason" and a "right of thought" are declared "our last and only place of refuge," and the argument is that a persistence of disciplined inquiry will bring enlightenment. But even assuming this actual result, what then? To see thus clearly, we now grow to see, is to be astonished by a visible darkness stretching back across the forty-nine stanzas before this one and forward to forty-four that directly follow it, all linked to "the electric chain of that despair" (st. 172) which is the Byronic byword. You shall know the truth and it will not set you free: that is an essential part of the message here.

It is not the whole of the message – or rather, the text is imagining itself beyond its discursive form. The chain of despair is electric, forbidding rest or any but momentary comforts. To be Byronic is precisely *not* to be laid asleep in body to become a living soul. So beyond the dream of reason and its right of thought is the driving verse, the famous passion emblemized by those astonishing enjambments that fractured for ever the purity of the Spenserian inheritance:

I know not why—but standing thus by thee
It seems as if I had thine inmate known,
Thou Tomb! And other days come back to me
With recollected music, though the tone
Is changed and solemn, like the cloudy groan
Of dying thunder on the distant wind;
Yet could I seat me by this ivied stone
Till I had bodied forth the heated mind,
Forms from the floating wreck which Ruin leaves behind;

And from the planks, far shatter'd o'er the rocks,
Build me a little bark of hope, once more
To battle with the ocean and the shocks
Of the loud breakers, and the ceaseless roar
Which rushes on the solitary shore

Where all lies founder'd that was ever dear:
But could I gather from the wave-worn store
Enough for my rude boat, where should I steer?
There woos no home, no hope, nor life, save what is here . . .

There is the moral of all human tales;
'Tis but the same rehearsal of the past;
First Freedom, and then Glory—when that fails,
Wealth, vice, corruption—barbarism at last,
And History, with all her volumes vast,
Hath but *one* page, – 'tis better written here
Where gorgeous Tyranny hath thus amass'd
All treasures, all delights, that eye or ear,
Heart, soul, could seek, tongue ask—Away with words! draw near.

"Admire, exult, despise, laugh, weep, – for here / There is such matter for all feeling: –" (104–106). And so on, relentlessly. It has been said that Byron's verse can't be appreciated in brief quotation. These stanzas illustrate why (and how) that's true. This is verse observing its own passion of thought, the passion of its insistence, its determination to think and think again and again. The imagined "refuge" – the dreams of home, hope, and life – are precisely "here," in these moving lines that signal a decision never to cease this side of an absolute extinction. Nor is there any thought that the thinking will come out "right," for this is thinking that lives in its expenditures. Unlike Wordsworth (once again), Byron's writing begins and thrives in disillusion. At its finest moments it is either ludic or it is failing. Like Beckett, however, the texts rise to unbuild themselves repeatedly. In the process they cast not dark shadows but a kind of invigorated negative textual space. So here "meaning" slips free of every conclusion, including the idea of conclusiveness, and fuses with its eventuality.

Lyric self-expression marks a Romantic ethos, and this verse fairly epitomizes its style. So for a hundred years "Byronism" in poetry was another name for "Romanticism." At that point, with the emergence of Modernism's neo-classical demands, a different style of Romanticism was summoned from the deep Romantic chasm. This was called "The Greater Romantic Lyric."[8] It is not a form that Byron cultivated, and on the one occasion when he undertook it, in Canto III of *Childe Harold*, he did so only to heat it to meltdown. His practice forecast what would emerge in late twentieth-century Romantic scholarship, starting with the immensely influential work of Geoffrey Hartman and Paul DeMan. Romantic lyricism, we came to see, was a field of "aporias" and brave self-conflictions. But this was not to deconstruct the art of Romanticism, it was to break off from a neo-classical reading of that art. (To point this out here, let me hasten to add, is not to say that the neo-classical reading is "wrong," it is merely to signal its case and its kind.)

Byron's cultural re-emergence in the late twentieth century is thus an historical fate. Who else could redeem Romantic self-expression from the conceptual heavens that threatened it? Byron's lyric style became Romanticism's dark angel when his work was officially cast off and set apart. That critical move, which can be given a precise historical locus as we know, would insulate Byron from the aesthetic challenge raised by deconstruction. His work was invisible through deconstructive lenses exactly because it is a discourse of failure, plainly imperfect – a "spoiler's art" whose first aim is to spoil itself.[9]

In the end, however, Byron's poems, like all imaginative work, will be left living after every post-Modernist conceptual form has turned to dry-as-dust. Byron's certain relevance at this particular time lies in the vitality of his dark eminence. "There is a very life in our despair," he famously declared, and the truth of that remark comes not from its idea but from the language which it thrives (so to say). The prose of philosophy and criticism is itself a ludic self-contradicted discourse, even a discourse of failure – deconstructive prose pre-eminently so. Rarely does either discipline admit or seek forms to display those features. A key social function of imaginative form is to offer models of such thinking. And just now Byron may be the paradigmatic model – a "poet's poet," as we used to say.

ONE WORD MORE

Finally, I must say something about the essays' critical style and procedures, which seem to me a function of their general subject – Byron and Romanticism. I've already noted how unlike these essays are compared to the typical work published in this series. The focused interests of editors, bibliographers, and textual scholars (in the most traditional sense of the term) play over these writings of mine, as do the "close reading" procedures of my earliest critical models. This book gives two cheers for their old democracies. Given the privilege they assign to imaginative writing as a touchstone of critical thought, the essays attend upon their subjects' minute particulars, their embodied thinking. At those elementary levels of perception one gains, I believe, a peculiarly clear view of (a) the play of contradictions that constitute all imaginative work, and (b) the performative involvement of the writing itself in its own contradictory elements.

"If this be but a vain belief" – or rather, *how it is and must be* a vain belief – may at least begin to be seen in the critical context these essays have been permitted to enter, and whose differential they have sought.

NOTES

1 See "The Rationale of HyperText," in *Electronic Text. Investigations in Method and Theory*, ed. Kathryn Sutherland (Oxford: Clarendon Press, 1997), 19–46.

2 See "Hideous Progeny, Rough Beasts: Editing as a Theoretical Pursuit," in the 1997 presidential address to the Society for Textual Scholarship, *TEXT II* (1998–1999), 1–16.

3 The 1970 book in dialogue was *Swinburne. An Experiment in Criticism* (Chicago: University of Chicago Press). *The Romantic Ideology* (Chicago: University of Chicago Press, 1983) was consciously written in recollection of some distinguished late eighteenth-century pamphlets.

4 A couple of examples: "Marxism, Romanticism, and post-Modernism: An American Case History," *South Atlantic Quarterly*, 88 (Summer 1989), 605–632; "Literary History, Romanticism, and Felicia Hemans," *Modern Language Quarterly*, 54:2 (June 1993), 215–236 (reprinted in *Revisioning Romanticism. British Women Writers 1776–1837*, ed. Carol Shiner Wilson and Joel Haefner [Philadelphia: University of Pennsylvania Press, 1994], 210–227). "The Alice Fallacy; or, Only God Can Make a Tree. A Dialogue of Pleasure and Instruction," *Chain* 3:2 (Fall 1996), 108–134 (reprinted in *Beauty and the Critic. Aesthetics in the Age of Cultural Studies*, ed. James Soderholm (Tuscaloosa: University of Alabama Press, 1997), 46–73).

5 See *The Republic*, Book x, 607b–608b.

6 See Peter Ochs, *Peirce, Pragmaticism, and the Logic of Scripture* (Cambridge: Cambridge University Press, 1998), 4–5.

7 It is a signal limitation of Ochs's book that he doesn't take up the physical scriptures of Peirce's existential graphs. The term "scripture" in Ochs in fact is a purely ideated term.

8 The phrase of course refers to the justly celebrated essay by M. H. Abrams.

9 For a fuller exploration of this important feature of Byron's work see below, chapter 9.

PART I

CHAPTER I

Milton and Byron

> I am too happy in being coupled in any way with Milton, and shall be glad if they find any points of comparison between him and me.
>
> Byron to Thomas Medwin

WHEN we think of Milton's influence upon English Romanticism the poets who first come to mind are Blake, Wordsworth, Keats, and perhaps Shelley. As for Byron, Milton rightly seems an altogether less dominating forebear since we remember only too well his distaste for blank verse, even Milton's blank verse:

> Blank verse, . . . [except] in the drama, no one except Milton ever wrote who could rhyme . . . I am aware that Johnson has said, after some hesitation, that he could not "prevail upon himself to wish that Milton had been a rhymer" . . . ; but, with all humility, I am not persuaded that the *Paradise Lost* would not have been more nobly conveyed to posterity . . . in the Stanza of Spenser or of Tasso, or in the terza rima of Dante, which the powers of Milton could easily have grafted on our language.[1]

Byron had a number of other criticisms of Milton's poetic craftsmanship, so one is not surprised that Milton did not haunt his work. Nevertheless, Milton's importance for Byron, both in his art and his life, was by no means insignificant.

To speak of Milton's influence upon Byron is, I believe, immediately to close the discussion under two principal headings. The first of these is well known and has to do with Byron's Satanism and the poetic tradition of the criminal hero. Though fairly and frequently treated, the matter has still to be properly elucidated, and the first part of this essay will deal with certain areas of the subject which have not been explained.[2] The second way in which Milton was an important influence upon Byron involves Byron's interpretation and imaginative use of Milton's life. This aspect of Milton's influence did not appear until Byron exiled himself from England in 1816. At this time he began to elaborate an autobiographical myth which was shaped in no small way by his interpretation of Milton's personal and political history. To my knowledge, no scholar has yet seen fit to go into this curious matter. Since the subject is rather complex and little known, I will leave it until after we have looked into the more familiar problem of Byron's Satanism.

I

Though Milton's influence upon Byron's gloomy and problematic heroes begins at least as early as 1812, the subject has always (and properly) been studied from the vantage of 1821–1822, when *Cain* was published and the famous discussion of the play was begun. Byron defended *Cain* against the charge of blasphemy by calling Milton to his defense:

If "Cain" be blasphemous, "Paradise Lost" is blasphemous; and the words . . . "Evil, be thou my good!" are from that very poem, from the mouth of Satan, – and is there anything more in that of Lucifer, in the Mystery? "Cain" is nothing more than a drama, not a piece of argument.

I could not make Lucifer expound the Thirty-nine Articles, nor talk as the Divines do: that would never have suited his purpose, – nor, one would think, theirs. They ought to be grateful to him for giving them a subject to write about. What would they do without evil in the Prince of Evil? Othello's occupation would be gone. I have made Lucifer say no more in his defence than was absolutely necessary, – not half so much as Milton makes his Satan do. I was forced to keep up his dramatic character. *Au reste*, I have adhered closely to the Old Testament, and I defy any one to question my moral. Johnson, who would have been glad of an opportunity of throwing another stone at Milton, redeems him from any censure for putting impiety and even blasphemy into the mouths of his infernal spirits. By what rule, then, am I to have all the blame?[3]

When Leigh Hunt commented upon Byron's arguments later in *Lord Byron and some of his Contemporaries*, he cut through Byron's deliberately "mystifying" remarks. Byron's defence, Hunt says:

is not sincere. "Cain" was undoubtedly meant as an attack upon the crude notions of the Jews respecting evil and its origin. Lord Byron might not have thought much about the matter, when he undertook to write it; but such was his feeling. He was conscious of it; and if he had not been, Mr. Shelley would not have suffered him to be otherwise. But the case is clear from internal evidence. Milton, in his "Paradise Lost," *intended* nothing against the religious opinions of his time; Lord Byron did. The reader of the two poems feels certain of this; and he is right. It is true, the argumentative part of the theology of Milton was so bad, that a suspicion has crossed the minds of some in these latter times, whether he was not purposely arguing against himself; but a moment's recollection of his genuine character and history does it away. Milton was as decidedly a Calvinist at the time he wrote "Paradise Lost," and subject to all the gloomy and degrading sophistries of his sect, as he certainly altered his opinions afterwards, and subsided in a more *Christian* Christianity.[4]

Hunt's criticisms make it plain that Byron's remarks were not so much lies as obfuscations. Byron's careful prose leaves unsaid everything that is truly germane to the issue, for the fact is that Milton's poem is fundamentally fideistic whereas *Cain* is just as radically skeptical. This does not mean that Byron saw Lucifer as his play's moral exemplar; on the contrary, Byron clearly (and sincerely) represented Lucifer in a critical light. But if he gave his diabolic prince certain negative qualities, he also created for him a number of sympathetic contexts, as well as several powerful speeches. Lucifer's parting words to Cain are a stirring rhetorical plea for one of Byron's deepest convictions: intellectual freedom.

The mixed character of Byron's Lucifer makes him a fitting inheritor of that line of post-Miltonic criticism which liked to sympathize with the demon's grandeur or power or suffering. Most of Byron's ideas about Milton, and *Paradise Lost* in particular, have little to do with that odd fragment of literary history, for Byron's Miltonic preoccupations were often of a technical nature. But when Byron did comment upon the character of Milton's Satan, he clearly echoed those eighteenth-century critics who had done so much to establish the ground for the Romantic idea that Satan was the hero of *Paradise Lost.*

I must remark from *Aristotle* and *Rymer*, that the *hero* of tragedy and (I add *meo periculo*) a tragic poem must *be guilty*, to excite "*terror and pity*," the end of tragic poetry. But hear not *me*, but my betters. "The pity which the poet is to labour for is *for* the criminal. The terror is likewise in the punishment of the said criminal, who, if he be represented too great an offender, will *not be pitied*; if altogether *innocent* his punishment will be unjust" . . . Who is the hero of *Paradise Lost*? Why Satan – and Macbeth, and Richard, and Othello, and Pierre, and Lothario, and Zanga?[5]

Byron does not idealize Satan any more than he idealizes his own Lucifer. Rather, Byron's argument depends upon a humanized interpretation of the fallen angel. In this respect, Byron's view is the direct inheritor of that eighteenth-century critical tradition which, by attempting to defend the probability of Milton's rebel angel, developed an elaborate exegesis of his human qualities and reactions.

Unlike his remarks on *Cain* and Milton, Byron's commentary on Satan as the hero of *Paradise Lost* is completely sincere. Byron believed that the devil was equivocally represented in Milton's epic, and if Leigh Hunt was able to discern the assured fideistic character of *Paradise Lost*, Byron was equally certain that the poem was basically non-dogmatic. "Cain," Byron said, "is not a piece of argument". It represented neither the devil's party nor God's, for Byron had no intention (nor any inclination) to choose forms of worship with his poetic tales. In this matter Byron felt himself to be following Milton's lead precisely, for he could not see an unequivocal theology in *Paradise Lost.* Milton's epics, for Byron, mirrored the open mind of their creator. According to Byron, they "prove nothing".

> His great epics . . . prove nothing . . . He certainly excites compassion for Satan, and endeavours to make him out an injured personage – he gives him human passions too, makes him pity Adam and Eve, and justify himself much as Prometheus does . . . I should be very curious to know what his real belief was. The "Paradise Lost" and "Regained" do not satisfy me on this point.[6]

This text is the crucial one for understanding Milton's influence upon Byron's Satanism. It not only contains the germ of his attitude toward Milton the thinker, it explains why Milton's influence upon the Byronic hero took the peculiar form it did.

Byron's gloomy heroes have long been recognized as the descendants of Milton's Satan through the intermediacy of such famous hero-villains as Karl Moor, Ambrosio, and Schedoni. Indeed, when Byron made his notorious remark that Satan was the hero of *Paradise Lost* he was not commenting directly on *Paradise Lost* at all. His letter was a reply to his friend Francis Hodgson, who had made some severe criticisms of Gothic hero-villains, that "long series of depraved . . . profligates adorned with courage, and rendered interesting by all the warmth and tenderness of love . . . [They] cannot but have had the worst effect upon the minds of the young."[7]

Byron's answer to Hodgson justifies (to a certain extent) his repeated assertions that his tragic heroes were never meant to be taken as models for behavior. The histories of the Giaour, Conrad, Manfred, Lucifer, Cain, Christian, *et al.* are records of guilt and suffering, and for this reason Byron was right to object when critics accused him of immorality.

Byron defended *Cain*, his own many dark heroes, as well as the fascinating villains of Gothic literature, on the same principle which guided his reading of *Paradise Lost.* Milton's poem was intellectually problematic for Byron because all of Milton's characters seemed humanized. Following Pope and others, Byron criticized Milton's portrayal of God because He seemed altogether too mundane, and hence sounded ridiculous while delivering His long theological disquisitions. According to Byron, He never should have appeared in the epic at all. Similarly, Satan's character had been wrought with the greatest art, but the psychological result was the portrait of a criminal-hero. Guilty he most certainly was, but a pure principle of evil he was not.

This humanistic reading of *Paradise Lost* helped Byron to create his own famous portraits of the criminal-hero. If Byron wondered what Milton's true beliefs might have been, his own lifelong uncertainty and skepticism about ultimate philosophical and theological questions were continually represented in his Gothic and oriental tales and his metaphysical dramas. These poems were Byron's means not for asserting his philosophical convictions, but for exploring the intellectual questions which never ceased to bother him. Moreover, the crucial vehicles for his intellectual questionings were his notorious and deeply problematical heroes, all of whom, as we know, trace their heritage back to Milton's Satan.

Byron told his wife that he believed himself the avatar of a fallen angel. This bizarre conviction explains, among other things, his fascination with the Satan of *Paradise Lost.* Byron's early heroes are frequently associated in more or less explicit ways with Milton's fallen angel.

> He stood a stranger in this breathing world,
> An erring spirit from another hurl'd;
>
> (*Lara*, I, 315–316)
>
> Enough—no foreign foe could quell
> Thy soul, till from itself it fell.
>
> (*The Giaour*, 138–139)
>
> His soul was changed, before his deeds had driven
> Him forth to war with man and forfeit heaven.
>
> (*The Corsair*, I, 251–252)

All such figures are, for Byron, guilty but fascinating beings. They are Satanic, and the measure of his judgment upon them is taken in his lyric "Prometheus." Like Shelley, Byron distinguished between the divine rebellions of Satan on the one hand and Prometheus on the other. His Satanic heroes, all "errant on dark ways diverse," are properly self-destroyed. But Prometheus is the innocent victim of an arbitrary external power. Far from making war on man, as Byron's Satanic heroes do, Prometheus is marvellously humanitarian. In Byron's terms he is not a tragic figure at all.

But while this distinction between the Promethean and the Satanic in Byron is necessary, the poems quite clearly represent even the most reprobate of Byron's heroes in a sympathetic way. The following remarks of Byron to Lady Blessington explain the reason for his sympathetic portraits of bad men.

> It is my *respect for morals that makes me so indignant against its vile substitute cant, with which I wage war*, and this the good-natured world chooses to consider as a sign of my *wickedness*. We are all the creatures of circumstance, the greater part of our errors are caused, if not excused, by events and situations over which we have had little control; the world see the faults, but they see not what led to them: therefore I am always lenient to crimes that have *brought their own punishment*, while I am a little disposed to pity those who think they atone for their own sins by exposing those of others, and add cant *and hypocrisy to the catalogue of their vices*.[8]

Thus speaks Byron the genteel reformer. His famous tales of guilty adventurers are all exercises in which sympathy is evoked for the hero by forcing the reader to consider all the circumstances of the case. The reader is asked not to excuse but to seek understanding.

> There was in him a vital scorn of all;
> As if the worst had fall'n which could befall,
> He stood a stranger in this breathing world,
> An erring spirit from another hurl'd;
> A thing of dark imaginings, that shaped
> By choice the perils he by chance escaped;
> But 'scaped in vain, for in their memory yet
> His mind would half exult and half regret.
> With more capacity for love than earth
> Bestows on most of mortal mould and birth,
> His early dreams of good outstripp'd the truth,
> And troubled manhood follow'd baffled youth;
> with thought of years in phantom chase misspent,
> And wasted powers for better purpose lent;
> And fiery passions that had pour'd their wrath
> In hurried desolation o'er his path,
> And left the better feelings all at strife
> In wild reflection o'er his stormy life;
> But haughty still and loth himself to blame,
> He call'd on Nature's self to share the shame,
> And charged all faults upon the fleshly form
> She gave to clog the soul, and feast the worm;
> Till he at last confounded good and ill,
> And half mistook for fate the acts of will.
>
> (*Lara* I, 313–336)[9]

Such men are vital because they are so problematic. The verse runs us through a series of paradoxes and contradictory circumstances. Indeed, the rushing movement of these portraits is essential to their effect, for the reader is meant to be struck with a sense that, though one may understand the nature and causes of the detailed situation, one must always remain behindhand with solutions. Too many factors are inevitably involved in human affairs, something crucial is always beyond one's control. Just as the Byronic hero's life is confounded equally in his will and in his fate, so the reader's schemes for moral order – whatever they may be – are confounded by Byron's presentation. Our sympathy for such a man is the melancholy sign of human ineffectuality. Indeed, the Byronic hero illustrates in his life what the reader, meeting him, discovers in himself. They "prove nothing"; rather, they raise questions.[10]

To instil in the reader a dislocated and melancholy intelligence is the primary function of the Byronic hero, who is, therefore, another of Byron's devices for making war on "cant." All Byronic heroes are almost hypnotically fascinating. The monks in *The Giaour* fear to look upon the hero of that tale because his very appearance troubles their consciences. The effect he produces is typical of the whole species.

With all that chilling mystery of mien,
And seeming gladness to remain unseen,
He sad (if 'twere not nature's boon) an art
Of fixing memory on another's heart:
It was not love perchance, nor hate, nor aught
That words can image to express the thought;
But they who saw him did not see in vain,
And once beheld, would ask of him again:
And those to whom he spake remember'd well,
And on the words, however light, would dwell:
None knew, nor how, nor why, but he entwined
Himself perforce around the hearer's mind;
There he was stamp'd, in liking, or in hate,
If greeted once; however brief the date
That friendship, pity, or aversion knew,
Still there within the inmost thought he grew.
You could not penetrate his soul, but found,
Despite your wonder, to your own he wound;
His presence haunted still; and from the breast
He forced an all unwilling interest:
Vain was the struggle in that mental net,
His spirit seem'd to dare you to forget!

(*Lara*, I, 361–382)

One dares not forget the sight of such a man because he is a living challenge to the comforts of undemanding and conventional ethics. To have known the Byronic hero is to have discovered a new and terrifying problematics of morality.

> For infinite as boundless space
> The thought that Conscience must embrace,
> Which in itself can comprehend
> Woe without name, or hope, or end.
> (*The Giaour*, 273–276)

Sorrows and disasters hunt the Byronic hero because he remains, in some radical way, unprotected. Ordinary men *are* ordinary not merely because they do not suffer in the nets of circumstance which have trapped these heroes, but even more because they do not see the true complexities of good and evil. Ordinary men are protected by their ordinary mortalities, by cant.

> He knew himself a villain, but he deem'd
> The rest no better than the thing he seem'd;
> And scorn'd the best as hypocrites who hid
> Those deeds the bolder spirit plainly did.
> (*The Corsair*, I, 265–268)

As Marino Faliero observes: "I am not innocent – but are these guiltless?" (V, iii, 40). His question illustrates the reflexive purpose of the Byronic hero's life. Meditating on the obscure complexities of this figure, the reader is thrown back on himself. The Corsair is a fearful object of scrutiny not because of what he reveals about himself but because he threatens to expose to the observer his *own* hidden heart.

> Though smooth his voice, and calm his general mien,
> Still seems there something he would not have seen:
> His features' deepening lines and varying hue
> At times attracted, yet perplex'd the view,
> As if within that murkiness of mind
> Word'd feelings fearful and yet undefin'd;
> Such might it be—that none could truly tell—
> Too close inquiry his stern glance would quell.
> There breathe but few whose aspect might defy
> The full encounter of his searching eye:
> He had the skill, when Cunning's gaze would seek
> To probe his heart and watch his changing cheek,
> At once the observer's purpose to espy,

And on himself roll back his scrutiny,
Lest he to Conrad rather should betray
Some secret thought, than drag that chief's to day.
(*The Corsair*, I, 207–222)

The inscrutable appearance of Conrad is a mirror in which the observer sees his own life in a clarified extreme. To the reader the Byronic hero whispers, threatens a self revelation.

This special quality of the Byronic hero sets him apart from most Gothic villains, who served, however, as Byron's immediate inspiration. For the typical Gothic villain does not set out to promote a radical critique of established moral issues. Circumstances have indeed warped Ambrosio's character, as they have warped Karl Moor, but in both cases we never doubt the rightness of an essential, and discoverable, code of values. A sense of prevenient order is always present in the pre-Byronic treatment of the hero-villain. But Byron's tales and plays achieved their enormous influence, and sometimes bad reputation, because their heroes forced the reader to a more searching inquiry into norms for order and value. We say that they are skeptical, and problematic, for they do not allow things to come out right in the end. We are always left wondering about the events and puzzling over their significance.

This quality in, for example, *The Giaour*, or *Lara*, or *Cain*, is the necessary consequence of Byron's "existential" reading of Aristotle on tragic effect. The "end" of tragedy, Byron remarked, is pity and fear, but he says nothing about the purgation of these emotions and the restoration of a final sense of order. Byron's reading of Aristotle stays *in medias res* just as his tales and plays characteristically refuse to set the problems they raise within a context of comfort, understanding, and government.

Pre-Byronic hero-villains are sentimental figures because they finally set aside the intellectual issues which they themselves have raised for us. But the Byronic hero carries out his skeptical programs. This is why Byron's tales and plays are actively intellectual works, whereas *The Monk* and *The Italian* and *Die Räuber* at some point rein in their questionings and set the reader's consciousness at rest.

Byron seems to have sensed this moderating quality in most Gothic treatments of the hero-villain. Milton, however, the unwitting father of these figures, he specifically excepted. Milton's mind, Byron says, is as searching and unsettled as his own. Indeed, Milton's mind is not only not made up, it positively avoids "argument" on a system or "proof" for a set of fixed ideas. He too provokes one to wonder about the issues involved in his epics by his non-dogmatic handling of certain very dogmatically conditioned materials. Most modern scholars would agree with Leigh Hunt, and disagree with Byron, about the belief structure of Milton's epics. That is another scholarly issue altogether. What is certain is that Milton was a signal influence not only upon the details which make up a portrait of the Byronic hero, but upon Byron's peculiarly skeptical treatment of that hero and his milieu. The intellectual freedom which Milton championed assumed a new and wilder form when it rose again, under Milton's own influence, in Byron. One is probably safe in assuming that Milton would not have approved – would probably have disavowed – his wayward offspring. But then fathers from at least the time of Jahweh have always fallen out with those children most fashioned in their own image and likeness.

In April 1814 – less than a year before his marriage and just two years before he was to leave England for good – Byron composed a poem on one of his greatest heroes. The *Ode to Napoleon Buonaparte*, at once a lament and a denunciation, was soon to acquire a weirdly self-reflexive dimension. Of the fallen Emperor Byron writes:

> Since he, miscall'd the Morning Star,
> Nor man nor fiend hath fallen so far.
> (Stanza 1)

Byron's own fall from society, via his falling out with his wife, was a descent of similar notoriety, and – so it came to seem for Byron – of equal significance and magnitude. Of the Giaour Byron had written, in remembrance of Milton, that nothing "could quell / Thy soul, till from itself it fell." Napoleon too, the Ode tells us, is another hero fallen from himself. Byron was quick to see in his own life this pattern of eminence and degradation when the appropriate time came. In exile in Switzerland he writes to his sister:

> The fault was mine—nor do I seek to screen
> My errors with defensive paradox—
> I have been cunning in mine overthrow
> The careful pilot of my proper woe.
> ("[Epistle to Augusta]," 21–24)

The last two lines draw Byron into the Miltonic company of the self-fallen and self-condemned. But the first two lines of the passage, though not themselves Miltonic, distinctly echo an important Miltonic passage in *Manfred*.

There is a power upon me which withholds,
And makes it my fatality to live;
If it be life to wear within myself
This barrenness of spirit, and to be
My own soul's sepulchre, for I have ceased
To justify my deeds unto myself—
The last infirmity of evil. (I, ii, 23–29)

The allusion to "Lycidas"[11] ("Fame is the spur... That last infirmity of noble minds") occurs in a passage full of significance for Byron. *Manfred* is a nakedly autobiographical piece in which Byron tries to represent what sort of life can remain for a man once he knows not only that his soul is a sepulchre, but that he himself has made it so. In the "[Epistle to Augusta]," where he says that "The world is all before me,"[12] the way he finally takes is at least as solitary and problematic as Adam and Eve's. But in *Manfred*, if the circumstances are equivocal and lonely throughout, the hero comes not only to accept his own barrenness of spirit, but even to find in such desolation an unexpected gift (see the pun on "desert" in *Manfred*, III, iv, 136, quoted below). Echoing Milton once again, Byron establishes Satan as Manfred's ancestor: "on his brow / The thunder-scars are graven" (III, iv, 76–77).[13] But Byron's Satanic hero takes the famous dictum of Milton's fallen angel

The mind is its own place, and in itself
Can make a Heaven of Hell, a Hell of Heaven.
(*P.L.*, I, 254–255)

and alters its significance as radically as he had altered the significance of the "Lycidas" passage. Twice Byron echoes Satan's famous remark (III, i, 70ff., and III, iv, 129ff.) and in each case we are given a glimpse of the state of mind of a man who has freed himself of the last infirmity of his own confessed evil. Gone is the possibility of any "defensive paradox" or self-justification; if Manfred is to be born again, it will have to be from the knowledge of his own desert. And so it is.

The mind which is immortal makes itself
Requital for its good or evil thoughts,
Is its own origin of ill and end,
And its own place and time; its innate sense,
When stripp'd of this mortality, derives
No colour from the fleeting things without,
But is absorb'd in sufferance or in joy,
Born from the knowledge of its own desert.
(III, iv, 127–136)

In *Manfred* and several other poems of 1816–1817, Milton helped Byron to explore the nature and extent of his downfall. But as Byron let his mind turn more and more on Milton (the process began in 1816 about the time he took up residence in the Villa Diodati – of Miltonic memory), he began to see a broad but clear parallel between the trials, betrayals, and goals of Milton's life and the similar circumstances of his own. The result of this was a noticeable shift in Byron's Miltonic echoes and borrowings whenever he wrote within the context of his own life's drama. Manfred (like Byron's Dante) learns to avoid the last infirmity of his own evil nature not only by recalling "Lycidas" but even more by invoking the history of Milton Agonistes. When Byron tells us that he had been the cause of his own "proper woe," and when Manfred wonders, just before the "Lycidas" allusion, "If it be life to wear within myself / This barrenness of spirit, and to be / My own soul's sepulchre," we are, in both cases, being asked to recall passages in *Samson Agonistes*:

> Nothing of all these evils hath befallen me
> But justly; I myself have brought them on,
> Sole author I, sole cause. (374–376)
>
> To live a life half dead, a living death,
> And buried; but O yet more miserable!
> Myself, my sepulchre, a moving grave.
> (100–102)

Immediately and for some time after the separation, Byron seems to have been obsessed with the parallels between his own situation and that of Samson/Milton. Canto III of *Childe Harold* concludes with a general parallel between Samson and Byron (stanza 103). Even more particularly, the famous line near the end of "Stanzas to Augusta" – "In the desert a fountain is springing" – echoes the divine act which, in Samson's need, "caused a fountain at thy prayer / From the dry ground to spring" (581–582).

In the fourth canto of *Childe Harold* Byron drastically extended the range of his willed identifications with "fallen . . . and buried greatness." Prowling through the museums and libraries of history, Byron found that he was not only the avatar of numerous Western heroes, real and mythological, but that a remarkable number of dead poetic spirits found their second selves in George Gordon. This inclination to seek his own image throughout history produced those bizarre autobiographical exercises *The Lament of Tasso* and *The Prophecy of Dante*. But while many

Italian spirits march across the stanzas of *Childe Harold IV*, it is an English poet, Milton, who stands as Byron's unnamed but clearly invoked precursor.

Childe Harold IV has two subjects, one personal (involving the disastrous history of Lord Byron) and one political (involving the present state of Italian degradation). As the poem develops, it becomes clear that the two subjects depend upon each other. Briefly, Byron hopes to reacquire a vital personal control upon life through his poetry, which he gives over to the service of Italian *risorgimento*. But in setting about this task, Byron invokes England's other traduced republican genius. Milton too spoke out for freedom in another time of trouble, and Byron returns to him for a present guidance and a present strength.

> Yet, Italy! through every other land
> Thy wrongs should ring, and shall, from side to side;
> Mother of Arts, as once of arms; thy hand
> Was then our guardian, and is still our guide;
> Parent of our Religion, whom the wide
> Nations have knelt to for the keys of heaven!
> Europe, repentant of her parricide,
> Shall yet redeem thee, and, all backward driven,
> Roll the barbarian tide, and sue to be forgiven.
>
> (Stanza 47)

A pivotal stanza in *Childe Harold IV*, it looks forward to the so-called "Forgiveness-curse" stanzas (stanzas, 130–137) and backward to Milton's proud sonnet "Cyriak, this three years day" (Sonnet 22). The allusion to Milton is brilliantly apt, for with it Byron reminds us that his political career is as related to his more intimate history as Milton's political involvements were to *his* personal life:

> What supports me dost thou ask?
> The conscience, friend, to have lost [my sight] overplied
> In Liberty's defence, my noble task,
> Of which all Europe talks from side to side. (II, 9–12)

Later in the canto Byron extends the Milton parallels. The "immedicable wound" (167) suffered by England at the death of the politically liberal (it was believed) Princess Charlotte recalls the "immedicable soul" (126) of all those whose lives seem to be "not in / The harmony of things." Both phrases reach back to recover a pertinent series of verses in *Samson Agonistes*.

My griefs not only pain me
As a lingering disease,
But finding no redress, ferment and rage,
Nor less than wounds immedicable
Rankle, and fester. (618–622)

As it ensues, Byron takes at least the formal pattern for his behavior in Canto IV from Samson's. Though confessing his responsibility for the disasters of his life, Byron denounces the treachery of his unnamed familial connection. Samson does the same. Both Samson and Byron leave the execution of revenge to other lords (*SA*, 506–508; *CHP IV*, 130–133), both offer a fury of forgiveness, both speak to their consorts "At distance" (*SA*, 954), both represent their wives in recurrent ophidian metaphors. Furthermore, the image of an independent and powerful hero imprisoned in darkness and chains flits through Byron's poem, as it does through a number of other works of Byron's exilic period, most obviously *The Prisoner of Chillon* and *The Lament of Tasso* (both of which contain Milton echoes). In *Childe Harold IV*, this Samson-like image is given its most powerfully Miltonic turn immediately after Byron's allusive reference to man's "immedicable soul."

Yet let us ponder boldly; 'tis a base
Abandonment of reason to resign
Our right of thought, our last and only place
Of refugee . . .
Though from our birth the faculty divine
Is chain'd and tortured . . .
And bred in darkness, lest the truth should shine
Too brightly for the unpreparéd mind,
The beam pours in, for time and skill will couch the blind.
(127)

But not until *Don Juan* does Byron explicitly draw out the parallels he felt between his own life and Milton's.

The only two that in my recollection
Have sung of heaven and hell, or marriage, are
Dante and Milton, and of both the affection
Was hapless in their nuptials, for some bar
Of fault or temper ruin'd the connection
(Such things, in fact, it don't ask much to mar):
But Dante's Beatrice and Milton's Eve
Were not drawn from their spouses, you conceive.
(III, 10)[14]

In the very act of writing such a stanza Byron establishes his equality with these two poets. Like *Childe Harold IV*, the verses enact Byron's achievement of his place among the community of the world's poetic geniuses, only in this case Byron stands with them not because of his tragic history, but because of his urbanity and great wit. He does not meet them because of likenesses in personal history, but because of the verse skills he displays in the handling of those likenesses.

Earlier in his masterpiece – in fact, at the outset – Byron reached for an identification with Milton in a mood more severe, if no less witty.

X

If, fallen in evil days on evil tongues,
  Milton appealed to the Avenger, Time,
If Time, the Avenger, execrates his wrongs,
  And makes the word "Miltonic" mean "*sublime*,"
He deign'd not to belie his soul in songs,
  Nor turn his very talent to a crime;
He did not loathe the Sire to laud the Son,
But closed the tyrant-hater he begun.

XI

Think'st thou, could he—the blind Old Man—arise,
  Like Samuel from the grave, to freeze once more
The blood of monarchs with his prophecies,
  Or be alive again—again all hoar
With time and trials, and those helpless eyes,
  And heartless daughters—worn—and pale—and poor;
Would *he* adore a sultan? *he* obey
The intellectual eunuch Castlereagh?

("Dedication" to *Don Juan*)

Be recalling stanzas 130–133 of *Childe Harold IV* Byron underlines the Miltonic character of that poem's most intimately autobiographical passages, and reminds us that we were not wrong to hear in them the undersong of *Samson Agonistes*. Further, Byron also makes explicit the political and poetic inheritance to which, in his mind, he was the true heir. As the whole of the "Dedication" shows, Byron set out in *Don Juan* to dispute with those Miltonists, Southey and Wordsworth, the right to take Milton as their forebear. Wordsworth and Southey may affect the Miltonic style, may wear the trappings of his Muse, but it is Byron in whom Milton's living spirit survives. "Though fall'n on evil dayes," like Milton, Byron wittily recalls the invocation to Urania in Book VII of *Paradise Lost* in order to justify the ways of his "pedestrian Muses" to men.

Southey and Wordsworth may be off and flying on their time-serving and pompous steeds just as they are free to seek their fortunes in the world of Lord Castlereagh, Poet-Laureateships, and places "in the Excise." To let them have their way is to let them condemn themselves.

> For me, who, wandering with pedestrian Muses,
> Contend not with you on the winged steed,
> I wish your fate may yield ye, when she chooses,
> The fame you envy, and the skill you need;
> And recollect a poet nothing loses
> In giving to his brethren their full meed
> Of merit, and complaint of present days
> Is not the certain path to future praise.
> ("Dedication" to *Don Juan* stanza VIII)

Meantime, while these bastard children of Milton soar in their illusory poetic heavens, Byron will gather himself back to his father and begin *Don Juan* under the aegis of the human books of *Paradise Lost.*

> Return me to my Native Element:
> Least from this flying Steed enrein'd (as once
> *Bellerophon,* though from a lower Clime)
> Dismounted, on th' *Aleian* Field I fall
> Erroneus there to wander and forlorne.
> Half yet remaines unsung, but narrower bound
> Within the visible Diurnal Spheare;
> Standing on Earth, not rapt above the Pole
> More safe I Sing with mortal voice, unchang'd
> To hoarce or mute, though fall'n on evil dayes,
> On evil dayes though fall'n and evil tongues;
> In darkness, and with dangers compast round,
> And solitude; yet not alone, while thou
> Visit'st my slumbers Nightly, or when Morn
> Purples the East: still govern thou my Song,
> *Urania,* and fit audience find, though few.
> (*P.L.*, VII, 16–31)

NOTES

1 *The Works of Lord Byron. Letters and Journals*, ed. Rowland E. Prothero (London, 1898–1903), IV, 490–491 (hereinafter referred to as *LJ*). All poetry is quoted from E. H. Coleridge's standard edition in seven volumes (London, 1898–1903).

2 My remarks on this aspect of the relation between Byron and Milton are made against the background of the following critical studies: [Anon.], "The Two

Devils; or the Satan of Milton and Lucifer of Byron Compared," *Knickerbocker Magazine*, 30 (1847), 150–155; Arthur Barker, "... 'And on His Crest Sat Horror'. Eighteenth-century Interpretations of Milton's Sublimity and his Satan," *UTQ*, 11 (1941–1942), 421–436; Calvin Huckabay, "The Satanist Controversy in the Nineteenth-century," *Studies in English Renaissance Literature*, ed. Waldo F. McNeir (Baton Rouge, 1962), 197–210; Mario Praz, *The Romantic Agony* (London, 1933); Eino Railo, *The Haunted Castle* (London, 1927); C. N. Stavrou, "Milton, Byron, and the Devil," *UKCR*, 31 (1955), 153–159; Peter Thorslev, *The Byronic Hero* (Minneapolis, 1962); Joseph A. Wittreich, ed., *The Romantics on Milton* (Cleveland/London, 1970). Though numerous other studies treat the subject in brief or peripheral ways, these are the ones I found most useful.

3 *LJ*, VI, 15–16; *Medwin's Conversations of Lord Byron*, ed. Ernest J. Lovell, Jr. (Princeton, 1966), 129–130.

4 (London, 1828), 126–127.

5 *LJ*, V, 284.

6 *Medwin's Conversations*, 77–78.

7 *LJ*, V, 284n.

8 *Lady Blessington's Conversations of Lord Byron*, ed. Ernest J. Lovell, Jr. (Princeton, 1969), 172–173.

9 Compare also *The Corsair*, I, 249–260.

10 Byron's rhetorical management of these tales is a Romantic equivalent for the rhetorical techniques used by Milton which were most recently described by Stanley E. Fish, *Surprised by Sin* (London / New York, 1967). Both poets set intellectual traps for their readers, but Milton's technique is employed to strengthen the reader's faith, whereas Byron's supports a new philosophy that calls all in doubt.

11 This passage, "Lycidas," 70–71, is also echoed in *The Prophecy of Dante*, I, 110.

12 This was one of Byron's favourite lines from Milton: it is also echoed in *The Lament of Tasso*, *The Island*, *Childe Harold*, and *Don Juan*.

13 See *Paradise Lost*, I, 600.

14 Byron accepted the legend that Dante was unhappily married, just as he also liked to apply Dante's history (in this version) to himself. He even suggested to his wife, directly, that he was like Dante in having been cursed with a malicious spouse: see *LJ*, V, 1–2, and compare *The Prophecy of Dante*, I, 172–174n.

CHAPTER 2

Byron, mobility, and the poetics of historical ventriloquism

I

Byron's popularity – the fact that he was a bestseller and "famous in [his] time" – has always focused certain literary problems, not least of all, at the outset, for Byron himself. "Lord Byron cuts a figure – but he is not figurative" (67), Keats waspishly observed in a letter to the George Keatses. This is an envious and illuminating remark which reveals as much about Keats and his ambitions for a successful career as it does about the character of Byron's verse, the phenomenon of Byronism, and the changing structure of the institution of letters at the beginning of the nineteenth century. Later writers have sometimes condescended to Byron, particularly to the Byron of the pre-exilic period, as a factitious writer who had merely seized the main chance during the Years of Fame. Of course it is true that he was himself largely responsible for creating the enormous popularity of the Oriental and Byronic Tales. Nevertheless – so the story goes – he cranked out verse between 1812 and 1815 to various formulas and audience expectations. In this activity he was not so much a poet as he was a pander and whore to public tastes. It passes without saying that those tastes were corrupt. (The non-malicious version of this general view is that Byron invented the myth of himself as The Romantic Poet, thereby creating a new structure of authorship which answered to the changing conditions that were rapidly transforming the English literary institution.)

Byron himself was well aware of these events and social formations. His letters and his poetry alike reflect on these matters often. In May 1813, for example, at the peak of his London years, Byron writes to Thomas Moore about projects in poetry:

> Stick to the East; – the oracle, Staël, told me it was the only poetical policy . . . The little I have done in that way is merely a "voice in the wilderness" for you; and, if it has had any success, that also will prove that the public are

orientalizing, and pave the path for you. (*Byron's Letters and Journals*. Ed. Leslie Marchand (hereafter *BLJ*), III, 101)

Later, of course, he came to speak more critically, even disparagingly, of this kind of careerist calculation. In January 1822 he tells Douglas Kinnaird that "*my* object is not *immediate* popularity in my present productions which are written on a different system from the rage of the day"; and in another letter three days later: "Now once and for all about publication – I *[n]ever courted the* public – and I will never yield to it. – As long as I can find a *single* reader I will publish my Mind . . . and write while I feel the impetus" (*BLJ*, IX, 92, 94).

Byron arrived at this changed position largely because of the Separation Controversy and its aftermath, which exposed to critical analysis a whole train of Byron's most cherished ideas and illusions. The idea which dominates his "[Epistle to Augusta]" – that "I have been cunning in mine overthrow, / The careful pilot of my proper woe" (lines 23–24) – has its deepest filiations with Byron's public life and poetical career between 1807 and 1816, as a later passage of the same poem testifies:

> With false Ambition what had I to do?
> Little with Love, and least of all with Fame;
> And yet they came unsought; and with me grew;
> And made me all which they can make—a Name.
> Yet this was not the end I did pursue;
> Surely I once beheld a nobler aim. (97–102)

This critical examination of himself, his public life, and his poetical/moral goals will dominate most of his later years and will affect all aspects of his work in the most profound ways.

I have sketched this brief history in order to recollect two salient aspects of Byron's work, especially his later work. The first has to do with the historical/biographical dimensions of his poetry. To speak only of *Don Juan*, we are always aware when reading the poem that its most persistent subtext is the myth (or plot) of Byron's public life, which *Don Juan* reflects upon as an exemplary history – a tale which sums up, in an English perspective, the meaning of the entire European epoch stretching from the late 1780s to 1818 and the six following years (the period of *Don Juan*'s composition and publication). More particularly, Byron's work will, as a matter of course, generate itself by echoing and reflecting his own earlier poetical works. The most dramatic example of this outside of *Don Juan* is, I suppose, stanzas 51–52 of *Beppo*.

Oh! that I had the art of easy writing,
  What should be easy reading! could I scale
Parnassus, where the Muses sit inditing
  Those pretty poems never known to fail,
How quickly would I print (the World delighting)
  A Grecian, Syrian, or *Assyrian* tale;
And sell you, mixed with western Sentimentalism,
Some samples of the *finest Orientalism.*

But I am but a nameless sort of person,
  (A broken Dandy lately on my travels).

Part of the genius of this passage is that it manages to be at once critical and sympathetic toward Byron's career, his own earlier work, and the audience which found (and which continues to find) an interest and profit in such things. This poetry institutes a benevolent critique of itself and its world, on the one hand, and, on the other, of the verse which fashion will cultivate at various times – as well as the very concept and event of fashionableness itself.

Often, however – as we have already noticed in the passages from Byron quoted above – Byron's reflective thoughts about these matters conclude on a much more problematic, even a more severe, note. This fact reveals the second important aspect of Byron's poetry: its preoccupation with the social structure of its rhetoric. This preoccupation appears frequently as a problem in Byron's verse which can be phrased, in simple terms, in the following way: a writer must have an audience and hence must operate with certain specific sets of audience expectation, need, and desire (which will be more or less explicit or inchoate); at the same time, the writer cannot merely attend upon and serve audience. Rather, the audience's social character must be reflected back to itself so that it can "reflect upon" that reflection in a critical and illuminating way.

Byron's famous discussion of "Mobility" in Canto XVI on *Don Juan* constitutes a structural analysis of this set of relations, but one that is carried out in non-literary social terms. The passage specifically calls attention to the relation of mobility to the structure of the artist's life:

This makes your actors, artists, and romancers,
  Heroes sometimes, though seldom—sages never;
But speakers, bards, diplomatists, and dancers,
  Little that's great, but much of what is clever;
Most orators, but very few financiers . . .   (98: 1–5)

– are people, in other words, whose work or life demands that they treat with others in a broadly public or spectacular field.

In a note to this passage Byron defines *mobility* as follows: "an excessive susceptibility of immediate impressions – at the same time without *losing* the past; and is, though sometimes apparently useful to the possessor, a most painful and unhappy attribute." Lady Adeline Amundeville shows that she possesses this equivocal virtue when she is observed dealing with her guests at Norman Abbey.

> But Adeline was occupied by fame
>   This day; and watching, witching, condescending
> To the consumers of fish, fowl and game,
>   And dignity with courtesy so blending,
> As all must blend whose part it is to aim
>   (Especially as the sixth year is ending)
> At their lord's, son's, or similar connection's
> Safe conduct through the rocks of re-elections.
>
> Though this was most expedient on the whole,
>   And usual—Juan, when he cast a glance
> On Adeline while playing her grand role,
>   Which she went through as though it were a dance,
> (Betraying only now and then her soul
>   By a look scarce perceptibly askance
> Of weariness or scorn) began to feel
> Some doubt how much of Adeline was *real*;
>
> So well she acted, all and every part
>   By turns—with that vivacious versatility,
> Which many people take for want of heart.
>   They err—'tis merely what is called mobility,
> A thing of temperament and not of art,
>   Though seeming so, from its supposed facility;
> And false—though true; for surely they're sincerest,
> Who are strongly acted on by what is nearest.
>
> (XVI. 95–97)

These lines deserve some attention. If mobility is "an excessive susceptibility to immediate impressions," the passage also suggests that it is not *simply* a psychological attribute. Lady Adeline is at home in this social world; indeed, her entire life in the poem shows that she is governed by a *social* "susceptibility" to this kind of structure. She has at once a taste and a gift for managing social affairs of these kinds with brilliance. In the end, however, the passage shows that the psychological attribute and the social formation call out to each other, that they are, indeed, symbiotic and inter-dependent.

We will understand what Byron means when he says that such mobility is "a most painful and unhappy attribute" if we meditate on Lady Adeline's barely perceptible "look . . . / Of weariness or scorn." Juan glimpses an important aspect of her character and its social determinants when he observes her "now and then" – in the very midst of her social brilliance – "Betraying . . . her soul" in those looks of scorn and weariness. "Playing her grand role" involves, within a Romantic Ideology, a reciprocal danger: lack of authenticity. Thus Lady Adeline "betrays" her soul in at least two senses when she inadvertently reveals her mobility to Juan and to us.

What is crucial to see in all this is that mobility involves a structure of social relations and not simply a psychological characteristic. Byron *interprets* mobility in psychological terms, but his verse exposes this interpretation as a special (ultimately, a Romantic) view of what is clearly a much more complex state of affairs. Scarcely less important is an interesting paradox which Byron calls attention to: *mobility* appears as a set of social graces, a capacity to charm and to be all things to all men, but it arises, apparently, from a ground of "sincerity" in those kinds of people "Who are strongly acted on by what is nearest." Yet it *appears* the very height of insincerity and calculation. Which is it: "a thing of" one's spontaneous "temperament," or of one's role-playing and "art"? Is it "false" or is it "true"?

This set of paradoxes and contradictions gets registered for us in Lady Adeline's looks of weariness and scorn, and in Byron's remark that mobility is painful and a source of unhappiness. Lady Adeline's "soul" is rent by these paradoxes which her situation reflects but which her consciousness does not appear to understand (or even try to understand). When Byron reflects upon her situation he gains a clearer knowledge of the contradictions, but he too remains incapable of producing anything more than a demonstrative and aesthetic explanation (which is itself supplemented by the psychological explanation of his note). Reading Byron's verse, we *see* it all much more clearly than Lady Adeline does, for we are provided with a much more comprehensive vantage of the field of relations being played out.

The connection of social mobility to the Romantic artist's ideal of spontaneity and sincerity has often been noted by scholars, most trenchantly, perhaps, by George Ridenour. Thus we now commonly equate the "conversational facility" of *Don Juan* (XV, 20, 3), or what H. J. C.

Grierson terms the "strain of passionate improvisation" in Byron's High Romantic mode ("Lord Byron: Arnold and Swinburne," 11), with the mobility of Lady Adeline and the "actors, artists, and romancers" who are her equivalents. What is less often noted is the negative dimension which Byron sees in the artist of mobility. It is mildly shocking, but quite necessary, to understand that the dark shadow cast by the mobility of the spontaneous Romantic poet is called (in *Don Juan* Robert Southey, and sometimes William Wordsworth. Byron calls Southey an "Epic Renegade" at the very outset of the poem, in the "Dedication" (1, 5), and he links the recent Laureate with Wordsworth as instances of poets who apostasized their early republican principles in their later years. Southey's "conversion" (6, 3) "has lately been a common case" (1, 4), Byron says, but if such "Apostasy's . . . fashionable" now (17, 6), it was not always so. Milton rises up in Byron's "Dedication" as one who "deigned not to belie his soul in songs" (10, 5) which swerved from his initial ground and principles. Byron, of course, justifies himself with such an ideal of poetic and ideological behavior: "And, if in flattering strains I do not predicate, / 'Tis that I still retain my 'buff and blue'" (17, 4).

In Byron's "Vision of Judgment" Southey's political apostasy is elaborated into a general "literary character," a Grub Street avatar formed in the image of his own time.

> He said—(I only give the heads)—he said,
>   He meant no harm in scribbling; 'twas his way
> Upon all topics; 'twas, besides, his bread,
>   Of which he buttered both sides; 'twould delay
> Too long the assembly (he was pleased to dread),
>   And take up rather more time than a day,
> To name his works—he would but cite a few—
> "Wat Tyler"—"Rhymes on Blenheim"—"Waterloo."
>
> He had written praises of a Regicide;
>   He had written praises of all kings whatever;
> He had written for republics far and wide,
>   And then against them bitterer than ever;
> For pantisocracy he once had cried
>   Aloud, a scheme less moral than 'twas clever;
> Then grew a hearty anti-jacobin—
> Had turned his coat—and would have turned his skin.
>
> He had sung against all battles, and again
>   In their high praise and glory; he had called
> Reviewing "the ungentle craft," and then

Became as base a critic as e'er crawled—
Fed, paid, and pampered by the very men
By whom his muse and morals had been mauled:
He had written much blank verse, and blanker prose,
And more of both than any body knows.

He had written Wesley's life:—here turning round
To Satan, "Sir, I'm ready to write yours,
In two octavo volumes, nicely bound,
With notes and preface, all that most allures
The pious purchaser; and there's no ground
For fear, for I can choose my own reviewers:
So let me have the proper documents,
That I may add you to my other saints."

(Stanzas 96–99)

Like Lady Adeline when she is "occupied by fame" (*DJ* XVI, 95, 1), Southey too is ever "watching, witching, condescending" with those who might advance his literary career and projects. He will write on any topic, from any point of view, in any style or medium. He is, besides, keenly aware of all that is most current, and anxious to be borne along by that current. Finally, he understands how the institutions of literary production operate in his day. In his own summing up, Southey's is "a pen of all work" ("Vision" 100, 5) and he is a poet of skill and industry, without malice (or conscience), good-natured (and culpably unscrupulous). He has all of Lady Adeline's (and by extension Byron's) gifts, and would be an exact literary reflection but for one thing: his looks never betray the telltale glance "Of weariness or scorn." His mobility is complete but, in the end, un-Byronic, for Byron's Southey does not feel it as a "most painful and unhappy attribute."[1]

II

Byron's most profound presentation of his idea of Romantic mobility comes, as we might expect, when he draws himself and his own practice into the analysis. "Changeable too – yet somehow '*idem semper*'" (*DJ* XVII, 11, 3): thus Byron sought to describe both himself and his poem in his last, fragmentary canto. The characterization intersects with the entire constellation of ideas related to the concept of mobility, and thereby also gestures toward the similarities and differences which link Byron to his dark double, Robert Southey. In Canto III these similarities and differences are fully elaborated in the figure of the poet who comes to sing at Juan and Haidée's lavish banquet and festival.

Byron's introductory stanzas (78–86) describe the character of this poet as "a sad trimmer" (82, 1). This passage distinctly recalls what Byron had said earlier about Southey in the (abandoned) "Preface" to *Don Juan* and the (reluctantly cancelled) "Dedication." There the tone is much more savage, however, resembling in this respect the satiric passage cited earlier from "Vision of Judgment." All the (by now) familiar charges are brought forward – for example, in stanzas 80 and 85:

He was a man who had seen many changes,
  And always changed as true as any needle,
His polar star being one which rather ranges,
  And not the fix'd—he knew the way to wheedle:
So vile he 'scaped the doom which oft avenges;
  And being fluent (save indeed when fee'd ill),
He lied with such a fervour of intention—
There was no doubt he earn'd his laureate pension.

. . .

Thus, usually, when he was ask'd to sing,
  He gave the different nations something national;
'Twas all the same to him—"God save the king,"
  Or "*Ca ira*," according to the fashion all;
His muse made increment of any thing,
  From the high lyric down to the low rational:
If Pindar sang horse-races, what should hinder
Himself from being as pliable as Pindar?

These stanzas epitomize Byron's usual critique of the poet as renegade and unscrupulous time-server, and they sum up the general tone of Byron's presentation in the passage as a whole. But two other stanzas in the sequence disturb the proprieties which customarily govern Byron's satire in these situations. In stanza 84 Byron tells us that this poet

had travell'd 'mongst the Arabs, Turks, and Franks,
  And knew the self-loves of the different nations;
And having lived with people of all ranks,
  Had something ready upon most occasions—
Which got him a few presents and some thanks.
  He varied with some skill his adulations;
To "do at Rome as Romans do," a piece
Of conduct was which he observed in Greece.

These lines recall nothing so much as Byron himself: first, as the Levantine cruiser of 1809–1811, and second, as the poet and social lion of 1812–1814. Byron had fun at Southey's Laureate expense, and while he sometimes protested that he never courted his immense popularity or flattered his adulators, he knew that he had in fact "filed [his] mind" (*Childe Harold* III, 113, 9) during his Years of Fame. For Byron himself, those years were far from innocent of the "adulations" for which he denounced Southey. Of himself he could say, with far more certainty than he could of Southey, that he had written verse to foster his image and advance his career. Like Lady Adeline, however, such work was produced side by side with those self-revelatory looks (or poems) "Of weariness or scorn" which reflected critically on the "adulations." Indeed, the "adulations" themselves frequently displayed their own internal self-contradictions.

In the "sad trimmer" poet, then, we glimpse the face of Robert Southey, and this is no great surprise; but in the allusion to Southey the outlines of another, unexpected face are also glimpsed. This palimpsest produces an unstable and apparently self-contradicted text whose true biographical subject – Byron himself – emerges from beneath the layers of his own normal satiric displacements:

> But now being lifted into high society,
>   And having picked up several odds and ends
> Of free thoughts in his travels, for variety,
>   He deem'd, being in a lone isle, among friends,
> That without any danger of a riot, he
>   Might for long lying make himself amends;
> And singing as he sung in his warm youth,
> Agree to a short armistice with truth. (*DJ* III, 83)

This could be, and is in part, an oblique thrust at Southey's renegado turn from his youthful republicanism to his later apostasy. It is also, however, an even more oblique glimpse of Byron's political and poetical career up to 1816, which was marked by its own definite, if much less apparent, forms of ideological backsliding and dishonesty. Byron was much more "cunning in [his] own overthrow" than Southey was, but that he had pursued "False Ambition" and betrayed his soul's "nobler aim" he could not, and would not, deny (see "[Epistle to Augusta]," 97, 102). And so "for long lying" he aimed, in this passage, to "make himself amends" in the form of an imitation revolutionary Greek ballad, the famous "Isles of Greece."[2]

The poem is at once an admonishment, or call, and a fulfillment of his highest poetical ideals. And the fulfillment lies precisely in this: that when he *now* sings "as he sung in his warm youth" he reveals, self-consciously and deliberately, both his utopian goals (to which he rededicates himself) and his understanding that he has been the worst betrayer of those goals. He is the worst because he appeared, to himself and to others, as one of the staunchest supporters of such goals.

The ballad's subtle mastery emerges when this network of allusions, intertexts, and subtexts is fully comprehended. In general, Byron's fiction is that the ballad is sung by a Romaic poet in the late 1780s to an audience of his fellows who live quiescently under Turkish rule. It calls them from their lives of pleasure and political degeneracy to take up a more strenuous and principled course of action. At this level, it is a poem determined to raise the Greek national consciousness. Consequently, though its fictive date is the late 1780s, and though it recalls the Greek patriotic songs of the late eighteenth century (like Rhiga's "War Song"), its 1820 context is equally operative. In fact, the Greek war for independence was to commence in 1821, and Byron's early attachment to that cause would draw him in 1823 from Italy to western Greece and his famous death in 1824.

Don Juan's fictive level – that is, the plot of Juan's career in the poem's imagined time scheme stretching from about 1787 to its (unreached) conclusion in 1793 – is always calling attention to its narrative (or "real") level: that is, to the poem as a continuing historical event which unfolds before its European audience between 1818 and 1824, and which makes that context part of its subject. This interplay between a fictive and a narrative time scheme throws into relief a dominant fact about *Don Juan*: that it is fundamentally an autobiographical poem which comments upon and interprets the course of European history between 1787 and 1824. In the case of "The Isles of Greece," Byron's fictional Greek poet masks, only to reveal more clearly, the poem's true author. As always in *Don Juan*, Byron reveals and thereby manipulates his poetical machinery in a self-conscious drama of his own mind. We therefore observe this ballad as a vehicle for satirizing Southey and all other republican turncoats, for satirizing generally those who have betrayed the cause of the European political ideal of liberty which had its origin in ancient Greece and which appeared once again in various revolutionary movements during the late eighteenth and early nineteenth centuries (paradigmatically in America and France). So, when we read "The Isles in Greece" we are also to *see* Lord Byron satirizing Robert Southey in 1820.

At the poem's most complex level, we also *see through* Byron's satire of Southey into the innermost drama of his own mind. Consider the ballad's fifth stanza.

And where are they? and where art thou,
  My country? On thy voiceless shore
The heroic lay is tuneless now—
  The heroic bosom beats no more!
And must thy lyre, so long divine,
Degenerate into hands like mine?

An act of poetic ventriloquism multiplies the pronominal references in these lines. The Romaic poet sings here of himself and of Greece, but the English poet sings of England and Lord Byron. The ideal of Greece calls out to Byron's, and England's, identification with that ideal, just as the degeneracy of present-day Greece (whether conceived in the context of 1787 or of 1820) reflects upon England's, and Byron's, betrayals of their most cherished, and Greek-derived, ideals.

Two fictive voices sing "The Isles of Greece": the imaginary Romaic poet of 1787 and the imagined Robert Southey of 1820 and they sing of the ideals and betrayals of themselves and their respective countries. In the end, however, the two voices are incorporated as the poetically "actual" voice of Lord Byron, who sings of his own immediate psychic and political situation and the context in which it had developed.

'Tis something, in the dearth of fame,
  Though link'd among a fetter'd race,
To feel at least a patriot's shame,
  Even as I sing, suffuse my face;
For what is left the poet here?
For Greeks a blush, for Greece a tear.

A passage like this dramatically reveals the complex voicing techniques of the ballad, along with the related and equally complex network of references and levels of statement. In these lines the "Fame" is Greece's, England's, and Byron's; the "fetter'd race" is Greek, but also Italian (Byron is writing his poem in the Italian dominions of the Austrian Empire), and – even more generally – European ("There is *no* freedom – even for *Masters* – in the midst of slaves" [*BLJ*, IX, 41]). Thus, when Byron gestures to "the poet here," his words resonate in the widest European context of 1787–1824.

The ballad plays itself out as a contest between the rival claims of "The Scian and the Teian muse, / The hero's harp, the lover's lute" (2, 1–2). Representing a poetical career and its goals as a dialectic between the shifting claims of heroic and amatory verse (here, specifically, between Homer and Anacreon) is a pre-eminently Byronic structure of thought.[3] His entire life's work as a poet develops as a self-lacerating experience of their rival claims. Whenever Byron moves too definitively toward one of these poetical and political ideals he will call upon the other to limit, criticize, and judge its illusions and appeals. Byron's great lyric "On This Day I Complete My Thirty-Sixth Year" culminates this conflict by representing it as (by itself) a hopeless one. "On This Day" calls for its cessation by invoking the option of suicide.

Such is also the option toward which "The Isles of Greece" makes its final gesture.

> Place me on Sunium's marbled steep,
>   Where nothing, save the waves and I,
> May hear our mutual murmurs sweep;
>   There, swan-like, let me sing and die:
> A land of slaves shall ne'er be mine—
> Dash down you cup of Samian wine.
>
> (16)

As in the later lyric, when the poet here chooses death to break the impasse of his life, his choice involves a decision for the claims of heroism. What is important to see is that this is an historical choice, one demanded by time, place, and circumstance. The voice of the Scian muse plays through "The Isles of Greece" to remind us of the essential virtues of a truly civilized life, which would not include war and violence. But no such life is possible when the social structure is degenerate at its ground.

> Fill high the bowl with Samian wine!
>   Our virgins dance beneath the shade—
> I see their glorious black eyes shine;
>   But gazing on each glowing maid,
> My own the burning tear-drop laves,
> To think such breasts must suckle slaves.
>
> (15)

In such times the image of love itself becomes an occasion for swerving toward heroic values. Nevertheless, we have to see that the move toward the heroic is now regarded as deeply equivocal, a fate or doom embraced by those who are willing to sacrifice themselves by choosing an heroic life in order to secure, at some future date, the restoration of a civilized order.

Thus the ideological structures of "On This Day" and "The Isles of Greece" are all but exact equivalents. However, "On This Day" is a much more interiorized poem, and that difference is crucial. The fact that Byron's voice in "The Isles of Greece" is explicitly mixed with the voices of Southey and the modern Greek patriot, and implicitly with the entire Anacreontic and Homeric traditions, socializes the lyric in a number of important and specific ways. The history imbedded in "On This Day" is Byron's personal history and the drama is fundamentally psychic. In "The Isles of Greece," on the other hand, the complex voicing extends the world of which and for which the poem is speaking. "On This Day" is set in 1824, in Greece, and in Byron's mind – finally, in the relations which the poem establishes between these three *loci* and all that each implicitly involves. The layered voices in "The Isles of Greece" dramatically enlarge the poem's network of references, forcing the reader to consider the complex *relations* of those references. In the end – like *Don Juan* itself – the lyric implies that European history between 1787 and 1820 is all of a piece, and that the condition of Greece during the period is the very symbol of the condition of Europe. At the end of the eighteenth century Greece looked for freedom from Turkish rule as Europe looked for a revolutionary emancipation from inherited and archaic political order; in 1820, despite the intervening years of turmoil and promise, the *status quo* has been (at least formally and materially) preserved. Even more telling, however, is the poem's revelation of all of Europe's – including England's – complicity in this state of affairs. In 1809–1811 Byron began to fear the truth of such complicity and he expressed his fears in *Childe Harold's Pilgrimage I–II.*[4] In 1820 his fears have been fully realized. "The Isles of Greece" exposes, analyzes, and judges this complicity. The English Lord speaks as and for the failed Greek patriot and the turncoat Jacobin Southey. In *Don Juan*'s "Dedication" and elsewhere Byron will separate himself from Southey, Castlereagh, Matternich, and the forgers of Europe's spiritual slavery. Here, by contrast, he speaks with their voices and says, of himself and for all those who have judged themselves innocent: "*Hypocrite lecteur, mon semblable, mon frère.*"

In "The Isles of Greece" Byron's voice does, however, gain a certain frail integrity through its aspiration toward the whole truth, toward complete freedom from cant. The ballad reveals and denounces the canting life of its age by constructing a poem which gives lip service to the traditional Western ideas of love and honor. Its honesty appears as a double understanding: first, that these ideals, in their inherited forms at any rate, are conflicted and self-contradictory; and second, that lip service, in Byron's age, is the most which history could expect. Byron everywhere speaks of the degeneracy of his period, a condition he deplored in the political, poetical, and moral cant which was being delivered by contemporary ideologues like Southey. These are the voices who speak with authority of what is right and wrong, good and evil, angelic and satanic. Byron's voice, by contrast, undercuts and renders ironic every voice which pretends to assume this kind of authority. The shock and even the genius of this procedure lies in the poetry's final level of irony, where Byron deliberately assumes the *rhetoric* of a total and dependable authority. Byron's high style – which appears once again in this famous ballad – projects the ideal of the poet and hero *manqué*, the figure who alone (in both senses) can speak in an unbetrayed voice of his age's persistent betrayals:

> Thus sung, or would, and could, or should have sung,
>   The modern Greek, in tolerable verse;
> If not like Orpheus quite, when Greece was young,
>   Yet in these times he might have done much worse:
> His strain display'd some feeling—right or wrong;
>   And feeling, in a poet, is the source
> Of others' feeling, but they are such liars,
> And take all colours—like the hands of dyers. (III, 87)

Thus Byron sums up the significance of the ballad he has just presented. The statement displays the ironic equivocalness engineered in "these times," but it equally and forthrightly says that a poet "might have done much worse" than this. The remark recalls Southey's Laureate performances as well as Byron's own earlier work in which the truth he is fundamentally committed to had been subtly, cunningly betrayed. Like the several stanzas which follow, this one concludes in that typical Byronic gesture of resolute irresolution: an equivocal affirmation of the power of poetry, on the one hand, and an equally equivocal pronouncement upon its unreliability.

The Shakespeare echo at the end of the stanza recalls Byron's views on poetic mobility. The cynical tone in which the echo is made, however – so unlike the original passage – reminds us, in this case, that Byron's ventriloquism, or mobility, is everywhere marked by the "weariness or scorn" which Juan glimpsed in Adeline's accommodating looks. Paradoxically, Byron's cynicism is a liberating rather than a defeatist move because Byron is aware that the past – its deeds, its voices, its ideas – cannot be appropriated to the present through simple gestures of mobility or chameleonic acts. Byron turns a mordant eye on the inheritance of greatness (especially poetic greatness) because he knows that its ideal apparitions conceal human, equivocal truths. Indeed, when those equivocal human forms do not appear, the ideals enter the world as monsters.

In the ballad, the temptation to accept an idealized view of the voices and deeds of the past appears most clearly in the call to heroic action – for example, in stanza 8:

> What, silent still? and silent all?
> Ah! no;—the voices of the dead
> Sound like a distant torrent's fall,
> And answer, "Let one living head,
> But one arise,—we come, we come!"
> 'Tis but the living who are dumb.

But the fact is that these martial voices from the dead may (and have) issued calls to freedom *and* to tyranny. The "Turkish hordes" of stanza 9 have answered that call as surely as did the 300 who fell at Thermopylae. If "the living . . . are dumb" now to that call, their silence may be the honesty of Keats's aesthetic escapism, or the critical judgment of the sybarite Sardanapalus. Besides, Byron has seen the call answered too often and too well by the poets and ideologues of European imperialism: by a Southey in his Waterloo hymns, and by a Wordsworth who could proclaim that the carnage of battle is the daughter of God.

So in the ballad the voice of the Scian muse repeatedly undercuts the voice of the Teian – but not definitively. Anacreon's role, in this respect, is to introduce the note of "weariness or scorn" into the poem's act of heroic ventriloquism. In this way Byron tries to insure that he will raise up from the past a human rather than a demonic figure; and in this way he also manages to compose, in 1820, a song on behalf of human freedom which escapes incorporation by the Age of Cant. The crowning wit of the poem is that the song is offered to the reader as a familiar Byronic *tour de force* in which the poet's identity is submerged in a network of competing voices. Byron appears, in the end, as the self-conscious creator and observer of his own verse: the man who finds his mixed identity and equivocal freedom when he acknowledges the constellation of his own social determinants, the man who discovers his voice in a conscious and dialectical act of poetic ventriloquism.

NOTES

1 I suppose it does not need to be remarked that this representation of the Laureate is a travesty of his actual character. In fact, the worst that might be said of him would be the opposite, that he was narrow and self-righteous (Byron accused him of these vices as well, of course – elsewhere). For a good assessment of his character see Geoffrey Carnall, *Robert Southey*.

2 For an excellent discussion of the poem's Greek context, both classical and modern, see Kiriakoula Solomou's recent studies, "Byron and Greek Poetry," and "Influence."

3 We should recall here Byron's early translations of Anacreontic verse.

4 The whole of this book comprises a commentary on Greece and on Europe's relation to Greece's political condition under Turkish rule. Byron was deeply critical of the hypocrisy of English, French, and Russian philhellenism, as we see most clearly in the notes and appendices which he included in *Childe Harold's Pilgrimage: A Romaunt* (1812). Most telling of all – and almost never noticed – is Byron's reference to, and partial translation of, the Romaic satire of Greece, England, Russia, and France: the so-called "Rossanglogallos." See Solomou's discussion, "Influence," and "Byron and Greek Poetry," 186–190, 218–221, 210–318; see also Byron, *Poetical Works*, II, 213–215.

BIBLIOGRAPHY

Byron, George Gordon, Lord. *Byron's Letters and Journals*. Ed. Leslie Marchand. 13 vols. London: John Murray, 1973–1982. Cited in parentheses as *BLJ*.

Byron's Don Juan: A Variorum Edition. Ed. T. G. Steffan and W. W. Pratt. 4 vols. Austin: University of Texas Press, 1957.

The Complete Poetical Works. Ed. Jerome J. McGann. 7 vols. Oxford: Clarendon Press, 1980–1992.

The Works of Lord Byron: Poetry. Ed. Ernest Hartley Coleridge. 7 vols. London: John Murray, 1898–1904. The texts of Byron's poems – with the exception of the passages from *Don Juan*, taken from Steffan and Pratt, eds. – are taken from this edition.

Carnall, Geoffrey. *Robert Southey and His Age: The Development of a Conservative Mind*. Oxford: Clarendon Press, 1960.

Grierson, H. J. C. "Lord Byron: Arnold and Swinburne," *Wharton Lectures on English Poetry* 11 (1920).

Keats, John. *The Letters of John Keats*. Vol. II. Ed. Hyder Edward Rollins. Cambridge, MA: Harvard University Press, 1958.

Ridenour, George. *The Style of* Don Juan. New Haven: Yale University Press, 1960.

Solomou, Kiriakoula. "Byron and Greek Poetry." Diss. University of Aberdeen, 1980. See esp. 249–299.

"The Influence of Greek Poetry on Byron." *Byron Journal* 10 (1982), 4–19.

CHAPTER 3

"My brain is feminine": Byron and the poetry of deception

I

I begin with a mouldy anecdote, a late supplement to that once-flourishing industry – now part of the imagination's rust belt – called "Curiosities of Literature."

In 1894 a short article appeared in *Notes and Queries* under the heading "Byroniana." Its subject was a poem entitled "The Mountain Violet" which the author of the article, Henry Wake, attributed to Byron.[1] The case for authenticity was argued on two counts, one archival and one stylistic. The archival argument observed that the poem was printed in an anthology of verse collected by one Charles Snart under the title *A Selection of Poems*, published in Newark in two volumes in 1807–1808. Wake said that he was in possession of a set of Snart's edition with "Mrs. Byron" written in pencil in her hand on the front flyleaf, and with the following notation on the end flyleaf of Volume II: "66 from Nottingham Journal." The latter was a reference to "The Mountain Violet," which was printed on page 66 of Vol. II. The poem, it turns out, was in fact first printed in the *Nottingham Journal* on 9 April 1803. Neither printing atttributes authorship, but according to Wake the pencil notation at the end of Snart's book is in Byron's hand.[2]

Wake went on to argue that the poem's style showed remarkable congruities with the style of Byron's early verse. Such matters are difficult to decide, of course, especially when one is dealing with juvenilia. At that stage of a career, an author's style will be derivative, and one expects to observe features which will be common to any number of other contemporary writers. Nonetheless, the stylistic similarities are striking; and this fact, coupled with the archival evidence, led Wake to his attribution. Wake's judgment was seconded by the distinguished Byronist Richard Edgecumbe, who wrote a brief supporting article which appeared shortly afterwards in *Notes and Queries*. (I pass without comment the importance of Nottingham and Newark since, as all Byronists know, these are places strongly connected with Byron's early verse – the writing of it, the printing, the publishing.)[3]

I initially became interested in this minor literary incident when I began editing Byron's poetry – that was in 1970. "The Mountain Violet" had never been included in a collected edition of Byron's works, and I had to decide what to do in my edition. For sixteen years that poem remained in my files under the heading "Dubia" – in other words, in an editorial limbo, neither in nor out of the authoritative corpus. In 1986, however, I discovered the truth about "The Mountain Violet." Byron did not write it. The poem is the work of Charlotte Dacre, and it was published in her two-volume poetry collection in 1805, *Hours of Solitude*.

I made my discovery while I was reading Dacre's books, reading them for the first time, I am ashamed to say. It was a discovery I was very happy to have made. But the reading led to another, related discovery about Byron's poetry, and that second discovery is what I want to talk about today.

The title *Hours of Solitude*, for one who knows Byron, can suggest only one thing: *Hours of Idleness*, Byron's first published book of verse issued two years after Dacre's book. This verbal echo is in fact only one part of the massive act of allusion to Dacre which constitutes the title page of Byron's book: the format of the latter imitates Dacre's title page in the most remarkable way. As might be expected, the title page signals a series of textual echoes and allusions which are scattered through the "Original" parts of the book Byron subtitled "Poems Original and Translated." Indeed, Byron's misguided plea, in his book's Preface, for the reader's "indulgence" because the poems are "the productions . . . of the lighter hours of a young man, who has lately completed his nineteenth year" was a move he took over directly from Dacre. In her prefatory note "To the Reader" and then throughout the text, she called attention to "the age at which [her poems] were written" (that is, all before she was twenty-three, and many when she was sixteen or younger).

What most impressed Byron in *Hours of Solitude* were the poems of sentiment. The poems he addressed to various female persons in his first three books (the volumes culminating in *Hours of Idleness*), as well as lyrics like "The First Kiss of Love," call back to a number of similar poems in Dacre's work – for example, "The Kiss," "The Sovereignty of Love," "To Him Who Says He Loves," and so forth. In the last section of *Hours of Idleness*, which comprises a kind of critical reflection on all of his poetry to that point, Byron includes a new poem, "To Romance," where he reluctantly (and sentimentally) acknowledges a failure of the muse of sentiment.

This instance of a neglected influence on Byron's juvenile poetry might appear just another item in the shop of literature's curiosities. But the event has an aftermath of real consequence in the history of Byron's work. The event has perhaps an even greater consequence for an understanding of the history and significance of so-called sentimental poetry, especially as it was written by women – but that is a large subject which I shall not, unfortunately, be able to take up here. Today I shall concentrate on the smaller and more local matter, on Byron.

We start to glimpse the complications involved by recalling Byron's attack upon Della Cruscan poetry in *English Bards and Scotch Reviewers*. The celebrity of that group of writers had waned since Gifford attacked them in his nineties satires *The Baviad* (1791) and *The Maeviad* (1795).[4] Nonetheless, their influence on contemporary writing remained considerable and can be traced even in writers who are still given prominent positions in our somewhat skewed literary histories: in, for example, Moore and Shelley, as well as Keats and Byron. Dacre published under the Della-Cruscan-style pseudonym "Rosa Matilda,"[5] and in *English Bards* Byron attacks her under that name, and through her the late flowers of the Della Cruscan gardens:

> Far be't from me unkindly to upbraid
> The lovely ROSA's prose in masquerade,
> Whose strains, the faithful echoes of her mind,
> Leave wondering comprehension far behind.
> Though Crusca's bards no more our journals fill,
> Some stragglers skirmish round the columns still,
> Last of the howling host which once was Bell's,
> Matilda snivels yet, and Hafiz yells. (755–762)[6]

In an attached prose note Byron characterizes Dacre as a "follower of the Della Cruscan School," the author of "two very respectable absurdities in rhyme" as well as "sundry novels in the style of the first edition of the Monk" (*CPW*, I, 413). These remarks are laced with witty innuendo. "The first edition of the Monk" (1796) created such a scandal that Lewis was driven to delete and revise the sexual passages which were so offensive to many readers. Byron links Dacre's novel *The Confessions of a Nun of St. Omer* (1805), which was dedicated to Lewis, with the latter's notorious novel, and when he characterizes Dacre's poetry as "very respectable" he wants his irony to be taken. "Sentimental" poetry like that by Dacre, Mrs. Hannah Cowley ("Anna Matilda"), and Mary ("Perdita") Robinson (or by Moore and Byron and Shelley) did not go in for the sexual fleshliness that one finds in certain Gothic novels and plays; nonetheless, the sexuality of such writing was explicit even if the diction and imagery were kept, as Byron delicately puts it, "very respectable."

In this context let us recall the crucial bibliographical facts: that *Hours of Idleness* was published in June 1807, and that *English Bards* was initially composed between October 1807 and November 1808. It took Byron less than a year to break off his literary liaison with Rosa Matilda, and to publicize their separation. In fact, the breakup took somewhat longer than that, as one can see by glancing at Byron's first two books of verse, both privately printed. *Fugitive Pieces* (1806), Byron's first book, is distinctly marked by that sort of "very respectable" poetry which *English Bards* ridiculed in the "sentimental" verse of various writers, and particularly in the work of Dacre and in the work of his later close friend Tom Moore.[7] Byron's second book, *Poems Original and Translated* (1807), he himself characterized as "miraculously chaste"[8] because it represented a deliberate effort to tone down the "sentimentalities" which had so heated up, in their presumably different ways, the readers of *Fugitive Pieces*. By the time he gets to writing *English Bards* Byron has abandoned the sexually charged poetry – the "sentimental" poetry – which had initially seduced him. Byron becomes "very respectable."

In doing so, however, we have to recognize how Byron has changed the character of his own changes. His turn (between 1808 and 1816) from what he would later call "amorous writing" (*Don Juan*, [hereafter in references *DJ*] V, st. 2) to a concentration on satire, travelogue, and heroic poetry was a turn from "feminine" to "masculine" modes, a turn from Anacreon to Horace and Homer. When *English Bards* announced this shift in Byron's work by an appeal to Gifford, the poem was specifically invoking a memory of Gifford's own satiric attack on the Della Cruscans in his two popular satires of the 1790s. In Byron's case, however, the turn involved a key self-referential feature which was entirely absent in Gifford's work. Gifford had never felt anything but abhorrence for Della Cruscan and sentimental poetry, while Byron cut his poetical teeth on it. In this respect, *English Bards* represents a typically Romantic act of displacement. Charlotte Dacre, among other amorous sentimentalists, is ridiculed in Byron's satire, but in truth he simply attacks her for a kind of writing which he himself had been driven from because the writing had offended certain provincial readers.[9] The attack on Dacre in the satire is distinctly an act of bad poetic faith.

But Byron was not happy with himself for having bowed to the prudery of Southwell society in suppressing *Fugitive Pieces*, and *Hours of Idleness* was an effort to keep some faith with Charlotte Dacre even as he acceded to certain of the wishes of Southwell's "knot of ungenerous critics."[10] In *English Bards*, however, Byron made a complete – but as we shall see, not a final nor a clean – break with Rosa Matilda, and he did so because *Hours of Idleness* was still judged too mawkish and sentimental – this time not by a provincial audience, but by the mighty and male *Edinburgh Review*. Of course, Byron struck back at his accusers with his first famous satire, but in doing so he adopted the style and the language of his attackers. Byron became what he beheld, and in the process Rosa Matilda fell, in Byron's eyes, from grace. The process is one in which Byron tries to redeem himself and his work by making a scapegoat of writers and writing which had given literal birth to his own imagination.

And so "The Mountain Violet" drops away from the Byron canon. It is in fact a spurious text, quite inauthentic; nonetheless, it stands as a sign of a deeper kind of authenticity which Byron would struggle his entire life to regain.

II

"Sentimental" poetry – the term will be taken here in its technical and historical sense – was associated with women writers in particular, though a great many male poets wrote sentimental verse. As a pejorative term it came to stand in general for writing which made a mawkish parade of spurious feelings. In the late eighteenth and early nineteenth centuries, however, such work was as frequently deplored for immodesty and even indecency; and the attacks were all the more virulent because so many women, both as writers and as readers, found important resources in this kind of work. To many, and especially to those (men and women both) who felt called upon to guard public morals, the whole thing seemed improper or worse; nor were the attacks without foundation.[11]

Crucial to sentimental poetry is the centrality of love to human experience and – more significantly – the idea that true love had to involve a total intensity of the total person – mind, heart, and (here was the sticking point) body. Love could be betrayed at any of those centres, and a betrayal of the body (through either lust or a prudish fastidiousness) was as disastrous as a betrayal of the mind or heart. Indeed, a betrayal at any point was the equivalent of a sin, for the "sentimental" soul was equally diffused through the entire sensorium. The stylistic index of sentimental poetry, therefore, is a peculiar kind of self-conscious fleshliness. Dacre's poem "The Kiss" provides a good example of the style – for instance, the first stanza.

> The greatest bliss
> Is in a kiss—
> A kiss by love refin'd,
> When springs the soul
> Without controul,
> And blends the bliss with mind.

Sentimental poetry strives to be both emotionally intense and completely candid. Its purpose is to "bring the whole soul of man [and woman] into activity," an event which, in the context of such writing, means that it is to bring along the whole person – mind and body as well. So the paradoxes of this poem swirl about the demand for an experience that is at once completely impassioned ("without controul"), completely physical, and yet perfectly "refin'd" as well. The poem solicits a wild erotics of the imagination where blissful consummations occur in and through, or "with," the "mind."

Byron and all the Romantics wrote a great deal of sentimental poetry – this is precisely why they were attacked by modernist ideologues like Hulme, Babbitt, and Eliot. Keats and Shelley are probably our greatest sentimental poets, but even Wordsworth's verse is marked by sentimentality. Wordsworth, however, made a life's work out of "subliming," as it were, the project of sentimentalism – attempting to show that the "sensations sweet / Felt in the blood and felt along the heart" were actually the impulses of "something far more deeply interfused," something he called "the purer mind" ("purer," that is, because it had to be distinguished from the sort of mind that Dacre was describing).[12]

But as Wordsworth was moved by a spiritual transcendence of sensuality and sexuality, Byron plunged completely into the contradictions which sentimentalism had come to involve for him. While these contradictions no doubt have deep psychological roots, I am incompetent to explore such matters. What is clear, at the social and personal level, is that Byron reconstructed those contradictions in his work.

We begin to see this in the myth of the relations between men and women which he deploys in his poetry between 1808 and 1816. This involves a misogynist inversion of a central myth of the sentimentalist program. According to the sentimentalist idea, when an individual only pretends to the intensities and sensitivities of sentimental love, he (or she) betrays not merely the persons who are love-engaged, they betray love itself in its fullest expression. Byron accepts the sentimentalist terms of the entire transaction: that love-relations will be cast along the norm of heterosexuality; that the partner (in Byron's case, the figure of the woman) is his epipsyche; and that a total love-experience – physical, mental, and spiritual – is the goal.

The "reality-principle" in this myth (and the term must be put in quotation because it stands only for a myth of reality) is that Byron's sentimental beloveds (who turn out plural, if not legion) continually betray the contract of love.[13] At times Byron will implicate himself in these betrayals of love – for example in the early *Childe Harold* when, in the lyric "To Florence," he writes of the "wayward, loveless heart" of the wandering – in several senses – Childe. But even in his Childe Harold mode Byron typically represents himself as a man devoted to love yet continually driven from it, or deprived of it, by circumstance. Byron wants to imagine himself true to love, but cruelly kept from it by interventions beyond his control: the time will be right but the place will be wrong; both time and place will be right, but the social or political structure of the events will make an impediment; or all circumstances will be provident, except the ages of the parties; and so forth. In any case, love is lost – mysteriously, fatally lost, but not by the will of Childe Byron, who is at all times and in all places love-devoted.

That Byronic constancy maintains itself despite the fact that its ideal-object, the feminine beloved, appears as a figure of repeated deceits and betrayals. Sometimes the beloved is lost circumstantially (for example through an untimely death) but she also moves away by her "wandering," by attaching herself to someone else. Mary Chaworth, Susan Vaughan, Lady Frances Wedderburn Webster, even Lady Caroline Lamb: according to this legend, all prove to be, if not positively "false," then at least "fickle."[14]

This Byronic myth is set down between 1808 and 1816 in a series of lyrics composed with these and perhaps several other women in mind.[15] The three most important, and even astonishing, poems in this series are "[Again Deceived! Again Betrayed]", written to the servant-girl Susan Vaughan; the lyric addressed to Lady Caroline Lamb that begins "Go – triumph securely – that treacherous vow"; and lastly "When We Two Parted," a poem written in memory of Lady Frances Wedderburn

Webster. The 1816–1817 poems written to and about his wife and his sister, including *Manfred*, involve a culminant and critical turn upon the entire pattern, and establish the ground on which the last six years of Byron's poetry will be written.

Though a general myth of social and psychic dysfunction, the Byronic malaise is most acutely expressed as a failure of love. A central representation of the myth is forthrightly stated in the opening lines of the first of the works just mentioned, the lyric addressed to Susan Vaughan.

> Again deceived! again betrayed!
>   In manhood as in youth,
> The dupe of every smiling maid
>   That ever "lied like truth". —

The poem's idea is that Byron, for all his experience in love, simply never learns – that he is too fond, too sentimental. Not that he fails to recognize his own fickleness; as he points out in the third stanza,

> In turn deceiving or deceived
>   The wayward Passion roves,
> Beguiled by her we most believed,
>   Or leaving her who loves.

But the typography and syntax here deflect the self-accusation even as it presses its charges against the "smiling maid." What "roves" here is not "Byron" or even the speaker of the lines, it is "The wayward Passion," the latter word capitalized in order to depersonalize further Byron's involvement. Besides, Byron's persona in these transactions never smiles, like the deceitful "maid"; he is too heartbroken for that, too sentimental.

The poem, in other words, is a peculiar exercise in "lying like truth," a work which once again deceives and betrays sentimental love by its pretences to faithfulness and candor. The occasion of the poem, we know, was Byron's discovery that he was not the only lover of the Newstead servant-girl Susan Vaughan. In the illusion that he was, Byron was equally deceiving himself and deceived by her. But the greater deception of the poem, and the source of its strength, lies in its assent to its own self-deceptions. This is the deception which makes the poem turn its sting back on itself, like the famous scorpion in *The Giaour*. The epigraph Byron placed at the head of the poem appears finally not to be a comment on Susan Vaughan or women generally, but a gloss on the poem itself.

I pull in resolution and begin
To doubt the equivocation of the fiend
That lies like truth. (*Macbeth*)

Finally this poem shows itself to be most concerned with how the mind and its constructions wound and betray one's life. *Manfred* will be the culminant text in this important line of Byronic work. It is not the historical Susan Vaughan who is the deceiver in this poem, it is the *figura* of the woman which the work conjures up and sets in motion. It is, in short, Byron's own mind and imagination – the "author" of this figure of Susan Vaughan who uses his writing to "lie like truth" both about her and about the *persona* of himself offered in the poem. By the time this author writes *Manfred* he will be able to see the entire pattern of this kind of writing more clearly. "I loved her, and destroy'd her!" Manfred says of his epipsyche Astarte (2, 2, 117), thereby expressing what amounts, in this Byronic myth, to a double tautology (for both pronouns and verbs in this sentence are equivalent).

The poem Byron wrote about Lady Caroline Lamb is perhaps an even more breathtaking display of "lying like truth."

Go—triumph securely—the treacherous vow
Thou hast broken *I* keep but too faithfully now,
But never again shall thou be to my heart
What thou wert—what I feel for a moment thou *art.*

To see thee, to love thee! what breast could do more?
To love thee to lose thee 'twere vain to deplore;
Ashamed of my weakness however beguiled,
I shall bear like a Man what I feel like a Child.

At first these lines seem hard to understand – at least as we read them in their topical context, that is, in 1812, and at the height of Byron's torrid affair with Lady Caroline.[16] The poem distinctly recalls the lines to Susan Vaughan, which Byron had written only shortly before and which, in one of the two manuscript versions, he had begun "Again beguiled! again betrayed!" not 'Again deceived." Once again we meet the *figura* of the repeated deceiver whose name only changes. The problem is, however, that *in fact* Lady Caroline remained perfectly faithful to Byron in 1812. What does the poem have in mind, then, when it speaks of her "treacherous vow"?

The answer is: her marriage vow to her husband! The agony of the lover here, of Byron, lies in his awareness that he is love-devoted to a woman whose return of love for him involves a betrayal elsewhere. The poem therefore sets out to imagine the futurity of such a love-relationship, to imagine the certainty of Byron's loss of her and the corresponding certainty of her "career" of deceit.

> For the first step of error none e'er could recall,
> And the woman once fallen forever must fall;
> Pursue to the last the career she begun,
> And be *false* unto *many* as *faithless* to *one.*

Such words! – from a lover to his beloved, from Byron to a woman whom he knew had broken her marriage vow only for him! Priggish? Ungrateful? The lines defy adequate characterization because they represent such a fundamental betrayal of love and of truthfulness. Sentimental poets like Charlotte Dacre – and like Byron earlier (and later) in his career – declare that love may be betrayed not only by unfaithfulness, by "wandering," but equally by moral priggishness and prudery. This truly amazing poem shows how the two kinds of betrayal are, as the sentimentalist program insisted, reciprocals of each other, a dialectic of what Blake described as the love-torments of spectre and emanation.

"When we Two Parted" in a way completes Byron's portrait of this circle of deceptions – completes it, first, because the poem explicitly links itself to "Go – triumph securely"; and second, because Byron for the first time deliberately casts the poem as a work of deception.[17] In later years he told his cousin Lady Hardy, in what was only apparitionally a "private" communication, that the poem was written about his affair with Lady Frances Wedderburn Webster, and that when he published it in 1816 he printed it with a purposely "false date," 1808. The poem was actually written in 1815, he said, about events in 1814–1815.[18] The poem was published in Byron's slim volume of *Poems* (1816), the book which also contained the notorious "Fare Thee Well!" and which, as a whole, was fashioned as a kind of summing-up of Byron's life since he left school and entered the fast and false world. The "false date" suggested, among other things, that the events in Byron's life between 1808 (the "date" of "When We Two Parted") and 1816 (the year when Byron's wife left him – *left him*, as Byron so theatrically lamented in "Fare Thee Well!") represent a history of Byron's sufferings at the hands of lying and unfaithful women. And the crown of thorns in that series of sufferings was, *mirabile dictu*, Annabella Milbanke.

Byron states his poetical case against her in his "Lines on Hearing that Lady Byron was Ill," which he wrote late in 1816, while he was working at

Manfred. The poem turns her "illness" into a symbolic event, an outward and physical sign of an inward and spiritual condition. Lady Byron, the poem charges, was in fact the unfaithful one in their relationship, the wife who, whatever his faults, would not remain "faithful" to him when he was begirt with foes. Indeed, as Byron's "moral Clytemnestra" (37) she is made to epitomize Byron's wonderful idea of "moral" adultery:

> And thus once enter'd into crooked ways,
> The early Truth, which was thy proper praise,
> Did not still walk beside thee—but at times
> And with a breast unknowing its own crimes,
> Deceit, averments incompatible,
> Equivocations, and the thoughts which dwell
> In Janus-spirits—the significant eye
> Which learns to lie with silence—the pretext
> Of Prudence, with advantages annex'd—
> The acquiescence in all things which tend,
> No matter how, to the desired end—
> All found a place in thy philosophy. (47–58)

The terms are familiar: like Susan Vaughan and so many others, Annabella is a fiend of equivocations, a woman – *the* woman – who knows how to lie like truth, in this case, to "lie with silence." As applied to the historical Lady Byron, the charges are not unwarranted; nevertheless, the woman addressed in this poem is just as imaginery as the Susan Vaughan, the Caroline Lamb, and the Frances Wedderburn Webster we saw in the other poems. However applicable to Annabella, therefore, this passage has to be read primarily as the key element in a poetical structure of reflections, has to be read – in short – as a self-portrait, down to the very details of its own unconsciousness ("And with a breast unknowing its own crimes").

Byron's texts about unfaithful women were the schools in which he learned to lie with silence. His writing, he told his wife, was an art of equivocation, and its greatness, in a lyric mode, is that it comes in the end to fall under its own judgments:[19]

> For thou art pillow'd on a curse too deep;
> Thou hast sown in my sorrow, and must reap
> The bitter harvest in a woe as real! (22–24)

Like the other lyrics we have examined, Byron appears to address this poem to another person; nevertheless, it finally speaks to, and of, himself alone – that is to say, himself as an individual, *and* himself as a Romantic solitary. The poem is a deception at every level, and most patently at the level of its rhetoric, where its massive self-absorption comes masked as the spoken word. This work was spawned in "hours of solitude." The pronouns shift their referents because the curse Byron refers to is a kind of secular Original Sin: moral or imaginative righteousness, the sense that one knows what is true (one's self) and what is false (the Other), and that the truth one "knows" will set one free. The actual truth, however, as Blake equally saw, is nothing but a "body of falsehood" fashioned in a state of Urizenic solitude. Consequently, the function of poetry – of this poetry of Byron's – is to reveal that body of falsehood, to expose the lies which the mind through its imagination conjures up.

The unfaithfulness of Byron's many women, therefore, is in the end a Byronic *figura* of the betrayed and betraying imagination, which is a specifically male imagination. *Manfred* is a crucial work in Byron's career, then, because it fully objectifies the self-destructiveness of this imagination. Astarte dies not at a blow from Manfred's hand but by a look into his heart. Her "heart," Manfred's epipsyche, "gazed on mine and withered" (2, 2, 119). That catastrophic event involves the deconstruction of the self-deceived and self-destructive Romantic imagination. The death of Astarte is a poetical representation not of the death of a woman, Manfred's sister/beloved, but the death of an idea, an idol, even an ideology. Astarte is Manfred's homunculus, his imagination, and the triumph figured in this play is the triumph of Manfred's "life" over the long disease of his imagination. Manfred's death, in this sense, is the sign that he has finally found it possible to live (or at least to imagine living), has finally escaped those fatal and Romantic illusions of living and loving which *Manfred* names, significantly, Astarte.

Nothing more dramatically reveals the play's awareness of lying and equivocation, and of its own investment in such things, than the so-called "Incantation" uttered over the unconscious body of the play's hero. As I have argued in some detail elsewhere, this poem, first published separately by Byron as a curse and denunciation of his wife, is so incorporated into *Manfred* as to become a judgment on his play's hero, and thereby a judgment on himself.[20] The *Manfred* text of the curse "reads" the earlier, separately published text and exposes the reciprocal truth of its lying representations. "A Voice" speaks the truth over the unconscious Manfred – that his "unfathomed gulfs of guile," "the perfection of [his] art," "call upon" him through this voice, and "compel" him not merely to *see* that he is a hell unto himself: they compel him "to *be* thy proper Hell!" (1, 1, 242–251, my italics). Manfred's Romantic imagination, which represented itself to itself as a resort and an escape from an imperfect world, is actually an Original Sin committed against that world, a way of seeing that, just because it is *merely* a way of seeing and not a way of reciprocating, becomes a way of life which is properly called "Hell," the final solitude. The "Voice" that speaks over Manfred is, as it were, the silenced voice of Astarte, Manfred's epipsyche now not to be represented as a visible figure (which is her emanative form as Manfred's superego) but rather as an audible voice (which is her spectrous form as libido). The character Manfred is not permitted in his play to see or understand this action literally, but Byron's play – both as an intrinsic dramatic event and an extrinsic communicative exchange – is a declarative embodiment of that action. Thus, when Manfred at last falls in with Lady Byron and all of Byron's other figures of lying and betrayal, the entire structure of Byronic betrayal, initiated through Charlotte Dacre and *her* betrayal, is exposed and confessed.

In tracing this literary history I have taken for granted that we understand how literary texts – poems, novels, plays – are always deployed in the practical mode of "communicative exchanges": simply, that they are produced in some material way or another. (In terms of those exchanges, the choice to write and *not* to publish, or to circulate privately, is just as important as the choice to publish.) The bibliography of a literary work is therefore the archive, the memorial machine, which defines and preserves those exchanges.

In the case I have been dealing with here, several of the crucial texts were not published by Byron: the poem to Susan Vaughan was not circulated at all, the poem to Lady Caroline was allowed to circulate among a small group of Regency intimates, and the poem on Lady Byron's illness was also shown only to a few people. None of the texts appeared in print in Byron's lifetime. Furthermore, the crucial lines in "When We Two Parted" which repeat the misogynist message of "Go – triumph securely" were also not published by Byron; he took them out of the published poem and only revealed them later, toward the end of his life, in a letter to Lady Hardy.

In his published work between 1808 and 1816, therefore, Byron's myth of the fallen women is distinctly muted; indeed, the fact that an elaborate mechanism of concealments has been set in motion is itself concealed. "I speak not – I trace not – I breathe not thy name": this notorious line from what is perhaps Byron's most notorious unpublished poem may stand as the epigraph of the Byronic mode. The Byronic hero suffers under some secret sin, and the entire structure of alienations which he both exposes and represents is a function of that sin, which is never identified. The poems we have been reading, however, show quite clearly that the unrevealed sin is the offspring of a habit of imaginative deceptions and misrepresentations. It has no name, this sin; it is the sin which dare not, which cannot, speak its name precisely because it has imagined itself *as* the Unspeakable. And *that*, exactly, is what Byron's work in this period communicates: that the inability or unwillingness to communicate is always an essential feature of the communicative exchange.

III

From 1817 to the end of his life Byron's work is consciously preoccupied with Poetry and Truth. As in the first part of his career, therefore, he is much concerned with the topic of lies and deceptions, with what he liked to call, generically, "cant." But the issues are treated with greater self-consciousness, if not greater intensity and poetical force, in the later work. This comes about largely because from 1816 Byron tried to include himself in, even identify himself with, that company he had imaged as the forever fallen: the company of women. When the Byron of 1808–1816 writes about those who "once fallen for ever must fall," he struggles to distance himself from the judgment they are subjected to. His righteousness is the moral adultery he will imagine as, and call "Lady Byron," Annabella, Clytemnestra. That is to say, it is himself.

The Byron of 1817–1824, however, including his female imaginations, is very different. The difference is registered in the dramatic shift in public judgment. No longer the bad but adorable creature of Regency England, the Byron of the *Don Juan* period is an all-but-hopeless case even in the eyes of those reviewers who had earlier celebrated his work most loudly. And this general abandonment of Byron by the reviews is a true reading of his latest work, for the poetry of 1817–1824 has itself abandoned some of the key moral imaginations which drove and tormented the work of 1808–1816.

The Donna Julia of *Don Juan*, Canto I, is the governing type of his new feminine imagination. In a sense, of course, nothing has changed, for Julia is both a liar and an adulteress. In her incomparable letter to Juan, she even acknowledges that she is one of the forever fallen, bound fatally to "[p]ursue to the last the career she begun," that is, "To love again, and be again undone" (I, st. 194). The difference lies not in her circumstantial life, but in her consciousness of those circumstances. Julia knows herself – wants to know herself – *in herself*, and is not constructing her Self through stories of self-justification.

> Yet if I name my guilt, 'tis not to boast,
> None can deem harshlier of me than I deem:
> I trace this scrawl because I cannot rest—
> I've nothing to reproach, nor to request.
> (I, st. 193)

This is a new image of the Byronic epipsyche, a female *figura* who represents not so much sinfulness as the knowledge of sinfulness, a figure of sympathy and understanding. Julia is the figure who, in refusing to cast reproaches, heaps coals of fire – a curse of forgiveness – on her lover. In the lyric works we glanced at earlier, the male speaker – the Byronic *persona* – speaks to his faithless lover in very different terms. The power of such works comes precisely from their non-consciousness, from their ability to create what the writing does not understand – finally, to create and then themselves represent a figure of self-deception and lack of understanding.

Julia's letter is in the genre of those earlier poems. It represents, however, the Byronic epipsyche's response to her creator – as it were, the "word[s] for mercy" which Manfred had begged in vain to hear from Astarte (2, 4, 155).

> My brain is feminine, nor can forget—
> To all, except your image, madly blind;
> As turns the needle trembling to the pole
> It ne'er can reach, so turns to you my soul.
> (I, st. 195)

Here the structure of the Byronic myth of the feminine is fully revealed. For there are two writers of these lines: Julia, the "soul" and "image" and epipsyche of Byron and his alter-ego Juan; and Lord Byron himself, who here conjures a way (something Manfred failed to do) for that "image" to turn and speak to him in more than simply cryptic tones. The "Julia" of these lines says that her lover Juan is her "soul," her epipsyche. In making this revelation, however, she speaks as the epipsyche of her poetical creator Lord Byron, out of that structure of creation we have been looking at in Byron's various sentimental lyrics. This speaking image, Byron's feminine brain, thus makes explicit a concealed truth of the dynamic of sentimental love as it plays itself out in his poetry: that it is a mechanism of truth-telling, a procedure whereby figures of imagintion tell the truth about their creators, whether the latter are aware of those truths or not.

In moral terms, this change in the character of the Byronic epipsyche appears as a new set of ideas about what it means to tell the truth and what it means to lie.[21] *Don Juan* projects many kinds of lies and liars, of course, but the poem's quintessential figure of lying is, appropriately and characteristically, female. This feminine brain, which Byron ultimately defines as "mobility," reigns from Julia's bedchamber to Lady Adeline's drawing-room. Far from standing as a figure of reproach, however, Byron's feminine brain becomes in *Don Juan* a device – both a figure and a mechanism – of redemption.

This change is especially clear in Canto IX when Byron digresses from a thought about the duplicity "Of politicians and their double front, / Who live by lies, yet dare not boldly lie":

Now What I love in women is, they won't
Or can't do otherwise than lie, but do it
So well, the very truth seems falsehood to it.

And after all, what is a lie? 'Tis but
The truth in masquerade; and I defy
Historians, heroes, lawyers, priests to put
A fact without some leaven of a lie.

(sts. 36–37)

The stanzas weigh in the balance the lies of women and the lies of men (from politicians to priests). The difference lies in this: that the lies of the feminine brain are imagined to be clear, conscious, even brazen, whereas the male brain is unaware of either the substance, the structure, or even the fact of its lying. Indeed, it is this lack of consciousness which turns the lies of the male brain into that central Byronic nemesis called "cant." The hero of this late discourse on the art of lying is, of course, the Julia of Canto I, whose magnificent lying tirade against her cuckolded husband – delivered to his face, in her bedroom, while her lover hides under the bedclothes – is a vision of judgment against him. It is such a vision because the poem means to expose the figure of Julia to us fully – means to expose her even in her awareness of herself as a liar and an adulteress. In this exposure she stands in sharp contrast to Don Alphonso, whose presence in his wife's bedroom stands as the poem's first great figure of "cant," that figure of "double dealing" who conceals his lies and deceptions under a parade of openness and truth.

Both "lying" and "cant" are departures from the truth. Nevertheless, Byron comes to argue that the distinction between these two "forms of life" is neither trivial nor false. Everyone is involved in deception; only the canting person reifies these deceptions, seeks to turn them from images of falsehood into figures of "truth." The latter is precisely the extension of the meaning of the word "cant" which Byron's work carries out. Southey is therefore called not merely a liar in *Don Juan*, he is "that incarnate lie" (x, st. 13) – lying which has assumed a fixed and material existence. Southey assumes such a form almost necessarily because, in Byron's imagination, Southey's vision of judgment is a vision of absolute truth, of which he is the spokesman. Paradoxically, therefore, the Byron of *Don Juan*, like his feminine imaginations in that work, is a deceiver, whereas men like Southey are taken as the representatives of accepted Truth – "truth" being understood now, however, according to that excellent modern proverb, 'Truth is lies that have hardened."[22]

Manfred is once again the key text for constructing this distinction between lying and cant. As Manfred contemplates suicide on a cliff of the Jungfrau he observes:

> There is a power upon me which withholds
> And makes it my fatality to live;
> If it be life to wear within myself
> This barrenness of spirit, and to be
> My own soul's sepulchre, for I have ceased
> To justify my deeds unto myself—
> The last infirmity of evil. (2, 2, 23–29)

Manfred does not redeem himself from "evil" here, he redeems himself from the "last infirmity" which evil deeds tempt one toward: the justification of those deeds, the effort to (mis)represent them as something other than what they are. In determining to cease his processes of self-justification Manfred speaks most directly to the Byronic texts of 1808–1816, explicating them as texts in which these deceptive dramas of self-justification were playing themselves out.

The connection between self-justification and cant is concealed, or revealed, in the Miltonic allusion executed through the phrase "The last infirmity of evil." Here the text glances at Milton's "Lycidas" (II, 70–71), where "The last infirmity of noble minds" is identified as the desire for fame, for a "public approbation." This desire is a recurrent topic in *Don Juan*, where Byron both seduces and abandons the public's approbation, mocks it and pursues it. The success of the work might well be represented, in fact, by the resoluteness with which it negotiates those ambivalent impulses, just as that resoluteness will be usefully traced in *Don Juan's* ambivalent reception history. Indeed, the highest praise that might be given Byron's masterwork is that, although recognized as a masterwork, it never became a cultural touchstone. When the need has arisen for oracular consultations, we have usually gone to Wordsworth and *The Prelude* rather than to Byron or *Don Juan*. (This has been good for Byron, but bad for – a travesty of – Wordsworth.)

Marino Faliero offers another example of a canting self-justification which is pertinent to this discussion. It occurs in Act IV, just after Faliero has overcome his class scruples and determined to carry out the *coup* against the Venetian aristocracy. Faliero reflects on the fact that the oligarchs of Venice, after having insulted him, "trusted to" his aristocratic character, trusted

> To the subduing power which I preserved
> Over my mood, when its first burst was spent.
> But they were not aware that there are things
> Which make revenge a virtue by reflection,
> And not an impulse of mere anger; though
> The laws sleep, justice wakes, and injured souls
> Oft do a public right with private wrong,
> And justify their deeds unto themselves.
>
> (IV, ii, 100–107)

Here the Manfredian phrase works to expose the self-deception of Faliero. The Doge means that his "private wrong," his revenge against his fellow aristocrats, will work in the end a "public right," will bring social justice to Venice. But the Doge is massively self-deceived, for the foundation of his part in the plot against the nobles has nothing to do with social justice or public service and everything to do with a private grievance and personal revenge. The ringing, "noble" phrases ("though / The laws sleep, justice wakes," etc.) are *post facto* special pleading, rhetorical obfuscation. Nevertheless, as in Julia's letter, this text comes to us through two voices. One voice we hear is the Doge's self-deceived voice, whose self-justification and apparent firmness of purpose only mask a deeper moral "infirmity." But that voice is itself defined by a deeper textual voice, which turns the Doge's personal "revenge" into a "virtue by reflection" in a sense entirely unintended by the Doge. This deeper voice, in fact, translates the entire passage into a positive expression on behalf of personal integrity and social justice, the two values here falsely proclaimed by the Doge, and thereby actually revealed through the text.

IV

Byron's interesting new theory of the truth of art is obviously a critique of the Romantic theory of artistic truth, i.e. a critique of the idea of Romantic sincerity. Byron's theory is a defence of a certain kind of poetic artifice which he calls "the truth in masquerade." This remarkable phrase involves an important allusion, indeed, a self-quotation. I cited the originary passage earlier:

> Far be't from me unkindly to upbraid
> The lovely ROSA's prose in masquerade.

The allusion tells us that Byron's theory of truth as poetic artifice is itself a masquerade of some larger truth, including some deceptions and absences of truth. The allusion reminds us, for example, that Byron's theory has concealed origins in that primary type of the poetry of Romantic sincerity, sentimental verse. When Byron in *English Bards* calls Charlotte Dacre's verse "prose in masquerde" he is ridiculing her work along the same lines that he ridiculed, throughout his life, the greatest Romantic poet of sincerity, Wordsworth.

Of course, in *Don Juan* Byron's attack comes from one who repeatedly insists that his poetic artifice aims for a higher kind of sincerity. Furthermore, if the poetry of sincerity is, as Byron says, dull and prosy, *Don Juan* has made an explicit contract with "pedestrian muses" ("Dedication," st. 8). Indeed, if the phrase "prose in masquerade" could ever be applied to any English poem, it could be – as all readers have understood – applied to *Don Juan*, the poem in which Byron "rattle[s] on exactly as [he] talk[s]" (XV, st. 19).

We can sort through some of these complexities by recalling Byron's attacks on some other children of the sentimental muse. When *Don Juan* was first read, the poem struck a number of readers as wickedly obscene. Byron bristled at the charge, and argued that his work would never induce a person to lustful acts because it was a comic poem. "*Lust* is a *serious* passion and . . . cannot be excited by the *ludicrous*," Byron says, and he goes on to contrast his comic writing with serious and sentimental poetry such as his friend Tom Moore's work (*CPW*, V, 679n.). Elsewhere he pursues the same line of argument, only more vigorously, in his brilliant if malicious remarks on Keats's similar sentimental eroticism.

Byron's argument is that the verse of erotic sentimentality – Charlotte Dacre's "prose in masquerade," John Keats's "*p[i]ss a bed* poetry" (*BLJ*, VI, 200) – turns sex from a matter of the body to a matter of the brain. Sex in poetry becomes "serious" when it is delivered over to the imagination. At that point the pleasure of the text becomes not moral but, literally, erotic. It is in this sense that Byron will insist, and with good reason to support his position, that sentimental poets like Dacre and Moore and Keats are the true immoralists. Through them eroticism appears as a behavior of *conscience* – as "sex in the head." Unlike sentimental verse, which Byron calls "the *Onanism* of Poetry" (*BLJ*, VI, 217), *Don Juan* takes up its erotic subjects in a deliberately *un*sentimental way – "it strips off the tinsel of *Sentiment*" (*BLJ*, VI, 202), he says, and thereby causes offence among those who, while they want sex in poetry, want it in more "refin'd" forms.

Byron's argument, made in a context in which the Romantic ideology was establishing itself, will now seem to us, who stand on the other side of the ideology's historical reign, remarkably insightful. And in truth his imagination of the truth is here quite important. Nevertheless, this Byronic imagination is not "the whole truth, and nothing but the truth." It carries its own form of special pleading, and that (what must surely be unconscious) allusion to Charlotte Dacre and his earlier act of poetic betrayal returns in *Don Juan* as a critical opening in Byron's own text, unknown to itself.

Following the concealments and self-deception practiced in the poetry of 1808–1816, Byron's exilic poetry made a virtue of candor and truth-telling. I pass without comment the important contribution which sentimental poetry like Charlotte Dacre's made toward a poetic ideal of candour and the fulness of truth. These matters we have already touched on, and we have seen the depth of Byron's debt to that poetry. Like Blake's Swedenborg, Byron in 1816 had broken some of the nets that had bound him up, and his escape is registered in his later work. Nevertheless, part of the truth of *Don Juan* still operates in the mode of deception and untruth.

We observe this by interrogating Byron's masterwork on the issue of the erotics of the imagination, the issue of sex in the head. This is the territory occupied by people like Dacre and Moore and Keats, a territory Byron says he has abandoned, as he abandoned his canting homeland. Byron's critique of cant, however, was partly negotiated through a recovery of certain sentimental attitudes – a turn away from the muscular and moral values which so dominate his work between *English Bards* and *Childe Harold* Canto IV. Juan's liaisons with Julia and Haidée are both completely sentimental affairs. Furthermore, Byron's new poetic theory of "truth in masquerade" is grounded in a sympathetic meditation on a certain kind of "feminine" lying. Earlier that sort of deception had served only to drive a wedge between Byron and his sentimental attachments, but in *Don Juan* he begins to rethink the issues.

The behavior of Julia (at the beginning of *Don Juan*) and of Lady Adeline, *la donna mobile* (at the end), epitomizes how theatricality and masquerade – deliberate strategies of deception – can serve the cause of deep truth. These strategies will do so, Byron's work argues, only if they are deployed with complete self-consciousness – that is, only if the theatre of deception, or the masquerade, labels itself as such, and includes itself in its own illusory displays. (To the degree that these displays are sentimental productions, to that extent they are part of the theater of love in the full sentimentalist sense.) In this erotic theater, the central figure, for the man, must be the woman, "Whence is our entrance and our exit" (IX, st. 55).

A theory of art, however, once it is deployed through a work, becomes a two-edged sword, and the case is no different for *Don Juan.* Byron's critique of the sentimental eroticism of Moore and Keats, for example, seems hardly less applicable to many parts of Byron's epic, not least, I suppose, to the scenes in the harem. Criticism might conclude, from this kind of contradiction, that Byron was fabulously self-deceived in thus criticizing Moore and Keats; and criticism would no doubt be correct in this judgment. But the exposure of Byron's personal self-deception is far less significant than the way his poetry transforms truth and lies through the artifice of its masquerades. Indeed, the brilliance of the harem episode depends exactly on its having shown so clearly – despite Byron's quotidian pronouncements – the positive relation which operates between sex and the imagination.

This relation is (as it were) dramatized for us in the persons – in the dreams and imaginations – of the young harem women. But the narrator's specular involvement in that drama (and our involvement through him) is equally drawn into the orbit of the poem's theatricality. The harem episode is, in one very obvious sense, nothing more than a distinctly "male" sex fantasy, and hence a voyeuristic spectacle. The narrator is unaware of his voyeurist perspective, however – or rather, he sees nothing in his act of seeing to be critical of. *We* see this innocence of his mind in his blithe assumption that the scene and events could only be imagined as he has imagined them.

This assumption acquires a critical edge in Byron's poem, however, just because it is a contrived assumption, an artifice. Indeed, the essential wit of the episode arises from the narrator's *conscious* assumption of an innocent eye, his pretence – as in the narrative of Dudu's dream – that he is himself unaware of the word-plays and double meanings of his own discourse. Unlike Julia in her letter in Canto I, Dudu does not narrate her own dream; the narrator tells it for her in indirect discourse. That indirection underscores the theatricality of his talk, the masquerade in which he is involved. The critical consequence, however, is that the narrator is himself pulled on to the stage of the poem. In that event the narrator is released from the bondage of his own imagination. We are not only able, for example, to "see" and criticize his voyeurism, we come as well into contact with that supreme objectivity which poetic discourse, alone of our discursive forms, seems able to achieve. "Byron" would not have wanted to be told that his masterwork was itself deeply invested in sentimentalism and sex in the head; nonetheless, this is the case, and it is his own master-work which tells us so.

In the harem episode we see *Don Juan* operating under the illusion of its own self-consciousness. The narrator's amusement is the sign that he is satisfied with his understanding, that he possesses understanding. But his wisdom is an illusion of knowledge which, however, tells a truth about feeling. The harem episode is a theatrical display of a certain kind of "sex in the head" – an onanism of poetry fully the equal of Keats's. And it is an onanism of poetry precisely because its eroticism, founded in the sentimentalist project, here executes that project in a space of solitude. The harem episode is an image, in short, not of fulfilled but of frustrated desire. Its pretence to be something else – its pretence to display an ultimately fulfilled eroticism – is an essential feature of its deepest truth.

In Charlotte Dacre's poetry, "hours of solitude" are hours of critical reflection, hours in which one experiences the loss and deprivation of love and in which one recognizes the state of the loss. The harem episode in *Don Juan* means to imagine a way of escaping such solitude and loss, but in the event it succeeds in defining those illusions of escape which serve only to deepen one's awareness of what the experience of loss entails. In this respect the episode is something of a retreat from the philosophical achievement of Canto I. But the text does not revert to the style of the period 1808–1816. Byron's feminine and sentimental brain, which emerged between 1815 and 1817, made such a lapse impossible. The eroticism of the harem episode is in certain obvious respects ludicrous and self-deceived, but – like "The Eve of St Agnes," which is quite a comparable piece of work – the episode does not (at any rate) torture sexual feeling with moral instrumentations. It catches, therefore, the true voice of Romantic feeling – even if the feelings involved are not so rich or complex as the feelings at the conclusion of Canto I.

NOTES

1 *Notes and Queries*, 8th series, 6 (25 August 1894), 144–145; and for Sir Richard Edgecumbe's piece, noted below, see ibid., 515.

2 I have never seen these books described by Wake but his identification of the pencil notations is persuasive. Byron often wrote in pencil in books in this way, especially in his early years.

3 Byron's four early books were all printed in Newark, and of course Byron's life between 1803 and 1807 was closely connected to the Nottingham area.

4 A good brief summary of the Della Cruscan phenomenon is given in John Mark Longaker, *The Della Cruscans and William Gifford. The History of a Minor Movement in an Age of Literary Transition* (Philadelphia, 1924).

5 The Della Cruscans typically published under pseudonyms, and "Rosa Matilde" is a direct allusion to Mrs. Cowley's adopted cognomen "Laura Matilda." It is important to realize, however, that Dacre was not a Della Cruscan herself, but a slightly later writer who came under their influence. Dacre's work exhibits a much more self-conscious employment of the Della Cruscan style: see, for example, her poems "Passion Uninspired by Sentiment," "To the Shade of Mary Robinson," and "The Female Philosopher."

6 Citations from the poetry are to *Lord Byron. The Complete Poetical Works*, ed. Jerome J. McGann, 7 vols. (Oxford, 1980–1992); when it is necessary to refer to this edition, the abbreviation *CPW* will be used.

7 Throughout his life Byron commented on the erotic elements in Moore's verse, and especially on Moore's *Poetical Works of the Late Thomas Little, Esq.* (1801). This book, a minor classic in the sentimental style, went through numerous printings, and had an important influence on Byron's early work. For a fuller discussion see Jerome J. McGann, *Fiery Dust. Byron's Poetic Development* (Chicago, 1968), Chapter 1.

8 *Byron's Letters and Journals*, ed. Leslie A. Marchand (Cambridge, MA, 1973–1982), I, 103; hereafter cited as *BLJ*.

9 The fullest discussion of this event in Byron's life is in Willis W. Pratt's *Byron at Southwell* (Austin, TX, 1948).

10 "To a Knot of Ungenerous Critics" is the title of one of Byron's poetical replies to his Southwell critics: see *CPW*, I, 19–22 (and the related poem at 17–19).

11 Some of Gifford's best lines in *The Baviad* and *The Maeviad* involve witty sexual wordplays which call attention not only to the sensuality of Della Cruscan poetry, but to its self-conscious (and hence, from Gifford's point of view, irreal) sensuality. When Byron later saw a similar poetic mode in Keats's work, he ridiculed it as "the Onanism of Poetry" (*BLJ*, VII, 217) – a distinctly Giffordian line of attack.

12 In this respect Wordsworth's was a more successful deployment of the Della Cruscan program, whose sentimentality inclined toward a travesty of platonic engagement. This travesty, and Platonism, are especially clear in the

famous poetical "love affair" which Della Crusca and Anna Matilda carried on in the pages of the *World* in the years 1787–1789. The two had in fact never even met.

13 Thus Byron's male friendships come to represent a more stable form of love. Even such love is not completely steady, however, as a number of poems written to his male friends show. In the myth of love Byron deploys, only one figure is imagined as perfectly faithful – his sister Augusta.

14 See the work of 1813 called "A Song" ("Thou art not false, but thou art fickle"), *CPW*, III, 105–106.

15 Byron's misogyny appears in some of his early poetry as well, although his commitment to sentimentalism at that stage distinctly undercuts his anti-feminist views. See especially the poem "To Woman," printed toward the end of *Hours of Idleness* (*CPW*, I, 45–46).

16 For an extended discussion of this poem's text and context see Jerome J. McGann, "The Significance of Biographical Context: Two Poems by Lord Byron," in *The Author in his Work*, ed. Louis A. Martz and Aubrey Williams (New Haven, CT, 1978), 347–366.

17 For a full discussion of the linkage see ibid. The essential fact is that the stanza of "When We Two Parted" which Byron dropped from the printed version was originally a stanza in the poem to Lady Caroline Lamb.

18 See *BLJ*, X, 198–199.

19 See Malcolm Elwin, *Lord Byron's Wife* (New York, 1962), 394, 400. The matter is more fully discussed in chapter 4, below.

20 See n. 19.

21 For a related discussion of these matters see my "Lord Byron's Twin Opposites of Truth," in *Towards a Literature of Knowledge* (Oxford, 1989), 38–64.

22 This is the first line of Alan Davies's excellent prose-poem "Lies," reprinted in *Signage* (New York, 1987), 11.

CHAPTER 4

What difference do the circumstances of publication make to the interpretation of a literary work?

Framed in this way, the question is open to any number of responses: for the "interpreter," the critic, is entirely free to decide which material in the literary event shall be salient for interpretation. The "circumstances of publication," therefore, can make a big difference, or no difference at all, or they can make various kinds of intermediate differences that could be specified.

I do not say this to be sophistical, but to call attention to some of the critical assumptions which generated the question. The question assumes that "circumstances of publication" make a difference to interpretation, and that such a difference has been demonstrated in certain critical discussions, perhaps in some of the work that I myself have done. But the question is aware that these demonstrations create a theoretical problem for some of the most important governing protocols of our received critical ideas: for instance, that bibliography and interpretation are different modes of literary enquiry and do not (as it were) naturally correspond with each other; that the social (as opposed to the purely authorial) dimensions of textual events have no necessary or essential relation to literary meaning; in general, that hermeneutics must preserve a theoretical (as opposed to an heuristic) distinction between the "extrinsic" and the "intrinsic" in literary study.

I disagree with these three ideas. Indeed, my own assumptions – the frames of my critical practice – are in each case precisely the inverse of each one. To my mind, the circumstances of publication *always* bear upon literary meaning. The initial question posed to me, therefore, seems pertinent only as a procedural problem which I would frame in this way: what are the most useful illustrations I could give of the way the "circumstances of publication" make a difference to literary meaning?

Since 1977 it is a question I have been much concerned with. Indeed, when I first tried to show what kind of a hermeneutical difference "circumstances of publication" can make, I deliberately chose my examples from Keats – simply because in his work the distinction between "intrinsic" and "extrinsic" literary matters was thought to be clearly preserved. To argue the hermeneutical relevance of "extrinsic" matters in the case of Keats was to mount a *theoretical* attack upon ideas about textual autonomy; and at that time, in 1977, theoretical lines of attack were very much needed.

Now [1991], everything has changed. This symposium is itself eloquent testimony to the change that has taken place during the past ten years of literary studies. I do not have to adduce instances to persuade you that "circumstances of publication" make a difference to interpretation because I and many others have already laid down more than a sufficient number of examples.

So let me re-frame the question slightly, and ask: what difference does it make when "circumstances of publication" are *not* factored into the interpretive operation? I offer you two cases, one from Blake and one from Byron.

THE PROBLEM OF *JERUSALEM*, PLATE 3

The opening text page – plate 3 – of Blake's consummate work offers an address "To the Public." It represents a sort of Preface to the poem, a set of remarks, some in verse and some in prose, which were to help "explain" what the subsequent work imagines itself to be doing. *Jerusalem* is a public performance from "the mouth of a true Orator," Blake says; its audience is "the Human Race," and most immediately the nation of Great Britain; it is a work of deliberate art ("Every word and every letter is studied"), but equally a piece of unpremeditated verse – inspired work, "dictated" to its "printer" William Blake; and – though Blake does not indicate this explicitly – it comes from the same "God" who years before had dictated *The Marriage of Heaven and Hell*, a dweller in flaming fire whose voice is not easily distinguished from Blake's own mind and conscience. Finally, the work is executed through what Blake calls "my types," an obvious paranomasia that draws an equation between the poem's spiritual designs and its material orders.

Works of imagination traffic in paradox – those opposite and discordant qualities which we sometimes imagine poems are made to balance and reconcile. Plate 3 of *Jerusalem*, however, offers at least one paradox which the imagination will not comfortably seize as beauty. Physicalized on the plate itself, this paradox is eventual, not conceptual. Blake's text assures his reader that what he prints – his "types" – will not be done in "vain," but this opening page of *Jerusalem* has much of its own message gouged from the plate. The consequence is not simply a set of awkward transitions and distracting blank spaces, but positive incoherence.

We must remember that the condition of Plate 3 is not "momentary" or transitional in the sense that Blake simply neglected to make the necessary further alterations which would have restored coherence to his work. Blake had at least ten years, 1818–1828, when he might have "repaired" Plate 3 (assuming that we are to think of the plate as "damaged"). Or, if he *could* not restore a grammatological coherence to this plate – if, for example, the copper had been so multilated that it was no longer able to support a new text – still Blake had ten years in which to re-engrave the plate. He did not choose to do this. Instead, he preserved a scarred discourse as the opening of his text, so that Plate 3 must be regarded as what textual scholars sometimes call "the author's final intentions." Every surviving copy of *Jerusalem* exhibits a Plate 3 mutilated in just this way, including the copies he sold during those last ten years, including even the magnificent full-colored copy E which Blake prepared so carefully toward the end.[1] So far as we can tell, Blake wanted the reader's initial encounter with *Jerusalem* to be through this broken and ruptured text.

This is an extraordinary situation, but the interpreters of Blake's *Jerusalem* pay little attention to it when discussing the work.[2] We would have to *imagine* comparable examples in the history of literature and poetry before our period, for nothing equivalent exists in fact. What Blake has done in *Jerusalem* is what Milton might have done had he excised certain phrases and lines from the opening twenty-six verses of *Paradise Lost*: had he excised, that is, passages carrying real weight and significance for the proemium, and had he then printed and broadcast the poem with the lacunae left visible.

Blake did not *begin Jerusalem* as a broken text, he *finished* it that way. The difference is crucial. Such a text calls attention to itself as gestural, performative. However it is to have its "meaning" "interpreted," the mutilated text of Plate 3 is at least making the following representations: that the words and figures on such a page are arbitrary, and that they were put there by design (in at least two senses).

If what Blake did in producing his text seems extraordinary, however, even more astonishing is what the critics have *not* done in relation to his act of production. *Jerusalem* has elicited a great deal of commentary, but very little attention has been paid to the physical condition of Plate 3, or to the meaning of that physical condition. Such disinterest is all the more surprising because Blake scholars generally understand that Blake's meanings are intimately related to Blake's productive methods and physical media.

That most capacious and distinguished of Blake scholars, David Erdman is virtually alone in the attention he has given to the problem of Plate 3. He has expended most of his efforts, however, not in attempting to solve the riddle of the plate as we have received it, but in trying to restore the material which Blake took such pains to eliminate. Of course, the restoration of that material might tell us much about why Blake erased it in the first place; but as it turns out the restored passages are not in themselves especially illuminating on that issue. As a consequence, Erdman interprets the mutilated plate in psychological terms – as an exponent of Blake's unhappiness with his audience and his failure to establish contact with "the Public." Thus Erdman refers to Blake's "self-destructive deletions" which "withdraw . . . the affectionate terms addressed to the once-dear Reader, [and] effac[e without] . . . quite thoroughly effacing the poet's confessions of faith and enthusiasm" (Erdman 1964, 1965).

Given the general condition of *Jerusalem*, however, this is not a very compelling argument. The work exhibits no other signs of self-destruction, nor does the poem otherwise develop the theme of a breakdown of sympathy between author and audience. In any case, it is an argument which Erdman himself does not work to support in his editorial treatment of the text. In his standard typographical edition of Blake's *Complete Works*, Blake's mutilated text is editorially "corrected." Erdman's excellent work in recovering the erased passages results in a text – Erdman's edition – which puts back the passages that Blake had so deliberately removed.

I think that this was not the best editorial decision to make. The recovered passages would have been, I believe, much better placed in a critical apparatus, and the superior text left to stand as Blake had wanted it to stand: with its drastic lacunae dramatically visible. However we read the meaning of Plate 3 of *Jerusalem*, we will want to ground our readings in the mutilated text which Blake produced rather than the editorially corrected text so brilliantly restored by Erdman.[3]

BYRON'S "FARE THEE WELL!"

The problem with this notorious poem is much more complex than the Blake problem I have been discussing. As we know, Byron addressed the poem to his wife at the time of the separation controversies in the spring of

1816.[4] It descends to us largely through one line of interpretation, where it is read as a *cri de coeur* from a heartbroken husband. This is the way the poem was read by many people in 1816. Madame de Staël, for instance, and Sir Francis Burdett, and various reviewers all read it this way and praised it extravagantly (see Mayne 1924: 256; and Erdman 1970: 642 and n.). And Wordsworth read it this way as well, only he anticipated the common, later judgment that the poem is hopelessly mawkish: "disgusting in sentiment, and in execution contemptible . . . Can worse doggerel be written . . . ?" (de Selincourt 1970: III Part 2, 304).[5]

But another, very different reading sprang up when the poem began circulating in 1816, like tares among the wheat of that first reading. Byron's friend Moore – who was later to endorse the sentimental theory of the poem – was at first deeply suspicious of "the sentiment that could, at such a moment, indulge in such verses" (Mayne 1924: 642). Moore did not elaborate on his suspicions, but others did. The reviewer of *The Prisoner of Chillon and Other Poems* in the *Critical Review* of December 1816 paused to reflect on the earlier "domestic" poem:

> [M]any who disapproved most of his lordship's . . . publication of his "Farewell" address, as inflicting a parting and lasting pang upon his lady, thought that the lines were most delightfully pathetic, and wondered how a man, who shewed he had so little heart, could evince such feeling. They did not know how easy it was for a person of his lordship's skill to fabricate neatly-turned phraseology, and for a person of his lordship's ingenuity to introduce to advantage all the common-places of affection: the very excellence of that poem in these particulars, to us and to others, was a convincing proof that its author had much more talent than tenderness. (*Critical Review* [1816], 577–578)

As it happens, Anabella herself, the person to whom "Fare Thee Well!" was most directly addressed, read the poem in just this insidious way. It seemed to her yet another instance of Byron's "talent for equivocation . . . of [which] I have had many proofs in his letters."[6] On 13 February, a month before Byron wrote his poem, she explained this "talent" further and pointed out that she learned about it from Bryon himself:

> I should not have been *more* deceived than I was by his letters, if he had not pointed out to me in similar ones addressed to others, the deepest design in words that appeared to have none. On this he piques himself – and also on being able to write such letters as will convey different, or even opposite sentiments to the person who receives them & to a stranger. (Elwin 1962: 400)

"Every day," she added, "proves deeper art" in her husband. What she most feared was "this ambiguity of Language in the Law," that it would give Byron an advantage over her in the separation proceedings.

Anabella went on to add two observations which are equally interesting and shrewd. Byron's skill in manipulating language reminded her of a passage in *Lara* (I, 504–509) in which the deportment of that Byronic Hero is exposed as a text of such ambiguity that, reading it, one cannot be certain if it signals a heart filled with "the calmness of the good" or with a "Guilt grown old in desperate hardihood." And she added that this skill with words was one "he is *afraid* of" himself.

In a good recent essay Elledge has revived a variant of this insidious reading of "Fare Thee Well!" The poem, he argues, is "a portrait of indecision, taut with antithetical tensions"; it "charts . . . the depth and configurations of the poet's ambivalence . . . toward reconciliation with his wife" (Elledge 1986: 43). Although Elledge is, I believe, certainly correct in this reading of the poem, he does not go nearly far enough, either substantively or methodologically. In this respect the readings of both the *Critical* reviewer and Lady Byron seem to me more weighty and profound.

What Anabella and the *Critical* reviewer call attention to are the social contexts in which the poem was executed. Anabella was peculiarly alive to such matters because they touched upon her life in the most important ways. "Fare Thee Well!" was not simply a thing of beauty, an aesthetic object spinning in the disinterested space of a Kantian (or Coleridgean) theoretical world. It was an event in the language, of art, specifically located, and she registered that event in particular ways. To her the separation controversy came to involve two primary matters. There was first the matter of the law, and who, in the complex legal maneuverings, would have power over the other to influence various decisions (Lady Byron feared, for example, that Byron would seek to deprive her of custody of their daughter Ada). And second there was the (closely related) matter of public opinion, and who would enter into and finally emerge from the separation proceedings with what sort of public image.

When Byron sent her a copy of "Fare Thee Well!" soon after he wrote it, Lady Byron was quick to read it as a shrewd ploy to gain power over her in the context of those two areas of interest which most concerned her. At first she emphasized the "legal" reading, for she felt, as we have already seen, that Byron's various communications were designed to construct a sympathetic self-image in order to improve his bargaining position. "He has been assuming the character of an injured & affectionate husband with great success to some," she remarked in mid-February (Elwin 1962: 409). When Byron sent her a MS copy of the poem late in March, she wrote ironically to her mother of its apparent tenderness, "and so he talks of me to Every one" (448). But the poem did not disturb her greatly until she learned that Byron intended to print and distribute it privately in London society. This act, she feared, would turn "The Tide of feeling . . . against" her,[7] but she was dissuaded from her first impulse – to publish a rejoinder – by the counsel of Dr. Stephen Lushington.

The significance of all this becomes more clear, I think, if we recall that "Fare Thee Well!" was initially constituted as three very different texts, only two of which were manipulated by Byron, while the other fell under the co-authority of persons and powers who were hostile to him. The first of these texts is the one which originates in the MS poem addressed to Lady Byron, and which Byron caused to have circulated in London in late March and early April. The second is the text privately printed and distributed in fifty copies on 8 April, at Byron's insistence and over the objections of his publisher Murray. Byron's activities here are important to remember because they show that he was manipulating the poem, was literally fashioning an audience for it of a very specific kind. The original MS may have been addressed to his wife, but when copies of that poem began to be made and circulated, a new text started to emerge. The printed text in fifty copies represents the definitive emergence of that text, which was addressed past and through Lady Byron to a circle of people – friends, acquaintances, and other interested parties – whose "reading" and "interpretation" of the poem Byron wanted to generate, and of course influence.

In the most limited sense, Byron wanted his poem to be read as the effusion of an "injured and affectionate husband." Moore's later report in his *Life*, that the MS text he saw was covered with Byron's tears, represents in effect such an interpretation of the poem. But the fact that Byron was also managing a certain kind of circulation for the poem set in motion other forces, and other readings, which were only latent (so to speak) in the verbal MS text. The poem, that is to say, came to be widely seen – and read – as another event in Byron's troubled "domestic circumstances." It is this circulation of the verses which begins to change the meaning of the poem – indeed, which begins to change the poem itself. The words of the original MS do not significantly differ from the privately printed text; nonetheless, that first printed text has become another poem, and one which sets in motion an urgency toward the production of yet another textual change.

This new change is definitive when the privately printed text finally makes its appearance in the *Champion* on 14 April and thence throughout the periodical press. This is a new poem altogether. In the first place, it does not appear alone but alongside "A Sketch," Byron's cutting satire on Mrs. Clermont which he had also put into private circulation in fifty copies several days before he began circulating "Fare Thee Well!." The editors of the *Champion* text so printed and positioned "A Sketch" as to make it an exponent of the "real meaning" of "Fare Thee Well!": that is to say, it is used partly for the light it sheds on "Fare Thee Well!," as a way of exposing Byron's hypocritical malignancy. In the second place, the farewell poem is accompanied, in the *Champion*, by a long editorial commentary denouncing Byron's character as well as his politics, and explicitly "reading" the two poems as evidence of his wickedness.

The *Champion*'s text of "Fare Thee Well!" is, I would say, the definitive version of the (so to speak) *hypocritical* poem, just as the MS version sent to Lady Byron – which, interestingly, seems not to have survived – would be the definitive version of the *sentimental* poem. The "texts" which extend between these two versions dramatize this first, crucial stage in the poem's processes of transformation. But they do not conclude those processes. Even as the *Champion* text is completing that first stage of the poem's transformations, it has initiated a new stage, the one in which the two faces of this poem are forced to confront one another. And it is in this next stage of its textual development that "Fare Thee Well!" becomes most rich and interesting. This is the poem whose meaning focuses and culminates the controversies among the readers in Byron's day. The question is gone over again and again: is this a poem of love ("sentimental") or a poem of hate ("hypocritical")? The final contemporary text declares that in some important sense it is both. Byron himself produced the materialized version of this culminant text when he published the poem, with the telling epigraph from "Christabel," in his *Poems* (1816).

This is the text which Elledge has recently revived, a work full of painful and even frightening tensions and contradictions. And while I want to salute Elledge's success in rescuing Byron's poem from its impoverished sentimental readings, I must also point out Elledge's insistence – it stems from his New Critical background – that his is not a reading of a work of poetry so much as an exploration of a set of tense personal circumstances: "my concern is less with the poem as poem than with the dynamics of the relationship between poet-husband and audience-wife as Byron represents them" (Elledge 1986: 44n). He makes this statement because his notion is that "the poem as poem" is an abstract verbal construct, a "text" that not only can be, but must be, divorced from the social and material formations within which the work was instituted and carried out.

Such an idea commits one to a certain way of reading poetry which seems to me intolerable. But it is a way which is particularly destructive for a poet like Byron, whose poetical language is characteristically executed by invoking and utilizing its available social and institutional resources. More, Byron's work insists that this is the way of all poetry, though some poets and apologists for poetry argue that it is otherwise, that poetry operates in a space of disinterestedness and autonomy. "Fare Thee Well!" is therefore, in this respect, a kind of metapoem, a work which foregrounds Byron's ideas about what poetry actually is and how it works.

Byron himself seems to have recognized very clearly – that is to say, with pain and reluctance – the full significance of his poetic practice. In writing and circulating "Fare Thee Well!" he was the author and agent of the completed work, the one who finally would be responsible (of course not entirely responsible – just personally responsible) for all of the texts. Yet while Byron authored those texts, he could not fully control them – this, the fate of all poets, is sometimes called their "inspiration" – so that in the end he found that he too, like everyone else who would involve themselves with the poem, would have to trust the tale and not the teller. His discovery of this, a bitter revelation, would soon find expression in another of the "Poems on his Domestic Circumstances": the "[Epistle to Augusta]" which he wrote in the summer of 1816. Reflecting on that "talent for equivocation" which he flaunted before his wife, Byron would expose its equivocal character.

> The fault was mine;—nor do I seek to screen
> My errors with defensive paradox—
> I have been cunning in mine overthrow
> The careful pilot of my proper woe. (21–24)

Which is as much as to say of that most "cunning" of his poems to date, "Fare Thee Well!," that it tells more than one would have imagined possible, tells more than its own author wanted told.

I shall shortly return to indicate what I believe this kind of analysis signifies for any concrete "reading" of "Fare Thee Well!" But first I would ask you to reflect upon certain matters of general relevance for Byron's poetry. When we say that Byron's is a highly rhetorical poetry we mean – we should mean – not that it is loud or overblown, but that it is always, at whatever register, elaborating reciprocities with its audiences. These reciprocities, like all social relations, accumulate their own histories as time passes and more interchanges occur – and we then call these, as Donald Reiman has called them, "the cumulative effect" of the work.[8] New poetry is written – and read – within the context of those accumulations. The development of the various texts of "Fare Thee Well!" between March and November 1816 is a miniature example of how these reciprocities can get played out.

I want to emphasize that Byron wrote this way throughout his life. The masterpiece *Don Juan* is a work of, quite literally, *consummate* skill, because the whole of Byron's life and career is gathered into it. Without an awareness of, an involvement in, that poem's "cumulative effect" one will be reduced simply to reading its words: as Eliot in this connection *might* have said, *not* to have the experience *and* to miss the meaning.

Related to this rhetorical framework of the poetry is Byron's habit of manipulating his texts. To present a work through a "cumulative" context is to open it to changes and modifications, in fact, to new opportunities of meaning: not so much, as Coleridge would have had it, the "reconciliation" of "opposite and discordant qualities" as their artistic exploitation. "Fare Thee Well!" did not bring about any reconciliations, poetic or otherwise; it raised a tumult of new discords and conflicts. Yet it is those very tumults, and their artistic significance, which turned the period of Byron's separation – from his wife, from England – to a watershed in his career, and in his understanding of what was involved, for him, in his methods of poetic production.

To understand this better we have to retreat in time, to Byron's years at Harrow and especially Cambridge, when he took his first lessons in the art of literary equivocation. Byron told his wife that he had a talent for that sort of thing, and Louis Crompton's recent book *Byron and Greek Love* has shown that it was a mode of writing practiced by Byron's circle of Cambridge friends – a deliberate and quite literally a *methodical* set of procedures for saying one thing and meaning something else. Briefly, they cultivated a mode of homosexual double-talk.

One of Byron's first epistolary exercises in this equivocal style was in his letter to Charles Skinner Matthews of 22 June 1809; Matthews's answer to this letter is important because of its explicit discussion:

> In transmitting my dispatches to Hobhouse, mi carissime βυρον [Byron] I cannot refrain from addressing a few lines to yourself: chiefly to congratulate you on the splendid success of your first efforts in *the mysterious*, that style in which more is meant than meets the Eye ... [B]ut I must recommend that ... [Hobhouse]

do not in future put a *dash* under his mysterious significances, such a practise would go near to letting the cat out of the bag . . . And I positively decree that every one who professes *ma methode* do spell the term wch designates his calling with an e at the end of it – *methodiste*, not method*ist*, and pronounce the word in the French fashion. Every one's taste must revolt at confounding ourselves with that sect of . . . fanatics. (Crompton 1985: 128–129)

Byron's letter may in fact have been his "first effort" at writing in Matthews's particular dialect of "the *mysterious*," but it was a language he was already practiced in, and one which would receive its apotheosis in the incredible display of puns and coded talk that constitutes *Don Juan*.

Matthews's letter is also interesting because it suggests that the use of this kind of style is a game that can be played with, and that its practitioners should think of themselves as a kind of élite group with special gifts and powers. But it was also a style that ran grave risks for the user. Byron told his wife that he was afraid of his own skill with this method of writing. And well he might be, for it entailed the conscious deployment of duplicitous and hypocritical postures.

All of Byron's early tales are written in this equivocal style – which has become, in Byron's hands, a vehicle of immensely greater range and complexity than Charles Skinner Matthews would have imagined possible, had he lived to see Byron's displays. But the more Byron developed his talent for equivocation, the more he built a store of explosive and dangerous contradictions into his work. Those contradictions came to a head during the separation controversy, and in "Fare Thee Well!" they finally reached their flashpoint.

That the poem is not what the commonplace "sentimental" reading has taken it to be is exposed unmistakably for us in the initial period of its production and reception. Many readers were alive to its duplicities. The opening four lines, in fact, signal the poem's method by installing a grammatical pun of fundamental importance:

Fare thee well! and if for ever—
    Still for ever, fare *thee well*—
Even though unforgiving, never
    'Gainst thee shall my heart rebel.

The sense here urges us to take Lady Byron's as the "unforgiving" heart, but the grammar tells us that heart is Byron's own. The poem will operate under this sign of contradiction to the end. Noteworthy too is Byron's assertion that, though his heart is unforgiving, it will never "rebel" against hers: as if he were imagining their separation and mutual antagonisms succeeding to a second, darker marriage which would "never" be dissolved or put asunder.

In fact, the poem is replete with this kind of complex double-speaking. Ponder, for example, these four lines:

> Would that breast by thee glanc'd over,
> Every inmost thought could show!
> Then thou would'st at last discover
> 'Twas not well to spurn it so— (9–12)

It is a nice question what the inmost thoughts of an unforgiving and yet *un*rebellious heart would look like. Blake wrote a great deal of poetry about just such a heart, and he always imagined it as dangerous and fearful. And if we merely "glance over" Byron's lines here we may easily fail to "discover" their full truth: that the passage does not merely tell about the dark truths of unforgiving hearts; it is itself executing them. "'Twas not well to spurn it so" is a warning of possible danger, but as coming from *this* speaker it carries as well a threatening message and rhetoric.

Of course the poem delivers these kinds of messages obliquely, but in doing so it only increases the volatile character of the text. Because more is meant here than meets the eye directly, the censored materials exert enormous pressure for their freedom of complete expression. The parallel text in Canto III of *Childe Harold's Pilgrimage* meditates on the situation by comparing it to the fury of a storm breaking over the Alps:

> Could I embody and unbosom now
> That which is most within me,—could I wreak
> My thoughts upon expression. (st. 97)

And so forth: he longs for "one word [of] Lightening," one word of comfort that would "lighten" his heart of its weight of sorrow, one word of insight that would "enlighten" his understanding of his situation, and one word of power that would, like a bolt of lightning, "blast" and purify those places "where desolation lurk[s]" (st. 95).

Like Manfred – another creature of separation – who begs from Astarte "one word for mercy" (2, 4, 155), Childe Harold's longings remain incompletely satisfied. In all these cases the very effort to achieve some kind of completion, to reconcile the various contradictions, only seems to install them more deeply and more firmly.

Charles Skinner Matthews wrote gaily of his "mysterious" style of discourse, but it was a style which Byron, its supreme master, came to fear as he developed it through his years of fame. And well he might have feared it since it was a style which forced into the open the hypocrisies of those who read and write poetry as if it were simply a beauty or a truth, as if it were something that could be controlled – enlisted to the purposes of either those who produce it or those who receive it. "Fare Thee Well!" is Byron's farewell to the illusion that he could be the master of the artistic powers which were given to him. Written in hopes that it would allow him to control the dangerous cross-currents of his circumstances in 1816, the poem's bad faith – which is its genius – worked to undermine the actual despair latent in such petty hopes.

CONCLUSION

A number of important deficiencies tend to follow when circumstances of production are not factored into the interpretive operation. At the most elementary level – at what Blake called "the doors of perception" – readers will be inclined to see, and hence to deal with, only the linguistic text. In fact the poetic event always comprehends a larger scriptural territory, one which is bibliographically (as well as linguistically) encoded. The physical forms within which poetry is incarnated are abstracted from an interpretive activity only at the price of a serious critical blindness, and a blindness that brings with it little corresponding insight.

The problem emerges dramatically in the example from Blake, of course, but the very clarity of that example – the fact that it can be grasped as a local and immediate event – can be deceiving. Blake's illuminated texts do not lend themselves to the kind of physical variabilities which are common in the case of typographical texts. I am speaking here of the variabilities which develop when texts are transmitted over time to later readers. That transmission history tends not merely to erase the bibliographical terms in which the texts – the meanings of the texts – were initially encoded; it tends to make us unaware of the presence and significance of bibliographical coding in general. People tend not to realize that a certain way of reading is privileged when "Ode on a Grecian Urn" is read in *The Norton Anthology of English Literature*, and that it is a way of reading which differs sharply from what is privileged in Palgrave's *Golden Treasury* or in the *Oxford Book of Romantic Verse*; and when the poem is (or was) read in other kinds of formats – for example, in its first printing in the *Annals of the Fine Arts* – an entirely different field of reading is once again deployed. Furthermore, the work that descends to us descends through particular forms of transmission, and the work does not pass through those incarnations without having its meaning affected by them. We are able to discern patterns in a work's reception history precisely because those historical influences have inscribed themselves in the works we receive.

The example from Byron, however, underscores yet another important matter. Poetic works are not autonomous in either of the senses that the academy has come, mistakenly, to believe. That is to say, poems are neither linguistically self-contained, nor simply the expressed forms of a single – an authorizing and integral – imagination. The actual production of poems is one part of that social dialectic by which they live and move and have their being, one part of the communicative interchange which they always solicit.

The Byron example is especially instructive, I think, because it shows how those interchanges can never be brought under the control of the author. Poems are produced, used, and read in heterogeneous ways; unlike other forms of discourse, in fact, they require – they thrive upon – those diverse forms of life. Crucial parts of those interchanges are encoded in the bibliographical and productive histories of the poems we read. When we neglect those histories we simply condemn our readings to a culpable – because an unnecessary – ignorance.

APPENDIX

Several queries put to my paper by symposium respondents might be usefully pursued. I note a few of them here and give some brief (too brief I realize) comments.

1 "Does a literary scholar . . . ever have what one might call a 'natural' response of his own? Or is he for ever and only knowledgeable about the way the poem (or whatever) has been received in various constellations of historical circumstances?"

I would say that all responses are continuations of "historical circumstances." But because we can never comprehend the limit of those circumstances, novel and imaginative interventions are always taking place. We recognize such interventions, after the fact, as having certain historical routes (roots), and so after the fact we seem to diminish their singularities. But even after the fact one cannot comprehend the full range of "historical circumstances" within which any text is imbedded, within which it carries itself out. (I have treated these issues at greater length in my *Social Values and Poetic Acts*.)[9]

2 "Does *some* meaning remain in common to all historical readings of a poem? – for instance to the three readings of the Byron poem you mention?"

The three readings of the Byron poem illustrate, for me, not only a set of differentials, but the field of their integrity as well. When I figure that field socio-historically I mean to gesture toward a common reality which the three readings share, and I do not exclude from this the reality of a "total meaning." Each of the readings participate in that "total meaning"; but because the totality of that meaning is never complete (it is always being modified, sometimes by extensions, sometimes by losses and subtractions), the commonality of meaning always exists as a state of desire (as Wordsworth puts it, "something longed for, never seen").

3 "With Byron's 'Fare Thee Well!' you distinguish three different ways of reading. Shouldn't one also add a fourth: our reading of Byron's poem in an edition (in isolation) . . . ?"

Yes, one should add such a fourth reading, and a fifth as well: the latter being that which is represented by my own, which seeks to define the boundaries within which every act of reading will (or could) take place.

4 "Could one go on to develop a strong account of literature as social action? – e.g. of the Byron poem as a turning point . . . in the history of attitudes toward marriage and divorce?"

I think one can and indeed must develop precisely such an account, and I have been trying to work in that direction with my two most recent critical books, *Social Values and Poetic Acts* and *Towards a Literature of Knowledge*.[10]

NOTES

1 All discussions here of the copies of Blake's books draw heavily on the monumental work by Gerald E. Bentley, Jr (1977).

2 See Erdman (1964, 1965). The only other comments that are more than just passing references are in the excellent review of David Erdman's revised edition of *The Complete Poetry and Prose of William Blake* done by the Santa Cruz Blake Study Group (1984) and in Ferguson (1978). Unlike the Santa Cruz Blake Study Group, Ferguson does not really grasp the problematic character of the plate; see, e.g., his discussion at 166–167: "The deletions which

Blake made from this plate reveal a growing sense of determination, perhaps also of isolation, similar to that experienced by Ezekiel at the beginning of his prophetic work . . . So, Blake deletes any apologies for his poem, clearly demonstrating a new awareness of prophetic calling, and exhibiting a much tougher attitude toward the reader." This "reading" has not come to grips with the *textual* ground of the (hermeneutical) problem.

3 For a possible "reading" of the plate see McGann (1989: ch. 1). The present discussion of the plate from *Jerusalem* is part of the more extended treatment of Blake given in that chapter.

4 The essential critical discussions of the poem are Coleridge (1898–1904: III, 531–535); Erdman "'Fare Thee Well!' – Byron's Last Days in England," in *Shelley and his Circle 1773–1822*, Vol. III, ed. Kenneth Neill Cameron (Cambridge, MA: Harvard University Press, 1970), W. Paul Elledge, "Talented Equivocation: Byron's 'Fare Thee Well!'" *Keats–Shelley Journal*, 35 (1986), 42–61, and *Lord Byron: The Complete Poetical Works*, ed. McGann, 7 vols. (Oxford: Clarendon Press, 1980–1992), III, 493–494.

5 Ethel Colburn Mayne, *Byron* (London: Methuen and Co. Ltd., 1924), 256; Wordsworth's reading is given in a letter to John Scott, who put out the unauthorized printing of Byron's poem (see below).

6 Malcolm Elwin, *Lord Byron's Wife* (New York: Harcourt, Brace & World, 1962), 394.

7 Thomas Moore, *The Life, Letters and Journals of Lord Byron* (London, 1892), 164.

8 Donald Reiman. *The Romantics Reviewed* (New York: Garland Press, 1972), Part B, IV, 1779.

9 Cambridge, MA: Harvard University Press, 1988.

10 London and Oxford: Oxford University Press, 1989.

CHAPTER 5

Byron and the anonymous lyric

I

Although academic criticism in the twentieth century has maintained a studied disinterest in Byron's lyric poetry, nineteenth-century attitudes were (as usual) very different. The difference is manifest in Pushkin, Heine, and Poe, but it takes its most startling and perhaps most significant form in Baudelaire. A key figure in the history of the lyric even for those (for instance, T. S. Eliot) who denigrated Byron's importance, Baudelaire took Byron's work as a crucial point of artistic departure. In that (now largely ignored) context the conventional academic view of Byron has to be judged, simply and objectively, mistaken. Profoundly mistaken.

To explain the historical contradiction involved here would require a revisionary critique of the modernist reception of Baudelaire. My object is more simple. I want to sketch certain key points of relation between Byron and Baudelaire in order to describe the general formal character of Byron's lyric procedures. Such a study will also display the peculiar subjectivity of Byron's narrative and dramatic poetry, and hence the remarkable transformation that he worked upon a paradigmatic Romantic form, the lyrical ballad.

The connection between Byron and Baudelaire is most easily traced through the cultural history of dandyism. To study Byron in that context, however, can easily obscure the technical issues to be understood when we try to recover what nineteenth-century writers found so important in Byron's lyrical procedures. So far as poetry as such is concerned, dandyism is important for the rhetorical postures it involves. *Fleurs du Mal* engages an aesthetic of dandyism that Baudelaire studied in Byron's lyric work. This aesthetic is announced in *Fleurs du Mal*'s famous opening poem "Au lecteur," where key conventions of Romantic lyricism undergo an ironic meltdown. The sacred interiority of the Romantic *rêveur* and his complicit partner, the overhearing reader, is torn open in order to expose (and exploit) its spiritual emptiness.

The text needs no rehearsing. We might recall, however, the important rhetorical move at the poem's conclusion, where Baudelaire addresses the reader directly: "Hypocrite lecteur, – mon semblable, mon frère." Baudelaire turns the monstrous delicacy of the Romantic aesthetic – the "overheard" poem, in John Stuart Mill's well-known English formulation – into a weapon. Poet and reader are no longer permitted to imagine themselves saved by imagination. On the contrary, imagination is figured in the poem as hashish, source of illusion. The point of the text is not at all to escape illusion – to acquire an aesthetic redemption through either intense feeling or deeper understanding. Rather, it is simply to confront the reader with his damnation, to plunge him into the hell he has imagined he has *not* chosen and does not inhabit. In this text reader and poet – like Paolo and Francesca – are imagined floating in the dry heat of shared hypocrisies and a culpable linguistic innocence. (As we shall see, Byron read the famous episode from Dante's *Inferno* in precisely that way – as an emblem for a writing that would bring itself as well as its (Romantic) readers to a final, terrible judgment.)[1]

To write in this style, for Baudelaire, was to write under Byronic signs, as Baudelaire told his mother immediately after the publication of *Fleurs du Mal*.[2] This we have largely forgotten, just as we have forgotten the extraordinary stylistic means Byron developed for releasing that system of signs. Baudelaire understood what Byron was doing, however, and he followed Byron's example in his own poetry.[3]

In this connection, one of Baudelaire's most significant comments appears in his (unpublished) 1862 critical essay "L'esprit et le style de M. Villemain." Baudelaire's essay is an extensive critical survey of Villemain's dull academic work. In his brief abusive dismissal of Villemain's 1859 study of Pindar, *Essais sur le génie de Pindare et sur le génie lyrique*, Baudelaire glances at what he considers most significant in "le génie lyrique." He calls it "*le poésie lyrique anonyme*." An obtuse academic to Baudelaire, Villemain simply has no grasp of this crucial lyrical style:

> Il a pensé à Longfellow, mais il a omis Byron, Barbier et Tennyson, sans doute parce qu'un professeur lui inspire toujours plus de tendresse qu'un poète.[4]

This "tendresse" is a condition of feeling appropriate to the style of Baudelaire's "anonymous" lyricism. It is a feeling generated from the (paradoxically) cold style of the dandaical poet, who pursues every range of feeling – pain and pleasure, benevolence and cruelty. Baudelaire reads Byron as he reads Pindar, as a poet nearly anonymous. Because Byron is a Romantic poet, however, because he inherits the style of Romantic self-expression, he becomes for Baudelaire a poet of masks and poses, the manipulator of his own subjectivities. Pain or pleasure, benevolence or cruelty, good and evil: the poem (as it were) will decide what to take up among this range of human things and in what point of view to consider the subject-poet and his overhearing reader. Theatricality replaces Sincerity as the measure of Romantic style.

We begin to recover Baudelaire's approach to Byron by starting from a key Byronic text, the once so celebrated "Fare Thee Well!"[5] The academic disinterest in this notorious poem to his wife sounds the hollow echo of a reading that emerged at the moment the text began to circulate. This is Wordsworth's bourgeois reading, a reading generated through the criteria of lyrical sincerity. Wordsworth, who would become a model Romantic lyrist for twentiety-century academics, pronounced Byron's poem "doggerel" and the judgment has stuck. Wordsworth saw the poem as a failed and utterly debased effort at Romantic sincerity. "Fare Thee Well!" appears to him the emblem of a maudlin and factitious effusion – Byron posing as the sinner candidly self-exposed, confessed, and repentant.[6]

What Wordsworth could not see in this peom – what he probably could not imagine for it – was its deliberate hypocrisy. The sincerity of the poem is a pose, a mask that at once covers and reveals a deeper "sincerity." When Keats later sneered at Byron's theatrical self-displays – "Lord Byron cuts a figure – but he is not figurative" – he followed Wordsworth in turning away from Byron's lyrical rhetoric.[7] In making that turn he seems to have understood – as Wordsworth apparently did not – the choice involved. For Byron is a writer who strikes poses in his work; he has only a diminished fancy for Keats's ornamental luxuriance, and a perverse design upon Wordsworth's internal colloquies.

Byron adopts the conventions of Romanticism he inherited – spontaneous overflow, internal colloquy – in order to break them apart. His crucial move was precisely a rhetorical one because the key assumption of Romantic lyric is that the "true voice of feeling" cannot be studied, is not a matter of rhetorical conventions. A non-artificial paradise (or form of expression) is assumed to exist, and "sincerity" is thereby made the source and end and test of (Romantic) art. The drama of the Romantic lyric therefore typically traces a sublunary pursuit by the speaking poet for his own deepest and truest self. As a result, the poet *in propria persona*, the poet in what Coleridge and Wordsworth would call his "ideal self," structures the scene of Romantic lyric.

Byron did not repudiate his Romantic inheritance, he simply traced out the logic of its internal contradictions – what Baudelaire later saw as its hypocrisies. In simplest terms, Byron's poetry argued that "sincerity" *for the poet* has to be a convention, an artifice of language. To write a Romantic lyric that will not be utterly self-deceived, the poet must stand as it were anonymously before his own subjective presentations. "Hypocrisy" (or contradiction) will become a poetical issue – a subject for the poet and the poem – as soon as the illusion lying behind the poetical convention of sincerity is exposed. Byron's lyric style, in effect, is a satire upon a normative mode of Romantic writing. (As such, it is equally a satire and critique of the moral and social orders implicitly celebrated in that normative mode.) Byron's "ideal self" is "born for contradiction," not for (the bourgeois illusion of) balance and reconciliation. Anticipating Baudelaire (and recalling Milton), Manfred would call that illusion of synthesis "The last infirmity of evil" (*Manfred*, 1, 2, 29).

Byron's critique of Romanticism thus argued that a style of art (Romanticism) was being transformed into an article of (bad) faith. Coleridge's famous definition of "poetic faith" as the "willing suspension of disbelief" is very much to the point here.[8] As in Coleridge's other technical discussions of poetry, this passage underscores the primacy of "disbelief" so far as poetic artifice is concerned. Coleridge imagines highly self-conscious readers of poetry – readers who deliberately "suspend" their awareness that the poetic scene is a play of language. Problems will arise, however, if the "suspension of disbelief" should lose its hold on the artifice involved – if a reader or poet should slip into a delusion and take the poem for "truth," take it (in its Romantic form) as an artistic representation of the poet's inner subjective feelings or state of mind.

As Byron observed the cultural development of Romantic ideas, he saw a widespread capitulation to such delusions. Other writers had made similar observations – T. H. Matthias, for example, and William Gifford, and the writers of the *Anti-Jacobin*. Though *English Bards and Scotch Reviewers* follows their critical line on Romanticism, it stands apart in one crucial respect. Byron's satire climaxes as an exercise in self-criticism. In making this move Byron's text also raised the troubling (Romantic) question: is the self-critique "true," or is it a matter of art? In what sense should Byron (or his readers) "believe" the self-critical representations of a text like *English Bards*? (The question would soon be raised again, even more problematically, in Byron's next published satire, *Waltz* [1813].)[9]

Byron's importance for Romanticism lies exactly in his determination to force a confrontation with that question. To do so Byron placed himself at the centre of his work and made a Brechtian theater of his Romantic self-expression and sincerity. In his work these Romantic forms are deployed *as if they were real*. Byron's is not merely the poetry of a bleeding heart, it is a poetry that comes complete with bleeding heart labels. Whereas in (say) Wordsworth and Coleridge the question of the truth of poetry remains a theoretical matter, in Byron's work it is the central and explicit subject of the writing.

The manifest sign of this fact about his work remains the biographical obsession that dominates the reading and criticism of his poetry from the outset. The obsession represents a desire to have the textual scene validated by an extra-textual measure of truth (which in Romantic terms would have to be a personal, subjective, or psychological measure – the emergence into view of "the real Lord Byron"). That truth, famously, remains elusive – like most Romantic forms, "something longed for, never seen." The artifice of Byron's work thereby reinstalls a "primary imagination" of disbelief into the scene of writing and reading. His is an art of seduction in which the seducer is as abandoned (in both senses of that word) as the object of his seduction. Byron's poetry constructs an artifice of the living poet himself, "Byron" (as it were) *in propria persona*. Suspended thus between belief and disbelief, the poetry opens itself to the consequences that follow when a Romantic "contract" between poet and reader is put into play. Unlike Wordsworth, Byron is not trying to draw up such a contract – to install the romantic artifice as a style of writing, to create the taste by which his work is to be enjoyed. Byron's relation to Romanticism is secondary and critical. Accepting (provisionally and artistically) the power and authority of Romanticism's conventions, Byron institutes an anatomy of their world.

To do this meant that Byron had to construc[illegible]fices of himself in his work – illusory and theatrical selves tha[illegible]mmon up their necessary reciprocals, an audience of responsive [illegible]s. Most famous of these is the figure of the suffering poet, who[illegible]ience) reciprocal is the sympathetic reader. (Poe, Heine, and Baudelaire represent the antithesis of that sympathetic reader; they are all "Byronic" readers, cynical and perverse.) Byron inherited the figure of the suffering poet from his Romantic forebears, and especially from Wordsworth and Coleridge. In the benevolent lyricism of those early Romantics this relationship comprises a dynamic wherein "feeling comes in aid of feeling." The dynamic operates on the assumption that nature and society are permeated by a spirit of benevolence – in traditional terms, by a loving God. *Lyrical Ballads* and Coleridge's early poetry constructed the model for this kind of poetry. *Lyrical Ballads* is especially important because it tells the story of Wordsworth's and Coleridge's education into the truth and reality of this spirit of benevolence.

Byron's work comes to reimagine the import of that message. When feeling comes in aid of feeling in the Byronic/Baudelairean world the dynamic of sympathy breaks free of the horizon of benevolence. Their's is no mere debunking move, however. Byron begins with the traditional Romantic assumption that the poet is a man like other men but endowed with more lively sensibilities and so forth.[10] And he adopts the Romantic course of trusting his own vision, his own imaginative grasp of experience:

> 'Tis to create, and in creating, live
> A being more intense, that we endow
> With form our fancy, gaining as we give
> The life we image, even as I do now.
> (*Childe Harold III*, st. 6)

The gods summoned by this "being more intense" turn out Lucretian, however, not Christian, and they rule according to the mighty working of a primal duplicity. Aphrodite, *Alma Venus Genetrix*, Egeria: a "shape and image . . . haunt[ing] the unequenched soul" in its eternal passage through an existence as radically contradicted as the paradoxes Byron fashions to explain it, like the famous "unreach'd Paradise of our despair":

> Who loves, raves—'tis youth's frenzy—but the cure
> Is bitterer still, as charm by charm unwinds
> Which robed our idols, and we see too sure
> Not wealth nor beauty dwells from out the mind's
> Ideal sh[illegible] of such; yet still it binds,
> The fa[illegible] still it draws us on,
> Re[illegible] whirlwind from the oft-sown winds;
> The s[illegible] heart, its alchemy begun,
> Seems ever near the prize—wealthiest when most undone.
> (*Childe Harold IV*, st. 123)

If passages like this – they are all over Byron's work – appear demonic, they measure the cost of that "being more intense" summoned by Byron. Indeed, they incarnate the presence of that being and hence draw our "gaze of wonder," like the Giaour.

What they do *not* draw, or even cultivate, is a reader's sympathy or empathetic response. What avenue for sympathy lies open for readers when the lyric voice clearly has no sympathy for himself? The verse is at once intense and indifferent, a poetry of self-expression in which the self has nothing to gain except further encounters, calculated and implacable, with its own folly and pain, blindness and insight. Such writing is exactly what Baudelaire called "anonymous" – mannered and theatrical, the poetry of dandyism. The verse performs a kind of Faustian rite in which Byron agrees to use himself up – to *use* himself, treat himself like a thing to be coldly anatomized and observed. The reward? Simply increased self-awareness.

We see Byron writing in this way very early, even in a juvenile poem like "Damaetas." The strength of this mordant analysis of a wicked youth comes from its poetic deception. Byron publishes the poem in *Hours of Idleness* under a cunning classical heading. The Theocritean name carries a sly homosexual overtone, but that obliquity is merely the sign of a deeper deceptiveness. More important and revelatory is the suppressed title of the work: "My Character."[11] In this poem Byron tells a slant truth about himself, and in slanting the truth he tells a further and more revealing truth: he dramatizes his own hypocrisy.

A master of this style, Byron turns it loose upon all the poetic forms of Europe's cultural inheritance. That fact about his work – the scope of Byron's formal poetic undertakings – explains the immense impact that his poetry had upon later writers. When he takes up the epigram – he wrote many – the same effect appears:

> Tis said *Indifference* marks the present time,
> Then hear the reason—though 'tis told in rhyme—
> A King who *can't*—a Prince of Wales who *don't*—
> Patriots who *shan't*, and Ministers who *won't*—
> What matters who are *in* or *out* of place
> The *Mad*—the *Bad*—the *Useless*—or the *Base*?[12]

"[T]hough 'tis told in rhyme": that conventional gesture of poetic modesty comes as the prolepsis of what the last line names directly. This poem is, in its chosen political terms, a mad, bad, useless, and base piece of work, the moral equivalent of the world it is attacking. It is a small but superb poem, an affront and an offence – quite literally a terrible truth. In a sense Auden's later sentimentality would not have approved, this is a poem that "makes nothing happen." It exposes and exploits the secret hidden within Kant's bourgeois aesthetic of disinterestedness.

But among Byron's shorter poetic forms, the love lyrics illustrate his stylistic achievements most fully. "Fare Thee Well!" is more than a cruel and pathetic piece of hypocrisy; it is a dramatic presentation of the illusion resting at the heart of the Romantic lyric, with its commitment to a "willing suspension of disbelief" on the part of poet and reader alike. We do not begin to enter the dangerous space of "Fare Thee Well!" until we see how, in the horizon of Romanticism's moral and aesthetic senses alike, it is a *bad* poem. It is bad not simply because it is a cruel poem, intentionally designed to hurt his wife personally and damage her in public. It is bad because, in a sense, it is hardly "poetry" at all, more like a psycho-political broadside in verse. It is also bad because this anti-aesthetic design is pursued in a cunning way, by the manipulation of a mask of Romantic sincerity. That pretense of sincerity deepens into an oblique exposure of Byron's own pretenses of art. The last infirmity of the poem's evil, then, comes in the failure of its designs. (This failure of the poem takes place on its own anti-aesthetic terms – that is to say, in an immediate and real way, when Byron is expelled from normal society, when he leaves England in disgrace.)

Sincerity that masks a "spoiler's art," poetry that is not poetical: the writing is radically self-contradicted in the context of its cultural inheritance. It imaginatively transcends that historical moment when its immediate failure and disgrace get culturally (re)inscribed, when the poem is (academically) judged a simple piece of factitious Romantic trash. That misreading of the poem comes from a culture's determination to cherish a doubled illusion: first, that poetry expresses the best that has been known and thought in the world; and second, that criticism may be confident in its visions of judgment. If the history of critical condescension toward "Fare Thee Well!" registers the collapse of Byron's Romantic authority, it equally testifies to the endurance of Baudelaire's hypocritical reader.

Byron's significance as a lyric poet lies in the range of ironizing and critical techniques that he brought to the new lyrical forms of Romantic sincerity. These techniques extend from the most sentimental kinds of "romantic irony" (already at work in his earliest poetry, for example *Hours of Idleness*) to corrosive and nakedly self-imploding forms. Though Byron's work shuttles between these two stylistic poles, his originality – and hence his importance for Heine and Baudelaire – must be located strictly at the latter end, in his critical exploration of the conventions of Romanticism and the inheritance of sentimentality.

Byron's work has caused great difficulty for many readers, however, because his critical stance so often appears cynical, desperate, or – perhaps worst of all – indifferent. Subjecting Byron's *oeuvre* to a programmatic hope for some kind of social accommodation, Carlyle would later call it "The Everlasting Nay." Thus would he execute upon Byron his middle-class, Victorian version of Hegel's "negation of the negation." Baudelaire's reading is structurally the same as Carlyle's and Hegel's, but politically deviant. Baudelaire has greater sympathy for the devil – he celebrates Byron's satanism – because his politics are resolutely opposed to bourgeois order.

If we are to read Byron well, then, the issue of his satanism – his non-benevolent sympathy and "tendresse" – must hold the center of our attention. Because Baudelaire did exactly that, his understanding of Byron runs deep. Why, then, would the importance of Byron escape so many twentieth-century readers? The answer, I think, is finally political. While modernists like Eliot could translate Baudelaire's myth of the aristocrat/priest/dandy into a reactionary literalism, it was a move that could not be made on Byron. Baudelaire was appropriated because his satanism – unlike Byron's – remained linguistic, and because a postmodern consciousness had not yet established the spectacular and mordant equivalence between *res* and *verba* that we now take for granted. In Byron, however, that equivalence is – as we shall see – exactly the issue of the work.

II

Thus far I have tried to define the general style and structure of Byron's lyrical dandyism. To understand the originality of this work, we have to inquire further into his relation to certain conventional styles of Romantic irony.

As Schiller's famous essay argued, "the sentimental" in literature is a figure of literary self-consciousness. In the analytic dyad naive/sentimental, "naive" is a term generated by the critical power of the idea of the sentimental. "Naive" poetry exists, first, because it has been turned upon by a critical self-consciousness; and second, because that self-consciousness – in a paradoxical move – declares "the naive" to be the primary and generative term so far as poetry is concerned. In this sense, to be sentimental is already to have deployed a form of "romantic irony."

Macpherson's fragments from Ossian, and more especially the subsequent controversies over those works, nicely illustrate the polemic involved in Schiller's position. So far as English Romantic poetry is concerned, the project of the *Lyrical Ballads* corresponds to the project of Schiller's essay. In Wordsworth's and Coleridge's work, ballad is to naive what lyrical is to sentimental. Wordsworth's critical formulation of the dialectic came in the Preface of the *Lyrical Ballads* when he distinguished "emotion recollected in tranquillity" from the "spontaneous overflow of powerful feelings." Poetry springs from the latter and depends upon it as a primary source of "feeling." As an artistic and compositional practice, however, poetry for Wordsworth is a recollective and secondary event. It is an act of self-consciousness. It is, in Schiller's sense, "sentimental."

Romantic writing thus involves a negotiation of two kinds of feeling: on one hand, spontaneous and naive feelings (for example, in the poetry of Robert Burns, or in the characters in "The Idiot Boy"); on the other, reflexive and internalized feelings ("the bliss of solitude"). More than anyone else, Wordsworth defined this dialectic for English poetry. It is, as we know, a story of loss and gain – loss of the naive, acquirement of the sentimental:

> We will grieve not, rather find
> Strength in what remains behind;
> In the primal sympathy
> Which having been must ever be . . .
> In years that bring the philosophic mind.
> ("Ode. Intimations of Immortality," 180–183, 188)

That "mind" is precisely *not* the Enlightenment mind. It is philosophical because it stands opposed to the critical intelligence of the *philosophe*, a figure specifically (and ironically) invoked in Wordsworth's phrase "philosophic mind." Not a contentious and worldly mind, Wordsworth's is a "purer mind," affective and childlike – a mind turned from murderous and socially divisive dissections toward healings, consolations, and "tranquil restoration."

The so-called Greater Romantic Lyric dramatizes the workings of this type of mind.[13] (For the reader of such work, the poems are an educational machinary disseminating the Wordsworthian mind through the culture at large.) The conventions of the form are well known: a movement into a scene of solitude, typically a solitude in Nature; a meditation on and within that place, which serves as a figure (and map) of lost regions of a more primal self; an encounter with the lost self and its desires, more or less direct; finally, a separation that leaves the mental traveller more deeply attached either through the pain of this (now self-conscious) loss, or through a faith in a suprapersonal order of benevolence that maintains these attachments beyond one's personal will or control. The exemplary Romantic form of that conceptual order (which is "sentimental" and self-conscious) was elaborated in Germany by Hegel.

Byron's deviant relation to this Romantic program becomes clear when we study the dynamic of his various natural meditations. For example, as Childe Harold is travelling from Spain to Albania in Canto II of his poem, his maritime solitude becomes the locus for a Romantic colloquy (sts. 22–27). The Childe's meditation is specially notable because it is a kind of second-order meditation. This is not simply a meditation within a natural solitude, the Childe is meditating upon the idea of such meditations. The thematic core of the passage contrasts the solitude of nature, which appears bountiful, with the solitude of society. Although the latter displays as much energy as the former, it appears a corrosive and destructive energy and hence something to be fled. The idea of taking flight culminates the meditative sequence:

> More blest the life of godly Eremite,
> Such as on lonely Athos may be seen,
> Watching at Eve upon the giant height,
> That looks o'er waves so blue, skies so serene,
> That he who there at such an hour hath been
> Will wistful linger on that hallow'd spot;
> Then slowly tear him from the witching scene,
> Sigh forth one wish that such had been his lot,
> Then turn to hate a world he had almost forgot.

The conclusion deliberately works a shocking inversion of the conventional Romantic topos of nature. Structurally the text repeats the Wordsworthian ideas (a) that feeling is primary, and (b) that "powerful feeling" (the naive) is dialectically connected to "tranquil" emotions (the sentimental). Here, however, that dialectic undergoes a reinterpretation of great importance. In simplest terms, Byron's passage through a Romantic meditation on nature does not conclude in a Wordsworthian "tranquil restoration" but in a characteristically Byronic turn to passion and savagery. Most startling of all is the presentation of hatred as the emblematic sign of Byron's "naive" poetical condition.[14]

This Byronic structure of feeling – the pursuit of primal and naive spontaneities through an adverse study of memory and sentiment – dominates all his work. Canto III of *Childe Harold's Pilgrimage*, so often read as Byron's "Lakist Interlude," in fact represents his definitive anatomy and rejection of Wordsworth's "philosophic mind." This happens literally in sts. 106–107, where Byron pledges his allegiance to the *philosophes* Voltaire and Gibbon, and to their programs of critical conflict with the conventional world. Furthermore, he takes this position following his conscious pursuit of the meaning of Romantic revery and Romantic nature.

The structure of the canto as a whole replicates the structure of the brief passage we just examined from Canto II. Byron (no longer wearing the mask of the Childe) departs "the world" and its scenes of violence and conflict. This violence appears in unmasked political forms early in the canto, when Byron calls back the climactic events of the Napoleonic War. That political scene comprises the emblem of wars that are at once more primal, more personal, and more secret.

Like Manfred, Byron begins by seeking forgetfulness and an escape from the tumult of emotional conflict. His conscious desire is that the strife of his passions might undergo moderated and sympathetic transformations: in the earlier words of the Giaour, "To rest, but not to feel 'tis rest." The famous "Wordsworthian" scenes in the canto, however, which are charged with such transformative powers, barely detain Byron. He engages those scenes as the Childe had engaged them in Cantos I–II, and as Manfred would shortly engage them again: as vehicles for restoring a commitment to elemental passion – indeed, as vehicles for gaining an immediate recovery of such passion.

In this connection, two passages in Canto III are especially significant. The poem climaxes in the famous Jungfrau Storm sequence, where the full force of Byronic passion is exteriorized. Following the logic of Byron's initial conscious desires, the storm breaks only to bring a clear sky and images of peacefulness and love. Concealed within the storm, however, are Byron's deepest and most savage feelings – feelings at once completely personal and wholly elemental:

> Could I embody and unbosom now
> That which is most within me,—could I wreak
> My thoughts upon expression, and thus throw
> Soul, heart, mind, passions, feelings, strong or weak,
> All that I would have sought, and all I seek,
> Bear, know, feel, and yet breathe—into *one* word,
> And that one word were Lightning, I would speak;
> But as it is, I live and die unheard,
> With a most voiceless thought, sheathing it as a sword.
>
> (st. 97)

Because the object of Byron's stormy passion is not actually named, this text's true "thought" – the wit here is typically Byronic – remains literally "voiceless." Byron speaks his mind by holding his tongue. The effect is to represent the presence of a psychic force that dwarfs even the Jungfrau's storm. No language is adequate to the enormity of Byron's desire – because that desire must match the enormity of its reciprocal, the righteously inverted betrayal of desire executed by Byron's unnamed enemies. (Readers have always recognized the enemy being imagined here in textual silence: on one hand, the collective Spirit of English moral hypocrisy, on the other the Spirit's immediate avatar, Byron's "moral Clytemnestra.")[15] Byron's savage desire in this passage is therefore literally beyond nature, an *un*natural response to the behavior and the desire of his antagonists. Theirs is the anti-nature of moral virtue, Byron's is the anti-nature that demands a morality beyond the order of moral virtue.

The demand cannot be met in the normative orders of time and space (traditional nature), history and society (Hegelian Spirit). The sheathed sword of stanza 97 represents an insurgent but hopeless energy:

> Their breath is agitation, and their life
> A storm whereon they ride, to sink at last,
> And yet so nurs'd and bigotted to strife,
> That should their days, surviving perils past,
> Melt to calm twilight, they feel overcast
> With sorrow and supineness, and so die;
> Even as a flame unfed, which runs to waste
> With its own flickering, or as a sword laid by
> Which eats into itself, and rusts ingloriously.
>
> (st. 44)

Exactly forecasting the textual events of the Jungfrau passage, this stanza explains the demonic, Lucretian character of the "Love" figured in the benevolent apparition of Clarens (sts. 98–104) following the Jungfrau storm. Byron presents the scene at Clarens as a special moment of clarity, the immediate reciprocal of the deceased storm. Far from an emblem of a universally benevolent Nature, the Clarens passage is exactly that – a mere moment in the being of Byron's ominous Lucretian silence. The wonderful irony of the passage comes from the historical association of Clarens with Rousseau. A Byronic figure of absolute contradiction, Rousseau is at once representative of natural benevolence and the "apostle of affliction" (st. 77): the self-torturing terrorist of freedom, devoured by love (see sts. 76–84).

Byron's argument throughout the canto is the same: that no "abundant recompense" (existential or artistic) can accommodate one to the departure of elemental emotional life or naive art. More than this, he argues that the installation of a program of such recompenses – whether psychological or poetic – installs a secret ministry that, when allowed to run its full course, will ultimately draw one back to the elemental. For Byron, the dialectic of loss and gain is endless, nor does it culminate in any "higher order" or synthesis. According to this argument, death itself, which Manfred deliberately undertakes, puts no period to the dialectic. As Byron says in the fourth canto of *Childe Harold's Pilgrimage*:

> But there is that within me which shall tire
> Torture and Time, and breathe when I expire;
> Something unearthly, which they deem not of.
> (st. 137)

To achieve this peculiar kind of immortality requires a perpetuation of resistance and strife, a refusal of what Wordsworth called "primal sympathy." It is to choose instead, with Blake, primal energy, primal conflict.

III

Byron turns all his subjects into lyrical forms. He protested when his contemporaries identified him with Harold, the Giaour, the Corsair, Lara, and so forth. Because these *figurae* are consciously manipulated masks, one has to read them – as Coleridge might have said – in terms of a "sameness with difference." The poetry lies exactly in the relation, in the dialectical play between corresponding apparitional forms: on one side, the spectacular poet – the man cut into a Keatsian figure, the person translated into what the Byronic texts call "a name";[16] on the other, the various fictional and historical selvings. In Byronic masquerade we have difficulty distinguishing figure from ground because the presumptive ground, "the real Lord Byron," becomes a figural form in the poetry.

The anonymous lyric depends upon this stylistic procedure and sets up a hypo-critical contract with the Romantic reader. The texts deliver a merciless revelation of a uniform condition – a kind of "universal darkness," but beyond the imagination of *The Dunciad* because Byron's revelatory text has itself been imagined in the darkness.

> I am not of this people, or this age,
> And yet my harpings will unfold a tale

Which shall preserve these times when not a page
  Of their perturbed annals could attract
  An eye to gaze upon their civil rage
Did not my verse embalm full many an act
  Worthless as they who wrought it: 'tis the doom
  Of spirits of my order to be rack'd
In life, to wear their hearts out, and consume
  Their days in endless strife, and die alone;
  Then future thousands crowd around their tomb,
And pilgrims come from climes where they have known
  The name of him—who now is but a name.

(*The Prophecy of Dante*, I, 143–155)

Is this text "about" Byron or is it about Dante, about Italy or about England? Is Lord Byron recollecting the great Tuscan poet, or are we to read it the other way round – with this textual Dante prophecying his future British avatar? Furthermore, this structure of convertibility turns everything into its opposite. Byron/Dante declares "I am not of this people, or this age" but his verse "embalms" the "worthless" acts of the age. As the remarkable wordplay in "harpings" suggests, a Mephisto comedy plays about this text. The word "embalm" is especially volatile since it connects the poet's work with corpsed forms – as if he (Dante/Byron) were a literal figure of the nightmare life-in-death that he perceives all about him. To consult such a poet one has to visit his tomb, where one encounters merely his "name." The tombstone's engraved letters enter the text as a sign that even before death the poet lives a post-mortem existence.

In his Preface to the poem Byron associates his "prophecy" with the vision of Cassandra, whose prophetic truth shares the doom of Troy. Like Cassandra and Dante – like some utterly bleak democrat of Wordsworth's Preface to *Lyrical Ballads* – Byron is "a man like any other men," but his endowment "with more lively sensibilities" gives him the darkened eye of a seer like Cassandra:

  All that a citizen could be I was;
Raised by thy will, all thine in peace or war,
  And for this thou hast warr'd with me,—'Tis done:
  I may not overleap the eternal bar
Built up between us, and will die alone,
  Beholding, with the dark eye of a seer,
  The evil days to gifted souls foreshown,
Foretelling them to those who will not hear.

(IV, 144–151)

This is no self-celebrating text. Byron's citizenship – the social and cultural position he sought and achieved – establishes his special identity with his own world. Like the Napoleon of *Childe Harold* Canto III, the Byron of this poem is at once "the greatest [and] the worst" of citizens (st. 36), the literary Alcibiades of his country. The anonymous lyrical style delivers the famous poet over to his text, however, turning him into a symbolic form. As such, the form is both beautiful and ineffectual – the very type of that dead knowledge that Manfred's Faustian quest revealed ("The Tree of Knowledge is not that of Life").

Byronic mobility, like Keats's chameleonism, is therefore "a most painful and unhappy attribute" in virtually every respect – at least if acts are to be measured in functional terms. The Byronic text stands aloof from the dialectic of loss and gain, rewards and punishments, in which it is yet so deeply – so wholly – involved. Its satanism rests ultimately in that posture of aloofness, as if it were indifferent to questions of judgment and valuation. Good and bad, better and worse, are terms to be evaded. Like Byron's Paolo and Francesca, the texts seek (and execute) something beyond our conceptual categories of judgment (whether moral or aesthetic).

> The land where I was born sits by the Seas
> Upon that shore to which the Po descends
> With all his followers in search of peace.

The speaker here is originally Francesca, but through the texts' masquerade we translate that name into its immediate equivalent, Teresa. Francesca of Rimini, Teresa of Ravenna: the text applies to both. In his role as poet and as lover Byron is then textually disposed as Dante and Paolo.[17] In truth, however, the "Byron" of this ventriloquist work seeks a gender translation as well, and identifies himself with Francesca as much as he does with her poet and her lover.[18]

As in Byron's equivalent text "To the Po," the river here is a figure of intense and ceaseless passion – Turgenev's "torrent of spring." All of the river's tributaries and "followers" ride this river toward an extinguishing sea, where Lucretius's Aphrodite stands observing her universe.

> Love, which the gentle heart soon apprehends,
>   Seized him for the fair person which was ta'en
>   From me, and me even yet the mode offends.
> Love, who to none beloved to love again
>   Remits, seized me with wish to please so strong
>   That, as thou seest, yet, yet, it doth remain.

Damnation itself has not quenched the passion that "Seized him" and "seized me," as the next two lines emphasize:

Love to one death conducted us along,
But Caina waits for him our life who ended.

Damned to hell herself, Francesca utters a cold prophetic curse upon her murderer. But the persistence of her passion, and of her love, is only underscored by the curse, which is the emblem of her Byronic satanism.

All these "Souls" are, in Byron's nicely ambiguous translation, "offended." Dante/Byron has "such a sympathy" in these offenses of love that he pursues his inquiry and deepens his identification:

We read one day for pastime, seated nigh,
  Of Lancelot, how love enchain'd him too;
  We were alone, quite unsuspiciously.
But oft our eyes met, and our cheeks in hue
  All o'er discoloured by that reading were;
  But one point only wholly us o'erthrew.
When we read the long-sighed-for smile of her
  To be thus kissed by such a fervent lover,
  He who from me can be divided ne'er
Kiss'd my mouth, trembling in the act all over.
  Accursed was the book, and he who wrote.
  That day no further leaf we did uncover.

The real force of this text depends upon our reading it is Byron's – as yet a further event in an eternal story of abandoned love. The book of the tale of Lancilot, Dante's text, Byron's: all are "Accursed" because all are committed, in Byron's view, to the immediate intensities of a mortal life. Paolo weeps as Francesca tells her accursed tale, Dante "swooned as dying" in sympathy with their condition, and Byron replays the entire complex story in both his verse and his life.

Byron finds himself, in 1820, in the same hell as Dante and the damned lovers. As Virgil – who will never achieve salvation – leads Dante through this hell, Byron internalizes the entire transaction. Becoming all the textual characters, Byron invents the myth of the *poète maudit*, whose work now falls under Francesca's curse of love. In Byron's text (unlike Dante's), the poet literally tells the tale of his own damnation, including the damnation of his poetry. What is worse (from a moral and aesthetic point of view), the text does not ask its readers to transvalue the values by which it will be condemned. All is accursed. If a benevolent (and invisible) God watches over all the events in Dante's text, and if this God reigns even in the love-hell of Paolo and Francesca, the children of Byron's text are children of a lesser god. Byron's anonymous and oneiric work takes possesion of all its features. Consequently, here there is no God but god, and his name is Byron. (He is also called Dante, Francesca, Paolo, Virgil, Teresa, Gianciotto, and Satan.) He is a god in name only.

In Baudelairean reading of Byron, then, the translation of "Francesca of Rimini" is a key text for the clarity with which it lays out the terms of Byron's lyrical dialectic. The Byronic mode is to *take for its text* Lord Byron's "personal life." Like the "Sun of the sleepless" – Byron's startling term for the imagination – the lunar poem then casts it revelatory light upon its subjects.[19] It is a light, however, "That show'st the darkness thou canst not dispel": "Distinct, but distant – clear but, oh how cold." This is a light that shines in the darkness, but, unlike John's salvific light, in comprehending the darkness it is equally comprehended by it. Byron's dark yet clarified knowledge emerges because he has agreed to collapse his "personal life" and his "poetical life" – because a final distinction cannot be drawn between the man who suffers and the poet who sees. Lord Byron's "personal life" is on one hand a fever of passionate intensities, and on the other a cold set of representations: at once a life and a reflection, a self and a text. The work is engulfed in that dissolving, disillusioning ambiguity – an ambiguity which, however, it also embraces.

NOTES

The editor of the *Byron Journal* asked me to write an essay for this issue [1992], to mark the completion of my project of editing Byron's *Complete Poetical Works*. This essay does not address editorial matters. It represents a reading of Byron that has slowly come to dominate my thinking during my past (almost thirty) years of involvement with his work.

1 See Byron's translation of the episode from Dante (*Complete Poetical Works*, ed. Jerome J. McGann, IV [Oxford: Oxford University Press, 1986], 280–285); hereafter cited as *CPW*. Byron's obsession with this emblematic story is evident throughout his work: several of the poems in *Hours of Idleness* recall the Dante passage (e.g., the "Lines Written in Letters of an Italian Nun and an English Gentleman . . . ," ibid., I, 131 [poem no. 75]), as does the love of Selim and Zuleika in *The Bride of Abydos* and Mazeppa and Theresa in *Mazeppa*. Byron puts a quotation from the passage at the head of the first Canto of *The Corsair*, and of course the tale figures in Don Juan's first two affairs, with Donna Julia and with Haidée.

2 See the letters to Madame Aupick of 9 July 1857 and 19 February 1858 (Baudelaire's *Correspondance*, ed. Claude Pichois [Paris: Gallimard, 1973],

I, 410–411, 451). The major work of *Fleurs du Mal*, "Le Voyage," is an act of homage to Byron, whom Baudelaire defined as the "charactère oriental . . . *le sceptique* voyageur" (Baudelaire, *Oeuvres Complètes*, ed. Claude Pichois [Paris: Gallimard, 1976], II, 213). See Baudelaire's letters to Sainte-Beuve, 21 February 1959, and (two days later) to Maxime du Camp (*Correspondence*, 553–554 and nn.).

3 Heine and Poe also understood Byron's method and imitated his work – and of course Heine and Poe are two of Baudelaire's other early poetical models.

4 *Oeuvres Complètes*, II, 194.

5 This brief discussion of "Fare Thee Well!" sketches the argument I elaborate more fully in "What Difference do the Circumstances of Publication Make to the Interpretation of a Literary Work?" in *Literary Pragmatics*, ed. Roger D. Sell (London and New York: Routledge, 1991), 195–204 (see also this volume, ch. 4). For two related discussions see as well my "The Book of Byron and the Book of a World," in *The Beauty of Inflections* (Oxford: Oxford University Press, 1985), 255–293; and "My Brain is Feminine': Byron and the Poetics of Deception," in *Byron, Augustan and Romantic*, ed. Andrew Rutherford (Basingstoke: Macmillan, 1990), 26–51 (see also this volume, ch. 3).

6 Wordsworth's judgment came in a letter to John Scott, who published the first unauthorized printing of the poem in his newspaper the *Champion*. See *The Letters of William and Dorothy Wordsworth*, rev. edn. by Mary Moorman and Alan G. Hill (Oxford: Clarendon Press, 1970), III, ii, 204.

7 See *The Letters of John Keats*, ed. Hyder Edward Rollins (Cambridge, MA: Harvard University Press, 1958), II, 67.

8 *Biographia Literaria*, ed. James Engell and W. Jackson Bate, Bollingen Series 70 (Princeton: Princeton University Press, 1983), II, 6.

9 Katrina Bachinger's brief comments on the extremely complex ironies of this work are the best criticism of the poem that I know. See her "The Sombre Madness of Sex: Byron's First and Last Gift to Poe," *Byron Journal* (1991), 131–136. (*Waltz*, incidentally, was not "published" in 1813, it was privately printed then. Technically, its first "publication" was in the pirated Paris edition of 1821.)

10 See Wordsworth's Preface to *Lyrical Ballads*, in *Lyrical Ballads*, ed. R. L. Brett and A. R. Jones (rev. edn., London: Methuen, 1965), 255.

11 For the publication history and the titles see *CPW*, I, 51–52 and 367.

12 See *CPW*, III, 91.

13 The phrase is M. H. Abrams's, from his celebrated structural study of the Romantic lyric: "Structure and Style in the Greater Romantic Lyric," in *From Sensibility to Romanticism*, ed. Gordon Haight and Harold Bloom (New Haven: Yale University Press, 1965), 527–560. Abrams says that "Only Byron, among the major poets, did not write in this mode at all" (527). This is wrong, I think, on two counts at least: first, Blake did not write in this mode (he is, like Byron, a rhetorical poet); and second, Byron did write in the mode, through he took considerable liberties with the form, See, e.g., "Churchill's Grave"

and "To the Po"; and *Childe Harold's Pilgrimage* has a number of set-piece passages that correspond to the form.

14 Baudelaire was especially pleased with Byron's sympathetic approach to feelings of hatred. See his letter to Michel Levy, 15 February 1865 (*Correspondence*, II, 462).

15 The classic statement of this reading is in Macaulay's 1831 review of Moore's *Letters and Journals of Lord Byron* (see *Byron. The Critical Heritage*, ed. Andrew Rutherford ([New York: Barnes and Noble, 1970], 295–316).

16 See "[Epistle to Augusta]", 100, and *The Prophecy of Dante*, Canto I, 155.

17 The Paolo indentification is made not merely through Byron's relation to the Francesca/Teresa figure, but also through his relation to Dante, whose younger brother (poet) he is (as Paolo was the younger brother of Francesca's husband Gianciotto).

18 For Byron's "feminine" sympathies see Susan Wolfson's two important essay " 'Their She Condition': Cross-Dressing and the Politics of Gender in *Don Juan*," *ELH*, 54 (fall 1987), 585–617; " 'A Problem Few Dare Imitate': *Sardanapalus* and 'Effeminate Character," *ELH*, 58 (fall 1991), 867–902. See also Sonia Hofkosh, "Women and the Romantic Author – the Example of Byron," in *Romanticism and Feminism*, ed. Anne K. Mellor (Bloomington and Indianapolis: Indiana University Press, 1988), 93–114, and chapter 3, above.

19 "Sun of the Sleepless!" is the title of one of the *Hebrew Melodies*; see *CPW*, III, 305. At line 4 Byron's poem recollects Dante's Paolo and Francesca passage by echoing one of his favorite texts – the Dante passage he appended to Canto I of *The Corsair*: "How like thou art to joy remembered well!"

CHAPTER 6

Private poetry, public deception

> *[P]oetic reference is not only a question of "the world in the work" but "the work in the world"*
>
> – Barrett Watten, *Total Syntax*

When readers today, especially academic readers, think of "the politics of poetic form" in connection with Romanticism, the names that usually come to mind are Blake and Shelley (for the opposition), or Wordsworth and Southey (for the establishment). In the context of 1790–1830, however, and throughout the Euro-American world of the nineteenth and much of the twentieth century, the name that would have been first on everyone's lips was Byron. A political activist in England where he spoke in parliament against capital punishment, later a social pariah who left England for Italy and Greece where he was deeply involved in revolutionary political groups, he finally – famously – died on the west coast of Greece, in the guerilla encampment of Greek Suliotes whom he had joined and personally financed to fight against the Turks for the liberation of Greece.

English public opinion, after worshipping at his shrine for almost five years (1812–1816), finally decided he was the single greatest threat to the country's public morals and social order. This judgment of Byron is written for anyone to see in the English public press of the years 1816–1824. It seems astonishing to us today, and yet it is the simplest fact. We are surprised partly because we do not easily imagine any single person having the kind of political significance which Byron evidently did have. We are astonished as well, however, because Byron's political life seems to have been so ineffectual – in contrast, for example, to a person like Lenin. But most of all we are surprised because we have come to think of Byron's Romanticism not as a political force but as a purely personal one: Byron the great lover, the man not of political but of erotic affairs, the broken dandy of the fast and luxurious world of Regency England.

I will be asking you to rethink the terms of this framework in which Byron and his work have descended to us. And I believe it is important to do so, at this point in time especially, because the contradictions implicit in Byron's personal and political investments have great relevance to our own immediate circumstances.

We begin to glimpse that relevance when we remember perhaps the single most important fact about him and his work: that he was the first writer in English to become a brand name, even a commodity fetish. He was himself well aware of this phenomenon, and was actively – consciously – involved in generating what Benjamin was later to see as an auratic field of poetical relations. Benjamin saw Baudelaire as the poet who defined the character of writing in an age of mechanical reproduction. But to Baudelaire, Byron was the true model and point of origin; and Baudelaire was right.

To understand this better we shall have to go over the ground of Romanticism, and the critique of Romanticism which Byron's work generated. Byron's departure from England in 1816, heaped with obloquy, would be the emblem of his subsequent cultural and ideological fate. Romantic ideologies came to dominate writing in English for the next hundred years and more, but those ideologies would carefully circumscribe the antithesis embodied in Byron's own Romanticism. This would be done by refusing to take seriously Baudelaire's and Nietzsche's readings of Byron's work, by marginalizing him into various inconsequential territories – poet of Regency high life, poet of sentimental love, Satanic poseur, king of light verse and depthless adventure narratives set in exotic places. In his own day, and throughout Europe in the nineteenth century, Byron was felt to be mad, bad, and dangerous to know. He was generally not read so in the English-speaking world for one simple yet profound reason: his work called into question the most basic premises of writing as they had been recast in the English Romantic movement. Byron's work argued that poetry is a discourse not of truth but of illusions and deceits – what Blake earlier called "bodies of false-hood"; and he went on to show the social structure, the rhetoric, by which such illusions are maintained. Briefly, he revealed the secrets of the imagination, made those secrets public information – much as Brecht in the twentieth century would say that the theater should do. For trying to leak the files of the pentagon of the poets, Byron would be silenced.

I

Sincerity: this is one of the touchstones by which Romantic poetry originally measured itself.[1] In a poem's sincerity one observed a deeply felt relation binding the poetic Subject to the poetic subject, the speaking voice to the matter being addressed. Romantic truth is inner vision, and Romantic knowledge is the unfolding of the truths of that inner vision.

Hypocrisy is the antithesis of sincerity. One can be sincere and yet speak incompletely, inadequately, or even falsely, but it appears a patent contradiction to think or imagine that one could be sincere and at the same time speak deliberate falsehoods or develop subtle equivocations. To do so is to declare that one is "two-faced," and hence lacking that fundamental quality of the sincere person: integrity.

In this context, rhetorical and premeditated verse may be imagined *prima facie* incapable with respect to truth and knowledge. The poetry of sincerity – Romantic poetry, in its paradigmatic mode – therefore typically avoids the procedures of those public forms of poetry, satirical and polemical verse. When Romantic poetry opens itself to those genres, it opens itself to the horizon of its antithesis, to the horizon of hypocrisy.[2]

This last move is, of course, exactly what Byron did. We should not be surprised, then, that he is the one English Romantic who has been commonly charged with – who has had his work charged with – hypocrisy.[3] This consequence reflects an important and (if I may so phrase it) two-faced fact about Byron as a writer: that he cultivated rhetorical modes of verse, and that *he was a Romantic poet who cultivated those modes.* The distinction is crucial. *Don Juan* is a machine for exposing many kinds of hypocrisy – cant political, cant poetical, cant moral, Byron called them – and there is no one, I suppose, who would gainsay the extraordinary scale of Byron's achievement. Nevertheless, what we have still to see more clearly is how this satire of hypocrisy is grounded in Byron's Romanticism, and how the latter is the very seat and primal scene of what it means to be hypocritical. In the end we will discover a poetic truth-function which Byron, alone of the English Romantics, elaborated and deployed. An essential feature of this work is the understanding that hypocrisy and the true voice of feeling cannot be separated (even if they can be distinguished). Paradoxical though it may seem, this is a discovery which may be imagined with peculiar – perhaps unexampled – clarity through the styles of Romanticism.

At the heart of the Romantic ideal of sincerity are two related problems, the one a contradiction, the other an illusion. The contradiction is concealed in the Romantic idea(l) of self-integrity. Byron summed up this problem with great wit and trenchancy:

Also observe, that like the great Lord Coke,
 (See Littleton) when'er I have expressed
Opinions two, which at first sight may look
 Twin opposites, the second is the best.
Perhaps I have a third too in a nook,
 Or none at all—which seems a sorry jest;
But if a writer would be quite consistent,
How could he possibly show things existent?
(*Don Juan* XV, st. 87)[4]

This anticipates exactly the critique of the Romantic idea(l) of subjectivity that would be raised so powerfully by Kierkegaard in his analysis of Hegel's paradigmatic representation of the truth-content of that ideal. Kierkegaard's *Concluding Unscientific Postscript* ridicules the "German philosopher" – "Herr Professor" – for the abstraction of Hegel's concept of subjective and phenomenological truth, which cannot be "realized for any existing spirit, who is himself existentially in process of becoming."[5]

I will summarize briefly Kierkegaard's argument on this matter because it helps to clarify the import and structure of Byron's work. According to Hegel, the idea(l) of identity is a dialectical synthesis of "Twin opposites." It is achieved when Otherness, that which is not the subject, is "negated" in the process of knowledge we call consciousness. The objective knowledge that is gained is not positive but phenomenological: not particular subjective or empirical truths, but the metaphysical truth of the process itself.

To this position Kierkegaard raised a simple but difficult problem – his famous "aut . . . aut," the "either/or." Assuming (with Hegel and the entire metaphysical tradition) the principle of identity, Kierkegaard argued as follows: either the truth that is achieved is identical with consciousness, or it is not truth. If the process is the truth, the process is solipsistic (it involves mere tautologies); if it is not solipsistic, contradiction – untruth – remains part of the process. The "negation" that is part of the Hegelian process is either the phantom of a negation or it is a true negation; in the first instance it may be transcended, in the second it may not, but in either case knowledge and truth remain unachieved.

A writer, therefore, cannot "possibly show things existent" and at the same time "be consistent." This contradiction operates because the "process" of subjectivity is an existential and not a logical (or dialectical) process. Kierkegaard's lively prose style is itself an "existential" critique of German philosophical discourse, a revelation of what it actually means to "show things existent." But in this respect Byron's verse far surpasses the Danish philosopher's arguments:

> If people contradict themselves, can I
> Help contradicting them, and every body,
> Even my veracious self?—But that's a lie;
> I never did so, never will—how should I?
> He who doubts all things, nothing can deny.
> (xv, st. 88)

The lines enact the contradictions they confront. In this passage Byron at once asserts and denies his self-integrity. His contradiction of himself is a lie, the lines declare, but they also declare that his "veracious self" is a lie, and hence they equally give the lie to his denial of his self-contradiction.

The passage, in short, turns itself into an illustration, or an instance, of the problem it is proposing to deal with. It is Byron's poetic, "existential" equivalent of the logical paradox of the lying Cretan. Byron's verse here proposes such a paradox, but it includes its own activity of making the proposal within the paradox, as yet another face of the contradiction.

Later I shall look further into *Don Juan*'s contradictions, but in order to do that we need to understand better the illusions which correspond to those contradictions. If a contradiction exposes itself at the core of Romantic self-integrity, we confront an illusion in the Romantic idea(l) of spontaneity and artlessness. Romantic sincerity only *presents itself* as unpremeditated verse; in fact it involves a rhetoric, and contractual bonds with its audiences, which are just as determinate and artful as the verse of Donne, or Rochester, or Pope. The rhetoric of sincerity in Romanticism is a rhetoric of displacement; the audience is not addressed directly, it is set apart, like the reflective poet, in a position where the discourse of the poem has to be overheard. Among the important consequences of this basic maneuver is the illusion of freedom which it fosters – as if the reader were not being placed under the power of the writer's rhetoric, as if the writer were relatively indifferent to the reader's presence and intent only on communing with his own soul.

Byron's work and his audiences, by contrast, always tend to preserve a clarity of presence toward each other. This remains true even when Byron is working in lyrical forms. In general, it is as if Byron in his work were not simply meditating in public, but were declaring or even declaiming his inmost thoughts and feelings out loud, and directly to others. (The procedure has been aptly described as "trailing his bleeding heart across Europe.") The difference from the usual Romantic practice is crucial.

II

We observe that difference very early in Byron's work. The first important publication in his career as a poet was in fact a text which he did not write himself, though he had provoked it. I mean Henry Brougham's shrewd notice of Byron's juvenile *Hours of Idleness* (1807). Brougham registers and then ridicules Byron's efforts to control and manipulate his audience:

> the noble author is peculiarly forward in pleading his minority. We have it in the title-page, and on the very back of the volume; it follows his name like a favourite part of his *style.* Much stress is laid upon it in the preface, and the poems are connected with this general statement of his case, by particular dates. (Rutherford, 28)

Brougham understands how the texts of Byron's poems are integrated into the format of the book in general so that the reading of individual texts will be framed and controlled by various intratextual markers. When Brougham pillories Byron, therefore, it is not so much because the poetry is maudlin or sentimental, but because he detects calculation and insincerity in the work.

In *English Bards and Scotch Reviewers* Byron strikes back. Though the work is formally a critical review of the current state of poetry and British culture, the poem is in fact a riposte to the *Edinburgh Review* notice, an act of self-justification.

> Still must I hear?—shall hoarse FITZGERALD bawl
> His creaking couplets in a tavern hall
> And I not sing, lest, haply, Scotch Reviews
> Should dub me scribbler, and denounce my Muse?
> Prepare for rhyme—I'll publish, right or wrong:
> Fools are my theme, let Satire be my song.
>
> (II, 1–6)

This is an unusual opening move because Byron does not entirely separate himself from the "Fools" who are his poem's theme. The touch of recklessness in the determination to "publish, right or wrong" is fairly paraded in these lines. What Byron gains by that move is an effect of honesty, as if he were – despite his faults as a writer and a person – more candid and morally courageous than those who will be the objects of his satire (that is, bad poets like W. J. Fitzgerald and proud reviewers like Brougham).

One notes as well the imperative address to the reader in the fifth line ("Prepare for rhyme"). This maneuver reminds us of the general literary situation which prevails in Byron's writing even at this first stage of his career. The work, that is to say, operates through a textual interplay which is carried out in the public sphere.

The special strength of *English Bards* is a function of the Brougham review. Charged by Brougham with insincerity in his earlier book, Byron responds in *English Bards* with a new and more powerful style of sincerity. His polemic is grounded in a significant and daring initial decision: not to deny the charges brought against *Hours of Idleness*. Byron does not even deny Brougham's *ad hominem* critical implications – that Lord Byron, the author of the book, reveals himself in it as a somewhat foolish, calculating, and untrustworthy person.

Byron, in other words, accepts "sincerity" as the critical issue. Launching an *ad hominem* rejoinder to his Scotch reviewer (whom Byron at the time mistakenly thought was Francis Jeffrey) and his critical cohorts at the *Edinburgh Review*, Byron admits his weaknesses as a writer and his faults of character. This admission is a new sign of his sincerity, and it is the foundation on which Byron reconstitutes his character in this new poem.

Being, as he says, the "least thinking of a thoughtless throng, / Just skilled to know the right and chuse and wrong" (689–690), Byron is a model neither as a poet nor as a "Moralist" (700). Nonetheless, he refuses to disqualify himself from satire. He has "learned to think, and sternly speak the truth" (1058), and the truth is that cultural rectitude in Britain has become random and ineffectual – a praiseworthy poet here, a judicious critic there, but none of them – and least of all Lord Byron – installed (or installable) in a position of authority. Byron's poem exposes the lack of a cultural consensus. More than that, it shows how, in the absence of such a consensus, the merely "righteous" will move to seize authority.

> Thus much I've dared; if my incondite lay
> Hath wronged these righteous times let others say;
> (1067–1068)

Lines like these solicit and even glory in their contrariness. At once aggressive and indifferent, the couplet – which concludes the poem – summarizes the tonal character of the satire as a whole, just as it anticipates the tonal perspective of the celebrated writings soon to follow: *Childe Harold* in particular, but all the Baudelairean Oriental tales as well, and of course *Manfred*.

The challenge reminds us, however, of the equally important matter I touched on earlier: that the structure of the work is communicative exchange. Throughout his career Byron's books cultivate direct communication with the people who are reading them – addressing such people (often by name) and responding to what they are themselves saying (as it were) *to* Byron's poems. His work assumes the presence of an audience that talks and listens – an audience that may hear as well as overhear, and that may have something to say in its turn.

We recognize this procedure in numerous passages from *Don Juan*. The exchange structure is especially interesting when Byron reflects upon or responds to criticisms directed at his work by contemporary readers.

> They accuse me—*Me*—the present writer of
> The present poem—of—I know not what,—
> A tendency to under-rate and scoff
> At human power and virtue and all that;
> And this they say in language rather rough.
> (VII, st. 3)

In such cases – they are numerous – the act of writing makes itself one of the principal subjects of the writing. This is not to say that we are simply witnessing a poem that is written about poetry. That is what we should say, correctly, about much of *The Prelude* or "The Fall of Hyperion" or a host of other excellent Romantic poems. The situation is slightly but significantly different in Byron's case. Here the act of writing has thoroughly materialized and socialized the field of the imagination's activity. In such circumstances we observe how poetry is like most human events – a dynamic interchange between various parties each of whom plays some part in the total transaction.[6] Those parties are never completely visible or present to consciousness – in Byron's poem or anywhere else; but a poem like *Don Juan*, by calling attention to certain of its communicative actions, allows one to glimpse the radical heteronomy of the exchanges that are taking place.

Byron is quite sensitive to the presence of his many readers – indeed, his acts of writing are equally acts of imagining them into existence, and then talking with them. Stanzas 27–32 of *Don Juan*, Canto I, narrate the marital troubles of Donna Inez and her husband Don Jose, but the subtext – the domestic circumstances of Lord and Lady Byron – exposes the actual structure of Byron's writing here:

> For Inez call'd some druggists and physicians,
> And tried to prove her loving lord was *mad*,
> But as he had some lucid intermissions,
> She next decided he was only *bad*. (st. 27)

And so on. One may read these lines, and the entire passage, without any knowledge whatever of the autobiographical allusions; or one may read them with no detailed and particular knowledge, though with some general sense that personal allusions are being made; or one may read them from the inside, as it were, as a person learned in the various references. *Don Juan* has imagined and written to all three of these audiences.

But it has also done more. Besides all those later readers (like ourselves) who are learned in such texts by study and application, the passage has imagined various contemporary readers. Their presences are called to our attention through the surviving proofs of Byron's poem, which were read and annotated by Byron's friend John Cam Hobhouse. In these annotations Hobhouse's principal object was to persuade Byron to moderate various aspects of the satire – for example, the personal swipes at Lady Byron.[7] Alongside the passage just cited Hobhouse wrote, disapprovingly: "This is so very pointed."

The proofs with Hobhouse's annotations were sent to Byron, who entered a dialogue with his friend by adding his own marginalia in response to Hobhouse's strictures. Against that comment by Hobhouse, for example, Byron wrote: "If people make application it is their own fault." The remark is entirely disingenuous, of course, but it emphasizes his awareness of "the people" who might "make application" in texts like these. Hobhouse is one of those people – but then so is Lady Byron; and these two readers, equally imagined through this text, will read in very different ways.

This proof material raises two points which I want to emphasize and pursue. First, the "application" which Hobhouse makes in his reading underscores the variety of *possible* applications: even if we limit the reading group to "the knowing ones," we can see how differently the passage will be read by Hobhouse, Lady Byron, Augusta Leigh, and so forth. Second, those different readings do not stand outside the text; on the contrary, they are part of the work's imagination of itself. Byron is a reader of his own text here, as his marginal note to Hobhouse indicates. And when we consult the reviews of the first two cantos we find a series of other readers who have been imagined by the writing and who turn upon Byron's texts in various states of outrage, annonyance, disgust. Our later varieties of amusement are to be reckoned up here as well.

Byron's poem thus incorporates a large and diverse group of people into itself. The group includes specific persons, like Hobhouse, Lady Byron, and a host of named or otherwise targeted individuals – literary people (friends, acquaintances, enemies, or simply people he knew or had heard of), politicians, public figures, lovers, and so forth; but it also includes various social, ideological, religious, and political groups (like the bluestockings, the landed aristocracy, the London literary world, the government, the opposition, and a variety of Christian readers). These people are "in" Byron's poem not simply because they are named or alluded to – not simply at the narratological level – but because Byron's text has called them out – has imagined them as presences at the rhetorical and dialogical levels. Because Byron has pulled them into the world of his poem, the poem is forced to overstep its own aesthetic limits, and to move among *them*, in *their* world.

The various public's responses to the poem are therefore included in the writing's imagination of itself. Byron's readers seem most present in those passages where the text appears most shocking or tasteless. The parody of the decalogue in Canto I; the scenes of cannibalism in Canto II; the aftermath of the siege of Ismael when the "widows of forty" are made to wonder "Wherefore the ravishing did not begin!" (VIII, st. 132): these passages horrified early readers, and many of them still retain their offensiveness. The effects are wholly calculated, however, though for certain readers this fact only increases the offense which they represent.

Byron's calculations are meant to draw readers into the orbit of the poem, to insist upon their presence. The stanzas in Canto I (209–210) where Byron declares that he "bribed my grandmother's review – the British" to write an approving article on *Don Juan* are a good instance of what is happening in Byron's text. The allegation is patently outrageous – an amusing poetical flight which calls attention to Byron's general awareness that his poem might cause "some prudish readers [to] grow skittish." The editor of the *British Review*, however, William Roberts, took it all in high seriousness, and was moved to issue a public denial of Byron's imaginary declaration.[8]

William Roberts thus becomes an accomplice in Byron's writing. *Don Juan* seeks that kind of complicity, imagines its presence at every point. We laugh at Roberts's foolishness for having risen to Byron's bait here, but the more important matter to grasp is that Roberts's reaction *has to be included in our understanding of Byron's poem*, has to be seen as "part of" the work.

Roberts's reaction calls attention to some of the poem's most important discursive procedures. We confront the same kind of situation, for example, when Hobhouse annotates the texts that allude to Lady Byron. Where the poem reads (in reference to Donna Inez and Don Jose)

> She kept a journal, where his faults were noted,
> And open'd certain trunks of books and letters.
> (I, st. 28)

the text is glancing at one of Byron's most cherished beliefs about his wife and her deviousness ("You know," Byron wrote to his sister, "that Lady B[yro]n *secretly opened my letter trunks before she left Town*").[9] Hobhouse annotates the *Don Juan* text "There is some doubt about this," meaning that he is not sure that Lady Byron actually ransacked Byron's belongings in January 1816. What is remarkable here is the *way* Hobhouse is reading, the way he, like Roberts, refuses to distinguish between the fictive and the factive dimensions of the text. Hobhouse reads the poem as if it were literal statement at the level of the subtext.

Byron's response to Hobhouse's annotation is even more interesting. Against his friend's expression of doubt about the factual truth of Byron's poetic allusion, Byron writes this in the margin:

> What has the "*doubt*" to do with the poem? It is at least poetically true—why apply everything to that absurd woman. I have no reference to living characters.

Here disingenuousness unmasks itself as hypocrisy. Byron's argument that his work should not be read outside its purely aesthetic space is belied by his own continual practice. What Byron's remark indicates, however, is his reluctance to accept fully the consequences of the writing procedures he has set in motion. The writing has collapsed the distinction between factual and fictional space, and it calls various actual readers into its presence. Byron's annotation shows that he still imagines he can control those readers, that he still imagines it is his poetic privilege to keep them in control and to require them to read "in the same spirit that the author writ." But a larger "spirit" than Lady Byron's husband supervenes the act of writing here. The poetry, written "in" that larger spirit, exposes that man as another partisan reader of the poem, and hence as a reader who can claim no authoritative privilege. Hobhouse's critical reading of Byron's text is written in, is part of, that larger satirical spirit. The generosity of Byron's satirical project is that it has licensed his work to bite the hand that feeds it.

III

To the degree that *Don Juan* is committed to telling the truth, the undermining of the narrator's authority has important implications. In laying "Byron" open to criticism, the writing takes away a fundamental Romantic truth-function. Sincerity, the integrity of the "veracious self," will not survive the poem's own processes. The poem responds to this situation by developing a new theory of truth, the idea of "truth in masquerade":

And after all, what is a lie? 'Tis but
  The truth in masquerade; and I defy
Historians, heroes, lawyers, priests to put
  A fact without some leaven of a lie.
The very shadow of true Truth would shut
  Up annals, revelations, poesy,
And prophecy.

This being the case, Byron concludes:

Praised be all liars and all lies!
(XI, sts. 37–38)

The project of *Don Juan* is itself an instance of the truth in masquerade: for while six volumes of the work were published under Byron's authority, they were all issued anonymously. Note or text, the name Byron never passes the lips of the poem. That Byron was its author everyone knew, nor did he try to conceal the fact; but he did equivocate, as we see from the "Reply" he wrote (but never published) to the attack made on *Don Juan* in Blackwood's *Edinburgh Magazine* of August 1819.

With regard to *Don Juan*, I neither deny nor admit it to be mine – everybody may form their own opinion; but, if there be any who now, or in the progress of that poem, if it is to be continued, feel, or should feel themselves so aggrieved as to require a more explicit answer, privately and personally, they shall have it.
I have never shrunk from the responsibility of what I have written.[10]

Byron here insists on maintaining the fiction of the author's anonymity even as he all but acknowledges the poem as his production. Not to come forward explicitly as the author of *Don Juan* meant that the work could operate as a masquerade performance whose many roles and attitudes would all have to be understood to have been assumed by one person. Furthermore, the work is properly to be designated a masquerade rather than a theatrical performance because the encounters with the poem's audiences do not take place across the distance marked by a proscenium. The poem engages its interlocutors – even when those people are a group or a class – in much more intimate and personal ways. The style is, as the work says, "conversational."

Still, the truth that lies in masquerade remains contradictory. In his enthusiasm for his new theory of truth the narrator exclaims "Praised be all liars and all lies!" But the propositions concealed in that sentence – that all liars and lies are worthy of praise, and that the speaker of the sentence assents to this idea – are both belied by *Don Juan*. The text is happy to praise many lies and liars, even the lies of lying women which the younger Byron, drowning in his sentimental sexism, once had so much trouble with; and the narrator stands behind the text in all those instances. But one liar stands outside the pale: "shuffling Southey, that incarnate lie" (X, st. 13).

The exception is extremely important so far as *Don Juan* is concerned. I pass without comment the obvious fact that Southey's exceptional position gives the lie to – contradicts – the universal praise of liars. This is important, but not so important as another contradiction. To the degree that Byron can perceive untruth incarnate in Robert Southey, to that extent Byron comes forward in his masquerade as one possessed, however unselfconsciously, of truth. A kind of negative ground of truth, Southey becomes one of the still points in the turning world of *Don Juan*. The veracity of the Byronic self is defined through its differences from and with Robert Southey.

But even here we encounter a problem, as one may see very easily from that passage in Canto III which centers in "The Isle of Greece" ballad. At the plot level, the ballad is sung by the Romantic poet kept by Lambro on his island fastness. The song becomes the occasion for a series of reflections on poets like Southey who sell themselves to authority, or fashion their work to catch the main chance. The textual difficulty arises because, in developing the attack on Southey's crassness and lack of integrity, the poem uses details and illustrations which are drawn from Byron's own work and career. As we saw earlier, in drawing the portrait of the "sad trimmer" poet (III, st. 82) in the likeness of Robert Southey, Byron's poem creates an unusual palimpsest in which the faces of Southey and Byron, those arch antagonists, are super-imposed on each other. The two men are, in the full meaning of that paradoxical phrase, "Twin opposites."

When truth operates in masquerade, then, even negative grounds of truth fail to keep their identity. If bad "moralists like Southey" (III, st. 93) are not the reeds on which the poem can lean, perhaps – as numerous readers have suggested – we are to count on the play of *Don Juan*'s ironies. Integrity and stability lie in the work's flaunting of its own contradictions, in the Romantic irony we observed playing through the passage about Byron's "veracious self" in Canto XV. There Romantic irony is invoked, as so often in the poem, to expose and transcend its own contradictions.

But Romantic irony is not the work's ground of truth either. We glimpse this even through the example of Southey, who is not known in *Don Juan* through plays of Romantic irony. He is known rather through hatred – the same way that Brougham and Castlereagh are known. The poem's equation of Byron and Southey, therefore, cannot be assimilated into *Don Juan*'s ironical self-understanding, for it is an equation which, though real, stands outside – in true contradiction to – the horizon of the work's self-consciousness. Byron can be witty at his own expense, or at Southey's expense, but his wit is not engaged in face of the Byron/Southey parallel. His wit cannot be engaged here because Southey is not in the end a figure of fun for Byron, he is a figure of all that is hateful and despicable.

The issue of Southey and the presence of anger and hatred in *Don Juan* are the touchstones by which we can measure the poem's contradictions. The argument in the margins between Byron and Hobhouse, noted earlier, eventually spills, like so much else, into the public text:

> And recollect [this] work is only fiction,
> And that I sing of neither mine nor me,
> Though every scribe, in some slight turn of diction,
> Will hint allusions never *meant*. Ne'er doubt
> *This*—when I speak, I *don't hint*, but *speak out*.
>
> (XI, st. 88)

Which is all very well except that the poem not only practices such an art of allusions, in Canto XIV it explicitly declares itself committed to the mode. *Don Juan* is written in a secret code, the text declares, because the work contains so "much which could not be appreciated / In any manner by the uninitiated" (XIV, sts. 21–22). It is important to see that these two passages – these two positions – do not cancel each other out in the poem. *Don Juan* is constructed to show that there is a sense in which – or perhaps one should say that there are times when – both assertions apply; just as there are occasions when each of these attitudes would have itself belied by the text.

Thus *Don Juan* does something more than set in motion Byron's version of Kierkegaard's either/or problematic. The poem's contradictions deconstruct all truth-functions which are founded either in (metaphysical) Identity or (psychological) Integrity, as we have seen. In their place is set a truth-function founded (negatively) in contradiction itself, and (positively) in metonomy: to the negative either/or dialectic *Don Juan* adds the procedural rule of "both/and." That procedural rule is Byron's version of what Hegel called "the negation of the negation."

The latter, in its Byronic form, means that the terms of all contradictions are neither idealistically transcended nor nihilistically cancelled out. They simply remain in contradiction. The both/and rule means that the writing of the poem must "invariably" produce not simply the dialectic of "Opinions two," but somewhere "a third too in a nook," that third being, minimally, that awareness of the unresolved character of the original opposition.

It is through its many forms of contradiction that the poem declares its truth-function to consist in the setting of problems and not the presentation of solutions. The point of the work is to test the limits of what it itself is able to imagine, and to carry out those tests by setting imagination against imagination.

The poem, we should therefore say, learns from itself, even though the knowledge it acquired must remain provisional, subject to change, and even sometimes unassimilated at the authoritative level of its consciousness. Byron's private argument with Hobhouse in the margins of the proofs of Cantos I–II would eventually find itself publicly displayed in the contradictory passages set down in Cantos XI and XIV respectively, where those two imaginations expose their respective limits. This kind of thing happens repeatedly in the work. The writing seems bound to imagine the truths in its own lies as well as the falsehoods in its own truths. In *Don Juan*, Byron's imagination of Southey has a fatal appointment to keep with his imagination of himself.

This structure of provocations does not arise, however, from the ideology of Byron's own "creative imagination." It is rather the consequence of *Don Juan*'s rhetoric, which insists upon the presence of an objective world of various readers. One of these readers is the person we call Lord Byron, the writer of *Don Juan*, though even in *his* case, as we have seen, the person subsists in a multiplied – perhaps we should say, a fractured – identity. But it is the many other readers – Hobhouse, Lady Byron, the reviewers, the public in general – who stand as the work's most plain figures of otherness and objectivity. "Prepare for rhyme," *Don Juan* in effect says to them all – and in so saying the work lays itself open to the preparedness – the self-consciousness – it insists upon in those it has summoned.

Don Juan is seriously interested in what they all have to say – the foolish things of William Roberts, the more thoughtful things of his friend Hobhouse, the critical and antagonistic things of everyone. In Canto VII, for example, when Byron protests against those who attacked him for underrating and scoffing "At human power and virtue, and all that," Byron defends the morality of the work "as a *Satire* on the abuses of the present states of society" (*BLJ* X, 68), and on the illusions of those who were unable to see those abuses.

But the reviewers and pamphleteers insisted that *Don Juan* was somthing far different. Jeffrey's notice in the *Edinburgh Review* (Feb. 1822), while respectful of the work in certain ways, summarizes the negative line of attack. *Don Juan* is "in the highest degree pernicious" to society because it, like all Byron's writings, has "a tendency to destroy all belief in the reality of virtue."

Though *Don Juan* vigorously dissents from such a judgment, it also assimilates the judgment to itself, adds its own assent to that judgment even as it maintains, at the same time, its dissenting line.

That both/and maneuver is unmistakeable, for example, at the beginning of Canto XIII. In Canto XII Byron had reiterated his position that *Don Juan*'s goal is the "improvement" (st. 40) of society: "My Muse by exhortation means to mend / All people" (st. 39). But at the opening of Canto XIII this passion for virtuous improvement, it appears, has waned somewhat:

I should be very willing to redress
  Men's wrongs, and rather check than punish crimes,
Had not Cervantes in that too true tale
  Of Quixote, shown how all such efforts fail.

Cervantes smiled Spain's Chivalry away;
  A single laugh demolished the right arm

Of his own country;—seldom since that day
  Has Spain had heroes. While Romance could charm,
The world gave ground before her bright array;
  And therefore have his volumes done such harm,
That all their glory, as a composition,
Was dearly purchased by his land's perdition. (sts. 8, 11)

The argument repeats the most commonplace line of attack taken toward *Don Juan* by contemporary readers. Its force here as a self-critical move is only emphasized by the explicit parallels which *Don Juan* draws at various points between itself and *Don Quixote*. Furthermore, since Byron has been deliberately pursuing this quixotic line at least since the first two cantos of *Childe Harold*,[11] the repetition of it here underscores the "truth" of the idea which Jeffrey had formulated for so many: that all of Byron's writings, and not just *Don Juan*, tend to undermine "the reality of virtue."

Byron's work is so replete with turnabouts of this kind that we tend to read its basic structure as dialectical, and hence to approach its truth-functions in an epistemological frame of reference. This is to see the work as fundamentally critical – the great pronunciamento of what Carlyle would call the "Everlasting Nay." But the critical spirit that drives Byron's work is inadequately represented as a dialectical form. True, the work itself frequently encourages such a representation:

And if I laugh at any mortal thing,
  'Tis that I may not weep; and if I weep,
'Tis that our nature cannot always bring
  Itself to apathy, for we must steep
Our hearts first in the depths of Lethe's spring
  Ere what we least wish to behold will sleep:
(IV, st. 4)

This passage begins with a dialectical gesture as the first two lines put us on the brink of a neatly turned antithesis. With the third line, however, we veer off unexpectedly – not in the direction of the laughter initially imagined but toward "apathy" and forgetfulness. These, it turns out, are neither wanted not attainable here, though they are raised up as imaginable goals. In the end the passage does not tell us what would follow if the text were to "weep" instead of laugh. Forgetfulness, indifference, and laughter would, by the logic of this argument, all be equally possible.

This famous passage displays in miniature an important point: that in Byron's writing, contradiction is not dialectic, it is asymmetry. Metaphoric transfers yield to the transactions of metonymy which themselves branch out along rhizomatic lines. The order of things in the work therefore turns out to be wholly incommensurate:

> Ah!—What should follow slips from my reflection:
> Whatever follows ne'ertheless may be
> As apropos of hope or retrospection,
> As though the lurking thought had followed free:
> (XV, st. 1)

Writing "what's uppermost, without delay" (XIV, st. 7) may equally mean description, narration, direct address; it may mean to write spontaneously or reflectively; it may mean gathering similes in a heap, developing an argument, opening a digression. It might mean copying out something (a quotation, a pharmaceutical prescription) or it might mean not writing anything at all, but simply editing.

The "ever varying rhyme" (VII, st. 2) of *Don Juan* seems to me a direct function of its choice of a rhetorical rather than a lyrical procedure. The decision has pitched the work outside the bounds of its subjectivity and forced it to take up many matters which it may have imagined but which it could not comprehend. As a result, the writing will not – indeed, cannot – achieve anything but provisory and limited control over its own materials. It continually enters into contradictions, but the contradictions do not typically emerge out of a structure of their own internal logic. Rather, contradictions come to the work at odd angles – for instance, through structures of the unforeseen and the haphazard:

> For ever and anon comes Indigestion,
> (Not the most "dainty Ariel") and perplexes
> Our soarings with another sort of question:
> (XI, st. 3)

What undermines authority in *Don Juan* is the presence of many competing authorities, all of whom have been called to judgment. Some of these authorities are not human beings at all but circumstantial powers: Indigestion, for example, or puberty (or age), boredom, or different kinds of chance events (like the assassination of the military commandant of Ravenna, Luigi dal Pinto).[12] If all are summoned to judgment, all are equally capable of introducing unauthorized topics and problems – surprises for or threats to the text which have to be taken into account.

The poem may then consciously engage with these materials or not, and when it does (or when it does not) its engagements (and refusals of engagement) will themselves be highly idiosyncratic.

Don Juan develops its masquerade by pretending to be equal to itself and to all its heterodox elements. This pretense to understanding and truth is carried out, however, in the contradictory understanding that it *is* a pretense; and the ground of that contradictory understanding is the presence of others who are to observe and respond to the pretenses being made.

That differential of a real otherness is most clearly to be seen in the texts that resist incorporation by Romantic irony. Because Byron's masquerade is not all in fun, for example – because many persons have been invited who are each other's mortal enemies – *Don Juan*'s pretenses are not all embraceable in a comic generosity. Benevolence may be universal, but it is not everything. Savagery and tastelessness are therefore *Don Juan*'s surest signs of a collapse of its integrity, a rupture in its pretensions to the truth. Did Byron's text imagine or anticipate the public outcry that would be raised at the passage which sneered at Southey's and Coleridge's wives as "milliners of Bath" (III, st. 93)? Was it equal to that outrage and to the meaning which the outrage represented? We would have to say that it *was* only if we also said that, in this passage, meaning deploys itself as an unreconciled differential.

At the end of Canto XIV, when the narrator teases us about the possible outcome of Adeline's and Juan's relationship, he forecasts the actual event which will prove crucial to their lives in the plot of the poem.

> But great things spring from little:—Would you think,
> That in our youth as dangerous a passion
> As e'er brought man and woman to the brink
> Of ruin, rose from such a slight occasion,
> As few would ever dream could form the link
> Of such a sentimental situation?
> You'll never guess, I'll bet you millions, milliards—
> It all sprung from a harmless game of billiards.
>
> (st. 100)

A superb masquerade of truth, the passage is not at all what it may appear: for concealed in its reference to a "harmless game of billiards" involving Juan and Lady Adeline is a private recollection of just such a game once played in 1813 by Lady Francis Wedderburn Webster and Byron.[13] But of course it was not a game of billiards at all, it was a game of hearts. In his wonderful description of the scene at the time to Lady Melbourne, Byron observed that

> we went on with our game (of billiards) without *counting* the *hazards* – & supposed that – as mine certainly were not – the thoughts of the other party also were not exactly occupied by what was our ostensible pursuit. (*BLJ* III, 134)

Lady Frances and Lord Byron played out the truth of what was happening in a masquerade. They were making love, not playing billiards, but the larger truth – as Byron's letters at the time show – was that the lovemaking was itself masked in a series of sentimental moves and gestures.

Don Juan pretends it is forecasting the lives of its fictional characters, but while its mind is on that game of billiards, it is on something else as well, a different game of billiards which was, like the other game, not simply (or "harmlessly") a game of billiards at all. The text here, in other words, executes a complex set of pretenses as a figure for the kind of truth which poetry involves.

That truth is best seen, perhaps, in the interpretive stanza which follows the one I just quoted.

> 'Tis strange—but true; for Truth is always strange,
> Stranger than Fiction; if it could be told,
> How much would novels gain by the exchange!
> How differently the world would men behold!
> How oft would vice and virtue places change!
> The new world would be nothing to the old,
> If some Columbus of the moral seas
> Would show mankind their souls' Antipodes.
>
> (XIV, st. 101)

Once the mask of truth is exposed in the first stanza, we understand how the thematized discussion in this stanza is equally a mask of truth. This happens because the text has revealed itself as a dialogical event in which various parties may be imagined to be participating. We may imagine, for instance, Lady Frances reading this interpretation, or Lady Melbourne, or any number of Byron's "knowing" friends – or, for that matter, other readers, people who are unaware of the subtext. Each would have a different way of interpreting the interpretation. Furthermore, in each of those cases the authoritative interlocutor, let us call him "Byron," would undergo an identity shift, for the masque of truth would have to play itself out differently in each of the exchanges.

When truth comes in masquerade, propositions and states of affairs are called into question, are called to an accounting; and this includes the propositions and states of affairs which the poetical work itself appears to aver or define. Thus we might say of the poems, after Sidney, that if affirms and denies nothing – that it is, in our contemporary terms, a "virtual" reality. That idea is often represented in *Don Juan*, as when the text insists that it denies, admits, rejects, and contemns "nothing." But "in fact" the work denies, admits, rejects, and contemns various things, though sometimes – as in the text I am alluding to – it "in fact" denies, admits, rejects, and contemns "nothing." *Don Juan* is not a virtual reality, it is a particular deed in language. It is – to adapt a phrase from Bruno Latour's work – poetry in action.

What is "true" in the poem therefore always depends on context and circumstances. The concept of truth itself is revealed as open to change. What does not change, I think is the structure in which knowledge and truth are pursued and (however provisionally or idiosyncratically) defined. This structure is rhetorical and dialogical – not an internal colloquy but a communicative exchange.

Finally, that structure is to be seen as a masquerade for two important reasons: that the parties to the exchange may be concretely defined, and that they may share each other's consciousness. The both/and form of the masquerade establishes the possibility of identity precisely by putting identity in question. In the same way, the pretense involved in the masquerade, being kept in the foreground, sets in motion an exchange of awarenesses from both sides of the encounter.

This is perhaps to put it all far too abstractly, so I close by asking you to imagine the billiard passage being read by different parties, and to measure the differentials of truth which would emerge through those readings. After you imagine it being read (say in 1823, the year the text was published) by Lady Frances, then imagine Lady Frances's husband, Byron's friend Wedderburn Webster, coming to the passage ten years after that billiard game at Aston Hall which, at the time, Webster knew nothing about. If you make the latter imagining you might recall as well – would Webster have recalled it? – that on the very evening of the perilous billiard game Webster, in company with his wife and his other guests, loudly proposed a bet to Byron "'that *he* [Webster] for a certain sum wins any given *women* – against any given *homme* including *all friends* present[']" (*BLJ* III, 136); and recall as well (would Webster have had the moral strength to make such a recollection?) that Byron "declined" the challenge with, as Byron put it, "becoming deference to him & the rest of the company." What *truth* Webster's reading would have involved – *however* he read the passage!

The point is that Webster's reading, though we do not have it or even know if it were made, is part of this text's imaginings – and *that* is an important truth about *Don Juan*, and about Byron's writing in general.

DISCUSSION

JEROME MCGANN: . . . I feel a little odd, because there's no reason for most of you to be as invested in Byron's work as I am, and I'm not sure how familiar you are with the sort of thing he does, especially since Byron, although tremendously famous to the nineteenth century and even to the beginning of the twentieth century, in the English–American world of cultural studies, [has] come to seem an odd, if not distinctly marginal writer – as opposed to, for example, the centrality, especially in the Romantic frame of reference, of, say, Keats or Wordsworth.

DEBORAH THOMAS: Why do you think that is?

MCGANN: Well, because of the dominance – the acceptance of the rules of the poetry of sincerity. Byron's poetry never is sincere in that sense. Even his most sincere poetry is always masked in some way, it always has a hidden secret. It's always looking at itself and *aware* that it is doing something according to a convention. Sometimes, he is the prisoner of the convention, even when he is aware that he is the prisoner of the convention; at other times he is not – he plays with the convention.

JAMES SHERRY: Where does this poetry of sincerity come from?

MCGANN: If you read Keats's "On First Looking Into Chapman's Homer," or probably any Wordsworth poem, you know you are reading a poetry which takes itself seriously. John Stuart Mill said that this kind of poem had the structure of "overheard" musings. That was a very powerful structure, because it gave a kind of sacredness to the musings of the poet. The poetic space was not to be invaded by persons from Porlock. You were to stand back and sort of watch the poet in a vatic posture. The sign of the poem's sincerity was the fact that it was in communion with these higher things: you weren't paying attention to the world, you weren't talking, it wasn't a rhetoric.

Wordsworth just denounced Byron's work as factitious, as doggerel, as poetry that – well, remember Keats's famous comment on Byron: "Lord Byron cuts a figure but he is not figurative." It's a shrewd comment. What he means is that Byron is like the Elvis Presley of his day, or James Dean or something like that [laughter]. He's very conscious of the transactions that are going on between himself and his audience. Keats sees that, doesn't like it, and satirizes it. Byron has his own way of denouncing Keats, equally witty, perhaps, and to the point. He calls it the onanism of poetry, he says [Keats] is frigging his imagination, which is true.

SHERRY: Is Byron consciously going after the other Romantic poets? Is he trying to undercut them? And if so, where does he go wrong, how does he lose out in this duel?

MCGANN: Yes he is. It seems to me it's a sociological problem. Byron very definitely is aware of his class situation [in the] special sense that he knows his class is doomed. It's like he's alive and already dead. So it's a kind of dialogue where he can look at a scene from outside. He has that special privilege of a person who no longer has any stake in what's happening. He knows it's a middle-class world. The middle class and its power structures, its ideologies, are winning. That means that he will lose. He's resentful of that, [but] it gives him a peculiar kind of privilege.

At the beginning of his life, Byron imagined that he would in fact be an aristocrat to join this middle-class revolution. He saw himself as a liberal reformer. He went into Parliament on those terms, and he quickly became completely disillusioned with this procedure. It took him about two weeks to realize that he was not cut out for this role [laughter]. So, he became cynical, nihilistic, with all the stylistic and poetic privileges that come with that.

Now, Keats, Wordsworth, and especially Coleridge, who is the main ideologue and cultural guru of Romantic theory, promulgate a series of aesthetic positions that Byron eventually will come to just vomit on [laughter]. But they are the positions that will dominate the theory of poetry for 150, 175 years, more, even to our own day. It seems that only in the theater of post-Modernism are these ideas actually beginning to crumble. Up until the Vietnam War, it seems to me they held perfect and total sway. They do not hold sway anymore.

SHERRY: I get the impression that Byron was a victim of who he was.

MCGANN: It's hard to see him as a victim, though. I mean, he was so successful. He's a byword, as everyone in this room must know, of the person who is beautiful, rich, successful. He couldn't be more famous or successful in all of his outward circumstances, and yet through all that he is unhappy. That's the meaning of Byronism: to be completely successful and beautiful and happy and so forth, and to have everything you want, and to be desperately unhappy [laughter].

NICK LAWRENCE: Was his fame due to the middle class?

MCGANN: Yes. But it's a very complicated situation, because it's the Regency. When you think of Romanticism – if you have any reason to think about Romanticism [laughter] – [you're not likely to] think about the Regency, [about] Holland House and certain fast, upper-class worlds. The Regency period was fast and immoral – as the movie says, "Live fast, die young, and have a good-looking corpse." That might have been its motto. [The Regency] was not at all the middle-class world [with the] bourgeois set of parameters [that usually come to mind with] Romanticism. [But] Romanticism and the Regency were one, historically. And to that extent

Byron is more truly of his age, whatever you want to call it, than probably any other writer at that time (except perhaps George Crabbe, whom nobody ever reads anymore) because he ran in both these worlds: the aristocratic and the middle-class . . .

[With the ascent of the middle class], the aristocracy either gets out, the way Byron sort of dropped out, or agrees to become middle-class. But it is allowed to keep its trappings. You can stay rich, you can keep your houses, you can keep all the emblems, but you have to perform emblematic ideological functions within a middle-class society. To me that is a definition of Victorianism. But Byron was nihilistic; he said no. It was a suicide.

LAWRENCE: I'm interested because he often championed early eighteenth-century satire when none of the other Romantics did. If the Romantic ideology has dominated academia's reception of poetry, it has also managed to exclude a serious satirical tradition.

MCGANN: Among the Romantic writers, Blake, Shelley, and Byron write satire. The others do not. Wordsworth specifically said he hated satire. Later on, Tennyson, famously, denounced satire as an immoral mode.

Part of what I was trying to talk about here was that style or that way with language: because satire has to be a public discourse, there have to be transactions across. In the poetry of sincerity, that's precisely what you forbid. You have an overheard situation. The poet looks in his heart, or her heart, and writes. And then you as a reader sort of look over the shoulder and participate: but you don't have an exchange going on between the writer and the reader, [which] is the nature of a satiric discourse.

LAWRENCE: Do you think it is class-related, as a genre? Because the early eighteenth-century satirists were often middle-class, too.

MCGANN: I don't know whether I'd say it is class-related, but it is related to a desire to manage social dysfunctions. It's like system-management: you don't want satire as part of the system because Romantic satire says that the system is dysfunctional. It's not unlike the sort of thing we see in the Bush campaign now, or [with] Reagan, where it is imperative that you speak positively; if you want to speak negatively [it must] be within the limits of negativity.

One of the reasons why Byron is a kind of impossible writer through this whole period is that he really is a nihilist. Baudelaire knew it, and Nietzsche knew it. He was not assimilable. There are things that he will do that are simply not to be done. You write a poem about a siege and then the people who take the town come in and they start looking around and they are *not* raping [laughter]. The text is very careful to say: Now of course in all these kinds of situations there is always a lot of raping going on, but in *this* one no raping occurs. And then the "Widows of forty," who are in their houses, open their shutters and say, "When is the raping going to happen!" People read this in *Don Juan* and they were horrified. It's a kind of joke that you're not supposed to tell.

Because of this, because of this aspect of Byron's writing, it's difficult for the culture, seen in an Arnoldean sense, to take him to its bosom. You don't teach your children this kind of thing.

There is lot of tastelessness in *Don Juan*, or what has been called tastelessness. I think that those passages are important to pay attention to. They are at the limit [which] the culture will not accept. Mostly, a culture wants to absorb its archive. It wants to take it and say: We love it, it's wonderful, here is another example of why our civilization is great. "The best that has been known and thought in the world." But Byron writes: "Wherefore the ravishing did not begin!" Arnold could not have said that [laughter]. But Benjamin would say that.

That kind of writing is not allowable in a framework that is defined by works like the *Biographia Literaria* or "The Preface" to *Lyrical Ballads* or any or Arnold's – the usual run of texts that stand behind curricular delivery systems of English–American poetry.

BRUCE ANDREWS: Speaking of cultural delivery systems, I wondered if you could talk about the consequences of the modernists' appropriation of Romantic ideology and specifically what happens as they repress this self-acknowledgment of conventionality, this self-acknowledgment of dialogue that you are talking about in Byron.

MCGANN: Here I think there is a difference between early modernism and late modernism. I really think that there was a distinct break with the conventions of the nineteenth century, say in 1912 with *Tender Buttons* and all the early efforts of modernism. It seems to me that what you're describing doesn't happen until later. A good example of it would be – which I think is a great poem – "The Four Quartets." It's quite a late poem, but it illustrates what you're saying. As I read, say, *The Waste Land* – leaving aside the problem of its plot, which is kind of despicable – its local procedures, section-by-section, its Poundian procedures, seem to me tremendous.

ANDREWS: I was talking about the canon as you end up confronting it in the academy, in which a work like *Tender Buttons* obviously doesn't exist. I know very little about the reception of Byron among those figures in the early period of the century. That's what I was curious about, because if that acknowledgment of this communicational transaction, this economy of dialogue, was present, it seemed that it would have given all its practitioners a great resource to break through this self-enclosure that you get with the other Romantics.

MCGANN: Byron was a tremendous lost resource.

It is in fact true that Pound began *The Cantos* with Byron and Browning in mind. Now Browning didn't have anything to do with Byron. They're very different, but stylistically they have a lot in common, at least from Pound's point of view. The ur-*Cantos* are consciously aware of Byron's model. He then becomes more interested in Browning and the whole sort of Byron thing drops away. Remember the ur-*Cantos*, how consciously satiric they are. That drops away.

Pound was really interested in the problem of voice: how to get many voices operating within a poetical text. And he saw *Dan Juan* as an obvious [model]. The problem is that when Byron manages voices, he is a [fantastic, seductive] mimic. And so, if you read the text through a Browning filter, you won't see the rhetoric that I've been trying to describe to you here.

STEPHEN LOWEY: In his era, do you think he was misread?

MCGANN: The thing that most strikes me about the reception history of Byron is that the best readers I think were the readers who were reading him at the time. The reviewers, friends, enemies: they know what's happening. Many of them hate it, but then they should. Byron calls out that hatred, deliberately.

DON BYRD: There are different kinds of time involved here. You probably wouldn't say that Wordsworth or Coleridge were best read by their contemporaries.

MCGANN: No. Wordsworth said he had to create the audience for his poetry.

BYRD: To a certain extent they're writing in "eternity." I wonder if underlying the Romantic ideology isn't, in some sense, a kind of academic ideology, and I don't mean that in any narrow sense, but the remembering function – the way a culture remembers itself. The one thing that an academy can't do is confront the circularity of the issue of its sincerity about sincerity or its insincerity. This is the one place that that self-referential moment that Byron makes so much use of comes alive for an academic tradition: how sincere are we going to be about sincerity, and can we actually transmit the idea of insincerity in some way without involving ourselves in a logically impossible situation? So it seems to me that the kind of writing-in-time that Byron represents, that some of the fine poets in this room represent, perhaps isn't by its very nature the kind of poetry that is not going to be remembered, in that high sense.

MCGANN: You raise an impossible question [laughter]. My way of trying to come to grips with that ultimate paradox is: I think of Arnold when he says that great writing, or whatever writing, is the best that has been known and thought in the world. And then, sixty year later, Benjamin says: "Every document of civilization is at the same time a document of barbarism." And it seems to me that if you are going to carry out academic writing, you have to carry it out under those two epigraphs. I don't know how you can do it. You somehow have to manage it, though. But you cannot give up either one. If you give up the Arnold, from a critical perspective what you do is you hand the archive over to people who really oughtn't to have it. So you cannot. There is some sense in which the best that has been known and thought in the world are these terrible things that Byron does, and yet if you assimilate them and pull them in and they lose their edge, then . . .

BYRD: . . . then they're not that anymore. And so exactly the self-referential paradox that Byron exploits so beautifully in a way makes it impossible for that to be done with a historical canon.

MCGANN: I suppose in the end what happens is that contemporary writing rewrites the past.

One personal object I have in view at this point – I don't think I'll ever write again about Romanticism, maybe here and there but not in any major way – [is] to be able to find a way – it's a pedagogical problem – to help people in a classroom situation to read the archive within the frames of reference of contemporary writing.

CHARLES BERNSTEIN: It seems to me that a lot of what you are saying about the complexity of the issue of sincerity also applies to left and oppositional poetry: that much of this writing has not taken to heart, or to non-heart, the limits of the Romantic ideology of sincerity. Even in rejecting the vatic role of the poet, some of this writing nonetheless relies on unambiguously positive images and values of, say, a community, or various programmatic goals or aims. The Byronic mode that you propose here is as antithetical to that as it is to the Arnoldian values you discuss.

MCGANN: No question. The writers that you are talking about are not interested in [the sort of consideration I'm suggesting here]. And they're right not to [be], I think, given what they believe about how writing ought to be carried out. [But] I believe they have miscalculated the social-historical situation. They have adopted an avant-garde position in a kind of traditional sense: that you can adopt an unproblematic negative position, and that by it you can actually have some political leverage. I think that's wrong.

NOTES

1 For two good generic discussions of sincerity in Romanticism see David Perkins, *Wordsworth and the Poetry of Sincerity* (Cambridge, MA, 1964); Lionel Trilling, *Sincerity and Authenticity* (Cambridge, MA, 1972).

2 Romantic drama – for example, the drama of Coleridge, Shelley, or Byron – presents a special case of Romantic absorption. No literary mode is more socialized than the drama: this is an historical and an institutional fact which declares itself in the relation which persists between theater and drama. The development of "closet drama" – which is what happened in Romanticism – clearly breaks down that relationship, or at least throws it into a crisis. The separation of the drama from the theater is an index of Romanticism itself.

3 The charge was first raised in the controversy over Byron's "Poems on his Domestic Circumstances," and particularly in relation to "Fare Thee Well!" John Gibson Lockhart's comment on *Don Juan* – "Stick to *Don Juan*: it is the only sincere thing you have ever written" (quoted in *Byron: The Critical Heritage*, ed. Andrew Rutherford [New York, 1970], 183; hereafter cited as "Rutherford") – nicely captures the problem of Byron's sincerity, for that view exactly flew in the face of the dominant line of contemporary criticism. The latter would have been able to say much the same thing that Lockhart said, only for *Don Juan* it would have substituted *Childe Harold*.

4 *Lord Byron. The Complete Poetical Works*, ed. Jerome J. McGann, 7 vols. (Oxford, 1980–1992) v, 614. All quotations from the poetry will be from this edition.

5 Soren Kierkegaard, *Concluding Unscientific Postscript*, trans. Walter Lowrie (Princeton, 1941), 171.

6 This is not to suggest that (say) *The Prelude* or "The Fall of Hyperion" are not themselves just as involved in communicative exchanges as Byron's work; on the contrary, in fact. Byron's work simply foregrounds these exchanges in a clearer way.

7 The annotations discussed here and below are to be found in the editorial notes for the relevant passages from *Don Juan*, in *Lord Byron. The Complete Poetical Works*.

8 Byron extended an absurd textual situation by writing a (prose) response to Roberts which he signed "Wortley Clutterbuck" and published in the *Liberal*. For further details see William H. Marshall, *Byron, Shelley, Hunt and the Liberal* (Philadelphia, 1960), 86–88, 113–114.

9 *Byron's Letters and Journals*, ed. Leslie A. Marchand (London, 1973–1982) v, 93. Hereafter cited as *BLJ*.

10 The text here is from *Lord Byron. Letters and Journals*, ed. Rowland E. Prothero (London, 1898–1901), iv, 475.

11 See especially Byron's Preface to Cantos i–ii where he ridicules the Romanticism of the chivalric order.

12 See Canto v, sts. 33–39.

13 For details see Leslie A. Marchand, *Byron. A Biography* (New York, 1957), i, 413–418.

CHAPTER 7

Hero with a thousand faces: the rhetoric of Byronism

I

> I did not, when a slave, understand the deep meaning of those rude and apparently incoherent songs. I was myself within the circle; so that I neither saw nor heard as those without might see and hear.
>
> (*Narrative of the Life of Frederick Douglass, an American Slave*)

> And feeling, in a poet, is the source
> Of others' feeling; but they are such liars,
> And take all colours—like the hands of dyers.
>
> (*Don Juan*, III, st. 87)

> I saw, that is, I dream'd myself
> Here—here—even where we are, guests as we were,
> Myself a host that deem'd himself but guest,
> Willing to equal all in social freedom.
>
> (*Sardanapalus*, IV, i, 78–81)

We think of Byron as the most personal of poets, recklessly candid, self-revealing to a fault. Like most long-standing literary judgments, this one still strikes home. Nevertheless, its truth involves a paradox best defined by a later English writer who is in many ways Byron's avatar. "Man is least himself," wrote Oscar Wilde, "when he talks in his own person. Give him a mask and he will tell you the truth."[1] Perhaps no English writer, not even Wilde himself, executed this theory of the mask so completely as Byron. "Before Oscar Wilde was, I am."

Many of Byron's masks are famous, Childe Harold being, I suppose, the most famous of them all – and the prototype of those subsequent masked men we call Byronic Heroes. But Byron was operating *en masque* from his first appearances in print. His three early books of poetry, now known collectively as his *Hours of Idleness*, construct a fictional self for establishing contact with his audience. When the role is attacked and ridiculed in public by Henry Brougham, Byron rewrites his character in *English Bards and Scotch Reviewers*. Childe Harold, evolving from these earlier fictional selves, mutates quickly and repeatedly: the Giaour, the Corsair, Lara, Manfred are all masks of Byron in the Childe Harold line. But then so is the figure of Napoleon in Byron's famous *Ode* of 1814. Indeed, Napoleon is the first of Byron's historical self-projections, a collateral line which includes, among many others, Voltaire, Rousseau, Dante, Tasso, Pulci, and a series of remarkable worldly characters who lived during the Italian Renaissance.

The autobiographical aspects of *Sardanapalus* are equally plain and need no rehearsing. But the work is not to be read simply as if Byron = Sardanapalus, Zarina = Annabella, and Myrrha = Teresa. These historical associations are invoked by indirection and only as special forms of desire. "Sardanapalus" is recognizably "Byron" because we register certain symmetries between constructs in the play and correspondences in the world. Insofar as the play is an autobiographical work, it is carried out in masquerade.

The symmetry between the triangle Byron / Annabella / Teresa and Sardanapalus / Zarina / Myrrha, for example, acquires force because of other, related symmetries. Crucial here are certain intertextual markers. Myrrha is less a portrait of the historical Contessa Guiccioli than she is the latest incarnation of the Byronic female known by various names, including Leila, Zuleika, Gulnare, and Kaled.[2] (At the most abstract political level she represents the desire for freedom of those who feel themselves in bondage.) She is, in short, the incarnation of Byronic dreams about Romantic love and Romantic revolution – highly equivocal dreams, needless to say. For her part, the character of Zarina resembles Byron's wife only as she corresponds to certain of his more Romantic, post-separation fantasies: Lady Byron not as the princess of parallelograms or his moral Clytemnestra, but as an angel in the house. Zarina, Byron's imaginary portrait of the forgiving wife, recalls the woman addressed in 1816 by "Fare Thee Well!" and "Lines on Hearing that Lady Byron was Ill."

Such characters – they are typically Byronic – face in two directions, "referentially" toward certain socio-historical frameworks, and "reflexively" toward the poetical environments within which they are aesthetically active. What is distinctive about Byron's imaginative works, including the dramas, is that they make the play of those double-faced relationships their principal field of attention. Thus, we do not read "The Lament of Tasso" as a study of the Italian poet, but as a poetical representation of Byron in a contemporary act of imagining himself as Tasso.

The subject of the poem is neither the Renaissance Italian poet nor the Romantic English poet, it is the masquerade of their relations as they get played out in the poem. The poetical subject is personal only in a dramatically indirect way.

This important distinction has to be kept clearly in mind for those texts that carry autobiographical references. Lord Byron-as-Sardanapalus is a masquerade which gives Byron the power to expose and explore certain interesting and important subjects. To stay for a moment with the evident domestic salient of that masquerade, the play represents Zarina acting out the role of the forgiving wife. This is a role in which Byron tried, quite unsuccessfully, to cast his wife from the earliest period of their separation in 1815. It is the role he offered, and she refused, most famously in "Fare Thee Well!" But in the more elaborate fictional world of *Sardanapalus*, Byron – for better and for worse – gets his wish.[3]

The key text here is Act IV of Byron's play, which contains one of Byron's most elaborately coded examples of secret (or half-secret) writing. At the level of the semi-private code, the text is addressed to the three women who, in 1821, most dominated his conscious thoughts: that is to say, Teresa Guiccioli, Augusta Leigh, and Lady Byron. A reading of Act IV imagined from each of their very different points of view seems to me a necessary reference point for any further acts of reading. In this essay, however, I shall concentrate only on the interpretive horizon which opens up when we think of the text in relation to that psychic field which in Byron's discourse is named "Lady Byron."

This small drama of the king and queen is one of the play's most fascinating interludes. In the historically correlative events recalled through the play, Lady Byron rebuffed all of Byron's repentant confessions of error and efforts at reconciliation. To her he was simply bad and untrustworthy, and his overtures were seen as part of a cunning policy to regain power over her. In Byron's play, however, things appear, and turn out, very differently. Lady Byron as Zarina does indeed, once again, rebuff "her lord" and his professions of repentance, but this time she appears not as cold and removed, but as sympathetic and benevolent.

The scene opens with an interchange between the king and queen that is astonishing in its autobiographical directness:

> *Sar.*: Your brother said,
> It was your will to see me, ere you went
> From Nineveh with— [*he hesitates*
> *Zar.*: Our children: it is true.

I wish'd to thank you that you have not divided
My heart from all that's left it now to love—
Those who are yours and mine, who look like you,
And look upon me as you look'd upon me
Once— (IV, i, 251–258)

Lady Byron's greatest fear, throughout the separation, was that Byron would seek to gain custody of their child. This he did not try to do. Through this text Byron has addressed his wife all but explicitly, recalling to mind how he dealt with her about their daughter Ada. In the drama, this interchange is important as an unmistakable cue to the intimate talk that is going on just below the public level of the play.

Later in the scene Zarina listens to her husband catalogue his sins and errors. The queen, however, brushes all such recriminations aside. She refuses to think in such terms. Love, however wronged, conquers all: that is her theme.

Sar.: Our annals draw perchance unto their close;
But at the least, whate'er the past, their end
Shall be like their beginning—memorable.
Zar.: Yet, be not rash—be careful of your life,
Live but for those who love.
Sar.: And who are they?
A slave, who loves from passion—I'll not say
Ambition—she has seen thrones shake, and loves;
A few friends who have revell'd till we are
As one, for they are nothing if I fall;
A brother I have injured—children whom
I have neglected, and a spouse—
Zar.: Who loves.
Sar.: And pardons?
Zar. I have never thought of this,
I cannot pardon till I have condemn'd.
(IV, i, 269–308)

The text clearly exhibits Byron's poetry of masquerade, where what he liked to call "realities"[4] are represented in the form of conscious pseudodisguise. Byron wants his audience (and in particular certain of his audiences) to see both the similarities and the differences between Zarina, Sardanapalus, and their immediate life-originals. Seeing them, however, exposes the text's witty and wicked ironies. Zarina's way of refusing to pardon her husband amounts to a critical commentary upon a similar resoluteness in Lady Byron toward her husband.

But of course Zarina here functions – as she does throughout the play – not as "Lady Byron" but as Lord Byron's emanation – an imaginary Lady Byron whom he conjures partly to reproach the real living woman (even as the fictional wife refuses to reproach Byron's masquerade-figure, the Assyrian king). The strength of the text emerges precisely from the explicitness of the masquerading talk, from the evidently self-serving character of Byron's textual manipulations. But Byron's ironies turn back upon himself – the ironies are perceived as self-serving – because the text as a masquerade is necessarily opened to points of view that must and will see what is being said here in ways that do not correspond to Byron's ways.

Such a scene multiplies interesting complications. Most immediate – at the simple level of the plot of the play – is the problem of how to separate the now-reconciled husband and wife. This is managed jointly by Sardanapalus and Salemenes, Zarina's brother and the king's principal supporter and advisor. Salemenes comes to drag the reluctant and fainting queen from her husband because, he says, she and her children must be saved from the impending disaster. The king ruefully agrees to this policy, which he also translates into more personal terms:

> Zarina, he hath spoken well, and we
> Must yield awhile to this necessity.
> Remaining here, you may lose all; departing,
> You save the better part of what is left . . .
> Go, then. If e'er we meet again, perhaps
> I may be worthier of you—and, if not,
> Remember that my faults, though not atoned for,
> Are *ended*. Yet, I dread thy nature will
> Grieve more above the blighted name and ashes
> Which once were mightiest in Assyria—
> (IV, i, 384–387, 390–395)

All this would translate into the merest claptrap were we not seeing the text as a masquerade involving two fictional characters who are never named in the play, Lord and Lady Byron. When we register those invisible presences, the texts turn deeply and even savagely comical. Here, for example, the projection of Lady Byron in perpetual grief for the "blighted name and ashes" of her estranged husband is grotesque, set against the "realities." But is that image any less grotesque than Sardanapalus' thought, repeated throughout this scene, that his wife is too good for him?

In handling his text as a masquerade, Byron is manipulating it for certain personal ends – in this case, as in the earlier "Fare Thee Well!" to forge indirectly a sympathetic image of himself. Byron is of course quite conscious of what he is doing. At a crucial point in this scene, as Salemenes is attempting to force the queen away, she resists:

> *Zar.*: I must remain—away! you shall not hold me.
> What, shall he die alone—*I* live alone?
> *Sal.*: He shall *not die alone*; but lonely you
> Have lived for years.
> *Zar.*: That's false! I knew *he* lived,
> And lived upon his image—let me go.
> (IV.i. 406–410)

Salemenes does not mince words with his sister: the king is an adulterer who has neglected his wife and who will die in the arms of his mistress. To Zarina, however, all that is mere "reality," for she is devoted to an imaginary form of Sardanapalus, to a sublimed "image."[5]

Read literally, the text will appear clumsy and sentimental – though we shall also come to see that we cannot altogether dispense with this literal reading, that it is a necessary feature of the poetical effect. As a masquerade, however, the text is something different, and far more complex. We probably respond first to the shocking aspect of the scene – to the exposure of an imagination of sexual and domestic relations which, in the Romantic period, is most strongly revealed in the texts of Blake, Mary Shelley, and Laetitia Elizabeth Landon. What is shocking here is not the simple fact of the illusionism of these Romantic ties, but the darker truth that the victims of these illusions are also their conscious constructors. Zarina is devoted to an "image" of Sardanapalus because she is Lord Byron's emanation in this text, the index of his illusory desires.

This aspect of the scene emerges only when we observe Byron the poet as the principal character in the text, the key figure generating the *agon* of his perceptions and misperceptions. Byron puts on a mask and is able to tell the truth about himself – a truth that comes across only because the text at the literal level is an imaginary execution of the denial of that truth. The text displays Byron, and perhaps his wife as well, as figures who have been playing a masquerade of their domestic and amatory connections. In *Sardanapalus* Byron translates Zarina's benevolent posture toward her husband into a mordant reflection upon Lady Byron's coldness and intransigence. But this critical reflection necessarily reverses direction when it is situated in the aesthetic space of the play, where the transformational laws of metaphor and metonymy rule.

Those laws, however, also reverse the cruelty of the text, and allow us to glimpse one of its unguessed and more sympathetic horizons. Thus, when we read the phrase "He shall *not die alone*" as a reference to Myrrha, and a dramatic prolepsis of the play's final immolation scene, the masquerading text (with its referential demands) also summons Lord Byron and contemporary Greece into the play. Byron will not die in Missolonghi until 1824, and *Sardanapalus* was written in 1821. Nevertheless, by making his historical self a character in his poem, Byron opens this passage to the futurities which are so essential to this play's desire. Those futurities are most fully represented in the king's final long soliloquy, at the end of the fifth act. However we read that last, highly equivocal text, this much is clear: that Byron's poem is able to realize an imagination of its own self-transcendence, a survival from the wreckage of its self-deceptions and stupidities:

> But there is that within me which shall tire
> Torture and Time, and breathe when I expire;
> Something unearthly, which they deem not of,
> Like the remembered tone of a mute lyre.
>
> (*Childe Harold iv*, st. 137)

By representing itself in these heroic terms, such a survival seems, in the *Childe Harold* context, at once splendid and ridiculous. Domestic disorders, Byron's middle-class sorrows, undermine his grand gestures. But a play like *Sardanapalus* makes it very clear that the transcendence here spoken can only be constructed on comic, even ridiculous, grounds. The grotesque features of *Childe Harold*'s sublimities are essential to the work, and ultimately function to satirize and deconstruct the reader's correspondently sublimed poetical expectations. Byron's Sardanapalus enters into his glory precisely because he is a fop, and because Byron's text is unembarrassed by that fact. The autobiographical equivalent of the king's absurdities are Byron's petty self-justifications and deceptions, which are equally a subject of the text. In *Sardanapalus*, as in *Manfred*, Byron sets his poetical house in a place of excrement, the foul rag-and-bone shop of his cruel and ridiculous heart. That heart thereby exposes its truth precisely by striking sympathetic poses, by putting on masks that cover a will to power. An exorcism of the will to power follows upon these cunning masquerades, and the possibility of a redemption that will not merely disguise further enchantments.

II

Let me try to generalize what Byron is doing in these kinds of texts before I turn to a few more examples of the method. Briefly, Byron puts on the mask of Sardanapalus in order to tell certain truths about the life he has known and lived. From a structural point of view, the scene with Zarina should be read not as if it were a drama, addressed to a large and general audience, but as if it were a masquerade, a closet drama performed by and for the actors involved. In the present instance I am imagining it as it is addressed to Lady Byron by Lord Byron. Other interpretive emphases are imaginable, and are anticipated in the text. For example, though the figure of Myrrha/Teresa does not appear in this scene, her presence is strongly felt, so that the text is also imaginable as a masquerade in which she too is involved. Whatever the frame of reference, Byron's masquerades are requests (or perhaps temptations) for someone to play a correspondent part in the imagined scene. *Beppo* and *Don Juan* are full of these wicked and seductive invitations. The Sardanapalus/Zarina relationship is a poetical figure, a fiction disguising the correlative relationship Lord Byron/Lady Byron.

As in the famous cases of *Manfred* and *Don Juan*, Byron makes personal allusions to his texts that he expects his audience(s) to register. Unlike Wordsworth's Lucy poems, where the personal elements are forced to operate at an unconscious level, Byron's work uses masquerade as a device for breaking down the censors of consciousness. Particular readers are called into the texts by Byron's constructive imagination. As a consequence, Byron – or rather, Byron's textual seductions and manipulations – becomes the principal subject of his own fictions.

The best gloss on texts of this kind, therefore, is a passage like the following, from *Manfred*:

> There is a power upon me which withholds
> And makes it my fatality to live;
> If it be life to wear within myself
> This barrenness of spirit, and to be
> My own soul's sepulchre, for I have ceased
> To justify my deeds unto myself—
> The last infirmity of evil. (I, 2, 23–29)

Byron, like Manfred, ceases to justify himself in his Romantic imaginations only when he makes those imaginations the self-conscious subject of his work. There is a power working upon Byron forcing him to display those aspects of the imagination that are seldom exposed to view: those self-justifying desires and needs that constitute, according to this penetrating text, a person's ultimate "barrenness of spirit." In Byron, as in all the Romantic poets, the "last infirmity of evil" is exactly the belief that one can know one's self, and hence be master of the (poetical) deeds that are the (illusory) self's justification.

In *Sardanapalus* the imagination of Zarina (i.e., both Byron's imagination of her, and her imagination of her lord) is so arranged as to move at the plot level outside the dynamics of justification and even forgiveness. The two terms are closely related for Byron, of course, as we know from the famous passage toward the end of Canto IV of *Childe Harold*, where Byron – now in acknowledged masquerade as Childe Harold – utters his thunderous forgiveness-curse upon his enemies and detractors.

> a far hour shall wreak
> The deep prophetic fullness of this verse,
> And pile on human heads the mountain of my curse!
>
> That curse shall be Forgiveness.—Have I not—
> Hear me, my mother Earth! behold it, Heaven!—
> Have I not had to wrestle with my lot?
> Have I not suffered things to be forgiven?
> (sts. 134–135)

The self-justification is one with the curse, and the equivocal words descend alike on the just and the unjust, on the speaker and on all those for whom, and to whom, he speaks.

Act I of Shelley's *Prometheus Unbound* involves a conscious interpretive replication of this text from Byron. As we would expect from Shelley, his is a text that presages ultimate freedom through knowledge and the deliverance of mind. In Byron's case, however, "The Tree of Knowledge is not that of Life" (*Manfred*, I, i, 12), and it never is. Rather, as the same text from *Manfred* declares, "Sorrow is knowledge" – which is not at all the same thing as to say "Knowledge is sorrow."

In the Byronic world, if one is truly committed to an intellectual existence, then one must forgo all those resolutions whose ultimate *figura* is happiness. The intellectual life, as Blake also saw, is a perpetual *agon*, and Byron's Satan, at the end of Act II of *Cain*, gives the most complete expression to Byron's conception of a "spiritual" and intellectual existence:

> *One good* gift has the fatal apple given—
> Your *reason*:—let it not be oversway'd
> 'Gainst all external sense and inward feeling:
> Think and endure, and form an inner world
> In your own bosom—where the outward fails;
> So shall you nearer be the spiritual
> Nature, and war triumphant with your own.
>
> (II, ii, 460–466)

Satan here is explicitly Byron's emblem of the spiritual life. His posture and his words are magnificent, but they achieve that condition only because they have consciously chosen the tree of knowledge over the tree of life, and hence have chosen sorrow over happiness.

The greatness of this text, however, depends upon our seeing that it is addressed to someone else – most immediately to Cain, but finally to anyone, ourselves included. The speech is a challenge and a temptation in which a great prize is offered to those who can choose it; but it is a prize for which one must pay a terrible price: in the end, "all that a man" or a woman hath. Satan's great knowledge, his supreme consciousness, may be had, presumably, by anyone. To acquire it, however, one must consciously choose to share his consciousness, one must consciously choose damnation and what damnation represents, the pain of ultimate loss, an existence of perpetual suffering. Anything less – anything more resolved or synthetic – is here, paradoxically, a departure from the life of knowledge.

This discussion of Byron's ideas about knowledge as suffering is relevant to *Sardanapalus* and to Byron's poetry of masquerade. Zarina's benevolent posture toward her husband recalls, for example, Julia's farewell letter to Juan when she tells him simply "I've nothing to reproach, or to request" (I, st. 193). In each case mildness descends upon the text like a new vision of judgment. "Elle vous suit partout" is the sign under which Juan's life of emergent unhappiness and disaster unfolds, paradoxically, under a comic and satirized horizon. In *Sardanapalus* Zarina's love is the spring that releases the king to his tragi-comical sorrows. To this point in the play Sardanapalus has been relatively untouched by either sorrow or knowledge, despite the fact that his entire world stands on the brink of extinction. The more he is judged (as good or bad or both) by those around him – by Salemenes, by the conspirators, even by Myrrha – the more he seems to gravitate to an amoral, Lucretian existence ("Eat, drink, and love; the rest's not worth a fillip" [I, ii, 252]). Zarina's refusal to judge him comes, therefore, as a redemptive sign, and opens for Sardanapalus space for a vision of judgment:

My gentle, wrong'd Zarina!
I am the very slave of circumstance
And impulse—borne away with every breath!
Misplaced upon the throne, misplaced in life.
I know not what I could have been, but feel
I am not what I should be—let it end . . .
I was not form'd
To prize a love like thine, a mind like thine,
Nor doat even on thy beauty—as I've doated
On lesser charms, for no cause save that such
Devotion was a duty, and I hated
All that looked like a chain for me or others.
(IV, i, 329–340)

Masquerading in public as Sardanapalus, Byron frees himself to deliver this set of judgments on himself.[6] Devoted to an image, Zarina now can listen to that illusionary icon deliver up some of its melancholy truths, like some new statue of Memnon.

Such a text pitches us back to Byron's "[Epistle to Augusta]" of 1816 – but most emphatically *not* to the two other pieces he addressed to his sister at that time. Those other two poems were published as part of his domestic warfare, as part of his campaign to make a public triumph over his wife and her supporters. In that campaign Augusta was to function as the gentle foil to his ferocious wife, so that the two published pieces "to" Augusta came as massive acts of public self-justification. Like "Fare Thee Well!" the two sets of "Stanzas" to Augusta are duplicitous and hypocritical works, and all the more wicked for the way they involved Byron's sister in their machinations.

The "[Epistle to Augusta]" is, by contrast, a private poem addressed directly to Augusta and written to remain in manuscript. Not a poem in masquerade, it is a personal meditation on the conditions that call out the poetry of masquerade.

With false Ambition what had I to do?
Little with love, and least of all with fame!
And yet they came unsought and with me grew,
And made me all which they can make—a Name.
(97–100)

Byron wants to keep the poem in manuscript, addressed only to Augusta, because he is struggling to imagine himself as something other than a text, an "image," a "name." It is a vain and self-contradictory desire, belied even as it is expressed, and when the "[Epistle to Augusta]" does finally appear – when it is posthumously published – it comes to its more general audience as a fiction or masquerade of Byron's desire for a pure self and a poetry of sincerity.

By attempting to situate his poem in private, in a space imagined as set apart from the murky and impure conflicts of right and wrong, of good and evil, Byron approaches his vision of judgment:

> The fault was mine—nor do I seek to screen
> My errors with defensive paradox—
> I have been cunning in mine overthrow
> The careful pilot of my proper woe.
>
> (21–24)

It is a splendid poem in which a person who has completely lost his way seeks to make nothing from that loss. Candor and self-knowledge come and go as untransformed and untransformative conditions. The dialectics of loss and gain implode in an imagination that no longer tries to draw illusory distinctions between them: "But now I fain would for a time survive / If but to see what next can well arrive" (31–32). This is the wisdom that, according to Manfred, is "born from the knowledge of its own desert" (*Manfred*, 3, 4, 36). It is the wisdom that casts a cold eye on life and death alike. Let life go on or, as Sardanapalus says, "let it end": when the illusionistic character of existence is Byronically constructed, either event is equally imaginable, because existence is being imagined beyond the dialectics of desire and indifference. The consummate expression of such an intelligence appears as *Don Juan*, which is Byron's Memoirs written in the form of masquerade, and under the following thematic sign: "In play, there are two pleasures for your choosing – / The one is winning, and the other losing" (*DJ*, XIV, st. 12).

III

After Yeats (and to a certain extent Pound), when we think of a theory of masking we imagine it as a device toward "the heart's discovery of itself."[7] In this view the mask is a vehicle for introspective revelation – for that Socratic self-understanding we commonly pair with science as one of the two types of knowledge human beings have imagined for themselves.

The type of masking that Wilde both theorized and executed, and that we see displayed throughout Byron's work, is quite different. Not that their masks could not be used for introspective exercises. Byron certainly meant to use the mask of Childe Harold in order to objectify himself to himself, in order to know himself more clearly; and the same is true of those many other masks he fashioned, particularly in the years 1812–1815. Nevertheless, even as Byron employed this type of masking he clearly found the method unsatisfactory:

> Could I embody and unbosom now
> That which is most within me,—could I wreak
> My thoughts upon expression, and thus throw
> Soul, heart, mind, passions, feelings, strong or weak,
> All that I would have sought, and all I seek,
> Bear, know, feel, and yet breathe—into *one* word,
> And that one word were Lightning, I would speak;
> But as it is, I live and die unheard,
> With a most voiceless thought, sheathing it as a sword.
>
> (*Childe Harold* III, st. 97)

Mask after mask is fashioned but to no redemptive avail. Worse, as *Manfred* and the "[Epistle to Augusta]" show, the masks rise up to reproach Byron as mere nominal and imaginary forms: names, images, illusions. They are his circus animals, the creatures of his cunning schemes of self-bafflement, because they are, after all, only his constructs, only his self-imaginings. They perform according to his poetical orders, whether he is aware of those orders or not. At best they give him only further *figurae* of what he is, further ranges of desire he, by himself, might imagine.

It seems clear to me that in 1816 Byron finally grasped the problem of the self-limits of imagination. The Separation Poems, *Childe Harold* Canto III, and especially *Manfred* are the texts through which Byron moved his poetry beyond the device of masks and into the dangerous scenarios of masquerade. Where masking is personal and introspective (or, as on the Greek stage, impersonal and mythic), masquerade is interpersonal and social. In the masquerade Byron's creative or constructive self moves into a space where he can no longer imagine or control the range of interactive relations that the masquerade makes possible. Byron writes and directs the intimate dramas of his work, but he finds himself, *as writer and director*, taking part in the action, and therefore falling subject to the action: as participant in the interpersonal exchange, and as the spectacular focus of a more generalized attention. The knowledge that emerges from this dynamic is neither subjective nor objective, it is social: an objective display of interpersonal relations lying open to an indefinite range of alterations from within and from without.

Of course, because Byron – unlike Wilde – operates out of a Romantic ideology, these masquerades in his work come to us in a subjective mode. Wilde is not a character in *The Importance of Being Earnest* or *The Picture of Dorian Gray* as Byron is a character in the *Ode to Napoleon Buonaparte* and *Manfred* and *The Lament of Tasso*. *Sardanapalus*, for its part, makes a gruesome and pitiless comedy of Byron's domestic and erotic relations. The play licenses Byron to imagine those relations in a series of connected masquerades that call out to certain specific persons, and invite them to assume certain roles. In making those invitations, however, Byron has brought imaginations into his texts that are not his in any sense, and that may wield their own authority, including authority over his own imaginations. At least three (but usually four) individuals are needed if one is to play at masquerade.

Besides one's conscious self, there is, in addition, the mask one assumes. The mask has a life of its own and cannot simply be manipulated by the poetical mind. In Canto III of *Don Juan*, for example, Byron stages a complex masquerade with his famous "The Isles of Greece" lyric. Lambro's court poet is represented as Robert Southey in a revealing costume. But this masked figure is also the emanation of the poet himself, who enters the text under its double disguise. As the satiric exposure of Southey unfolds in this text, therefore, it also turns back upon its maker, and the poem creates an extraordinary identification of Byron with his most hated "self," the Poet Laureate. The costume which Byron had fashioned for Southey becomes, for Byron, a kind of Nessus-shirt.[8]

A similar kind of double-disguise operates in the first two acts of *Sardanapalus*. In this case we have to register one of the play's witty topical allusions. It comes at the first entrance of the king who appears, according to the stage direction, "*Effeminately dressed, his Head crowned with Flowers, and his Robe negligently flowing, attended by a Train of Women and young Slaves*":

> Let the pavilion over the Euphrates
> Be garlanded, and lit, and furnish'd forth
> For an especial banquet; at the hour
> Of midnight we will sup there: see nought wanting,
> And bid the galley be prepared. There is
> A cooling breeze which crisps the broad clear river:
> We will embark anon. (I, ii, 1–7)

This pavilion is the play's principal emblem of the king's despotic oriental voluptuousness. It is not, however, exactly what it appears to be. Through it Byron is glancing satirically at George IV, who spent millions furbishing the Brighton Pavilion as his exotic pleasure dome. The "Paradise of Pleasure and *Ennui*" (*DJ*, XIV, st. 17) that, for Byron, summed up the world of the Regency is recalled to our attention in the sybaritic scenery of Byron's play.[9]

In Canto XIV of *Don Juan* Byron refers directly to the Brighton Pavilion, which he properly identifies with King George. "Shut up – no, *not* the King, but the Pavilion, / Or else 'twill cost us all another million" (st. 83). The satire of this text helps to explain the more equivocal function of the pavilion in *Sardanapalus*. If the Assyrian king is in one obvious respect a mask of Byron, he is, in another, a mask of George IV. As a mask of the English king, Sardanapalus becomes a double-disguise in exactly the same way that Lambro's court poet does in *Don Juan*. Playing masquerades of this kind forces Byron to become what he beholds, to reflect himself in the guise of the last, and most contemptible, of the English Georges.[10]

To write in this way is to be cunning in one's own overthrow. In these cases we are astonished at the boldness of Byron's self-exposures, at the self-conscious level of his critical moves. Byron puts on a mask, or a double-mask, and seems to invite it to exert its own power over him. By plunging his desires and consciousness into his poetical medium, he surrenders his imagination and authority to alien orders, both malign and benevolent. The masking texts are summoned to speak the truths the poet *in propria persona* might not otherwise be able to tell.[11]

Three times in his work Byron donned the mask of Napoleon – in the 1814 *Ode*, in Canto III of *Childe Harold* (1816), and finally in *Don Juan*, Canto XI.[12] Although in each case the tone shifts with the poetical genre, in all three the mask asserts its independent authority. Each time the text passes a judgment upon the figure of Napoleon, a translation occurs:

> An empire thou couldst crush, command, rebuild,
> But govern not thy pettiest passion, nor,
> However deeply in men's spirits skill'd,
> Look through thine own, nor curb the lust of war.
> (*Childe Harold* III, st. 38)

In poetic privacy to his sister, Byron will say the same things of himself. Here the mask of Napoleon becomes Byron's occasion of making the truth public.

> But quiet to quick bosoms is a hell,
> And *there* hath been thy bane; there is a fire

And motion of the soul which will not dwell
In its own narrow being, but aspire
Beyond the fitting medium of desire.
(st. 42)

Of this "fever at the core" the text will say that it is "Fatal to him who bears, to all who ever bore." Yet this fatality, though in one sense a "bane" and malignant condition, is in another a redemption, for it springs the self free from "its own narrow being" and from every "fitting medium of desire." The mask of Napoleon is what Blake would have called "the death" of Lord Byron.

The autonomy of the mask, so far as the poetry of masquerade is concerned, is matched by the integrity of the individual masquers. Byron cannot play these deceptive games alone, his texts necessarily draw others into the fictional spaces he invents. The poetry invites others to play a part in its action, and if the masks Byron assumes have set limits on those that can be assumed in turn by others, the outcome of these textual interactions stands beyond anyone's, including the author's, control.

Manfred is a good index of the dangerous freedom offered through these masquerades.[13] In its original context at least three specific women could have been seen, or could have seen themselves, in the role of Astarte: Lady Byron, Augusta, and Mary Chaworth-Musters. We know that the first two did assume the role: Augusta saw herself as Astarte and was filled with anxiety, whereas when Lady Byron first identified with that figment, she registered a kind of satisfaction.[14] In each case the text becomes a kind of precipice that draws one on – like Manfred, like Byron – either to the self or to the destruction of the self.

Canto XIV of *Don Juan* opens as an exercise in negotiating these precipitous kinds of text. The passage addresses the reader directly on the problem of meaning, but in doing so it casts the reader in the role of an interpreter, and specifically an interpreter of poetical texts – most immediately *this* text. The passage represents its mysteries as an abyss of the self, "our own abyss / Of thought" (st. 1), so that knowledge appears as the possibility of ultimate self-revelation.

  You look down o'er the precipice, and drear
The gulf of rock yawns,—you can't gaze a minute
Without an awful wish to plunge within it.

'Tis true, you don't—but, pale and struck with terror,
  Retire: but look into your past impression!

And you will find, though shuddering at the mirror
 Of your own thoughts, in all their self-confession,
That lurking bias, be it truth or error,
 To the *unknown*; a secret prepossession,
To plunge with all your fears—but where? You know not,
And that's the reason why you do—or do not.
(*DJ*, XIV, sts. 5–6)

A text of this kind does not have a meaning, cannot be solved. It is rather temptation and threat, promise and invitation. More, it declares that poetry is of such an order, and that its significance unfolds as a dynamic of how its players do or do not choose to act in its terms. Byron's readers may succumb to, play with, or resist his spectacular intimacies. The history of his work's reception is a complex and fascinating story of responses that have been as widespread as they are diverse. By the law (or lawlessness) of these texts, every reader becomes, like "Every Poet," "his *own* Aristotle" (*DJ*, I, st. 204).

Being released into such a freedom, however, will prove as problematic for the reader as for Byron. This is the point of the admonitory passage from Canto XIV of *Don Juan*. Byron's intimates and family connections are not the only ones who come to play a part in *Manfred*. The notorious secrecies of that drama are the sign under which the general reader gets enlisted in the masquerade as spectator and interpreter. This is the role, or mask, that Byron's work always prepares for us. Of course a poem's interpreter – like those "attendant Lord and Ladies" of the play, or the audience in the theater – can seem safely removed not so much from the work's complications, but from any dangers that might be imagined a part of those complications. But in Byron, as the passage from Canto XIV of *Don Juan* makes plain, one is required to assume those roles at a risk. Indeed, a major function of this work is to remind readers that they do not stand at a remove from the action. Like Brecht's audience, they are forced to play a role, and hence to confront themselves in the objectivity that their role constructs. Baudelaire, one of Byron's greatest readers, understood perfectly the dynamics of the process: "Hypocrite lecteur, mon semblable, mon frère."

We think of 1816 as a watershed moment in Byron's career, and we are right to think so. In 1816 he was forced by "circumstance, that unspiritual god" (*CHP*, IV, st. 125) to confront the hypocrisies of Romantic imagination – its hypo-crises and its hypo-criticisms alike; in general (and in terms of a contemporary idiom), its "hyped" condition. But we should not forget that the poetry of 1816–1824 is in certain important ways only an extension of the earlier work. The Byronic Hero, fashioned (in every sense) between 1812 and 1815, is a hero with a thousand faces – what William Burroughs in our own day called a "soft machine." Sardanapalus, Satan and Cain both, Mazeppa, Tasso, Fletcher Christian and Torquil, Juan and his narrator: like the Byronic Heroes of 1812–1815, these are all figures of the same order, poetical constructions designed to summon their rhetorical doubles, Baudelaire's hypocritical readers. Now we tend to privilege the later figures and works, but certain of the earlier texts – *The Giaour* and *Parisina* especially – yield nothing to the poetry of Byron's exile. Both of those tales – does this even need to be said? – are evident masquerades.

NOTES

1 See "The Critic as Artist," in *The Artist as Critic. Critical Writings of Oscar Wilde*, ed. Richard Ellmann (Chicago: University of Chicago Press, 1982), 389.
2 For a good related discussion of Byron's treatment of such figures see Cheryl Fallon Giuliano, "Gulnare/Kaled's 'Untold' Feminization of Byron's Oriental Tales," in *Studies in English Literature*, 33 (1993), 785–807.
3 The text of Byron's poems, including *Sardanapalus*, is taken from *Lord Byron. The Complete Poetical Works*, ed. Jerome J. McGann (Oxford: Oxford University Press, 1980–1992), in seven volumes. *Sardanapalus* is in vol. VI, jointly edited by McGann and Barry Weller. Prose references are to *Byron's Letters and Journals*, ed. Leslie A. Marchand (London: John Murray, 1973–1982), here cited as *BLJ*.
4 See Byron's comments upon *The Bride of Abydos*, where he spoke of it as running too close to realities in *Poetical Works*, III, 435.
5 For an extended discussion of these sublime imaginary dialectics between Byron and Lady Byron – and, in general, between Byron and various women who were attached to him in his life – see James Soderholm's important study *Fantasy, Forgery, and the Byron Legend* (University of Kentuckey Press, 1996).
6 For Sardanapalus/Byron to speak of himself as "the . . . *slave* of circumstance" (my emphasis) underscores the problematic nature of the masquerade here. Byron was an abolitionist at a time when the slave trade was an important issue in England (one recalls his famous aphorism that "There is no freedom, even for masters, in the midst of slaves" [*BLJ*, X, 41]); and of course Sardanapalus is a monarch in a slave-holding society. It is, in other words, the presence of Byron in the character of the king (and of the king in the character of Byron) that gives such an edge to the word "slave" in the poetical context.
7 See *Per Amica Silentia Lunae* in *Essays* (London: Macmillan, 1924), 485.

8 For a full discussion of this text see my "The Book of Byron and the Book of a World," in *Social Values and Poetic Acts* (Cambridge, MA: Harvard University Press, 1988).

9 Byron told John Murray that his play had no contemporary references to "politics or personalities" (*BLJ*, VIII, 152), but his disclaimer can hardly be taken seriously – indeed, his remarks were probably meant to be seen as slyly disingenuous. See the discussion of these matters in *Poetical Works*, VI, 610–611.

10 On the Marine Pavilion see Lewis Melville (pseud. for Lewis Saul Benjamin), *Brighton, Its History, Its Follies, and Its Fashions* (London: Chapman & Hall, 1909), esp. chap. III, "The Prince of Wales and the Marine Pavilion." The Pavilion was begun in 1787, and when its last additions were completed it had cost altogether over £70,000. The public was first admitted to view the Pavilion in 1820. It was this public viewing that triggered Byron's poetical response in *Sardanapalus*, just as it was the completion of the constructions in 1822 that was the immediate occasion of *Don Juan*, Canto XIV, st. 83.

11 In an excellent study ("'A Problem Few Dare Imitate': *Sardanapalus* and 'Effeminate Character'") Susan Wolfson likewise remarks on the conflicting forms of Byron's self-projections in the play: "Byron's Ravenna was already under foreign domination, and the politics were all concerned with revolt and subversion. Byron was participating with money, advice, and collaboration. In this respect he was acting as one of the rebel satraps, rather than as Sardanapalus" (874). See the essay in *ELH*, 58 (1991), 867–902.

12 There is a sense in which he also donned that mask in *The Age of Bronze*.

13 Lady Byron said of *Manfred* that it was meant "to perplex the reader, exciting without answering curiosity" (see Malcolm Elwin, *Lord Byron's Family* [London: John Murray, 1975], 175).

14 The Hon. Mrs. George Villiers, who was the confidante both of Byron's wife and of his sister as well, had no trouble reading the text of *Manfred* as a masquerade of the truth. For a good discussion of these matters see Ralph Milbanke, Earl of Lovelace's *Astarte* (London: Chiswick Press, 1905), chap. 3.

CHAPTER 8

Byron and the lyric of sensibility

In our recent revaluations of Romanticism we have certainly neglected Byron's lyric work – a signal neglect since his influence on nineteenth-century lyric was so great. But to take up this topic is also quickly to discover that the issues involved are large ones. When you open the subject of Byron's lyric poetry, you reopen the subject of Romantic forms in general.

It is a commonplace of literary history that Romanticism instituted a poetic renewal, in particular a renewal of the lyric. With the coming of modernism, when another upheaval of poetic imagination took place, Romantic forms came under severe critical scrutiny. The critique focused on the conventions of Romantic subjectivity and the idea – or the ideology – of "spontaneous overflow." Those two famous "fallacies" of writing – "the intentional fallacy" and "the affective fallacy" – are obverse and reverse of the same coin. The one is a warning to critics, the other a warning to poets: "Beware Romanticism."

I recall these matters in order to supply a background for M. H. Abrams's celebrated essay "Structure and Style in the Greater Romantic Lyric."[1] His argument doesn't need rehearsing. Briefly, Abrams drew on New Critical approaches to seventeenth-century poetry (in particular its various "poetries of meditation") to fashion his influential description of Romantic lyric form. The persuasiveness of Abrams's essay comes partly from his excellent analysis of a special kind of lyric – the express subject of the essay – and partly from an oblique set of moves to avoid the main line of modernist attack. The association of a "greater romantic lyric" with seventeenth-century writing, which is implicit in the essay's argument, is a shrewd maneuver. Abrams thereby connected Romantic poetry with a heritage of lyric writing that had come to define how criticism ought to think about poetry in the twentieth century. Abrams went on to show – rightly, to my mind – that the poetic locus called "romantic nature" could be used, was in fact used, as a transcendental ground for wayward or disturbed subjectivity. The drama of such uses Abrams called "the greater romantic lyric." From this vantage Romantic poetry would be seen not as emotional overflow but as a redemption from such overflows – not an expression of personality but rather what Eliot preferred, an "escape from personality."

Our problem with Abrams's account lies not in what it does but in what it leaves undone. "Byron and the Anonymous Lyric" was partly written to show "the structure of" another key form of Romantic lyricism.[2] The "structure" of the latter is very different from the one sketched by Abrams. Its lord is not rule but misrule; for emotion recollected in tranquillity it substitutes a derangement of the senses; in place of redemption, a Batail-lian expenditure. If a colloquy with Nature is essayed, Byron's Nature is more Lucretian than Rousseauist – as dangerous as it is dependable, and marked more by indifference than by love or benevolent ministries. If Romantic writing induces and displays emotional crisis, Byron gives a distinctive tone to the crisis. The great paradox of the Byronic lyric, first explicitly noted by Baudelaire, is that it tends to an impersonality – an "anonymity" – quite unlike those "first affections" pursued in Abrams's Wordsworthian and Coleridgean lyrics. What Baudelaire, Nietzsche, and Flaubert valued in Byron's writing was exactly its psychic coldness – that Byronic move to entertain or undergo extremes of emotional experience with a kind of indifference of consciousness.

In this respect the case of Byron exposes an even larger truth about the diversity of Romantic lyricism. The Romantic meditative forms pursued by Coleridge and Wordsworth, as well as the Satanic excesses (of thought and feeling alike) engaged by Byron, are both secondary historical developments so far as Romanticism is concerned. Each evolves from two earlier related lyric styles that supplied fundamental terms for Romantic lyric of whatever kind. This earlier poetry corresponds to what modernism would turn so sharply against: a writing that privileges and expresses feeling as such.

One strain of such writing appeared in the verse of the Della Cruscan poets, who dominated the poetry scene during the 1790s.[3] Drawing inspiration from recent traditions of sentimental writing, and in particular the tradition of Sterne, the Della Cruscans made the self-conscious pursuit of love the center of their work. This love ranged from a kind of universal benevolence at one end – many of the Della Cruscans were Jacobins or at least sympathizers with the goals of Jacobinism – to the intensities of personal, erotic engagement at the other. At its best and most distinctive, Della Cruscan poetry pursues a metaphysics of sentimentality. The work is therefore marked by extreme paradoxes, the most important being its cultivation of exquisite or powerful feelings alongside a heightened intellectual awareness.

The movement launched itself in 1785, when a group of English expatriates privately printed a collection of verse in Florence. *The Florence Miscellany* is a book of poetry dedicated explicitly to pleasure: as Mrs. Piozzi remarks in her Preface, these writings grew from having "glistened innocently in Italian Sunshine; and . . . imbibed from it's rays the warmth of mutual Benevolence" (6). Mrs. Piozzi's comment connects an ideology of sentimental feeling ("mutual Benevolence") with an imagination of unspoiled natural environment and pure (in both senses) physical pleasure. Some of the early Wordsworth, much of Coleridge, and even more of Burns, recollect or run parallel to this writing's dramatic portrayal of the marriage of self-conscious wit to animal spirits.

Della Cruscan love poetry is most notable for its startling mixtures of incongruous signifying markers: it pursues at once spontaneity and extreme artifice, it privileges natural settings in the most urbane and sophisticated tones, it exalts love in erotic terms that emphasize and even privilege the so-called lower senses (touch and taste especially). It maps the geography of "the feeling mind" (II, 26) and the "sensate heart" (II, 171).[4] In its notorious cultivation of poetic extravagance we trace a style committed to a Lockean *idealization* of experience.

In these endeavors the writing and exchange of poetry become essential. Della Cruscan verse typically develops as a dialogue of love (most famously between Della Crusca/Robert Merry and Anna Matilda/Hannah Cowley) where dialogue itself enacts the experience and stimulates the desire. In the world of Della Crusca, lovers meet only in the fields of their own immediate language, where

> The lustre of poetic ray
> Should wake an artificial day.
> (I, 11)

In this proto-Baudelairean paradise the cultivation of the literal and the immediate generates an experience of unreality and extravagance.

> Let but thy lyre impatient sieze,
> Departing Twilight's filmy breeze,
> That winds th' enchanted chords among,
> *In lingering labyrinth of song.* (I, 87)

As so often in this style of verse, the distinction between the literal and the natural, between poetry and reality, is attacked and undermined. What rules here are the conscious intensities of erotic desire:

Let the mean bosom crave its *love's return*,
Thine shall with more distinguish'd ardors burn:
To *know* the passion—yes, be that thy strain,
Invoke the god of the mysterious pain!
("Anna Matilda," "To Reuben," I, 54–55)

Erotic passion functions through extreme self-consciousness. To experience it properly requires one to "*know* the passion," to be on fire at once in the body and in the mind. The fires are to be deliberately set and carefully maintained at the most intense level (the ideal of intensity being represented here, and generally in Della Cruscan writing, through the sign of love's "pain"). The poetry instructs one to *choose* an abandonment to the sovereignty of Eros.

In the last passage that theme locates itself perhaps most remarkably in the word "distinguish'd," which carries its full freight of diverse meanings. Cowley demands "ardors" of several kinds and each is to be known and experienced separately, clearly, distinctly: not a lump of "sensations sweet" but one ardor as it were at a time, each gaining its qualitative fineness partly because the ardors can and should be physical and quantifiable.

These rules (of love and of art alike) require a poetry that chooses and consciously constructs its freedoms – a poetry that puts its own choices on display. Once again, Cowley:

And be thy lines irregular and free,
Poetic chains should fall before such Bards as thee . . .
Bid her in verse meand'ring sport;
Her footsteps quick, or long, or short,
Just as her various impulse wills— (I, 33)

As the sign of a conscious design, irregular verse here marks a decision to forgo what Cowley punningly calls all "Vapid Content." Cowley wants to enact rather than merely deliver a poetic message, and she writes in avoidance of poetic regularities, which are imagined as merely following a debased pleasure principle here named, contemptuously, "the bliss of TASTE." She is pursuing orders of pleasure and of poetry at once higher and lower, more natural and more artificial:

Hast thou known Love's enchanting pain—
Its hopes, its woes, *and yet complain*?
Thy senses, at a voice, been lost,
Thy madd'ning soul in tumults tost?
Ecstatic wishes fire thy brain—
These, hast thou known, *and yet complain*?
Thou then deserv'st ne'er more to FEEL . . .
Ne'er shalt thou know again to sigh,
Or, on a soft idea die;
Ne'er on a *recollection* gasp;
Thy arms, the air-drawn charmer, never grasp.
("To Della Crusca," I, 34)

This is a poetry of Romantic wit where a marriage is made between an intense eroticism and contemporary speculative philosophy. Its lack of apparent spontaneity – the *forwardness* of its rhetoric – is not a fault but a measure of its self-consciousness. Such writing drew the fire of conservative critics like William Gifford for arguing (note: *arguing*!) that pleasure, love, and philosophy were related activities and were all to be deliberately, artistically pursued. (The Sadean parallels are real enough and should be critically explored.)

In the early 1790s Coleridge – who after all named one of his children Hartley – wrote in similar ways.[5] His late masterpiece "Constancy to an Ideal Object" at once recollects and repudiates those youthful commitments. His initial repudiation, sketched in "The Eolian Harp," came in part because, unlike Hannah Cowley, he was troubled conceptually by the idea and ideal of a phenomenal existence. Cowley's lines wittily "grasp" her ideal object as an art of living through the wordplay of an internal rhyme ("arms"/"charmer"). But Coleridge came to give a negative inflection to the erotic death that Cowley textually reconstructs for herself. As a result, he lived without dying on his "soft idea," and he tried to explain his failure philosophically as a kind of flaw in nature. But it wasn't. It was simply – and profoundly, and terribly – a flaw of character and a fear of art. (Let me say here that his greatest poetry succeeds exactly as it is an expression of his fear of poetry.)

The Della Cruscan influence would eventually pervade the Romantic movement, despite the efforts of "Anti-Jacobin" writers (like Gifford, Mathias, and Polwhele) to stem its tide. There were of course other important sentimental poets, some closely related to the Della Cruscan school (like Seward, Hayley, and Darwin), some less so, like Charlotte

Smith. Smith's *Elegiac Sonnets* – at least thirteen editions were printed between 1784 and 1811 – evolved an important and distinctive style of sensibility. As in Della Cruscan verse, Smith's work locates a scene of sentiment and intense feeling. But her poetry is not at all the self-validating activity it is for the Della Cruscans. Rather than a game for generating textual pleasures and sensations, Smith's art of poetry is courted and practiced as an emblem of cruelty and illusion.

The opening sonnet of her celebrated book of verse defines her project perfectly.

> The partial Muse, has from my earliest hours
>   Smil'd on the rugged path I'm doomed to tread,
> And still with sportive hand has snatch'd wild flowers,
>   To weave fantastic garlands for my head:
> But far, far happier is the lot of those
>   Who never learn'd her dear delusive art;
> Which, while it decks the head with many a rose,
>   Reserves the thorn, to fester in the heart.
> For still she bids soft Pity's melting eye
>   Stream o'er the ills she knows not to remove,
> Points every pang, and deepens every sigh
>   Of mourning friendship, or unhappy love.
> Ah! then, how dear the Muse's favors cost,
> *If those paint sorrow best—who feel it most*![6]

The force and cunning of that key phrase "dear delusive art" – its own "dear delusive art" – only appear when the sonnet reaches its couplet climax, where the double-edged meaning of "dear" is plainly exposed. This text pursues a dark reading of its famous Horatian pretext. Instead of the laurel wreath, Smith expects from poetry either a crown of thorns for her heart or a madwoman's garland for her head. These equivocal gifts come from a Muse whose apparent attractions conceal their true import. The smiles and the "sportive hand" associate ironically with the "fantastic garlands," and the Pity starts only a widespread *lacrymae rerum*.

Smith's opening sonnet is as much an elegy for art as for anything that her art might think to lament. Its conclusive gesture of self-pity is badly misread if it is read as either artistic incompetence or emotional indulgence. The true "cost" of undertaking poetry is the discovery of poetry's delusions, which are then (i.e., here in this text) played out as dark comedy. Smith's poetic vocation entails a special knowledge of sorrow: that poetry's knowledge shall produce no powerful acquirements, but simply bleak insight. Most bleak of all is the awareness that even this knowledge will only be gained in the event, as the actual experience of writing and fulfilling poetry's incompetent promise. Smith's self-pity is thus the poem's key textual event, the poem's objective correlative for its indictment of the pretensions of art. (Ironically enough, therefore, the modernist critique of Romanticism's "sentimentality" entails not merely a misreading of verse like Smith's, but a sentimental investment of its own in poetry's high cultural mission.)

In Smith's hands, poetry becomes a machine of truth functioning through the pitiless dialectic of "Fancy" and "Reason," dream and consciousness:

> When welcome slumber sets my spirit free,
> Forth to fictitious happiness it flies,
> And where Elysian bowers of bliss arise
> I seem, my Emmeline—to meet with thee!
> Ah! Fancy then, dissolving human ties,
> Gives me the wishes of my soul to see;
> Tears of fond pity fill thy softened eyes;
> In heavenly harmony—our hearts agree.
> Alas! these joys are mine in dreams alone,
> When cruel Reason abdicates her throne!
> Her harsh return condemns me to complain
> Thro' life unpitied, unrelieved, unknown.
> And as the dear delusions leave my brain,
> She bids the truth recur—with aggravated pain.
> (*Elegiac Sonnets* [1789], Sonnet XXXVIII)

The force of these lines comes from the deliberate and reflexive turn they make on Smith's own work, represented here (initially) by an intramural reference to her recently published novel *Emmeline* (1788). As the locus (literally) of "fictitious happiness," the novel is the sign of the human effort to gain "the wishes of [the] soul." But the poem's chinese-box structure – it records and reflects upon an imaginary dream of an encounter with the domain of the fictional – implodes upon itself, leaving a residue of undesired, unimagined, and disorienting "truth." In Smith's work, the reason for dream (or poetry) is to reveal the sick dreams of reason, the traumas of conscious benevolence. This poem is itself another instance of such traumatic revelation.

Like all the other canonical Romantics, Byron learned much of his art from several late eighteenth-century sentimental sources, including the Della Cruscans and Charlotte Smith. Smith's poetry stands behind the visible darkness of, for instance, the Thyrza lyrics. The remarkable "scorpion" passage in *The Giaour* elaborates the argument that Smith had developed in her sonnets. Her "aggravated pain," a deliberate construction, is the direct ancestor of Byron's Giaour's "guilty woes." Each cultivates what James later called "an imagination of disaster":

> So do the dark in soul expire,
> Or live like Scorpion girt by fire.[7]
> (433–434)

Smith set a model for living in such an unrefining fire, and for imagining its equivocal virtues. The brilliant syntactic wordplay of Byron's couplet's first line, which intimates either a material or a spiritual suicide, recalls various poems by Smith, especially her sequence of sonnets "Supposed to be written by Werter."

For better and for worse, Byron brought a Brechtian theatricality to textual strategies like the elegiacs of Charlotte Smith: perhaps for the worse in poems like "If sometimes in the haunts of men," certainly for the better in another Thyrza elegy, the small masterpiece "Stanzas" ("And thou art dead, as young and fair"). Constructed as a series of perverse turns upon the inheritance of the poetry of lament, the poem casts a cold eye upon itself, its poet, its audience, its forebears. It is a text that would bear no illusions, not even the illusion of disillusion:

> The love where Death has set his seal,
> Nor age can chill, nor rival steal,
> Nor falsehood disavow:
> And, what were worse, thou can'st not see
> Or wrong, or change, or fault in me.
> (23–27)

The poem's basic unit is a distinctively artificial nine-line stanza, metrically paced 4–4–4–3–4–4–3–4–4 and rhyming ababccbdd. There are eight of these stanzas, whose formal complexity shuts down – in particular at the crucial seventh line – any possible apparition of expressive freedom. In thus flaunting its cold technical correctness, the verse underscores its key themes of loss and deficiency. Byron's lines are out of joint psychically, morally, and even culturally.

In the passage just quoted, this warp appears with dramatic obliqueness in the odd allusion to *Antony and Cleopatra*. If the reference shocks us by its incongruence, and it does, it helps us to see Byron's analogous ineptitude in face of his loss. He is a figure of ("worse") incompetence by his virtues and fidelities, which here are turned to signs of vice.

Byron's perverse experience thereby cuts back upon his Shakespearean inheritance, wringing Cleopatra's "infinite variety" into a figure of the grotesque.

Such a move, we must realize, poisons the very ground of an English conception of poetry and culture, for this precise Shakespearean text had become the touchstone of Shakespeare's poetical greatness. Byron deals, quite literally, a mortal blow to received ideas about the authority of poetry and imagination. Recollecting Shakespeare, he discounts the cultural capital that has been made of the original work. In a love-elegy for John Edleston, the oddness of the Shakespeare allusion is doubly witty, and of course doubly perverse. Dangerous ambiguities play all about the action of poetry, which is not – Byron insists – what high culture imagines it to be. And so in reading Byron's text we are teased to recall the whole of the original Shakespeare passage, where the unnerving truth about poetry – that it *is* unnerving – will be found:

> other women cloy
> The appetites they feed; but she makes hungry
> Where most she satisfies; for vilest things
> Become themselves in her. (II, ii, 241–244)

Born from and for death in several senses, Byron's is a poetry of spoliation where, like Samson among the Philistines, he pulls the temple down upon himself and everyone who comes to witness his prisoned strength.

> It is enough for me to prove
> That what I lov'd and long must love
> Like common earth can rot;
> To me there needs no stone to tell
> 'Tis Nothing that I lov'd so well.
> (14–18)

In Byron, and as by tradition, Memory is the mother of the muses, as this poem's epigraph reminds us: "Heu quanto minus est cum reliquis versari quam tui meminisse." But here the offspring of Memory are stillborn.

The logic of Byron's thinking is sketched in a poem written shortly before these "Stanzas," the lines "Written Beneath a Picture":

> 1.
> Dear object of defeated care!
> Though now of Love and thee bereft,
> To reconcile me with despair,
> Thine image and my tears are left.

2.
'Tis said with Sorrow Time can cope;
But this I fear can ne'er be true:
For by the death-blow of my Hope
My Memory immortal grew.

Written under the sign of art, the lines enact the contradictory powers of imagination. Like the "image" of his unnamed love, the poem seems fated to eternalize its ground of experience – as the text's powerful set of upper-case abstractions indicate (Love, Sorrow, Time, Hope, Memory). In establishing their authority these powers, these symbolical forms, appear to have erased the material name and figure of the beloved. As a consequence, among the symbolical forms that loom over this small text, only "despair" comes as a mortal figure, dressed in lower case.

Thus the celebrated power of art over Time is here weighed out and found wanting: not because art fails to "defeat" Time, but exactly because it does gain its customary measure of triumph. With poetic immortality comes the evanishment of immediate experience – the "Dear object of defeated care" – and the emergence of a figure of "Hope" delivering its own death-blows, and a figure of Memory doomed to transcendence.

The "Stanzas" ("And thou art dead, as young and fair") do not immortalize Thyrza in "powerful rhyme," therefore, they mortalize him. Left with memories alone, the work ensures that no one, least of all the poet or his readers, shall make capital of those revelations. Three references to Shakespeare, all perverse objects of defeated care, signal Byron's determination to see that only loss shall be built upon loss.

The flower in ripen'd bloom unmatch'd
  Must fall the earliest prey,
Though by no hand untimely snatch'd.
  The leaves must drop away:
And yet it were a greater grief
To watch it withering, leaf by leaf,
  Than see it pluck'd to-day;
Since earthly eye can ill but bear
To trace the change to foul from fair.
(37–45)

As with the earlier allusion to *Antony and Cleopatra*, these two recollections of *Macbeth* call attention to themselves by their oddness and ineptitude. Something seems missing, or wrong, as if the poem possessed an awareness that escaped us. Whatever they might be taken to "mean" in a thematic sense, the allusions function rhetorically as Byron's personal signature. Their very unnaturalness underscores the textual presence of a dark design in the text.

We register that design in two principal ways. Choosing to write his poem under the aegis of Antony, Cleopatra, and Macbeth, Byron suggests that those massive Shakespearean pretexts somehow forecast a pattern for Byron's personal life. But the allusions also form an indirect address to Byron's readers, who have their own claims upon the Shakespearean inheritance. Byron's odd quotations are signs of a cultural disturbance. Such stylistic moments prophesy the coming of the celebrated Byronic Hero, who will unsettle his readers with similar uncertainties. That is at once the hero's meaning and function in the Byronic economy of art.

In this context the "Stanzas"' second *Macbeth* allusion seems especially effective. The awkwardness of the inverted construction "to foul from fair" recalls the more orderly and expected "from foul to fair," which is a phrasal index of the compensatory logic of traditional elegy. When Byron wrecks this phrase he makes more than his immediate text difficult to read. Once again we realize that Byron has made Shakespeare the spring of his mordant rhetoric: "Fair is foul, and foul is fair."

Byron's use (and misuse) of Shakespearean pretexts may return us to the poem's first quotation – the epigraph from Shenstone's celebrated inscription "On an Ornamented Urn," which Shenstone composed for his cousin "Miss Dolman . . . who died of the smallpox, about twenty-one years of age." The whole of the Shenstone text is as follows:

> Ah Maria
> puellarum elegantissima,
> Ah flore Venustatis abrepta,
> Vale!
> Heu quanto minus est
> cum reliquis versari,
> quam tui
> meminisse![8]

Byron's last stanza recollects (and almost translates) the epigraph, thus:

> Yet how much less it were to gain,
> Though thou hast left me free,
> The loveliest things that still remain,
> Than thus remember thee!
> (64–67)

In traditional elegy the recollection *is* the event of the writing, so that Byron's "thus" refers to his own text. But his point becomes ironical because the English syntax of "how much less . . . than" makes only a highly equivocal rendering of the Latin original "quanto minus . . . quam." The latter speaks unambiguously on the question of what is "less" (i.e., "cum reliquis versari") and what is more ("tui meminisse"). Turned into Byron's verse, however, a Latin clarity translates to an English problem, for the English text leaves one uncertain about the status of losses and gains. Indeed, one reading only signifies the option of relative degrees of loss either in the gaining of (life's present) "loveliest things" or in the remembering of the dead Thyrza.

The text's ultimate irony is reserved for the wordplay Byron teases from the Latin phrase "cum reliquis versari." The normal reading of this phrase might be rendered something like "to be occupied with others (people and/or things)." But the root of "versari," as the English word "verse" reminds us, leaves the Latin word perpetually open to the meaning "to make verses." Historically this meaning seems not to have been exploited by earlier writers. In Byron's poem, however, the meaning is all but irresistible, at least after one has finished reading the final stanza, where "gain" is translated (literally) into a syntax and economy of diminishing returns.

In Byron, therefore, the poetry is not in the pity but in the pitilessness. To write anything about loss, especially anything poetical, threatens to make a mockery of the event. This thought, yet another commonplace of elegy, Byron literalizes in order to display the truth about loss – that it is irreparable – and the truth about elegy – that it is at best a bad (which is to say, for Byron, a *good*) joke.

Such humor is bleak enough. In Byron's work it plays alongside another comic style that he learned from a different sentimental source, the Della Cruscans. Like their master Sterne, Hannah Cowley and her poetical comrades tend to enlighten (in several senses) the scene of love's trials, even to the point of comedy. Once again Byron makes himself their student, as we see so plainly in the splendid late poem "Could Love for ever." This work makes a game of its self-consciousness and urbanity by parading (and parodying) a kind of step-by-step logical argument. It is, in this respect, the fulfillment of various Della Cruscan exercises of his youth – for example. "The Edinburgh Ladies' Petition to Dr. Moyes and his Reply."

I draw two morals from this fragment of a forgotten poetical history. First, Byron's lyrics can help us recover a body of writing – indeed, a whole complex stylistic tradition – that has been badly misunderstood and neglected. I mean the many forms of sentimental poetry, and in particular the work of those inaugural figures who shaped the tradition during the years 1780–1830. Second, and reciprocally, the recovery of that tradition will throw our received critical views of Romanticism into an entirely new light. Or perhaps I shouldn't say "entirely new." What we will discover, I think, is a path to reconnect with critical understandings that flourished in the nineteenth century, before modernism tried to raze that landscape and set new rules and proprieties for poetry and imagination.

NOTES

1 See the reprint of the original 1965 text in *Romanticism and Consciousness*, ed. Harold Bloom (New York: W. W. Norton & Co., 1970).

2 In the *Byron Journal* (1992), 27–45, and above, chapter 5.

3 For an extended discussion of the Della Cruscans see my "The Literal World of the English Della Cruscans," in my *The Poetics of Sensibility* (Oxford: Clarendon Press, 1996), 74–93.

4 The references here are to that other major source of Della Cruscan texts, *The British Album*, 2 vols. (London: William Bell, 1789).

5 See especially the poems of 1792–1794 (e.g. "Kisses," "The Sigh," and "The Kiss," among others). These are explicitly Della Cruscan works.

6 My text is the facsimile reprint of the 1789 edition, with an Introduction by Jonathan Wordsworth (Oxford: Woodstock Books, 1992).

7 My Byron texts are from *Lord Byron. The Complete Poetical Works*, ed. Jerome J. McGann (Oxford: Clarendon Press, 1980–1993).

8 *The Poetical Works of William Shenstone*, with Life, Critical Dissertation, and Explanatory Notes by George Gilfillan (New York: D. Appleton and Co., 1854), 279. The epigraph comprises only the second half of the inscription, but Byron recollects the first half in his (crucial) fifth stanza.

CHAPTER 9

Byron and Wordsworth

I

They met intimately just once, in the spring of 1815, at Samuel Rogers's house. Wordsworth "talked too much," according to Rogers, but Byron wasn't put off. At home afterwards he told his wife Annabella that "I had but one feeling from the beginning of the visit to the end – *reverence*" (Lovell, *His Very Self and Voice*, 129). And that's all we know about the only meeting between the two dominating English poets of the period. To us now, that foregone scene might easily recall the Romantic passage in *The Age of Bronze* where Byron describes the great forensic rivalry of Fox and Pitt:

> We, we have seen the intellectual race
> Of giants stand, like Titans, face to face—
> Athos and Ida, with a dashing sea
> Of eloquence between. (13–16)

So will distance lend enchantment to a view of people and events. Imagined more closely, the meeting of Byron and Wordsworth must have been riven with awkwardness. Both were conscious of the other's eminence. Rogers had arranged his dinner specifically to bring them together. They were also well aware of Byron's public comments on Wordsworth's poetry – his review of the 1807 *Poems*, and his general critique mounted in two passages of *English Bards and Scotch Reviewers* (235–254 and 903–905). Byron must have been somewhat chagrined by the recollection of those writings, for while they clearly showed great respect – if not exactly "reverence" – for Wordsworth, they were also forthright, as Byron always was, with their disapprovals. For his part Wordsworth had privately acknowledged his own equivocal view of Byron's work, and he always chafed before the spectacular fame that

Byron so quickly – and in Wordsworth's view, so undeservedly – had gained.

Within a year these tenuous relations would slip into deeper aversions. The public scandal of Byron's marriage break-up moved Wordsworth to speak privately of Byron as an "insane" person and of his poetry as "doggerel." He arrived at these judgments after reading John Scott's attack on Byron in his newspaper *The Champion*, where Scott also published – without permission – Byron's two unpublished poems "Fare Thee Well!" and "A Sketch from Private Life." As Mary Moorman has noted, however, Scott's malicious prose was "not severe enough" for the outraged Wordsworth, who urged Scott in a letter to renew and deepen the attack. Needless to say, this was not Wordsworth's finest hour. His letter moved Scott to write two further pieces on the wicked Lord. These were the texts that both focused and fuelled the campaign of vilification, which climaxed with Byron's departure from England.

Byron never knew the secret part that Wordsworth played in what he called his "home desolation." Some say that he learned later how Wordsworth – again in a private letter – had denounced his poetry as "immoral and vicious." Wordsworth certainly believed that Byron heard about the letter, and he attributed the attacks on him in *Don Juan* to Byron's knowledge of what he had written. But nothing in Byron's correspondence or conversations indicates that he knew of this letter either. His sense of honor was acute. Had the letter come to his attention he would have responded to Wordsworth with the kind of rage he felt for Southey when he learned in the summer of 1818 that the Laureate was spreading scandalous gossip about him.

Byron hated Robert Southey, he did not hate Wordsworth – though he *would* have hated him had he known the whole truth. Byron had some fun with Wordsworth's name – he called him "Wordswords" and "Turdsworth" – but these were games of language, rhetorical flourishes in his argument with Wordsworth's politics and his programmatic ignorance of Pope. What Michael says to Sathan in "The Vision of Judgment" anticipates Byron's imagination of the rivalry of Fox and Pitt, and pretty well sums up Byron's view of his relation to Wordsworth throughout his life:

> Our different parties make us fight so shy,
> I ne'er mistake you for a *personal* foe;
> Our difference is *political*, and I
> Trust that, whatever may occur below,

> You know my great respect for you; and this
> Makes me regret whate'er you do amiss—
>
> (491–496)

The substance of this passage will gloss any one of Byron's many commentaries on Wordsworth: the judgments, both prose and verse, published in 1807 and 1809; the long letter to Leigh Hunt of 30 October 1815 in which Byron critiques both *The Excursion* and the 1815 *Poems*; the unpublished prose note to his Wordsworth imitation "Churchill's Grave"; and even the more savagely worded criticisms laid down in his 1820 rejoinder to John Gibson Lockhart's review of *Don Juan* in *Blackwood's Edinburgh Magazine* (August 1819). True, the "reverence" Byron felt for Wordsworth, registered in 1815, collapsed in the course of the "intellectual war" (*Don Juan*, XI, 496) he undertook against the Lake School under the twin banner of the traduced genius of Pope and the betrayal of enlightened political ideas. That such a reverence existed, however, and that it was genuine, seems very clear. That it was also "antithetically mixt" (*Childe Harold's Pilgrimage III*, 317) goes without saying – we are talking of Byron after all – but it should not go without close examination. The subject holds far more than purely biographical significance. In Byron's critical reverence for Wordsworth we can trace some of the volatile contradictions that organize the Romantic movement in England.

II

Most discussions of Wordsworth and Byron begin with Shelley, who – as Byron later told Thomas Medwin – "used to dose me with Wordsworth physic even to nausea" in Switzerland in 1816. He goes on to say that "I do remember reading some things of his with pleasure. He had once a feeling of Nature, which he carried almost to a deification of it:– that's why Shelley liked his poetry." Byron goes on to suggest that Wordsworth lost "the faculty of writing well" when he lost "his mental independence" and became a "hireling" of British imperialism. Nonetheless, Byron acknowledges "a certain merit" in the stylistic "simplicity" that Wordsworth famously developed in the *Lyrical Ballads* – a book he clearly knew intimately – and he adds that Wordsworth "now and then expressed ideas worth imitating" (Lovell, *Medwin*, 194). These comments have led many readers – including Wordsworth himself – to find the third canto of *Childe Harold* full of an unacknowledged and second-rate Wordsworthian "feeling of Nature."

There is no question that Byron made Shelley's reading of Wordsworth a central part of the third canto of *Childe Harold*. But we want to remember that the poem is a Byronic and not a Shelleyan – and least of all a Wordsworthian – exercise. That is to say, its reflexive structure is energetic and existential, not meditative and conceptual. The form asks us to receive the poem as if it were an experiential record – a fact about the work blatantly announced in the remarkable opening stanzas, where a dream sequence offers itself to the reader as an immediate experience rather than a recollective construction. In this frame of reference, ideas – including the poem's Wordsworthianisms – come to us as part of the poem's running eventualities, as thoughts borne along with the imaginary passage of the imaginary Childe Harold. In this "being more intense" Byron passes through a certain space of time – a few months in 1816 when he journeyed from England to Switzerland in quest of spiritual and psychic stability. Shelley's Wordsworth comes as part of that passage, a gift from a friend who thought a Wordsworthian "feeling of Nature" might help to alleviate the tumult of Byron's condition.

But Shelley's "physic" ends in "nausea." Byron emblemizes this result in the discrepancy between the "forgetfulness" he desired at the start, and the even more acute sense of his own "identity" and place in the world that he has at the canto's end. Byron's absorption into a sense of nature's transcendental processes is not a culminating or defining event, it is one experience among many. When Wordsworth is laid asleep in body to become a living soul he sees into the life of things, and that sight, once gained, brings the promise of a final peace: for Nature

can so inform
The mind that is within us, so impress
With quietness and beauty, and so feed
With lofty thoughts, that neither evil tongues,
Rash judgments, not the sneers of selfish men,
Nor greetings where no kindness is, nor all
The dreary intercourse of daily life,
Shall e'er prevail against us, or disturb
Our cheerful faith, that all which we behold
Is full of blessings. ("Tintern Abbey," 125–134)

This famous passage, and the whole of the poem which it moralizes, gets recalled, and refused, at the end of Byron's canto when he addresses his daughter as Wordsworth had addressed his sister. Canto III of *Childe Harold* is an undertaking and rejection of the Wordsworthian ethos (or "physic"), an event defined in the different "blessings" each poet imagines at the end of his poem. Whereas in Wordsworth these are assigned to a transhuman source and conceived as both full and perpetual, in Byron the case is otherwise. Byron's blessings are human and individuated – they are specifically his own, sent specifically to his daughter (and in other poems of 1816, specifically to his sister), nor are they validated in any non personal terms. They are also equivocal because they are lost and helpless. Byron knows that the love gifts he is sending will be prevented from any immediate arrival. Consequently, nothing in this poem is certain except the intention of the speaker, an intention which circumstance – "that unspiritual god" – has driven into a conditional existence. The canto ends in a flurry of subjunctives that culminate in the canto's penultimate declaration: "Fain would I waft such blessing upon thee."

The explicitness of Byron's rejection of Wordsworthian doctrine defines one of the poem's most important figures. It is the emblem of his identity and self-consciousness. His "Alpine Journal," which he wrote for his sister, repeats the message of Canto III of *Childe Harold*. One of the great acts of English prose attention, the journal stands as both coda to and commentary on the poem. For thirteen carefully articulated days Byron records the minutest particulars of his physical and mental experiences. Nothing falls out of focus, nothing of the world, nothing of Byron, nothing past and nothing present:

> stopped at Vevey two hours (the second time I have visited it) walked to the Church – view from the Churchyard superb – within it General Ludlow (the Regicide's) monument – black marble – long inscription – Latin – but simple – particularly the latter part – in which his wife (Margaret de Thomas) records her long – her tried – and unshaken affection – he was an Exile *two and thirty years* – one of the King's (Charles's) Judges – a fine fellow. I remember reading his memoirs in January 1815 (at Halnaby).

It is the first day of his trip, with the grand passages of the Swiss Alps still to be seen. Byron remains rapt in his present, where (however) the recent disaster of his marriage runs through the interstices of his careful prose. For that event is as present to him as the churchyard at Vevey, or the memoirs of General Ludlow. Moving through the journal we realize that no part of the human world seems to escape his interest or attention: the peasant dancers at Brientz; the corporal at Chillon Castle "drunk as Blucher"; the copy of Blair's *Sermons* "on the table of the saloon" in the

Chateau de Clarens, where Byron is led through the "bosquet de Julie" by a "Guide full of *Rousseau* – whom he is eternally confounding with *St. Preux*." Every detail fascinates, and all carry him home:

> In the evening four Swiss Peasant Girls of Oberhasli came & sang the airs of their country – two of the voices beautiful – the tunes also – they sang too that Tyrolese air & song which you love – Augusta . . . they are still singing – Dearest – you do not know how I should have liked this – were you with me – the airs are so wild & original & at the same time of great sweetness. – The singing is over – but below stairs I hear the notes of a Fiddle which bode no good to my nights rest. – The Lord help us! – I shall go down and see the dancing. –

For both Byron and Wordsworth, "feeling comes in aid of feeling" in these kinds of encounter. But as Ruskin would acutely note, the Wordsworthian process involves a technique of soft focus that melts the "whats" of the experience in a meshed network of "hows," a process of the soul's "Remembering how she felt, but what she felt / Remembering not" (*The Prelude*, II, 316–317). In Byron, on the other hand, the course of the particulars remains sharply drawn. The difference is especially remarkable when the poets are engaged with a "feeling of Nature":

> Arrived at the Grindenwald – dined – mounted again & rode to the higher Glacier – twilight – but distinct – very fine Glacier – like a *frozen hurricane* – Starlight – beautiful – but a devil of a path – never mind – got safe in – a little lightning – but the whole of the day as fine in point of weather – as the day on which Paradise was made. – Passed *whole woods of withered pines – all withered* – trunks stripped & barkless – branches lifeless – done by a single winter – their appearance reminded me of me & my family. –

The text should be compared with Wordsworth's equally great description of his passage through the Gorge of Gondo in *The Prelude* (Book VI, 617–640). Wordsworth's descriptive scene is an organized series of representative sublimities, all

> like workings of one mind, the features
> Of the same face, blossoms upon one tree;
> Characters of the great Apocalypse,
> The types and symbols of Eternity,
> Of first, and last, and midst, and without end.

Byron's "one mind" is only his own as it observes, relates, remembers. Wordsworth's "Apocalypse" and "Eternity" insist on the truth of their transnatural referents, whereas for Byron "Paradise" is simply – wonderfully – a figure of speech. A thought from Blake defines the differences exactly: Wordsworth's imagination deals in "forms of worship," Byron's in "poetic tales."

At the conclusion of his journal, as at the conclusion of Canto III of *Childe Harold*, Byron recurs to the "physic" that Shelley had been offering to his friend. The brief Alpine tour had involved the most intense kind of encounter with mountain gloom and mountain glory. Byron reflects on the experience:

> I am a lover of Nature – and an Admirer of Beauty – I can bear fatigue – & welcome privation – and have seen some of the noblest views in the world. – But in all this – the recollections of bitterness – & more especially of recent & more home desolation – which must accompany me through life – have preyed upon me here – and neither the music of the Shepherd – the crashing of the Avalanche – nor the torrent – the mountain – the Glacier – the Forest – nor the Cloud – have for one moment – lightened the weight upon my heart – nor enabled me to lose my own wretched identity in the Majesty & the Power and the Glory – around – above – & beneath me. –

The passage faces in two directions: back to Canto III of *Childe Harold*, which he had just finished writing; and forward to *Manfred*, which Byron had begun shortly before his September trip into the Bernese Oberland and which he would complete the following spring, in Venice. At that point Byron was poised on the brink of *Beppo*, which is to say, on the threshold of *Don Juan*. Counterpart and antithesis to *The Prelude*, it is Byron's sweeping act of historical reflection – a work Coleridge might have called a "great philosophical poem," had Coleridge not abandoned enlightenment for transcendental philosophy. In this respect *Manfred* is the hinge work of Byron's career. It is also a poem deeply involved with Wordsworth.

To see this more clearly we should briefly recall an event that took place on Byron's last day in England. Just before leaving Dover for Europe Byron visited the grave of the satirist Charles Churchill. Sometime later – probably in June or July – he recollected that highly charged moment in his Swiss tranquillity (such as it was). The result became the poem "Churchill's Grave," a deliberate exercise in the style of "the simple Wordsworth," as Byron's note to the text declared.

> The following poem (as most that I have endeavoured to write) is founded on a fact; and this attempt is a serious imitation of the style of a great poet – its beauties and its defects: I say, the *style*, for the thoughts I claim as my own. In this, if there be anything ridiculous, let it be attributed to me as much as to Mr. Wordsworth, of whom there can exist few greater admirers or deplorers

than myself. I have blended what I would deem to be the beauties as well as the defects of his style – and it ought to be remembered that in such things, whether there be praise or dispraise, there is always what is called a compliment, however unintentional.

The equivocalness of this prose text runs through the poem as well, which involves a manifestly Wordsworthian encounter between a traveller – Byron – and the "Sexton" of the Dover cemetery. Byron later liked to twit Wordsworth as the "hireling" of a reactionary government, a poet who took his "place in the excise" (*Don Juan* "Dedication") in 1813 and then dedicated *The Excursion*, that "drowsy frowzy poem" (*Don Juan*, III, 847), to the man who gained it for him, Lord Lonsdale. Byron's first public allusion to the event comes in this short poem of 1816, in the most amusingly oblique way – that is, in the final words of the sexton to Byron, where he looks to be paid for his service.

> "I believe the man of whom
> You wot, who lies in this selected tomb,
> Was a most famous writer in his day,
> And therefore travellers step from out their way
> To pay him honour,—and myself whate'er
> Your honour pleases." (27–32)

Over the grave of Churchill – the neglected eighteenth-century satirist and Byron's alter ego here – Byron uses Wordsworth's poetical style to reflect on the difference between payment in honor and payment in cash. Byron wraps his critique of Wordsworth as hireling poet in the "compliment" of a "serious imitation" of Wordsworth's style. The irony of the passage is as wicked as it is brilliant. But nothing in this splendid poem is unequivocal, as its conclusion shows. Clearly Byron expects the reader to catch his ironical critique, for after he pays the sexton he remarks (this time in a different ironical register):

> Ye smile,
> I see ye, ye profane ones! All the while,
> Because my homely phrase the truth would tell.
> (36–38)

There is more truth here than the "fact" of Wordsworth's sinecure. There is as well a different "fact," a "deep thought" that Byron underscores in his poem's reflective conclusion:

You are the fools, not I—for I did dwell
With a deep thought, and with a soften'd eye,
On that old Sexton's natural homily,
In which there was Obscurity and Fame,
The Glory and the Nothing of a Name.
(39–43)

Churchill, Wordsworth, Lord Byron: at last, at the last of this poem, all come together – as Byron wrote elsewhere – "in the dark union of insensate dust" ("[A Fragment. 'Could I remount . . .'']," line 22). Wordsworth's sinecure slips into inconsequence when Byron weighs it in a more exacting scale. Indeed, Byron uses Wordsworth's recent public "honour" as a kind of "physic" for his own immediate feelings of "bitterness." Both are to be finally measured by his poem's epigram: "The Glory and the Nothing of a Name."

The "physic" of "Churchill's Grave" is distinctly Byronic (rather than Shelleyan or Wordsworthian). The poem's complex mixture of ironies ranges widely: from parodic game, through brilliant wit – part playful, part malicious, supremely cool – to its mordant, Byronic sententiousness. From Wordsworth's "style" Byron fashions his own "thought," a somewhat Mephistophelean argument coded in a medley-style of writing.

The poem is especially important because of its self-conscious manner of proceeding. Canto III of *Childe Harold* is no less a work of conscious *art*, but in its case it is an art of sincerity. As in Wordsworthian sincerity poems – "Tintern Abbey" is a perfect example – the reader of Byron's canto is asked to accept the illusion of an unmediated expression of feeling and thought, as if nothing intervened between the experience represented in the poem and its textual emergence. "Churchill's Grave" is completely different. It is a poem flaunting its artistry and constructedness, a fact emphasized in the various differentiations put before us in Byron's prose note.

I have spent this time on "Churchill's Grave" not simply because it has been sadly neglected. The poem is also important because it illuminates, as no other work of 1816 does, Byron's strange and difficult masterpiece *Manfred*. Of course *Manfred* is in certain ways a clear reprise on the third canto of *Childe Harold*. This fact is emphasized by Byron's "Alpine Journal," which could be – and has been – used to gloss both works. Besides, all these writings swirl in a vortex of memory and forgetting, another Wordsworthian subject to which I shall have to return. In *Manfred*, however, the dramatic presentation makes self-consciousness rather than sincerity the determining stylistic move. In this respect *Manfred* is a work that does not pretend to discover its own thought – which is what sincerity poems like "Tintern Abbey" and *Childe Harold III* do – but to put its thought on display, and thereby to make a deliberated exposition and argument, as in "Churchill's Grave."

Part of the argument is anti-Wordsworthian, as we might expect. Three explictly Wordsworthian surrogates appear in the poem. The first is the Witch of the Alps, an all but allegorical figure for the Shelleyan reading of Wordsworth. The Witch promises peace of soul to Manfred if he will "swear obedience to my will, and do / My bidding" (II, 2, 156–157). In refusing her offer Manfred is refusing what Byron saw as the Wordsworthian "deification of [Nature for which] Shelley liked his poetry." For, unlike Wordsworth and even Shelley, Byron thought the idea that "Nature never did betray / The heart that loved her" ("Tintern Abbey," 122–123) a serious intellectual error. Speaking for himself on the matter, and in his usual exacting way, he said he was "an Admirer of Nature," but not a worshipper. The other two Wordsworthian figures are easy to spot – the Chamois Hunter, who incarnates the virtues of Michael, the Leech Gatherer, and so forth; and the Abbot, whose ancestors include the Pastor in *The Excursion*. In separating himself from these characters Manfred serves to focus the argument with Wordsworth, and with Romanticism more largely, that we've already seen in *Childe Harold*. It's important to see that each of them, even the Abbot, is treated respectfully in the poem. Nonetheless, they are all refused.

It is also important to see that the Abbot has other, very different ancestors – in particular the monkish interlocutor of the Giaour, who of course is one of Manfred's own most important precursors. This Byronic/Wordsworthian overlap forecasts the even more remarkable overlap of Byron and Southey in Canto III of *Don Juan*, in the figure of Lambro's oral bard who sings "The Isles of Greece."[1] In each case Byron is not only developing a self-critical dimension to his poetical arguments, he is dramatizing the self-consciousness of his texts, forcing us to see that imaginations are being constructed. The 1816 drama opens with a soliloquy that emphasizes Manfred's intellectual and imaginative powers. A large part of the play's wit – and it is an exceedingly witty work – depends upon our realization that Manfred's power is a metaphor for Byron's. Manfred's story is as it were a play within a play. The drama of *Manfred* is the Faustian wizardry of Lord Byron.

The double take that we are offered in the figure of the Abbot is comical because the Abbot's ideological allegiances are contradictory. The first version of the play emphasizes this comical element much more clearly, and I also think much more effectively. In the original third act Byron creates a kind of romp with his play's gothic paraphernalia. Returning to make a last effort to save Manfred's soul, the Abbot is handed over to "the demon Ashtaroth" whom Manfred conjures from a little casket as "a gift for thee." He then commands Ashtaroth to carry the Abbot to the top of the Shreckhorn where he might glimpse what being "near to heaven" actually means in a mortal universe. Ashtaroth obeys, disappearing "with the Abbot" and singing an irreverent ditty about the ordinariness of evil:

> A prodigal son—and a maid undone—
> And a widow re-wedded within the year—
> And a worldly Monk—and a pregnant Nun—
> Are things which every day appear.

What is all this about, what is happening here? In one sense none of it is serious, for Manfred and Ashtaroth are as enveloped in a comic atmosphere as is the butt of their humor, the Abbot. The whole of the scene, even in its revised version, is partly a game of horror, not at all unlike the half-serious games with horror that "Monk" Lewis – one of Byron's favorite authors – plays so splendidly in his outrageous novel *The Monk*. (And of course, as we know, it was Lewis who recalled Goethe's *Faust* to Byron's attention in 1816.) But the comedy is as "serious," in another sense, as it is in "The Isles of Greece" episode, or "Churchill's Grave," or throughout *Don Juan*, which is a vast display of poetic wit and invention. Manfred's fabulous powers – to call spirits from the vasty deep, or from little caskets – are a trope for Byron's own. He is making a performance of those powers in *Manfred*, is literally staging them in a proto-Brechtian play. So the work appears as an exposition of, and implicitly an argument with, the illusionistic styles and ideas of Romanticism – that "wrong revolutionary poetical system," as Byron called it, in which he – like Wordsworth – played such a key role.

Philip Martin was the first modern critic to argue for this way of seeing *Manfred*. It is a work "proposing a wholly new and fundamentally dramatic relationship between author and reader," a "pre-conditioning exercise for *Don Juan*" in which Byron comes before us as a Gothic magician, "deliberately trifling with decorum" and scattering his play with "a ubiquitous quasi-burlesque tone" (116, 117). Concentrating on Act II scenes 3 and 4 – the scenes involving the demonic characters – Martin makes a splendid exposure of the play's farcical satire and of Byron's Mephistophelean posings. He does not remark on the play's affinity with

Byron's earlier parodic farce "The Devil's Drive," even though he shows in another part of his book the resemblances between the jokes in that early poem and similar comic moves in major works like *Cain* and "The Vision of Judgment." But we want to see the full pattern of this parodic and self-dramatizing poetry in Byron, for it involves what Paul West years ago, quoting Byron, labelled "The Spoiler's Art." Madame de Staël found the same style in the Mephistophelean passages of Goethe's *Faust.* She called it an art that deliberately cultivated defects of style, and in particular outrageous breaches of linguistic decorum ("les fautes de goût . . . qui l'ont déterminé à les y laisser, ou plutôt à les y mettre").[2]

Unlike De Staël, both West and Martin – especially Martin – abominate this kind of comic debunking. Without it, however, Poe and Baudelaire would have found little in *Manfred* to interest them, and Nietzsche's Byron would simply not have existed. Consider, for instance, the joke that climaxes the play's second act – a joke that neither West nor Martin register, perhaps because of its utter outrageousness. It locates a crucial moment in the action, for once Byron makes this stylistic move within and against his play all conventional understandings are hurled into an abyss.

When Astarte disappears, Manfred, one of the demonic spirits tells us, "is convulsed" and the demon comments ironically on Manfred's evident "mortal" weakness in seeking "the things beyond mortality." As Manfred pulls himself together "ANOTHER SPIRIT," impressed that he is able to make "his torture tributary to his will," observes majestically: "Had he been one of us he would have made / An awful spirit." What we have to deal with here is a singular moment of stylistic crisis exactly like those that De Staël found so central to *Faust.* Scots usage, which of course Byron knew very well and used to brilliant effect throughout *Don Juan*, permitted greatly divergent meanings to the word "awful": on one hand it could signify something awe-inspiring, on the other something mean and despicable. From the point of view of "correct" English usage, however, Byron knew that the latter meaning was still regarded (in 1816) as impossibly vulgar – a meaning in fact associated with the "low" usages of American and Scottish dialect. A year later, writing *Beppo*, Byron would again conflate these "low" and "proper" meanings when he describes that "bluest of bluebottle" authors William Sotheby as "A stalking oracle of awful phrase" (line 585).

But while the joke is formally the same in both works, the object and result in each case are very different. The point of the wordplay in *Manfred* is to suggest why Manfred, a mere mortal creature, is in fact superior to all common understandings of "spiritual" orders and beings. At the outset of the play Manfred does not understand the grandeur of his defective and limited human condition, does not realize why the fate of death opens up transcendental possibilities that are completely unavailable to creatures bound by spiritual conditions. In a word, he is "awful" in one sense because he is "awful" in another. But the effect of Byron's pun in the play passes beyond the word's rather transparent thematic meaning. We realize this when we reflect on Byron's joke in *Beppo*. There the word makes no assault upon the poem in which it appears because Byron plainly controls the wit of the text. The dramatic texture of *Manfred* alters the terms of the word's reception, as if it were the "choice" of the demon to speak in this way, as if a wholly inappropriate meaning of the word "awful" (from the demon's and the English reader's point of view) had found its way into his mouth. At such a moment the play's traditional decorum is hopelessly breached and the artistic integrity of the drama imperilled. At such a moment, in fact, as De Staël observed of Goethe and his *Faust*, Byron emerges unmistakably as a character in his own work, a kind of Samson wrecking the pillars of his art: Out of this chaotic moment emerges the Gay Science of Byron's comic immensities. The joke on the word "awful" in *Beppo* fully explicates the meaning of the joke in *Manfred*: against Sotheby's "sublime / Of mediocrity" (lines 581–582) Byron sets a new kind of poetic sublimity, the style of a deliberate and imperial artist who can as easily make as unmake his own worlds, and who can observe these acts in many tones and moods. Like Goethe in *Faust*, Byron in *Manfred* chooses to hurl his own work down from the heaven of fine art.

This is truly a joke from the regions beyond good and evil. It is also an important and a telling joke in the context of the play. The demon, being a spirit, is clearly unaware of the vulgar meaning of the word he uses. Byron, however – widely travelled and an avid student of language – supplies the demon with a word that literally *dramatizes* who is the master of all these poetical ceremonies.

The master is not Manfred, least of all the imaginary world of spirits and demons, but the author of the play named after its fictive hero. Byron uses comedy and burlesque to signal the self-consciousness of his production. But like Sterne before him, Byron insists upon locating himself, the ceremonial master, within the critical context of his own phantasmagoria. We admire and praise this manner when we encounter it in *Don Juan* and its associated writings, where the self-critical manoeuvres are handled with such un-self-critical elegance. But there is an important sense in which *Manfred* is a far bolder and more forward-thinking work than *Don Juan* – just as we can see that Wordsworth's linguistic experiments in *Lyrical Ballads* engaged more prescient and profound stylistic issues than his clear masterpiece *The Prelude*. For *Manfred* is the acme of his "spoiler's art." No other work of his dares to bring so much to judgment. It is all very well – and it is very well indeed – to essay the candor of the "[Epistle to Augusta]" with its admission that "I have been cunning in mine overthrow, / The careful pilot of my proper woe" (23–24). It is quite another matter to demand that your art take up literally unspeakable matters – Byron's "home desolation" as well as his love for his sister Augusta – and force them into a public sphere of discussion. The move involves far more than a breach of aesthetic decorum, it sets a whole new agenda for what we think about the limits of art. Which is precisely what Byron's great nineteenth-century European inheritors thought it did.

The contrivance of Byron's move spans, and requires, the entire work. This fact is nicely illustrated in the full dramatic management of that curse and judgment pronounced in the play's great "Incantation." Not many writers have found the courage, or the stylistic means, to unleash their conscience upon themselves, in public, in this way:

> Though thou seest me not pass by,
> Thou shalt feel me with thine eye
> As a thing that, though unseen,
> Must be near thee, and hath been . . . .
> And a magic voice and verse
> Hath baptized thee with a curse;
> And a spirit of the air
> Hath begirt thee with a snare;
> In the wind there is a voice
> Shall forbid thee to rejoice;
> And to thee shall Night deny
> All the quiet of her sky . . .
>
> By thy cold breast and serpent smile,
> By thy unfathom'd gulfs of guile,
> By that most seeming virtuous eye,
> By thy shut soul's hypocrisy;
> By the perfection of thine art
> Which pass'd for human thine own heart;
> By thy delight in others' pain,
> And by thy brotherhood of Cain,
> I call upon thee and compel
> Thyself to be thy proper Hell!
>
> (I, I, 212–215, 222–229, 242–251)

The stylistic procedure of the play does not let us forget that Manfred is the undisguised surrogate of Lord Byron. Nor has the work ever been read otherwise, and this passage is the clear origin of the entire *poète maudit* tradition that runs through so much of our art even to the present.

The great curse is the play's high moral equivalent of what enters from below as travesty and burlesque. These antithetical forces locate the poles of a work that is trying to say something reasonably honest about human sin, weakness, and self-deception. And also about the aspiration to truth-telling in works of art. What *Manfred* ends up arguing, in major part, is that such aspirations are as doomed to failure – to defect and to spoliation – as human beings are doomed to die. That thought is brilliantly dramatized in the final travesty of the play, when Byron deliberately "spoils" the splendid gesture made at the outset in the great Incantation. That first text had pronounced an irrevocable and apparently objective doom upon Manfred. But when the demons enter at the end to carry him off to the "Hell" we all know he deserves, the scene falls apart. Manfred simply refuses to go. So much for grand incantations of doom and damnation. When he answers the melodramatic demands of the demons with his own melodramatic *non serviam*, the spirits from hell lose their high style of talk and fall into a kind of Monty Python stuttering: "But thy many crimes / Have made thee –." And that's all they get to say. When the absurd "*Demons disappear*," only the Abbot remains to uphold the claims of sublimity. He implores Manfred to "Give thy prayers to heaven – / Pray – albeit but in thought – but die not thus." But Manfred sets his sights higher by setting them lower. Dying, Manfred is being "born from the knowledge of [his] own desert." The play's last important pun (on the word "desert") comes in to brilliant effect, spoiling the high rhetoric of its own linear loveliness. (How does one *speak* such a line when the word we hear in it is simultaneously *desert* and *dessert*?) And then it's over.

MAN. Old man! 'Tis not so difficult to die.
[MANFRED *expires*]
ABBOT. He's gone—his soul has ta'en its earthless flight—
Whither? I dread to think—but he is gone.

A death splendid for its unpretentiousness and lack of ceremony, and most of all for the vital signs of its language. Manfred, still a young man, leaves the world with a witty allusion to the old fears of the "Old man," the latter phrase playing ironically with the Christian – and specifically Pauline – source that it echoes. Missing the joke, the Abbot fears what he sees, desires to imagine a more glorious expiration, but finally "dread[s] to think" anything one way or the other. For Byron, who never wants to dread to think anything, the death – the whole ending – is just right.

III

What has all this to do with Wordsworth, you're wondering? I'll try to explain by asking you to think about the way Wordsworth treats the relation of remembering and forgetting. First for Wordsworth, paradoxically and platonically, comes forgetting, as we see it named at the outset of the "Immortality Ode." "Our life is but a sleep and a forgetting" because we are plunged into the maelstrom of experience. In a further paradox, however, Wordsworth argues that this occlusion in the body is the means for the emergence of the soul:

we are laid asleep
In body, and become a living soul;
While with an eye made quiet by the power
Of harmony, and the deep power of joy,
We see into the life of things.
("Tintern Abbey" 45–49)

This ultimate knowledge of a spiritual order develops through acts of remembering. Wordsworth sees a dialectic between two types of what he came to call "spots of time": moments of experience that impress us as both dark and powerful, full of obscure significance; and moments of reflection when the deep meaning of those dark moments gets exposed. The schema of this relation is laid out in the "Preface" to *Lyrical Ballads*. On one hand is the "forgetting" of immediate experience – the "spontaneous overflow of powerful feeling"; on the other is the "remembering" of reflexive thought – "emotion recollected in tranquillity." Wordsworth appears to have conceived the whole process as the operation of what he called "Imagination."

However that may be, it is a process that functions to repair or redeem our experience of loss and recurrent disaster. With time comes memory, or more exactly an imaginative remembering that overtakes one's inherited sense of loss and transforms it into something said to be "full of blessings." Stories are retold – "Michael," "The Ruined Cottage," pre-eminently *The Prelude* – so that we may re-perceive their originary losses and confusions in benevolent terms.

Byron too, of course, is a great poet of remembering. But a work like *Manfred* helps us to see how differently he engages with the process of remembering and forgetting. Like *Childe Harold III*, *Manfred* begins as a quest to extinguish memory, with all its train of vivid losses and "desolations." At the end of both works, however, as the "Alpine Journal" declares (not to mention all his subsequent poetry and prose), nothing has been forgotten and nothing is redeemed. "In my heart / There is a vigil" of ultimate losses, Manfred says at the outset of his play, and the pain of keeping this vigil brings a desire, or rather a temptation, to forget. The move toward suicide is simply the definitive sign of what he knows but is reluctant to accept: that so long as he lives he will never forget. As it turns out, he has what he calls a "fatality to live" and hence to remember always. Like the Giaour before him, Manfred keeps his "vigil" of losses and gains, powers and limitations, end-to-end. So does the Giaour, but his vigil is maintained under tormented pressures: "The cherish'd madness of [his] heart" (line 1151). In Manfred, by contrast, the pressure of the fatality of living turns more mixed and fluctuating, like the tones of his play – ultimately, like the tones of *Don Juan*. Above the latter, the entrance not to hell but to the tragi-comical human world, is written the following motto:

> In play, there are two pleasures for your choosing,
> The one is winning, and the other losing.

The Byronic ethos, then, has no need of the redemptive processes put into play through the Wordsworthian imagination. Or rather, the need for forgiveness and redemption does not locate something ultimate and transformational, it is one more need among the strange variety of needs that constellate in the fatality of living. This view of the matter gets argued very clearly in Manfred's governing desire to see Astarte once more and to extract "forgiveness" from her. The climactic scene, a piece of full-blown Gothic phantasmagoria, ends in the purest irresolution and anti-climax, fittingly underscored in the outrageous joke about the "awful spirit."

Manfred asks of Astarte, his epipsyche and imaginative ideal, "One word for mercy." She gives him what he asks when she responds with the word: "Manfred." This is the play's term of grace, one word naming something at once grand and ridiculous: this character, Byron's play. Both of the term's values, moreover, derive from an underlying commitment to the kind of self-conscious thought that Byron's play epitomizes: the clarity and candor of an Enlightenment ideal, what he calls "the right of thought" in Canto IV of *Childe Harold*, "our last and only place of refuge" (lines 1137–1138). Ultimately the "vigil" Manfred keeps is to the act of thought itself, and Astarte is the emblem of that act. Her supreme moment comes when she "gaze[s] on" the heart that Manfred opened to her awareness and, *with Manfred looking on*, "withered" at what she saw. In terms of this psychodrama, her disappearance after that event is the dramatic sign of Manfred's "last infirmity of evil" (II, 2, 29), that is, his desire to conceal or alter the full truth: in his own words, "To justify my deeds unto myself" (II, 2, 28).

At this point a Wordsworthian comparison can usefully be drawn. My example is *The Prelude*, which is Wordsworth's story of the Imagination: "what it is, and what it would become," how it was "Impaired" and how it was "Restored." The problem is that this uplifting story regularly, and I think inevitably, belies itself. Inevitably because Wordsworth's own aesthetic is committed to a dialectical "counter-spirit." So at the end of Book XII, when the tale of the restored Imagination is being completed and the benevolent theory of the spots of time fully set forth, Wordsworth's vision turns dark. The restored Imagination foresees its own death:

> The days gone by
> Return upon me almost from the dawn
> Of life: the hiding-places of man's power
> Open; I would approach them, but they close.
> I see by glimpses now; when age comes on
> May scarcely see at all. (XII, 276–281)

We are moved by such undefended sincerity, and would perhaps now rather wish that the poem had ended there, crowned in its own spoliation, the revelation of its failure.

It does not. The concluding Books, and in particular Book XIV, turn to dispel the darknesses raised by Wordsworth's narrative, and finally propose the work as an exemplary moral tale – a tale that our culture, alas, has often accepted at that face value. However that may be, the consequence in the poem is a series of dismal recapitulating texts that we may register as either deliberate acts of bad faith, or as moments of lapsed awareness induced perhaps by the "more habitual sway" of a certain kind of writing and thinking that Wordsworth programmatically cultivated. So, for example, when he assures us that his autobiography has not left out anything of consequence – that it has "Told what best merits mention" (370) and regularly determined to stand up

Amid conflicting interests, and the shock
Of various tempers; to endure and note
What was not understood, though known to be;
Among the mysteries of love and hate,
Honour and shame, looking to right and left,
Unchecked by innocence too delicate,
And moral notions too intolerant,
Sympathies too contracted. (333–341)

we are only too aware that Wordsworth knew very well how much of importance he deliberately left out – how many of those "conflicting interests" of "love and hate / Honour and shame" in particular. We now name them, generically, "Annette Vallon," and Kenneth Johnston's splendid new biography has somewhat lengthened the list. So a passage like this deconstructs itself, as does Wordsworth's declaration that finally

the discipline
And consummation of a Poet's mind,
In everything that stood most prominent
Have faithfully been pictured. (303–306)

The Wordsworthian program of sincerity is here exposed, by the law of its own dialectic, as a program of bad faith. Has he simply forgotten, this disciple of Memory? It is hard to believe. The structures of Memory that Wordsworth so cherished will return upon these passages – it will take some one-hundred years – and force them to deliver up their larger truths – not just the "facts" uncovered in certain birth records, but the truths preserved, as Wordsworth might have said, "behind" those facts. And the poem will grow all the greater for these postponed, contradictory revelations.

In *The Prelude* Wordsworth covers his sins. His first impulse in writing the poem had been to displace his tortured memory into the fictive terms of the story of Vaudracour and Julia. But as he went over the poem again and again, recollecting it in further tranquillities, if they can be called that, he air-brushed the memory from his text altogether. The paradoxical result of this – we all know our Freud – is a poetry indurated to its remarkable melancholy. "Loss" in Wordsworth is saved for ever, in secret, where its power feeds all that splendid and terrible verse. Wordsworth could not bring himself to cast an Incantation across his work, or make sure his readers had clear access to his deepest terrors – personal terrors that eclipsed – how sad to think so! – *The* Terror of the French Revolution. But because Wordsworth is a great poet his own work inevitably – art too has its fatalities – rose up against itself. One thinks of Pound's *Cantos*, that masterpiece of broken and misguided dreams. *The Prelude* is another masterpiece of another common human frailty: bad faith. Reading it one recalls that agonizing masterpiece, Wordsworth's "Elegiac Stanzas, Suggested by a Picture of Peele Castle," where the epigraph for *The Prelude* is written in two wondrous lines:

> The feeling of my loss will ne'er be old;
> This, which I know, I speak with mind serene.
> (39–40)

And what about Byron? Well, he writes *Manfred*, a text that comes as close as one could imagine – certainly in 1816 – to *uncovering* what Manfred describes to Astarte as "The deadliest sin to love as we have loved" (II, 4, 124). That Manfred is Byron's surrogate has never been in doubt. But seeing this, readers have rarely seen that Manfred is also, no less than figures like Oedipus and Hamlet, an Everyman. Manfred, Lord Byron: c'est moi. That is what the play argues, for better – Manfred is splendid – and for worse – Manfred is a coward, a hypocrite, a "deadly" sinner. Readers recoil from this revelation because Byron takes the revelation of sin to the limit and beyond. We are sinners who want to cover our sins, to mitigate their depth. This desire is precisely "the last infirmity of evil" that Byron wrote his play to engage. No cultural taboo has greater authority than the taboo against incest – no taboo, that is, except one: to think about and reveal a taboo, to open it to the light and "right of thought." This is what *Manfred* accomplishes. It is an act of remembering in public, an act that argues the need to preserve an eternal "vigil" to unedited memory and unconstrained thought. As the case of Wordsworth shows, this need is not just Lord Byron's. The "shut soul's hypocrisy" is a defining human impulse. Byron's friends burned his *Memoirs*. Bad faith comes with the best of intentions.

Acts have consequences, and one of the consequences of *Manfred* is *Don Juan*, a poem that takes the full measure of the fatality of living. For sheer range of affective awareness, only *The Canterbury Tales*, among English masterpieces, compares with it. *The Prelude*, like *Paradise Lost*, is an epic of redemption, for better and for worse. Blake took the measure of Milton's bad faith in a poem he named after the great Puritan; *The Prelude*, all unwillingly, took its own. But *Don Juan* and *The Canterbury Tales* are epics of life. Byron v. Wordsworth, Chaucer v. Milton: "These two classes of men are always upon earth and they should be enemies. Who ever seeks to reconcile them seeks to destroy existence." As Blake, that wise man, knew, we sinners have need of both.

IV

Coda: The literal world of Manfred

Picture a man burning up in a fog of thought. Picture the fog burning off. (Jean Day, *The Literal World* [1998])

In *Manfred*, Byron constructs an argument about the status of the creative imagination as understood in Romantic categories. The argument is mounted largely in stylistic terms, and in a consciously dialectical relation to audience reactions that Byron took as a point of departure. As such, the drama enacts the argument through the management of its characters and dramatic paraphernalia. The play's "realism," or the manner in which it executes an "imitation of life," is not situated at the level of the "Dramatis Personae" and their presumptive world of space, time, and circumstance. Those figures and their "world" provide Byron with the terms in which he casts his argument. The chief character, Manfred, functions primarily as a dramatic *figura* – literally, a representation – that can point to the work's true chief referent, Lord Byron, who is the play's persistent unseen or absent presence, the master of the play's literal revels. What we are asked to witness is a drama of the action of Byron's mind as it functions in a poetical, or as Coleridge would say in an "image making," mode. The play seeks to draw out judgments and conclusions about that kind of human action by putting the image-making faculty and its operations on full display. *Manfred* is therefore, quite literally, what Byron would later call "mental theatre."

Manfred's pride centers the action and the play opens as he passes critical judgment on his own Faustian powers. If supremacy of knowledge reveals the limits of knowledge, as Manfred argues, what is to be done? Manfred decides to pursue a final act of self-deconstruction, as if "Oblivion, self-oblivion" (I, 144) will remove the last vestiges of his proud illusions. To carry out this purpose he summons his powers to undertake their final task and last judgment. He begins by calling up an irreal world "by the written charm / Which gives me power" (I, 35–36) upon that world and its creatures. This highly reflexive statement locates the source of transnatural orders at a "literal" level. As Blake earlier observed, all gods reside in the human breast and *Manfred* comes to repeat that view. For the remainder of the play we will be forced to see all the transcendental creatures as the "subjects" of Manfred's ideas and purposes. The consequence of this representation is that we will also perceive Manfred as a second-order representation, the invented creature of an unseen but presiding power: literally, of Lord Byron.

The play's first act establishes these general dramatic terms of engagement. In addition, it dramatizes the problem that drives the action forward. Manfred's pride rests in the illusion he cherishes of his own power and self-sufficiency. The revelation of Manfred's unacknowledged limits comes first when his own summoned spirits trick him with an unexpected illusion. When he tells the spirits that "there is no form on earth / Hideous or beautiful to me" (I, 184–185), they cast up before him "*the shape of a beautiful female figure.*" Manfred is thrown into confusion by this image of Astarte precisely because he had forgotten that he had cherishings and attachments. Manfred's creatures come to humble his forgetful pride.

Two important consequences emerge from this event. First, we realize that Manfred is as yet unaware of the full range of his mind's powers and desires. Second, we see that his creatures have the ability to raise the level of his self-awareness. As the play unfolds we will also realize that Manfred's experience in this regard carries a more general imaginative argument about the function of art in a Byronic view. Artistic creations are not valued in themselves, as if they were self-subsistent things. Viewed in that way, creatures of imagination become "forms of worship" rather than "poetic tales." Byron's play is written to show what the "creative imagination" actually is: not the revelation of the reality of transcendental orders but the enactment of the power that human beings have to expose themselves to judgment and self-knowledge.

In a Romantic frame of reference – that is to say, in *Manfred*'s frame of reference – these purposes require special resourcefulness. For the power of the human mind is such that when it ceases to worship transcendental gods and spirits, it opens itself to the danger of "an ignorance . . . / Which is another kind of ignorance" (II, 4, 62–63): the worship of itself and its own powers. This temptation, a peculiarly Romantic one, is of course figured as Manfred's pride, which is in turn a trope for Lord Byron's own poetical gifts and pretensions. Undoing the power of that temptation entails another, yet more radically paradoxical move. Byron's play, it turns out, can only succeed by attacking itself, satirizing and exposing itself to itself. This move comes as Byron's invitation to the audience to observe the work of the play in its full dramatic reality – that is, to see the theatricality of the events as well as the procedures that establish their theatricality.

To carry through that purpose Byron constructs *Manfred* as a proto-Brechtian play about itself. The audience registers this level of the action as a drama of style keyed to various kinds of ironizing and comical elements.

Act I makes two ironical moves that set limits to Manfred's initial Faustian position. The first, already noted, culminates in the trick that the spirits play at the expense of Manfred's initial pretension to self-sufficiency. Then comes the Interlude of the famous "Incantation" when "*A Voice*" passes its majestic ironical judgment on the "senseless" Manfred. The next sequence, which runs from Act I scene 2 through Act II scene I, involves the exchange between Manfred and the Chamois Hunter. This event brings an abrupt stylistic turn, the first of many that characterize the play. A Wordsworthian solitary and figure of simple virtues, the hunter's most important function is rhetorical, not eventual. In his dialogue with Manfred we register a quasi-comical discrepancy between the discourse of these two men:

C. HUNTER . . . When thou art better, I will be thy guide—But whither?
MAN. It imports not: I do know
My route full well, and need no further guidance.
C. HUNTER. Thy garb and gait bespeak thee of high lineage—
One of the many chiefs, whose castled crags
Look o'er the lower valleys—which of these
May call thee Lord? I only know their portals;
My way of life leads me but rarely down
To bask by the huge hearths of those old halls,
Carousing with the vassals; but the paths,
Which step from out our mountains to their doors,
I know from childhood—which of these is thine?
MAN. No matter.
C. HUNTER. Well, sir, pardon me the question,
And be of better cheer. Come, taste my wine. (II, I, 4–17)

A passage like this recalls nothing so much as Wordsworth's stylistic innovations carried out through his *Lyrical Ballads* experiment, and in particular his comments on the relation of verse and prose. Shakespearean iambics sit awkwardly on the Chamois Hunter, who seems to speak in a clumsy and unnatural style, and Manfred's laconic responses come to set a frame around this quality in his humble interlocutor's speech. Cast in heroic verse, the hunter's virtuous simplicities seem overblown, as if he had forgotten the prose inheritance he should have received from the low characters in Shakespeare. In other contexts – *Don Juan*, for example – Byron will critique Wordsworth's theories about poetic diction. Here, by contrast, he utilizes them for theatrical purposes. At one level the drama is realistic and the interchange defines a difference in social class and attitudes. Because the play is Romantic and not Shakespearean, however, moments like this drift out of Shakespearean objectivity into subjective and self-conscious space. In that space – which is the space of all Romantic drama from *The Castle Spectre* to *Death's Jest Book* – we witness what Arnold would later call "the dialogue of the mind with itself." The drift is completely apparent in the following exchange:

> C. HUNTER. Man of strange words, and some half-maddening sin,
> Which makes thee people vacancy, whate'er
> Thy dread and sufferance be, there's comfort yet—
> The aid of holy men, and heavenly patience—
> MAN. Patience and patience! Hence—that word was made
> For brutes of burthen, not for birds of prey;
> Preach it to mortals of a dust like thine,—
> I am not of thine order.
> C. HUNTER. Thanks to heaven!
> I would not be of thine for the free fame
> Of William Tell; but whatsoe-er thine ill,
> It must be borne. And these wild starts are useless.
>
> (II, I, 31–41)

Thus does Byron bring Wordsworth to expose Byronic creativity to itself. As earlier the spirits had mocked Manfred's un-selfconsciousness, here the Chamois Hunter does the same with an ironical remark delivered in an unpretentious conversational register. To the Chamois Hunter, Manfred seems slightly ridiculous, perhaps even "mad," but ultimately pitiful. To a proud character like Manfred, these judgments bring a new wave of self-revulsion. He parts from the Chamois Hunter, who saved his life, a chastened and a wiser man: "I . . . can endure thy pity. I depart . . . I know my path – the mountain peril's past" (II, I, 91–92, 95). The symbolic valence of that last figure of speech is so patent ("mountain peril" = Manfred's pride) that the verse once again turns self-conscious and Romantic: we see right through Manfred's words (theatrical realism) to their expressive source (Byron's argumentative poetical purposes).

The next scene brings the Witch of the Alps and another abrupt change in rhetoric. Coming in the wake of the stylistic issues raised in the Chamois Hunter scenes, this event appears a Romantic-allegorical discussion of the function and status of art and poetry to the Faustian consciousness. The Witch offers Manfred permanent forms of beauty as a refuge from his psychic torments. His refusal, a hinge event in the play, entails Manfred's conscious assumption of responsibility for all of his "deeds." More crucially, he assumes this responsibility knowing that neither he nor his subject forms, of whom the Witch is one, can alleviate or redeem his sufferings, or define his desires. His next move after this encounter, then, is toward "what it is we dread to be" (II, 2, 179), that is, into the territory where human resources appear to have no purchase at all, into the land of the dead.

How can this possibly be done? Byron's solution to that apparently insoluble problem is stylistic. The unknown world, for a poet, will be the place where art comes to its end. This place is forecast in the following passage in Act I, where Manfred passes a mordant judgment on human beings as

> Half dust, half deity, alike unfit
> To sink or soar, with our mix'd essence make
> A conflict of [earth's] elements, and breathe
> The breath of degradation and of pride,
> Contending with low wants and lofty will
> Till our mortality predominates . . .
>
> (I, 2, 40–45)

In the climactic moment of the drama Manfred enters that world, which is the world of his own mind. It is a world later glimpsed in appalled horror by the Wordsworthian Abbot, who recapitulates Manfred's earlier description:

> This should have been a noble creature: he
> Hath all the energy which would have made
> A goodly frame of glorious elements,
> Had they been wisely mingled; as it is,
> It is an awful chaos—light and darkness—
> And mind and dust—and passions and pure thoughts,
> Mix'd, and contending without end or order,
> All dormant or destructive: he will perish . . . .
>
> (III, 1, 160–167)

This description of Manfred's mind is a figural definition of the play's own medleyed and "deliberately defective" style. When Manfred calls the dead in the drama's central scenes – Act II Scenes 3–4 – he moves to bring the uninhibited "chaos" of this mind into full play.

Manfred plunges suddenly into its Goethean *Walpurgisnacht* with the entrance of the Three Destinies, who sing their reckless comic lyrics about an amoral disordering order that in their view is the ground of existence. Historical nightmares return – a distorted and grotesque Napoleon, for instance – but here they come resurrected in even more shocking and ambiguous forms:

> The captive Usurper,
> Hurl'd down from the throne,
> Lay buried in torpor,
> Forgotten and lone;
> I broke through his slumbers,
> I shivered his chain,
> I leagued him with numbers—
> He's Tyrant again!
>
> With the blood of a million he'll answer my care,
> With a nation's destruction—his flight and despair.
> (II, 3, 16–25)

These summary words of the First Destiny epitomize the argument made in the play's set of ludic songs: "This wreck of a realm – this deed of my doing – / For ages I've done, and shall still be renewing!" (52–53). These ideas and images culminate in the monstrous joke on the word "awful," where the play's anarchic revelations achieve their self-conscious and deconstructive climax. The more Gothic paraphernalia Byron brings forward, the more ludicrous and "awful," in both senses of that word, does the action become. Like Samson, Byron is pulling down every conceivable Temple of Fame and Delight, most importantly the Temple of his own work and the Idea of Art that it instantiates. The paradox of the work is thus extreme and finally incommensurable. And if we think, like Carlyle, that its program amounts merely to some "Everlasting Nay," we will want to reflect on the Nietzschean implications of wrecks that are at once ageless and "renewing."

These are, quite simply, the wrecks of a new order of the Romantic imagination, for which *Manfred* is both argument and example. Instead of proposing as the rule of art a "willing suspension of disbelief" Byron offers a rule founded in the deliberate installation of disbelief. Manfred's final address to the setting sun emblemizes this demand for enlightenment: "Most glorious orb! Thou wert a worship ere / The mystery of thy making was revealed" (III, 2, 9–10). At such moments one realizes the affinities that put Blake and Byron in their critical relation to Wordsworth and Coleridge: "God appears and God is Light / To those poor souls who dwell in Night / But does a human form display / To those who dwell in realms of day." The paradoxical result of Byron's skepticism is the emergence of a non-natural, a wholly poetical and imaginative world. This new world appears as the enactment of the form of *Manfred*, which unravels itself as the mystery of its making gets revealed by its own maker. In this new order, forms of worship are translated back to poetic tales, their primal state. Purged of the obscurities of suspended disbelief, the human imagination discovers an ultimate, perhaps therefore a terrifying, freedom. After *Manfred* there are no redemptive schemes because the play gives it allegiance only to "this deed of my doing" and not to the rules that set limits to such deeds. The play knows the rules and acknowledges the power of those "dead, but sceptred sovereigns, who still rule / Our spirits from their urns" (III, 4, 40–41). Acknowledging is not the same thing as obeying, however, and obedience itself may be a choice to be made or unmade at discretion (or indiscretion). If *Manfred* (and Manfred) (and Byron) are defeated by what Foucault called "The Order of Things," they all also show how one might engage a process of "making death a victory" ("Prometheus," 59).

No gods, human or transhuman, survive the coming of this work, where pictures of the mind revive only from a specific mind, reminding us that words like "wreck" and "renewing" reference particular, mortal events. These events will be as simple and as catastrophic as the break-up of a marriage or an exile from home. If a play like *Manfred* suggests that these events also involve some kind of cosmic meaning, that is because the play attaches ultimate value to quotidian human emergencies.

Among those emergencies Death has been set apart as a summary and standard, a kind of ultimate sign that "The Order of Things" must be obeyed. *Manfred* argues a different view. Death in this play, as Manfred's death shows, need be no more imposing or terrible than the mortal person who undergoes its momentary authority – unless of course, as the Abbot's life shows, the individual imagination assents to the Myth of Death. Death does not have dominion in Byron's play, Manfred does; and Manfred's victory, which arrives with his death, becomes the final exponent and symbol of Byron's art of "deliberate defects." One may perhaps think forward to those fierce and clarified lines that climax Byron's great lyric "On This Day I Complete My Thirty-Sixth Year":

> If thou regret'st thy Youth, *why live?*
> The land of honourable Death
> Is here:—up to the Field, and give
> Away thy Breath!

NOTES

1 See my "The Book of Byron and the Book of a World," in *The Beauty of Inflections. Literary Investigations in Historical Method and Theory* (Oxford: Clarendon Press, 1985), 277–286.

2 De Staël, 291. Her entire discussion of *Faust* (270–293) is deeply relevant to an understanding not only of *Manfred*, but of *Don Juan* as well. Byron was clearly much influenced by De Staël's view of Romanticism. Her analysis of *Faust* hinges on her insights into the play's deliberated violations of decorum and mixtures of different styles (see De Staël, especially pp. 276 and 291). *Manfred* is thus in every sense a continuation of *Faust* along lines that De Staël's brilliant interpretation suggested to Byron. He first read her book in 1812 or 1813.

BIBLIOGRAPHY

Cooke, Michael G. "Byron and Wordsworth: The Complementarity of a Rock and the Sea," in *Lord Byron and his Contemporaries*, ed. Charles E. Robinson. London and Toronto: Associated University Presses, 1982, pp. 19–42.

Foucault, Michel. *The Order of Things. An Archaeology of the Human Sciences.* New York: Vintage Books, 1973.

Garber, Frederick. "Continuing *Manfred*," in *Critical Essays on Lord Byron*, ed. Robert F. Gleckner. New York: G. K. Hall and Co., 1991, pp. 228–248.

Gill, Stephen, ed. *William Wordsworth.* Oxford Authors Series. New York: Oxford University Press, 1984.

Johnston, Kenneth. *The Hidden Wordsworth. Poet. Lover. Rebel. Spy.* New York: W. W. Norton & Co., 1998.

Levine, Alice, and Robert N. Keane, eds. *Rereading Byron. Essays Selected From Hofstra University's Byron Bicentennial Conference.* New York and London: Garland Publishing Inc., 1993.

Lovell, Ernest J., Jr., ed. *His Very Self and Voice. Collected Conversations of Lord Byron.* New York: Macmillan, 1954.

Medwin's Conversations of Lord Byron. Princeton: Princeton University Press, 1966.

Marchand, Leslie A., ed. *Byron's Letters and Journals.* 13 vols. London: John Murray Ltd., 1973–1982.

Martin, Philip W. *Byron. A Poet Before his Public.* Cambridge: Cambridge University Press, 1982.

McGann, Jerome. *The Beauty of Inflections. Literary Investigations in Historical Method and Theory*. Oxford: Clarendon Press, 1985.

ed. *Lord Byron. The Complete Poetical Works*. 7 vols. Oxford: Clarendon Press, 1980–1992.

McVeigh, Daniel M. "Manfred's Curse," *Studies in English Literature* 22 (1982), 601–612.

Moorman, Mary. *William Wordsworth. A Biography*. 2 vols. Oxford: Clarendon Press, 1965.

Sperry, Stuart M. "Byron and the Meaning of *Manfred*," *Criticism* 16 (1974), 189–202.

De Staël-Holstein, Madame Anne Louise Germaine. *De L'Allemagne*. Paris: Didot, 1845.

West, Paul. *Byron and the Spoiler's Art*. London: Chatto and Windus, 1960.

PART II

CHAPTER 10

A point of reference

The concept – and the problem – of the referential aspects of literary works is so central to an adequate literary theory and critical practice that it must be addressed. Two things may be initially observed. First, referentiality appears as "a problem" in formalist and text-centered studies precisely by its absence. Though everyone knows and agrees that literary works have socio-historical dimensions, theories and practices generated in text-centered critical traditions bracket out these matters from consideration, particularly at the level of theory.[1] Second, referentiality appears as a problem in historically grounded criticism because such criticism has thus far been unable to revise its theoretical grounds so as to take account of the criticisms which were brought against it in this [the twentieth] century, and in particular the criticisms developed out of the theory of literary mediations. Involved here is the view, pressed strongly on various fronts in the past fifty years, that language and language structures (including, perforce, literary works) are modeling rather than mirroring forms. They do not point to a prior, authorizing reality (whether "realist" or "idealist"), they themselves *constitute* – in both the active and the passive senses – what must be taken as reality (both "in fact" and "in ideals"). To the extent that traditional forms of historical criticism have not been able to assimilate or refute such a view, they have been moved to the periphery of literary studies.

In recent years, however, textual and intertextual approaches have begun to yield up their own theoretical problems, and literary studies have witnessed a renewed interest in various kinds of socio-historical critical work. Marxist and Marxist-influenced criticism has been an especially important factor in this development, largely, I think, because the questions it poses are founded in a powerful and dynamically coherent tradition of critical inquiry. Feminist studies have also done much to expose the socio-historical dimensions of literary work. Because both of these critical approaches necessarily practice a hermeneutics of a repressed or invisibilized content, both have found no difficulty in assimilating the basic poststructural programmatic. At the same time, the traditional methods of historicist philology have also begun to reappear in interpretive studies. Bibliography, manuscript studies of various kinds, analyses of the forms, methods, and materials of literary production: these materialist and empirical branches of learning have been experiencing a renascence and at the same time have begun to rediscover their theoretical ground. Hermeneutical studies are increasingly realizing that the symbolic discourse which is literature operates with and through many forms of mediation besides "language" narrowly conceived. The price of a book, its place of publication, even its physical form and the institutional structures by which it is distributed and received, all bear upon the production of literary meaning, and hence all must be critically analyzed and explained.

When we speak of the referential dimensions of literary work, therefore, we have in mind several different things. In the first place, literary work can be practiced, can constitute itself, only in and through various institutional forms which are not themselves "literary" at all, though they are meaning-constitutive. The most important of these institutions, for the past 150 years anyway, are the commercial publishing network in all its complex parts, and the academy. The church and the court have, in the past, also served crucial mediating functions for writers. Literary works are produced *with reference to* these mediational structures, are in fact embodied in such structures, and criticism is therefore obliged to explain and reconstitute such structures in relation to the literary work. As we now realize more clearly than ever before, criticism must factor itself and its own mediations into its explanations. In the final accounting, "the work" and its mediations are as inseparable as are "the (original) work" and its (subsequent) critical explanations.

Historically considered, the problem of referentiality first appeared not as a fault line in empirically based critical studies, but much earlier, in the Kantian response to the philosophic grounds of empiricism. Derrida's influential account of the textual dynamic ("the joyous affirmation of the play of the world and of the innocence of becoming, the affirmation of a world of signs without fault, without truth, without origin, offered to an active interpretation")[2] recalls nothing so much as the opening of Kant's *Critique of Judgment*, in which not only is the radical subjectivity of the esthetic event founded, but it is founded via an explication of the judging subject rather than the "work of art." Coleridge's important variation on this Kantian move was to emphasize even more clearly the "ideal" content which the poetic text constitutes. Poetical works do not "copy" the phenomena of the external world, they "imitate" the ideal forms which we know through the operations of the human mind.[3] As a good recent critic of Coleridge has put the matter: "The 'reality' that poems 'imitate' is not the objective world as such, but . . . the consciousness of the poet himself *in his encounters with* the objective world . . . the poet's only genuine subject matter is himself, and the only ideas he presents will be ideas about the activity of consciousness in the world around it."[4] Coleridge's critique of the insistently referential aspects of Wordsworth's poetry – what he calls its "accidentality" and its "matter-of-factness" – is merely the critical reflex of his positive position: that "poetry as poetry is essentially *ideal*, [and] avoids and excludes all *accident* [and] apparent individualities."[5]

Coleridge is himself an impressive historicist critic, as his commentaries on the biblical tradition show. Nevertheless, his theoretical ground would eventually be appropriated by those idealist and subjectivist forms of criticism which emerged out of twentieth-century linguistics and semiology. If "poetry as poetry" has reference only to a field of subjectivity, then the criticism and interpretation of poetry which pursue the accidentalities and matters-of-fact of philology will themselves be necessarily misguided.

Coleridge's view is recapitulated, in a variety of ways, by all twentieth-century practitioners of purely immanent critical methods. C. S. Lewis's remarks in "The Personal Heresy" in 1934, and Cleanth Brooks's in *The Well Wrought Urn* (1947), typify the New Critical position on the matter of poetry's relation to socio-historical actualities.[6] That is to say, while the New Criticism was a vigorously antihistorical movement, and consciously in reaction to the philological and historicist methods which had come to pre-eminence in literary studies during the eighteenth and nineteenth centuries, it always made practical provision for certain "extrinsic" materials in the poetic product. The position is epitomized in Wellek and Warren's widely used handbook *Theory of Literature* (1947), where the concepts of "intrinsic" and "extrinsic" interpretation are enshrined. Equally characteristic are formulations like the following by Brooks, who means to have an organic–intrinsic idea of the poem, but cannot altogether evade the informational–extrinsic dimensions of the text: "If we see that any item in a poem is to be judged only in terms of the total effect of the poem, we shall readily grant the importance for criticism of the work of the linguist and the literary historian."[7]

In short, the intrinsic and text-centered approaches of the early and mid twentieth century made certain tactical accommodations and compromises in their critical programs and arguments. Indeed, it was precisely this compromised status of their theory which brought them to ruin at the hands of their ungrateful children, the deconstructionists. For the latter had no difficulty in showing that New Critical strategies were based upon an illusory and mystified form of the very empiricism which those strategies were consciously designed to displace. The idea of "the poem itself," of the stable (if paradoxical) object of critical attention, was swept away in the aftermath of structuralism. "De-ferral," "de-stabilization," "de-centering," "de-construction": the history of the emergence of these ideas during the 1970s is well known and needs no rehearsing again here. Nor will it be necessary to point out what is equally well known, that the deconstructionist movement was (and of course is) a form of immanent criticism's twentieth-century wilderness.

Two important aspects of these late forms of immanent criticism do need to be attended to, however. The first is the extremity of their antihistorical position. None of the earlier twentieth-century text-centered critics ever spoke, as J. Hillis Miller has spoken in one of his most celebrated essays, of "the fiction of the referential, the illusion that the terms of the poem refer literally to something that exists."[8] This bold pronouncement offers a final solution to the problem of the social actuality of poetical work, and it is quite typical of (at any rate) the American deconstructive establishment. The repudiation of referentiality is made, as Miller says, "according to the logic of a theory of language which bases meaning on the solid referentiality of literal names for visible physical object."[9] Here Miller intends to dispose once and for all of that Great Satan of so many humanists, "empiricism," by dismissing at last the supposed "theory of language" on which it rests.

In making his attack, however, Miller unwittingly exposes another important aspect of his critical position. That is to say, he reveals his assent to a particular concept of referentiality. A "solid" correspondence of "literal names for visible physical objects" is certainly *an* idea of referentiality, but it is manifestly an impoverished concept. This idea of how language "refers" to the actual world where those language forms called poems operate may reflect the view which someone (besides Miller) has held at some time or other. It is not, however, characteristic of the thought of the great traditional philological and historical critics. When Miller dismisses this concept of referentiality, then, he is trying to cast out a mere phantom. His dismissal thus fails to confirm his own critical practice.

Of course one can, with some searching, find other critics besides deconstructionists like Miller who have subscribed to excessively simple concepts of referentiality. When Daniel Aaron, for example, says that "the historian who writes about the past might be likened to a naturalist as he observes and analyzes specimens in a museum or perhaps animals caged in a zoo,"[10] his words betray a concept of referentiality that is quite comparable to Miller's. One is tempted to reply merely that this is not a persuasive idea, and that it runs counter to the lines of historical thought which have dominated critical thought for almost three centuries. But one might do better to quote, for example, Vico's stronger thought, that "human history differs from natural history in this, that we have made the former, but not the latter."[11] Indeed, it is Miller's sympathy with Vico's thought which has helped to set him, along with so many other recent literary critics, in opposition to "referentiality."

What is necessary at this juncture, therefore, is not to bracket the referential dimensions of poetry out of critical consideration on the basis of an impoverished theory of language and literary reference. Rather, we should be trying to recover and reformulate the idea of referentiality which underlies the thought of the great historical critics of the recent past. Only in this way will the full significance of Miller's excellent critical work – and the work of many other immanentist critics – be revealed. The American line of Derridean thought, in particular, would do well to recall the following passage from Derrida himself: "A deconstructive practice which would not bear upon 'institutional apparatuses and historical processes' . . . , which would remain content to operate upon philosophemes or conceptual signified[s], or discourses, etc., would not be deconstructive; whatever its originality, it would but reproduce the gesture of self criticism in philosophy in its internal tradition."[12] When Miller, in his essay "The Critic as Host," speaks of "deconstructive strategy" as "going with a given text as far as it will go, to its limits," he echoes Derrida, as he does when he goes on to add that all criticism, including deconstructive criticism, "contains, necessarily, its enemy within itself."[13] But the fact is that American deconstructionism does not go to those limits and does not expose its internal fault lines. On the contrary, it hides and obscures them at every turn. The enemy which deconstructive critics like Miller will not face is history, and the fault line of such criticism appears as its elision of the socio-historical dimensions of literary work.

At the beginning of his first book, *L'épithète traditionnelle dans Homère* (1928), Milman Parry consciously set his work in the line of the great tradition of modern historical scholarship.

> The literature of every country and of every time is understood as it ought to be only by the author and his contemporaries . . . The task, therefore, of one who lives in another age and wants to appreciate that work correctly, consists precisely in rediscovering the varied information and complexes of ideas which the author assumed to be the natural property of his audience.[14]

Parry is quick to observe that this scholarly project of "reconstructing that [original] community of thought through which the poet made himself understood" is a task "so complex as to be impossible of realization in an entirely satisfactory manner."[15] Nevertheless, the project must be pursued if we are to hope to have any reliable understanding of the culture of the past.

The twentieth-century attack upon the historical method in criticism, initially focused on the so-called intentional fallacy, soon became a broadly based critique of genetic studies in general. John M. Ellis's *The Theory of Literary Criticism: A Logical Analysis* (1974) has summarized and completed this line of critique. His argument is not merely that genetic studies cannot recover the "original context," but that the human meaning of literary works does not lie in that context. Rather, it lies in the context of immediate use: "If we insist on relating the text primarily to the context of its composition and to the life and social context of its author, we are cutting it off from that relation to life which is the relevant one."[16] In addition, genetic criticism limits and shrinks the dynamic potential of literary products by reducing their meanings to "static" forms, and by suggesting that certain "information" can supply "the key to the text" and its meaning.[17] Poststructural critics like Miller would merely take this (ultimately Nietzschean) line of thought to a more extreme position. Genetic criticism is the epitome of all critical forms which seek after the "univocal reading" of a text.[18] For deconstructionists, it does not matter whether the finished reading stands as an "originary" form to which criticism seeks to return, or an accomplished form which criticism makes in its own rhetorical praxis. All are unstable and operating under the sign of *différance*. Thus, "Nihilism is an inalienable alien presence within Occidental metaphysics, both in poems and in the criticism of poems."[19]

Ellis's view that criticism justifies itself in its social praxis is important and will be reconsidered below. Before taking up that matter, however, we have to inquire into the idea that genetic criticism offers static and univocal meanings for literary works. In fact, all the great historicist critics were well aware that their method could not do this. The ideal of reconstructing the originary material and ideological context, even if fully achieved, would provide the later reader only with what "the author assumed to be the natural property of his audience." The method does not offer static and univocal readings, it attempts to specify the concrete and particular forms in which certain human events constituted themselves. The "meanings" of those events, whether for the original persons involved or for any subsequent persons, are themselves specifically constituted events which can and will be reconstituted in the subsequent historical passage of the poem. The "reading" and the "criticism" of poems and the human events they represent set what Blake called a "bounding line" to human action. In this sense criticism – and historical criticism paradigmatically – does not establish the "meanings" of poems, it tries to re-present them to us in "minute particulars," in forms that recover (as it were) their *physique* in as complete detail as possible. Thus Parry says, of the historical reconstruction which his criticism brings about: "I make for myself a picture of great detail,"[20] *not* "I translate for myself and my world the meaning of the ancient texts." The originary "meanings" (Parry's "complexes of ideas which the author assumed") are themselves concrete particulars, not concrete universals; and their complexity involves diverse and often contradictory lines of relations. Historical criticism's great critical advance lay in its ability to reconstruct, in methodical ways, the differential and contradictory patterns within which poetical works constitute themselves and are constituted.

Parry and those like him understood very well that texts and the criticism of texts labored under various destabilizing forces.

> If I say that Grote's account of democracy at Athens is more revealing of the mind of an English Liberal of the nineteenth century after Christ, than it recalls what actually took place in Athens in the fifth century before Christ, and then go on to admit that the opinion which I have just expressed about Grote may in turn reveal even more my own state of mind than it does that of Grote (indeed, I know that I am expressing this thought here because I came across it about two weeks ago in one of the essays submitted for the Bowdoin prize essay contest and it struck me) – even in that case I am still doing no more than to try to attain a more perfect method for the historical approach to the thought of the past.[21]

This is Parry's version of "the critic as host," and it explains why he will state the following basic paradox of historical method: that by it "we learn to keep ourselves out of the past, or rather we learn to go into it."[22] Historical method in criticism clarifies and defines the differentials in concrete and specific ways for the originary and the continuing past, as well as for the immediate present (and the as yet unconstructed future).

These passages are taken from Parry's great essay "The Historical Method in Literary Criticism" (1936), where Parry also expresses "a certain feeling of fear" that this method will "destroy itself."[23] His fear recalls Nietzsche's critique of philological studies expressed in *On the Advantages and the Disadvantages of History for Life*, and anticipates the anti-historical arguments of the immanentist critical methods which, in the early 1930s, were just beginning to gain force and prominence. "I have seen myself, only too often and too clearly, how, because those who teach and study Greek and Latin literature have lost the sense of its importance for humanity, the study of those literatures has declined."[24] What Parry proposes is that scholars "create their heroic legend" of the importance of the historicity, not merely of truth, but of the search for truth: "Otherwise they will be choosing a future in which they must see themselves confined not by choice, but by compulsion, to be forever ineffective, if they would not be untruthful."[25]

In fact, however, historical criticism – at least as it was practiced in the Western academy – did not go on to fulfill what Parry called for. This failure occurred, I believe, because historicist criticism always tended to conceive its terms in a recollective frame. Thus "referentiality," in this program, tended to be construed as bearing upon persons and events which lay behind us, in a completed form of pastness. It is true that language "refers to" particular actualities. But if no historical critic of any standing ever understood this referential connection in the simple empiricist terms laid down by Miller, neither, on the other hand, did they explore the full theoretical implications of some of their most important historicist principles.

"I make for myself a picture of great detail." This is the heart of the historicist program. But the traditional historicists – even late figures like Parry – tended to "read" this picture with their gaze turned backward. Parry knew perfectly well that the picture he made for himself contained historical layers (himself, Grote, fifth-century Greece, as well as many intervenient distances), but when he actually *made* the picture for his audience, the layers and intervenient distances tended to disappear into the outlines of the originary picture. This blurring of the palimpsest seems most obvious to us, now, in the picture's avoidance of its projected future details. These we now call, in general, the "prejudice" (after Gadamer) or "ideology" (after the Marxist tradition) of the critical account.

Any present deployment of historical criticism will have to renovate the original program along such lines. The picture which the historical critic makes is one which includes a future as well as a present and a past, which includes, indeed, many pasts, presents, and futures. Historical criticism can no longer make any part of that sweeping picture unself-consciously, or treat any of its details in an untheorized way. The problem with Parry's brief anecdote about fifth-century Greece, Grote, and himself is that he was unable to incorporate the shrewd insight of this anecdote into his explicit programmatic scheme. As a result, the anecdote stands apart, an ancillary sketch which would not find its way into a single, larger picture of great detail.

In this context we can begin to reconstitute the idea of "referentiality" and even sketch the outlines of a renovated historical criticism. We begin with what Parry called the "detail." For a properly historical criticism – which is to say, in my view, a dialectical criticism – those much-maligned matters of fact are the postulates of a critical discourse. The historical particularity of a poem by Wordsworth or a novel by Austen have to be clearly specified in the act of criticism if that act is to proceed dialectically, i.e., if that act is not simply to project upon "the work" its own conceptual interests. Such elementary particulars establish the ground for a whole system of critical differentials that stretch across the continuing social life of a literary work from its point of origin to its current operations.

These matters ought to be clear enough. What also needs to be said, however, is that the "referent" of any discourse – whether the "original" creative discourse, the intervening discourses of the work's reception, or the immediate discourses of current criticism – cannot be conceived simply as an empirical datum. The matters-of-fact which poems and criticism embody (or constitute) are not – to borrow Coleridge's phraseology – "objects as objects"; rather they are objects-as-subjects, objects which have been (and continue to be) a focus of important human interests.[26] The poems themselves, because they are "social texts" and events, are also objects as subjects, but the poems acquire this character because they "have reference to" the larger (human) world of social interactions. Literary works represent, and are representative of, that larger world.

All this does not mean, however, that the task of criticism is a historicist reconstruction or glossing of a particular work's originary referential field. The critical ideal must be a totalizing one, for literary "works"[27] *continue* to live and move and have their being. The referential field of Byron's *Don Juan* is by no means limited to the period 1789–1824, though that is the explicit frame of the poem's narrativization. *Don Juan* "has reference to" a larger share of the past than the period of its immediate focus. Indeed, that focusing period, as reconstituted through *Don Juan*, is revealed to be itself a vehicle (or system of mediations) by which history is rendered up for human use. In the end, what we must see is that works like *Don Juan* have reference to – make use of and assume an interest in – some more or less comprehensive aspects of the past, and the present and the future as well. Because critical activity shares in that work, it too operates with its own various, and more or less explicit, socio-historical interests.

To recover the concept of referentiality, we might well begin by reminding ourselves that "facts" are not mere data, objects, or monads; they are heuristic isolates which bring into focus some more or less complex network of human events and relations. As such, "facts" always have to be reconstituted if those networks are to be clarified and redeployed. One of the special graces of poetic works – probably their chief social value – is that they are conceptual forms which operate at a high level of generality, on the one hand, and at an equally high level of particularity on the other. The particulars, the "matters-of-fact," are subjected to a general organizing structure which precisely *does not* reduce those particulars to conceptual finishedness, but instead preserves them in a state of (as it were) freedom. The particulars are grains of sand in which the world may be seen – may be seen again and again, in new sets of relations and differentials.

It may be useful to recall at this point the more traditional theory of literary imitation. Sidney's *Defence of Poesie*, the finest English representation of the Aristotelian doctrine of mimesis, concerns itself principally with what he calls "right poets," that is, those poets who in their art of imitation "borrow nothing of what is, hath been, or shall be; but range . . . into the divine consideration of what may be and should be."[28] When Coleridge, in the *Biographia Literaria* and his related essay "On Poesy or Art," distinguishes between what he calls "imitation" and "mere copying," he is recollecting the Aristotelian tradition.[29] In this view, what the poet imitates are not simply matters of fact or accidentalities or minute particulars; the poet imitates the essential qualities of his subject, human beings or individual persons in their generic distinctiveness. As a consequence, since human life – in contrast to the natural world – is distinguished by its spiritual or moral dimensions, the object of poetic imitation will have to be a re-presentation, via a judicious selection of phenomenal details, of noumenal realities.

The authority of this theory of imitation, along with its related concept of referentiality, began to be undermined with the development of eighteenth-century empiricism and modern historical thought. The rise of the novel is connected to the emergence of what we now call "realism," in which accidentalities and matters of fact are crucial to the deployment of a new type of poetic imitation. Among poets, Wordsworth has the distinction of being the first – in the Preface to the *Lyrical Ballads* – to intimate the relevance of these new ideas. Minute particulars of time, place, and circumstance gain in importance (for artists as well as for people in general) when the character of human morals is seen to be a function of social and political processes. Erstwhile "noumenal" realities are *functionally* related both to the determinations of given phenomenal circumstances, on the one hand, and, on the other, to the manipulations of current human perspectives and engagements. Briefly, it came to be believed that if one wanted to understand "human nature" in general, one had to proceed along two dialectically related paths: along the path of a thorough socio-historical set of observations, and along the path of the (now so-called) "sciences of the artificial."[30] For "human nature" was not (is not) "made" by God; it was (and continues to be) artfully, artificially, constructed by human beings themselves in the course of their social development.

What art "imitates," then, what it "has reference to," is this totality of human changes in all its diverse and particular manifestations. Since the totality neither is nor ever can be *conceptually* completed, however, art works must always intersect with it at a differential. That is to say, art must establish its referential systems – including its reference to the totality – in the forms of dynamic particulars which at once gesture toward the place of these particulars in the ceaseless process of totalization, and also assert their freedom within the process. Such freedom is relational, and it illustrates a key element in the maintenance of the process of dynamic totalization: that the particulars which are to count in art, the particular acts, events, circumstances, details, and so forth, along with the textualizations through which they are constituted, are those which in fact *make (and/or have made) a difference* – particulars which will be seen to have been (and to be still) positively engaged in processes of change. Whether these processes offer themselves as progressive or conservative does not in itself matter; in either case the reader's attention will be drawn, via such details, to the socially located tensions and contradictions, as well as the responses to such things, which poetry imitates and participates in. In art and poetry these particulars always appear as *incommensurates*: details, persons, events which the work's own (reflected) conceptual formulas and ideologies must admit, but which they cannot wholly account for.

In this context one may see the emergence of a new theory of representation that has modified the traditional Aristotelian theory. Modern idealist and deconstructive attacks on literary referentiality, and hence on any criticism which presupposes such a concept, assume – as the traditional theory had assumed – that no natural relation exists between "what is, hath been, or shall be," and "what may be and should be." (In traditional theory, the relation between the two is supernatural, whereas in the poststructural model the relation is at best arbitrary and at worst illusory.) Socio-historical criticism, however, argues that "what may be and should be" is always a direct function of "what is, hath been, or shall be," and its theory of representation holds that art imitates not merely the "fact" and the "ideal" but also the dynamic relation which operates between the two.

In addition, socio-historical criticism will both assume and display the *determinate* character of this dynamic relation. This emphasis upon the determinate is fundamental if "what is" is to stand in a *natural* or scientific relation to "what should be." But because knowledge is a project rather than a possession, it always falls short of a complete grasp of its objects. The determinate relation between "what is" and "what should be" is what Shelley had in mind when he spoke of "something longed for, never seen." The determinate is – in the alternative sense of that word – what exists by acts of determination. Knowledge as a project is knowledge grounded in a Platonic Eros, which is in the end both determined and determinative, in every sense of those two terms. Kant's "categorical imperative" is an analogous concept, though it seems to me that subsequent readers of Kant have misleadingly emphasized the categorical rather than the imperative salient in his thought.

This is the framework in which we are to understand the idea of the "incommensurate" in poetry and art – the "irrelevant detail," the "accidentalities," all those arresting particulars of fact, language, text, and event which seem to escape both the ideologies of the works themselves and the ideologies of criticism. Poetry aims to establish a holistic and totalizing act of representation, but this project or purpose can be achieved only in the dynamic condition of the work itself – which is to say that it must look to have, like the human life it reflects, an *actual* rather than a conceptual fulfillment, a completion in the continuous deed and event which are the poetic work. Accidentalities and incommensurates in art localize this permanent discontinuity between (as it were) "the consciousness" of the poetical work and its complete if unrealized self-understanding. The deep truths that poetry knows are, as Shelley observed, "imageless" even in the poems themselves; and that tension in the unrealized desire of the images points toward the absent totalization. The entire process was captured, in the most witty and understated way, by Pope when he spoke of poetry as "what oft was thought, but ne'er so well expressed."

In sum, poetical work epitomizes the referentiality of communicative action. Criticism moves in constant pursuit of the text's lost and unrealized points of reference all the verbal and eventual matters of fact which constitute the work's complex symbolic networks, and without which criticism cannot hope to *re*-constitute those networks. That reconstitution is not achieved, however, as some factive historicist reconstruction of the "original context" of the work. Poetry operates a form of finishedness, but that form cannot be finished in conceptual fact. On the other hand, when purely immanent criticism condescends to the historicist and philological effort to reestablish an image of some originary form of a poetical work, it has missed the point of why criticism must pursue referential particularity and concreteness. The project of historicist work, its insistence upon matters of fact and accidentalities, is a critical reflection (and redeployment) of poetry's incommensurable procedures. Far from closing off poetic meaning, factive reconstructions operate such an array of overdetermined particulars that they tend to widen the abyss which is the communicative potential of every poem. It is as if, reading Wolf on Homer, or Driver on Genesis, one were able to glimpse, however briefly, the deep and totalizing truth in and toward which literary works are always moving, and to feel as well how and why their images have preserved an imageless and referential import, and their significance has remained in process of realization.

What is needed at this juncture is a wide and diverse exploratory program in socio-historical theory and method. That purely immanent critical procedures will no longer do is apparent to all, even to those who have done most to establish and develop such methods.[31] What is not apparent is precisely how we should best advance the resocialization of literary studies. My own conviction is that what will have to be achieved – *methodologically* – is a criticism which joins together work that is at once empirically comprehensive and hermeneutically self-conscious: a conjunction, let us say, of what one finds in Robert Darnton's *The Business of Enlightenment*, on the one hand, and Frederic Jameson's *The Political Unconscious* on the other.[32] Such a criticism will also have to incorporate, in an antithetical way, the entrenched forms of purely immanent critical procedures, from New Criticism to the latest forms of intertextual studies.

Elsewhere I have set forth, in a brief way, my view of how historical criticism ought to proceed. The schema is based upon the "dialectic between the work of art's point of origin, on the one hand, and its point of reception on the other":

Although writing verse is itself a social act, only when the poem enters social circulation – in MS copies, in private printings, or by publication – it begins its poetic life. Once born, however, a poem opens itself to the widest possible variety of human experiences.

To determine the significance of a poem at its point of origin demands that we study its bibliography. That subject is the *sine qua non* of the field, for in the study of the poem's initial MS and printed constitutions we are trying to define the social relationships between author and audience which the poem has called into being. It makes a great difference if, for example, an author writes but does not print a poem; it also makes a difference whether such a poem is circulated by the author or not, just as it makes a very great difference indeed when (or if) such a poem is printed, and where, and by whom.

The expressed intentions, or purposes, of an author are also significant for understanding a poem. At the point of origin those intentions are codified in the author's choice of time, place, and form of publication – or none of the above, by which I mean his decision *not* to publish at all, or to circulate in MS, or to print privately. All such decisions take the form of specific social acts of one sort or another, and those acts enter as part of the larger social act which is the poem in its specific (and quite various) human history.

What we call "author intentions" all appear in his particular statements about his own work. Those statements may be part of a private or even a public circulation during his lifetime, but as often as not they only appear later, when (for example) conversations or letters or other ephemeral writings are posthumously given to the world (an event that likewise occurs under very specific circumstances). All publications of such material are of course social events in their own right, and they always modify, more or less seriously, the developing history of the poem.

Once the poem passes entirely beyond the purposive control of the author, it leaves the pole of its origin and establishes the first phase of its later dialectical life (what we call its critical history). Normally the poem's critical history – the moving pole of its receptive life – dates from the first responses and reviews it receives. These reactions to the poem modify the author's purposes and intentions, sometimes drastically, and they remain part of the processive life of the poem as it passes on to future readers.

From any contemporary point of view, then, each poem we read has – when read as a work which comes to us from the past – two interlocking histories, one that derives from the author's expressed decisions and purposes, and the other that derives from the critical reactions of the poem's various readers.

When we say that every poem is a social event, we mean to call attention to the dialectical relation which plays itself out historically among these various human beings.

The traditional function of historical criticism has always been taken to involve the study and analysis of these past sets of relations. Roy Harvey Pearce's famous essay "Historicism Once More" shows this quite clearly. But the historical method in criticism, to my view, involves much more, since every contemporary critic, myself at this moment included, focuses on something besides a poem written, read, and reproduced in the past. The critic focuses as well on the present and the future, that is to say on the critic's audience, in whom he discerns the locus of his hopes for the project which his criticism *is*. Any reading of a poem that I do is a social act not primarily between myself and (say) Keats's work, but between myself and a particular audience(s).

Since this is always the case, the same sort of historical awareness which we would bring to bear on the past history of a poem must be introduced into every immediate analysis. In this case, the analysis must take careful account of all contextual factors that impinge on the critical act. Most crucially, this involves the need for precise definitions of the aims and the limits of the critical analysis. Like its own object of study ("literature"), criticism is necessarily "tendentious" in its operations. The critic's focus upon history as constituted in what we call "the past" only achieves its *critical* fulfillment when that study of the past reveals its significance in and for the present and the future.

I should add that everything I have noticed here is always involved in every critical act, whether the critic is aware or not that such matters are involved in his work, and whether the critic is an historical critic or not. (A person may, for example, give a reading of "La Belle Dame Sans Merci" in total ignorance of the poem's bibliographic history. Students do it all the time, and so, alas, do some scholars. Nonetheless, that history is always *present* to a person's critical activity despite his ignorance of that history, and even despite his ignorance *of* his ignorance. It is simply that the history is *not* present to his *individual* consciousness.) One of the principal functions of the socio-historical critic is to heighten the levels of social self-consciousness with which every critic carries out the act of literary criticism.[33]

A more detailed outline of these procedures can be found in a related paper.[34] I offer this here not as something definitive but as a model against which others interested in these questions may react. An adequate program will emerge, however, only when literary students are once again moved to initiate a related series of practical and theoretical studies that correspond to what was produced in the great philological renascence of the late eighteenth and nineteenth centuries. That many of those studies now seem to us the epitome of academic Dryasdust does not mean – as it once seemed to mean – that socio-historical studies are peripheral (rather than central) to literary studies; it signifies merely that such modes of work have to be retheorized. Were it otherwise – were socio-historical methods actually marginal to hermeneutics – we would be able to dispense with literary scholarship altogether and simply "read" our texts.

We cannot do this because scholarship – the socio-historical acts by which criticism preserves and reconstitutes the past for immediate use – is the ground of every form of critical self-consciousness. We cannot know the meaning of our own current meanings without setting our work in a reflexive relation with itself and its history, including the history of which we are ignorant. And we cannot know that history outside its documentary and otherwise material forms. This is why historical criticism must also be material and sociological. It will be, finally, dialectical because the pasts reconstituted by present literary studies are established for *critical* purposes: to expose to itself the mind of the present in order that it may be better able to execute its human interests and projects for the future.

NOTES

1 The antihistorical line of the New Criticism and (generally speaking) of its structuralist aftermath is well known. The same limitation applies to the principal work of the deconstructionists, at least in America: see *The Yale Critics: Deconstruction in America*, ed. Jonathan Arac, Wlad Godzich, and Wallace Martin (Minneapolis, MN, 1983), especially the summarizing "Afterword" by Arac. See also the similar critical exposition in Suresh Raval, *Metacriticism* (Athens, GA, 1981), 209–238, especially 220.

2 Jacques Derrida, "Structure, Sign and Play in the Discourse of the Human Sciences," in *The Languages of Criticism and the Sciences of Man*, ed. Richard Macksey and Eugenio Donato (Baltimore, 1970), 264.

3 *The Collected Works of Samuel Taylor Coleridge. Biographia Literaria*, ed. James Engell and W. Jackson Bate (Princeton, 1983), II, 72–73 and n.

4 C. M. Wallace, *The Design of Biographia Literaria* (London, 1983), 113.

5 Coleridge, *Biographia Literaria*, II, 45–46.

6 See C. S. Lewis and E. M. W. Tillyard, *The Personal Heresy in Criticism* (Oxford, 1934), especially Essay 1, and Cleanth Brooks, *The Well Wrought Urn* (New York, 1947), Appendix 1.

7 Brooks, *Well Wrought Urn*, 227.

8 J. Hillis Miller, "Stevens' Rock and Criticism as Cure," *Georgia Review*, 30 (1976), 29.

9 Ibid., 28–29.

10 Daniel Aaron, "The Treachery of Recollection," in *Essays in History and Literature*, ed. Robert H. Bremner (Athens, OH, 1967), 9.

11 Quoted by Marx in *Capital* (New York, 1967), I, 372.

12 Quoted by Godzich in *Yale Critics*, 39.

13 J. Hillis Miller, "The Critic as Host," *Critical Inquiry*, 3 (1977), 443, 447.
14 Milman Parry, *The Making of Homeric Verse: The Collected Papers of Milman Parry*, ed. Adam Parry (Oxford, 1971), 2.
15 Ibid., 3, 2.
16 John M. Ellis, *The Theory of Literary Criticism: A Logical Analysis* (Berkeley, CA, 1974), 136.
17 Ibid., 137, 154.
18 Miller, "Critic as Host," 458.
19 Ibid., 447.
20 Parry, *Making of Homeric Verse*, 411.
21 Ibid., 409. We are aware, of course, particularly from the work of Hayden White, that the construction of a "picture" by historians is a narrativizing act which imbeds in itself an interpretive structure. But the "great detail" which underlies this narrativizing whole always exercises a counter-movement of more or less extreme resistance. The best historians, and historical critics, insist upon the significance of these details and matters of fact. See below for a discussion of incommensurate detail.
22 Ibid.
23 Ibid., 410, 413.
24 Ibid., 413.
25 Ibid.
26 The most complete analysis of the structures of human interests operating in culture and its products is set forth in Jürgen Habermas, *Knowledge and Human Interests*, trans. Jeremy J. Shapiro (Boston, 1971); see especially chapters 3, 8, and the appendix.
27 Throughout this chapter the distinction between poetical "works" and poetical "texts" is being preserved. The former refer to cultural products conceived of as the issue of a large network of persons and institutions which operate over time, in numbers of different places and periods. "Texts" are those cultural products when they are viewed more restrictively, as language structures constituted in specific ways over time by a similar network of persons and institutions. Barthes's critique of the concept of the poetical "work" was a salutary move against the naive idea of poems as stable and defined objects. His related effort to install the concept of "text" in literary discourse has much less to recommend it, since this concept – while it has promoted certain forms of dialectical thinking in criticism – has also broadened the gap between the empirical and the reflective dimensions of literary studies. See Roland Barthes, "From Work to Text," reprinted in *Textual Strategies: Perspectives in Post-Structuralist Criticism*, ed. Josué Harari (Ithaca, 1979), 73–81.
28 Sir Philip Sidney, *An Apology for Poetry or The Defence of Poesie*, ed. Geoffrey Shepherd (London, 1965), 102.
29 Coleridge, *Biographia Literaria*, II, 72–73 and n.
30 Herbert A. Simon, *The Sciences of the Artificial* (Cambridge, MA, 1969).
31 See Geoffrey Hartman, *Criticism in the Wilderness: The Study of Literature Today* (New Haven, CT, 1980), 259, as well as Michael Sprinker's critique of the

contradictions in Hartman's call for a resocialized criticism in "Aesthetic Criticism: Geoffrey Hartman," in *Yale Critics*, 43–65, especially 58–60.

32 Robert Darnton, *The Business of Enlightenment: A Publishing History of the Encyclopédie, 1775–1800* (Cambridge, MA, 1979); Frederic Jameson, *The Political Unconscious* (Ithaca, 1981).

33 Jerome J. McGann, "Keats and the Historical Method in Literary Criticism," *MLN*, 94 (1979), 993–994.

34 The related paper is Jerome J. McGann, "The Monks and the Giants: Textual and Bibliographical Studies and the Interpretation of Literary Works," in *The Beauty of Inflections: Literary Investigations in Historical Method and Theory* (Oxford, 1985), part 2, chap. 1.

CHAPTER II

History, herstory, theirstory, ourstory

Because "history" takes place as a matter of pluralities, it should always – like Herodotus' exemplary work – be written in the plural. But of course it is not, of course people tend to write Theirstories in the singular, tend to write *a* history of something or other, and tend to suggest thereby that history is integral, uniform, and continuous. We are all familiar with Thesestories – for example, with the commonplace view that there are basically three theories of history, the degenerative, the progressivist, and the cyclical (with due allowance made for the spiral variant, usually imagined as moving in an upward rather than a downward direction).

Thistory, thus imagined, creates problems for people who work as historians, a fact which people who work as anthropologists have been pointing out to them for some time now. But history thus imagined is worse still for people who write and study literature; indeed, the linear imagination of history was probably the single most important factor in separating literary work from historical studies in the twentieth century.

In literary criticism, for example, the classic argument against a historical method in criticism has been that facts in poetry are not like facts in history: a fact is a fact in history (whether we mean by the term "history" the historical event or the historical text), but in poetry facts transcend any one-to-one correspondence relation. In poetry facts are taken to be multivalent, or as we sometimes like to say, symbolic. They are open to many readings and meanings, and any effort to explicate them by a historical method, it is believed, threatens to trivialize the poetic event into a unitary condition. Furthermore, to the degree that a poem solicits a historical condition, to the degree that it seeks to define itself locally and topically, to that extent, it is argued, does the poem abandon its poetic resources. Byron's "Fare Thee Well!" became one of the most notorious pretenses to poetry in the language, so far as the academy was concerned, precisely because the academy *knew* that it was a poem written to his wife on the occasion of their marital separation, and because the academy therefore knew – or thought it knew – what the poem meant. Its meaning *is* simple because its meaning *was* simple; worse still, that meaning is and was sentimental and mawkish.

I will return to the example of "Fare Thee Well!" at the end of this brief essay. For the moment I want merely to emphasize that the historicity of the poem is no more linear or unitary than is the historicity of any other human event. The problem of understanding the historicity of poems is grounded in a misunderstanding of what is entailed in facts and events, whether poetical or otherwise. Every so-called fact or event in history is imbedded in an indeterminate set of multiple and overlapping networks. The typical procedure in works of history is to choose one or more points in those networks from which to construct an explanatory order for the materials. Furthermore, works of history commonly cast that explanatory order in a linear form, a sequential order of causes and consequences. These procedures are of course perfectly legitimate heuristic methodologies for studying human events, but they foster the illusion that eventual relations are and must be continuous, and that facts and events are determinate and determinable in their structure.

But in *fact* history is a field of indeterminacies, with movements to be seen running along lateral and recursive lines as well as linearly, and by strange diagonals and various curves, tangents, and even within random patterns. Such variations are a consequence not merely of the multiplicity of players in the field (persons, groups, institutions, nonhuman forces, chance events, and so forth), but of the indeterminate variations in scale and speed which operate in dynamic sets of events. Herodotus wrote his *Histories* out of his understanding of the play of such variations, and Tolstoy constructed *War and Peace* from a similar imagination. In our day Marshall Sahlins's *Islands of History*[1] used Captain Cook's voyage to Hawaii as a dramatic instance for showing how a set of events may be seen to have different and antithetical meanings because the same set of events is incommensurate with itself – because the same set of events is, appearances notwithstanding, *not* the same set of events, is not equal to itself but is multiple.

In telling Thatstory Sahlins wrote History (a history, or perhaps A-history). That is to say, he sought to define, for certain critical and heuristic purposes, a structure of particular events. He produced a new order of explanation which restored commensurability to the order of events whose problematic character he had initially exposed. (The new order involves the introduction of anthropological categories into a historical field.)

These matters are important for anyone interested in the relation of history and literary work because facts and events *in history* are likewise not integral or stable or commensurable with themselves. They are multiple, and normative historical texts seek to regularize them only because such texts are committed to using their materials to develop explanations and to moralize events. These regularizing procedures are essential to the tasks, for example, of history and philosophy; and while they operate as well in poetry (for example, in a poem's expository and ideological materials), even the most rationally grounded poetical work – Lucretius, say, or Pope – resists and scatters its regularizing orders.

This is why so many commentators have observed that poetry operates as a kind of second nature (or, more exactly, an imitation of the human world). As in the world it refigures, a poem (as it were) strives to become the locus of a complex agenting structure. Facts in poetry therefore appear as *facta*, and the Latin form of the word reminds us, as the English form does not, that facts are *made* things. The poem itself, the artifice of its madeness (*poiesis*), is thrust forward as the sign under which all its materials stand.

Brecht's crucial reflections on epic theater have helped to remind us that the ultimate subject of *poiesis* is the global event of the work: not simply the tragic story of Romeo and Juliet, but *The Most Excellent and Lamentable Tragedy of Romeo and Juliet*. The *Tragedy* is the globe (in several pertinent senses) that contains the tragic history, and when the *Tragedy* is seen as such it appears, in its turn, as a complex event (or, more strictly, set of events) carried out in a larger world.

In a poetical field we are asked to observe a play of complex interactions between the various agents who are responsible for the *poiesis*. Even lyric poems are "theatrical" in Brecht's sense. *Poiesis* is the display of active agents carrying out deeds which later agents (call them critics and historians) remake through their subsequent acts of reflection. So, if it is a fact that Byron wrote "Fare Thee Well!," that fact was (and still is) an event involving multiple agents and authorities. The *writing of* "Fare Thee Well!" is only one act (or fact) in the much more complex fact which (for example) literary critics are interested in when they study the work that goes by the name "Fare Thee Well!" If we look even cursorily at the *printing history* of the poem we discover very soon that "Fare Thee Well!" is a work which will be only partly (and very narrowly) defined by the horizon of its composition and its composer.

We have already examined some of the acts and events which are comprised under the title of the lyric "Fare Thee Well!"[2] The poem was written by Byron, initially, but even that act summoned a larger context that he had already partially imagined when he wrote the poem. But Byron had not been able to summon in his own consciousness the entire context of his work, or the ways in which other agents in the field of Byron's particular activities would make their own special contributions to the *fact* we (think we) know as the poem "Fare Thee Well." That larger context, which includes various particular people and institutions, is written into – is assumed in the structure of – the work we know as "Fare Thee Well!," though not all of what the *work* assumes was assumed by Lord Byron, the titular workman who made the poem. What all this means is that the poem is initially made in a certain way, and that we can glimpse the complexity of its initial facticity by (for example) looking at the different ways the poem was read by its various early readers: by Byron, Lady Byron, Thomas Moore, John Cam Hobhouse, Wordsworth, Mme. De Staël, and many, many others. These different readings overlap and converge at some points, but they veer away and differ at others. The diversity is an index of the work's factive heteronomy, and when we remember that many different agents read and refashion the work over time and across spatial and political boundaries, we begin to glimpse the abyss of human agencies which underly everything we call a fact. No one person or group of persons can control this enormous field of human activities, all the agents are swept up by inertias in which they have played their parts.

Normative historical texts try to regularize these complex eventual networks. The facts that come to us through these explanatory and moralizing agencies become those so-called empirical facts which most people think of when they think about facts. When Coleridge said that "objects *as* objects are fixed and dead," he was referring to this kind of empirical facticity.[3] Coleridge was wise to distinguish the empirical from the phenomenological order of things, as he did when he made that remark, but he was less shrewd when he suggested that the empirical order comprises "fixed and dead" objects. The factive object of the empirical imagination is itself a *factum*, a thing made to be (seen) in this way by certain agenting processes. The "object as object" is not dead, even though the life it leads is far removed from the life we solicit through poetry.

Among the Romantics, it was Blake who saw most clearly into the peculiar reality of the fact. His understanding is nicely exposed in the following passage: "The reasoning historian, turner and twister of causes and consequences, such as Hume, Gibbon and Voltaire, cannot with all their artifice, turn or twist one fact or disarrange self evident action and reality. Reasons and opinions concerning acts, are not history. Acts themselves alone are history . . . Tell me the Acts, O historian, and leave me to reason upon them as I please."[4] Blake's distinction between facts and reasonings underscores his view of the fact as a kind of deed or event which opens a field – which itself *constitutes* the opening of a field. By contrast, reasoning upon the facts entails for Blake the emergence of what Coleridge called the fixed and dead object. Blake's reasoning is a structure of thought which limits and organizes the active agencies of the factive realm. The latter, for Blake, comprises the *order* of imagination – with order in this sense principally signifying a performative rather than a structural phenomenon.

These poetical orders increase one's sense of the incommensurability of facts, events, and the networks of such things.[5] Poetry, in this view of the matter, does not work to extend one's explanatory control over complex human materials (an operation which, as we know, purchases its control by delimiting the field of view); rather, poetry's function is to "open the doors of perception," and thereby to reestablish incommensurability as the framework of everything we do and know. In this sense poetry is a criticism of our standard forms of criticism – which is, I take it, approximately what Aristotle meant when he said that poetry is more philosophical than history and more concretely engaged than philosophy. Its philosophical (critical) task could not be executed, however, if poetry took its direction from the orders of reason rather than from the orders of facticities and minute particulars.

If poetry operated solely within physical and biological horizons, we would perhaps say that it represents a kind of Second Nature, with the matter of its universes disposed according to a human rather than a divine consciousness. But the horizon within which poetry operates is sociological (or, more strictly, socio-historical). It represents not the natural but the human world, an eventual field with two important features that distinguish it from a natural world: first, it functions within the complex networks of various conscious agencies, and second (but contradictorily), those networks undergo constant and arbitrary change. This means, among other things, that whereas such a world is always both reflexive (like God) and integral (like Nature), its consciousness and integrity are both indistinguishable and incommensurable.

The antithesis of poetry displays that world for us through its special modes of acting within such a world. The clearest way I can think of to explain this is to contrast what I would call "poetry in action" with what Bruno Latour has called *Science in Action*.[6] The latter involves consciousness in immensely complex sets of goal-directed operations: literary criticism (including this essay) is a perfect instance of "science in action." The object of these activities is knowledge. Latour uses the analogy of a road map to define the complex networks of scientific activities, because the road map is for him the sign of the human preoccupation with destinations and the desire to be master of destinations.

When science is in action, the best road map is the one that most clearly defines the relative importance of different places on the map and the relative mobility which comes with the various roads. Old maps and new maps, good maps and bad maps, none of these are *prima facie* without importance or interest to science in action. Everything depends upon the object in view, the goal, the destination. An old map might be more useful, might function with more useful information, than a new one – depending on your goals and purposes.

When poetry is in action, the situation appears quite different. The poetical object in view is precisely not to set limits on the objects in view. Of course, poems will always have very specific goals and objects set for themselves – by the original authors, by various readers, early and late. Poems do not achieve their vaunted universality from the fact that their authors set out for themselves transcendental goals: were this the case, we would have no mute inglorious Miltons (Milton Friedman, Milton Eisenhower, Milton Berle? or perhaps Alexander Ha*milton*). Nor is it that they affirm nothing and deny nothing – explicitly didactic poetry is merely the index of the ideological dimension which is a necessary component of any use of language, including poetical language.

The poetical use of language is special insofar as it preserves materials which – according to any of the work's possible sociologics – may be experienced, through a poetical deployment, as heterodox, irrelevant, contradictory, enigmatic. Poetry operates with the same kind of sociologics which Latour observes in *Science in Action*, but it veers away from the pragmatistic horizon of scientific knowledge. It is consequently the framework within which a critique of scientific knowledge is alone possible, for this reason: only a poetical deployment of language can make one aware how every ordering of knowledge is at the same time, and *by the very fact of its orderliness*, a calling to order of what must be experienced simultaneously as noncongruent and irrational.

Near the outset of this essay I mentioned Byron's "Fare Thee Well!" as a kind of epitome of the factive poem – a work fairly defined by what Blake called "minute particulars." Some have taken those particularities as a sign of the poverty of the poem's merely local habitations. Others have read those particulars with a different negative twist: the poem is bad not because it is full of particularities, but because it is absurdly sentimental. But though Ronald Reagan has imagined, and said, that "facts are stupid things," they are by no means stupid – nor are they fixed and dead, as Coleridge thought. Byron understood, as all poets more or less consciously understand, that facts are what Blake would call the "vehicular forms" of social events. They are neither dead nor stupid, and "Fare Thee Well!" illustrates *that* fact very well.

Many – myself included – have missed the factive life of Byron's excellent poem because we have imagined its facts were, perhaps like the poem's author, "stupid things," and hence have imagined the poem to be as stupid and sentimental as this way of reading the poem. In *fact*, the poem is as much a work of revenge, hatred, and hypocrisy as it is a work of suffering, love, and cant-free talk. Its minute particulars tell a set of contradictory stories, and finally make up one story whose central subject is contradiction itself – a contradiction we know as the torments of love and jealousy which were realized and played out through the break-up of the Byron marriage. This poetical work is at once a part of and a reflection upon that immensely complex set of connected and contradicted events.

"Fare Thee Well!" tells HIStory, then – let us call it Byron's story, pretending that even his-story is unitary and unconflicted. But in venturing Thatstory the work also calls out HERstory – let us call it Lady Byron's story, on a similar heuristic pretense. Because neither of Thesestories are simple or commensurable (and least of all pretty or sentimental), in thosestories the work develops Theirstory as well. Theirstory, however, never belonged entirely to HIM and HER; from the outset it comprised numerous otherstories which wove themselves into the fantastic network of Thesestories. As the locus of Thistory, "Fare Thee Well!" makes possible a number of other stories, which we would probably not be entirely wrong to call ourstory. All Thesestories began among the first transmitters of the poem, and they continue to work their ways down to and beyond ourselves.

But that is what poetry is supposed to do. What we forget sometimes is the *fact* that it will do so only as it works with minute particulars – with those hard facts (linguistic, bibliographical, sociological) which can never be made commensurate with the meanings we lay over them. It is in this context that we should say, therefore, after Lyn Hejinian's excellent prose sequence, that "Writing is an aid to memory."[7] Normative histories and memorial forms tend to use writing in order to disable the contradictions and differentials which constitute the field of memory. But writing in Hejinian's poetical imagination functions to multiply those differentials, and thereby to increase our potential access to ranges and ways of remembering we might otherwise have hardly known.

NOTES

1 Marshall Sahlins, *Islands of History* (Chicago: University of Chicago Press, 1985).

2 See chapter 4, above. See also David V. Erdman, "'Fare Thee Well!' – Byron's Last Days in England," in *Shelley and His Circle: 1773–1832*, ed. Kenneth Neill Cameron (Cambridge, MA: Harvard University Press, 1970), IV, 638–665; and W. Paul Elledge, "Talented Equivocation: Byron's 'Fare Thee Well!,'" *Keats–Shelley Journal*, 35 (1986), 42–61.

3 See *Biographia Literaria*, ed. James Engell and W. Jackson Bate (Princeton: Princeton University Press, 1983) I, 279.

4 *The Complete Poetry and Prose of William Blake*, rev. edn. by David V. Erdman, with commentary by Harold Bloom (Berkeley: University of California Press, 1982), 543–544.

5 Of course some poems solicit an incommensurable reading more actively and thoroughly than others; moreover, certain texts which are not formally poetical – Plato's dialogues, for example, Gibbon's *Decline and Fall*, the essays of Montaigne, Herodotus' *Histories*, and so forth – are highly "poetical" in the sense of the term that I am using here (where, if metaphor remains the central sign of a poetical text, it is taken to be the figure which holds "opposite and discordant qualities" together in an antithetical and unresolved state). Poetry's central function, in this view, is to expose the differentials which play within the apparitions of wholeness and order.

6 See Bruno Latour, *Science in Action* (Cambridge, MA: Harvard University Press, 1987), esp. 215–223.

7 See Lyn Hejinian, *Writing Is an Aid to Memory* (Great Barrington, MA: The Figures, 1978).

CHAPTER 12

Literature, meaning, and the discontinuity of fact

Textual studies and editing are two exemplary fields of historical criticism. They are also fundamental, since all literary work is grounded in them. These subdisciplines of historical criticism have been dominated for many years by empirical and even positivist methods and goals, sometimes for good, sometimes for ill. That general context has led me to concentrate much of my work in textual criticism and theory. I have done so with two particular goals in view.

First, I wanted to attack traditional historicism in what has always been regarded as its fastness of strength, its (hitherto) impregnable inner tower: textual studies and editing. Second, I wanted to open a parallel critique of contemporary theory and hermeneutics, which has largely avoided a serious engagement with the problem of facticity and positive knowledge. The unwillingness or inability of most influential literary theoreticians of the past twenty-five years to enter the fields of textual criticism and editing is an eloquent historical fact. Even when theoretically sophisticated critics moved beyond a "hermeneutics of reading" into various kinds of "new historical" and "cultural" studies, they did so typically without having addressed the conflicting claims of fact and idea, writing and reading, history and interpretation.

In textual studies and editing, however, these issues cannot be evaded, because the editor's and textual critic's literary works are always encountered as specific, material historical forms. They have what Paul de Man, speaking for hermeneutics generally, said "literary texts" cannot have: "positive existence."

The condition of positivity led traditional historicists, including textual critics, to conceive their obligation as recuperating phenomena that had slipped into the past. Though the theoretical impossibility of such a goal was always acknowledged, its heuristic operation was pursued. The idea was to try to make as close an approach to the lost phenomena as one could manage. Moreover, the pursuit

(What mad pursuit? What struggles to escape?
What pipes and timbrels? What wild ecstasy?)

involved an engagement to recover not so much the lost phenomena as their lost meanings. The works of the past survive in documentary forms. In their historical passage these documents appear to grow more distant and difficult to understand. The traditional historicist – and here the textual critic stands as the supreme model – works to clear the documents of their accumulated detritus and obscurities, ideally exposing, and explicating, an original and complete truth that lies in the eternity of the past. Strict constructionists of the Constitution express an analogous goal when they speak of adhering to what the Founding Fathers intended.

Without arguing the matter – I have done so often elsewhere – let me say that this is not my view of what either textual criticism in particular or historical criticism generally entails. Historical method is for me strictly a form of comparative study. From that vantage, a historical criticism does not imagine that its object is to recover some lost original text or meaning. Such goals lie within neither its province nor its power. Normative goals of these kinds are hypothesized, as one commonly sees in the case of editing and textual studies. Norms are constructed, however, only to set in motion the special critical dynamic peculiar to every historical procedure: the method of comparative analysis. The basic form of historical method is not positivist – positivism is one of its Kantian "moments" – it is dialogical.

The points of departure for such a dialogue are, in the most general sense, the present and the past. The more deeply the dialogue form is engaged, the more clearly we perceive the multiple possibilities for situating what might be understood as the loci of presentness and pastness. Texts, for example, like the readings of the texts, are invariably multiple. When criticism constructs a "textual history" or a "reception history," the differential of the here and now is forced to confront a host of earlier, analogous differentials. The dialogue of history is endless both *between* the present and the past and *within* the present and the past.

Implicit in any historical criticism of literature is a crucial assumption: that literary works are certain human acts carried out within a larger world of other human acts. In this respect historical criticism distinguishes itself from hermeneutics, which is a method for elucidating symbolic forms. For historical criticism, "in the beginning was the deed";

and if that deed is an act of language – if we could also call it a "word" – it has to be first engaged as a rhetorical event rather than as a symbolic form. Though we may be interested in how a novel or a poem is a "virtual world" calling for an interpretation of its inner structure of relations, we cannot neglect in what ways and to what ends its virtualities have been deployed. A novel is also, necessarily, a certain kind of book (in fact, many kinds of book) written and disseminated in many different kinds of ways. The (formal) category we call "the novel" (as opposed to "the story") presupposes the institution of book production. For the historical critic, meaning(s) that might be educed from "the novel" are subsumed within a larger arena of meaningfulness: the social world of writing and reading books, the institutions for transmitting and retransmitting them.

In an epoch like our own, where the limits of knowledge are mapped onto models of language, the special character of historical criticism (as opposed to literary hermeneutics) may be clarified by asking the following question: must we regard the physical channels of communication as part of the message of the texts we study? Or are the channels to be treated as purely vehicular forms whose ideal condition is to be transparent to the texts they deliver? How important, for the reader of a novel or any other text, are the work's various materials, means, and modes of production? Does a work's bibliographical existence, for example, seriously impinge upon its symbolic form and meaning?

Normally, criticism leaves the documents to the bibliographers and the texts (so called) to the critics. In all of my works I have been arguing against this habit of thought – have been arguing that "reading" must cover the entirety of the literary work, its bibliographical as well as its linguistic codes. A recent essay on James's *The Ambassadors* brings an especially clear focus to the issues at stake.[1]

The key fact is that the first English edition and the first American edition, published within a month of each other in 1904, have chapters 28 and 29 in different orders. Until 1949 the two orderings were not noticed, and the novel was read in the order printed in the first American edition (which was canonized in the 1909 New York edition and all subsequent printings to 1949). In 1949, however, critical opinion reversed itself and decided – it was a scandalous moment in American literary studies – that the order in the first American edition was a printer's mistake. Editions after 1949 change the chapter order to the sequence in the first English edition. As it happens, a close critical study of the bibliographical materials reveals no mistake in the first American edition. The scandal turns out to be worse than was imagined in 1949. The scandal is that the novel makes sense no matter which order the two chapters are put in.

What is startling here is that both ways of reading the novel are authorized at the bibliographical level, not at the hermeneutic level. Our imaginations do not impose a meaning upon the work; it imposes meanings upon our imaginations. The originary work seems to have transcended, equally and at once, the law of authorial intention and the law of integral aesthetic form. In its bibliographical doubleness *The Ambassadors* establishes alternative ways of thinking and reading both with and without an order of intentions. James's novel lies open to two linear sequences of text simultaneously, and it has generated them as if by some fate, or deliberation, of its special textual condition.

The situation argues that text may be founded as an order of discontinuous phenomena. The question is, just how deeply are these orders of chaos grounded? Does the case of *The Ambassadors* expose a textual freak, an accident and exception that prove the rule of normal orders of conscious control? Or is it a dramatic instance of just how strongly, and in the end vainly, we resist the presence of aleatory orders?

When we think with a post-Heisenbergian imagination (or, alternatively, with a pre-Socratic one), we have no difficulty grasping the random order of things. We are not surprised by sin, by the operations of fate, by Lucretian swerves, by Mandelbrot sets. Seen through the text of the Bible, they reveal the necessity of a willful refusal of necessity. Seen through the text of *De rerum natura*, they declare the presence of love – Aphrodite, alma Venus genetrix – at the foundation of the human world. We have also developed distinctive twentieth-century literary and artistic methods for expressing analogous forms of order. (By "we" I mean Euro-Americans.) But in our scholarship and criticism we still behave as if randomness and contradiction were not essential to the order of things. Perhaps we merely execute our habits of contradiction.

However that may be, let me close by returning to the subject of historical criticism. The case of *The Ambassadors* is important because no amount of nonhistoricized analysis could have exposed what is going on in that work. Reciprocally, the historicized analysis shows the objective, the positive, existence of the work's contradictions. Meaning outstares the blindness or insight dialectic of the hermeneutic circle. The analysis exposes (by critical reciprocation) a chaotic originary order in the textual condition. In rough terms, facticity appears logically prior to the concept of facticity. That logical priority assumes a concrete material form.

We experience and define it as a historical priority. For all its historical character, the priority is a philosophical condition.

That condition explains why *The Ambassadors* needs to be faced as a complex (and evolving) set of material and socio-historical events. If it isn't, we shall encounter it at no deeper level than that of its semantics. We will be limited to either structural analysis or thematized reading. While both of these critical procedures are important, they require a historical dialectics to supply them with reflexive power. Criticism needs this vantage because the works it investigates are themselves eventual and interactive.

Eventual: While criticism wants to know what literary works are saying, even more it needs to know what they are doing in saying what they say.

Interactive: Literary work comprises a ceaseless dialogue of many agents. By their fruits we shall know them . . . and they us.

NOTE

1 Jerome McGann, "Revision, Rewriting, Rereading; or, 'An Error [not] in *The Ambassadors*,'" *American Literature*, 64 (1992), 95–110.

CHAPTER 13

Rethinking Romanticism

I

Until the early 1980s scholars of Romanticism generally accepted Rene Wellek's classic modern definition of their subject: "Imagination for the view of poetry, nature for the view of the world, and symbol and myth for poetic style."[1] This formulation represents, on one hand, a synthesis of an originary Romantic tradition of thought, and, on the other, the bounding horizon for much of the work on Romanticism done until fairly recently.

Today that synthesis has collapsed and debate about theory of Romanticism is vigorous – from cultural studies, feminist scholarship, even from various types of revived philological investigations. My own work has been much engaged with these revaluations, not least since the publication of *The Romantic Ideology* in 1983. Because these discussions have (inevitably) influenced my own thinking about Romanticism, as well as the more general problem of periodization, I want to return to the subject once again.[2]

Between 1978 and 1983, when I first addressed these issues, I was not concerned with the question of periodization as such. I was more interested in the conceptual representations of Romanticism – contemporary representations as well as subsequent scholarly representations. The periodization issue entered my purview obliquely – for example, in relation to the kinds of problems that arise when a clear distinction is not maintained between certain cultural formations (like Romanticism, modernism, or post-Modernism) and the historical frameworks within which they develop and mutate. So I worked to clarify the distinction between "the romantic period" (that is, a particular historical epoch) and "romanticism" (that is, a set of cultural/ideological formations that came to prominence during the Romantic period). The distinction is important not merely because so much of the work of that period is not "romantic," but even more, perhaps, because the period is notable for its many ideological struggles. A Romantic ethos achieved dominance through sharp cultural conflict; some of the fiercest engagements were internecine – the civil wars of the Romantic movement itself.

Later I shall try to examine these topics more closely. For now let me summarize the argument I began to elaborate in *The Romantic Ideology*. It seemed to me then, and it still seems to me: first, that Wellek's position flattens out the rough terrain of the cultural formation(s) we call Romanticism; and second, that Wellek's position fails to map the phenomena comprehensively because it is a specialized theoretical view derived from a Kantian/Coleridgean line of thought. In other words, between approximately 1945 and 1980 the most influential interpreters of English Romanticism examined their material with a historically determinate theory of their subject. To recognize the historicality of the theory is to understand more clearly its limits (as well as the powers). The recognition also helps one toward possible reimaginations of Romanticism – to think beyond the conceptual framework of Wellek's synthetic theory.

The limits of that interpretive line pressed themselves upon me because I was much occupied with Byron and his works. A Byronic vantage on the issue of Romanticism immediately puts in question Wellek's imagination/nature/symbol tercet. That Byron did not figure importantly in the representations of the Romantic period of 1945–1980 is not an anomaly, it is a theoretical and ideological fate.

The contrast between the view of Romanticism that dominated the period 1945–1980 and the nineteenth-century's view seemed to me equally startling. Once again Byron loomed as the unevadable locus of the issues. The continental vantage exposes the problems in their most telling form. From Goethe and Pushkin to Baudelaire, Nietzsche, and Lautréamont, Byron seems to stand at the very center of Romanticism. The nineteenth-century English view is slightly different. Though Byron remained an important resource for England and the English, he had emerged as a highly problematic figure. From different Victorian points of view Byron's famous "energy" (as it was called) seemed one thing – usually a positive thing – whereas his equally famous critical despair seemed something else altogether – typically, something to be deplored. Nineteenth-century England therefore kept opening and closing its Byron with troubled (ir)regularity.

As Coleridge and Wordsworth gradually came to define the "center" of English Romanticism in twentieth-century critical thinking, Byron slipped further from view. Wellek's intervention was a key event because he sought to integrate a European philological view with a correspondent line of English cultural thought. In the Romanticism that emerged from this synthesis, Byron's deviance seemed virtually complete. "Imagination" is explicitly *not* Byron's view of the sources of poetry, "nature" is hardly his "view of the world" (Byron is distinctly a cosmopolitan writer), and his style is predominantly rhetorical and conversational rather than symbolic or mythic. No one would, I think, disagree with this general representation of Byron, any more than one would deny that Wellek's formulation corresponds very closely to Wordsworth's and Coleridge's work. Wellek's triad can of course be traced through Byron's work, especially via a study of Byron's peculiarly antithetical ways of engaging nature, imagination, and myth. When this is done, however – for instance, in the guiding work of an Abrams or a Bloom – what one discovers are precisely traces and differences.[3] Observed through a theory of Romanticism like Wellek's, Byron appears either a problem or an irrelevance.

The difficulty is at its root a historical one. While Byron does not fit easily into Wellek's criteria for Romanticism, he cannot easily be removed from the historical phenomena. In the theoretical (and Romantic) line synthesized by Wellek, this Byronic contradiction was negotiated very simply. Although the splendor of Byron's miseries initially seemed an astonishment to many, they came at last to be judged a kind of vulgar theater of Romanticism, the debased margin of a complex cultural center: at best perhaps historically interesting, at worst probably factitious. The subject of Byron's late masterpiece *Don Juan* was set aside altogether so far as the question of Byron's Romanticism was concerned. For while here one could see, very clearly, a panoramic (dis)play of "romantic irony," Byron's work pursued its ironies in an apparently unsystematic and nontheoretical way. Byron's resistance to theory – famous in its time – troubled the Romanticism of his ironic masterpiece. It became a negative cultural sign that his work lacked depth and cultural seriousness. Himself at odds with so much of his age's systematic theorizing – "born for opposition," as he flamboyantly declared – Byron courted marginality and inconsequence from the very center of the Romantic fame he had acquired.

(Let me say in parenthesis that the recent "return of the Byronic repressed" does not simply reflect the editorial scholarship that has restored his texts to us during the past twenty years or so. At least as important has been the emergence of post-Modernism, with its Derridean concern for textual play and instability and its Foucauldian pressure to recover salient but neglected historicalities.[4])

Working from the antinomy of Byron, then, *The Romantic Ideology* drew out a dialectical critque of Wellek's ideological synthesis. Once begun, such a move lays bare a whole array of similar deviances concealed within the synthetic structure. For example, if Romanticism takes "nature" for its view of the world, then Blake falls out of the synthesis. "Nature" corresponds to a Romantic *Weltanschauung* as a scene of fundamental innocence and sympathy; conceptually opposed to the urban and the artificial, Romantic nature is the locus of what Wordsworth paradigmatically called "feeling." As an artistic resource it generates a constellation of anti-Enlightenment cultural formations that are critically recollected in phrases like "the meddling intellect," and Romantically transformed in phrases like "the philosophic mind." Because Blake also attacked key Enlightenment positions, one may overlook or set aside the manifest differences that separate his view of nature from, say, Wordsworth's or Coleridge's. But the fact is that Blake does not take "nature as his view of the world" any more than Byron does, though the antinaturisms of Blake and Byron are also noncongruent with each other.

A close investigation of the ideas that particular Romantic writers had about imagination, nature, and symbol or myth will disclose a series of similar fundamental differences. I recently tried to illustrate what might be demonstrated along these lines by tracing important distinctions between different Romantic ideas of imagination.[5] Memory is so important to the theories of Wordsworth and Coleridge, for instance, that their views deviate radically from Blake's. Imagination is a conscious activity for Coleridge, subject to the will, whereas for Shelley it is a faculty precisely distinguished by its total freedom from willful control. Keats evolved from Wordsworth a sensationalist theory of imagination that stands quite at odds with Shelley's more idealistic views. For that matter, Wordsworth's work is so deeply in debt to associationist theories of imagination that Coleridge himself wrote *Biographia Literaria* in large part to demonstrate the crucial differences that separated his aesthetic ideas from those of his early friend. (In doing so, curiously, he aligned himself closely with the criticisms initially raised by Wordsworth's most famous antagonist, Francis Jeffrey.)

Now it might be objected that this general line of critique against Wellek's synthetic representation of Romanticism simply returns us to a neo-Lovejoyan skepticism. Differences are so elaborated and insisted upon that we effectively abandon all hope of theorizing the phenomena. Instead we atomize, discriminating ever more particular forms within an enchafed but finally featureless Romantic flood.

To the extent that *The Romantic Ideology* was written as a critical polemic against what I took to be a false consciousness of Romanticism, its arguments might be used to bolster such a Pyrrhonist approach. My own view, however, is very different, as might perhaps be seen from more recent critical projects. These projects have not been specifically addressed to the question of Romanticism or to the problem of its periodization. I have been trying rather to develop a general set of research and teaching protocols for the historical study of literary work, regardless of "period." This more general aim grows from investigations into the changing relations of language and textuality, and particularly the changing relations of language and the textuality of literary or poetical work.[6]

From this perspective, Romanticism is inadequately characterized by a synthesis like Wellek's because the synthesis is too abstract and conceptual. The best work to utilize this synthesis has tried to resist that conceptual framework, to preserve the dynamism of the phenomena even as a continual resort is made to terms like imagination, nature, and symbol, with their fateful positivist inertias. Nor can we, nor should we, dispense with those terms, which are primary philological data of the originary historical efforts to forge Romantic experiences of the world.

What we have to bear clearly in mind, however, is the heuristic and constructivist character of those terms and the ideas they generate and pursue. "Imagination," especially as it was deployed in Romantic discourse, is a radically dialogical term. When Coleridge or Shelley, say, use the term in prescriptive and ideological frameworks, they try to limit the dialogism of the word, to set it within a defined conceptual position. The same is true with regard, let us say, to Wordsworth's or Byron's or Blake's expositions of terms like "imagination" and "nature." So we can speak of different (Romantic) "theories" of nature or imagination, and we can separate these different theories from each other. However, to the extent that Romanticism is executed not as a prescriptive but as a poetical economy – a dynamic scene of evolving tensions and relationships, as in a family – its primal terms and data cannot lapse into systematic rectitude. Romantic poetry, in short, constructs a theater for the conflicts and interactions of the ideologies of Romanticism.

In this sense, to define Romanticism with Wellek's tercet of keywords is not wrong so much as it is abstract and preliminary. If our critical point of departure is poetry and art rather than culture and society, we have to begin the study of Romanticism at least from a Bakhtinian vantage, as a disputatious scene whose internal tensions re-present the strife of historical differentials and ideological conflict. The period is notable, as I have said, for its various cultural/theoretical controversies, and in particular for the emergence of the manifesto as a distinct literary subgenre. The cultural forms of Romanticism are famously volatile and shape-changing because they typically hold their ideas and projects open to transformation – even to the point, as I shall try to show, of their own self-destruction.

A book like *The Romantic Ideology*, it has been argued, implicitly reifies this kind of Romantic dynamism as a transcendent aesthetic form or set of procedures. The charge is that *The Romantic Ideology* at times simply replaces Wellek's tripartite structural representation with a dialectical view that is, finally, no less conceptual, for all its appeal to dynamic forms. I have come to think this criticism a just one.[7] I also think it an important criticism, for it exposes a residual investment in a type of interpretive thought that I was explicitly trying to avoid.

As I see it, criticism should be seeking a dialectical philology that is not bound by the conceptual forms it studies and generates.[8] The paradox of such a philology is that its freedom would be secured only when it accepts the historical limits of its own forms of thought. It is not bound by its theoretical forms because it holds itself open to the boundary conditions established by other conceptual forms. This is a theory imagined not as a conceptual structure but as a set of investigative practices – and a set of practices that play themselves out under a horizon of falsifiability.[9]

II

If we take such an approach to a topic like "the romantic period," then, our object will not be to "define" the period but to sketch its dynamic possibilities. In this frame of reference it helps to remember that "periodization" is itself a critical tool fashioned in historicality as such. Periodization is a possible form of historical thinking that has been realized under specific socio-historical conditions of the European Enlightenment. We do not, after all, *have* to think in such terms. A current world-historical perspective will not sweep off the periodic table "Medieval, Renaissance, Enlightenment, Romanticism, Modernism," but it will certainly execute radical and across-the-board changes and options of meaning.

Modern historical method is a tool for bringing order – I would rather call it "possible order" – to cultural change and cultural difference. We want therefore to bear in mind the historicality of the method in order to hold it open to the full range of its possibilities, which necessarily entail the limits it is perpetually constructing and discovering. When we focus attention on a topic like the Romantic period, we may willingly (though perhaps not consciously) suspend our disbelief in the period as such, and hence take our studies in the period for pursuits of an *Urphänomen*. This is, in effect, what we observe in Wellek's approach to Romanticism and the Romantic period. The problem with Wellek's formulation is not so much that it is a limited view – all views are limited – but that it holds out against the possibilities of its own limitations. It does not invite a "suspension of disbelief *for the moment*" but for good and aye.

At issue here is how we pursue a historical method of literary investigation. Because historical method is strictly a form of comparative studies, its goal is not the recovery of some lost originary cultural whole. The presumption must rather be that the object of study is volatile and dynamic – not merely that it (in this case, "the romantic period") *was* an unstable and conflicted phenomenon, but that it continues to mutate as it is subjected to further study; indeed, that its later changes are the effects of such studies. (This situation explains why the basic form of historical studies is not positivist but radically dialogical.)

Thus the standard dates for the Romantic period – let us say, 1798–1824 – cannot be read as a mere statement of fact. Scholars of course understand the signifying mechanism involved here. "1798" stands for the coming of *Lyrical Ballads*, and "1824" stands for the death of Byron. But those events merely define the critical materials in terms of a simple historical allegory. Most scholars are also aware that the dates could be shifted – typical shifts at the *terminus a quo* are "1789," "1792," and "1800," while at the *terminus ad quem* the dates "1830," "1832," and "1837" (among others) are common enough. All signify some event that is implicitly being asked to carry important cultural meanings. The "facts" come legend-laden through the forest of history. We have to translate those legends, but we also have to realize what is implicit in *the fact of the legends*: that a historical moment (so-called) can and will be (re)constructed in different ways.

That realization should not be left to fend for itself, as it were. We want to get beyond assenting to "the play of difference," beyond describing instances of that play. A fully developed historical method ought to encourage the exploration of alterities. That goal would entail, however – to borrow a thought from Shelley – *imagining* what we know: constructing and deploying forms that will be equal to the pursuit of differential attention. We shall not advance the knowledge we desire, therefore, by continuing to work almost exclusively within the most traditional generic conventions of academic discourse. These forms, after all, evolved from nineteenth-century historicist philology and hermeneutics. As such, they are structurally committed to holistic accounts of history and integrated, self-consistent acts of interpretation.

Derrida has been a great spur (so to speak) to new kinds of critical in(ter)ventions. (The use of dialectal forms that give momentary exposure to language's differential possibilities is now common.) But the academy's turn in the past twenty-five years toward various philosophies of differential attention has remained largely conceptual. Not many critics or scholars have tried to translate these commitments into equivalent generic forms. The most innovative work here has come from extramural writers. Scholars could learn much from the criticism of contemporary poets like Susan Howe and Charles Bernstein.[10] Howe's exploration of *My Emily Dickinson*, for example, is an astonishingly inventive work of historical scholarship. The book's collage format permits her to deploy and then explore a series of nonlinear historical relations. Pivoting about a close reading of a single poem ("My Life had stood – a Loaded Gun"), the book slowly explores multiple intersections of public event and private life – intersections *in* the past as well as *between* the past and its possible futures.

When academics have tried to escape the limitations of traditional critical forms, response tends to be at best interested and wary, and at worst hostile or indifferent. In Renaissance studies one thinks immediately of Randall McLeod, perhaps the most innovative textual scholar of our time (in any period of work.)[11] In the Romantic period I would instance the recent work of Jeffrey Robinson, or Donald Ault's struggles (they recall McLeod's work) to force the physical medium of the text to become a critical tool and form of expression.[12] In my own criticism, especially during the past five years, I have been exploring the resources of dialogue as a mode of scholarly investigation.[13]

One thinks as well of the important *New History of French Literature*, which has made a deliberate effort to surmount the limits of narrativized history by subordinating narrative form to an incipient dialectic licensed by the discontinuous chronicle organization of the materials.[14] The *New History* does not seek a synthetic historical account of French Literature. On one hand the work underscores the limits of historical vision by emphasizing the extreme particularity of various accounts. On the other it tries to induce imaginations of new sets of historical relations between different and competing views of the material.

Implicit here is a general critical idea that has great power: to display the constructed and non-natural status of historical information. Insofar as narrative history aspires to a finished account, its rhetoric tends to represent the past as completed – a complex set of "facts" that require thorough research and fair disclosure. The *New History* is an index of a contrary view: that history is a continuous process, and that the past itself is, like the future, a serious possibility. The *New History* subordinates narrative (closure) to dialectic (engagement).

Its general procedures, however, can sometimes be as well or perhaps even better pursued in other expository modes. Consider the critical possibilities of the anthology form. These first became apparent to me in Yeats's great *Oxford Book of Modern Verse, 1892–1935* (1936). By opening his collection in 1892 with a (re)constructed text of Pater's prose, Yeats announced the arbitrary and polemical character of his work. At that point I began to realize the virtues to be gained by "writing" literary history in the editorial structure of the anthology. Several years later, when I was asked to edit *The New Oxford Book of Romantic Period Verse*, I seized the opportunity. Concealed within this project was the chance to give a practical demonstration of certain theoretical ideas about history, on one hand, and literary form on the other.

An anthology of this kind necessarily constructs a literary history, but the historical synthesis is subordinated in the formalities of the collection. The anthology focuses one's attention on local units of order – individual poems and groups of poems. As a consequence, these units tend to splinter the synthetic inertia of the work-as-a-whole into an interactive and dialogical scene. Possibilities of order appear at different scalar levels because the center of the work is not so much a totalized form as a dynamically emergent set of constructible hypotheses of historical relations. Built into the anthology form are what topological mathematicians might call "basins" of contradiction: orderly, expository, and linear arrangements that stand at a perpetual brink of Chaotic transformation.

As I began studying the anthology form more closely, I was struck by one of its dominant modern conventions. Since *Tottel's Miscellany* (1557) literary anthologies – even when they are trying to display some more or less comprehensive historical order – tend to arrange themselves by author. Palgrave's *Golden Treasury* (1861) might seem a great exception to this rule, but it isn't. Although poems by different authors are scattered through each of the anthology's four great books, Palgrave's Introduction makes its author-centered form very clear. The four "Books" of the *Golden Treasury* locate the four great periods of what Palgrave calls "the natural growth and evolution of our Poetry." The periods roughly correspond to the sixteenth, seventeenth, eighteenth, and early nineteenth centuries. For Palgrave, however, each of these four evolutionary phases have unfolded under the sign of a single dominant author "who more or less give[s] each [phase] its distinctive character."[15] Consequently, Palgrave tells us that each of the four books of his anthology "might be called the Books of Shakespeare, Milton, Gray, and Wordsworth" respectively.

Yet even as Palgrave's great anthology connects its Romantic-evolutionary account of English literary history to certain epochal figures, it deploys two interesting and antithetical forms of order. First, the anthology is formatted into four abstractly arranged "Books." Each book carries no heading other than "Book First," "Book Second," etc., without historical labels of any kind. Second, no effort is made within each book to foreground a local evolutionary cycle, or – for that matter – to isolate individual authors, not even the epochal authors. Each poem comes forward under a title and the author's name is tagged at the end. Neither are an individual author's works grouped into a subunit within the horizon of a particular "Book." The poems are arranged, so far as one can tell, by random and personal choice – Palgrave says simply that he has avoided "a rigidly chronological sequence" in order to pursue what he calls "the wisdom which comes through pleasure." That idiosyncratic remark underscores the anthology's deep commitment to a principle of subjectivity: "Within each book," Palgrave adds, "the pieces have . . . been arranged in gradations of feeling or subject."

What most strikes one about Palgrave's anthology, therefore, is not its rather (in)famous Arnoldian determination toward "the best original Lyrical pieces and Songs in our language." Rather, it is the book's complex structure. Palgrave puts into play several competing and even antithetical forms of order and attention. While the implicit conflict of these forms does not overthrow the book's ultimately Hegelian organization, it allows the reader recurrent waylayings from Palgrave's imperious instruction in his version of a "great tradition." For Palgrave's own project is built upon internal conflict and self-contradiction. On one hand he tells us that local randomness comes from a poetical desire towards "the wisdom which comes through pleasure." On the other hand he associates the "poetical" experience with total form. "In the arrangement," he says, "the most poetically-effective order has been attempted" – by which he means, explicitly, an evolutionary wholeness that he equates with and calls "the sense of Beauty."

> And it is hoped that the contents of this Anthology will thus be found to present a certain unity, "as episodes," in the noble language of Shelley, "to that great poem which all poets, like the co-operating thoughts of one great mind, have built up since the beginning of the world."

Rereading Palgrave made me understand that the differential order achieved (perhaps not altogether consciously) in his book might be deliberately essayed in my *New Oxford Book of Romantic Period Verse.* I have therefore made several important departures from the conventional format of a "New Oxford Book" anthology. The most significant departure involves the collection's general historical horizon. The historical scene is more atomized than it is cumulative or developmental: as it were, thirteen ways of looking at the Romantic period (or, in this case, forty-seven ways). Not unlike the *New History of French Literature*, the anthology follows a simple chronicle organization, year by year from 1785 to 1832. Within each year the poems are also arranged by elementary chronological sequence.

As a consequence, different authors appear recurrently rather than as coherent authorial units. Wordsworth and his poetry, for example, continually reemerge in new and perhaps unexpected sets of relations. Narrativizing literary events, by contrast, tends to rationalize such historical intersections under the laws of an expository grammar. Similarly, by making individual poems the base units of a "literary history" – as it were the "words" of its "language" – the *New Oxford Book* anthology cuts across what Palgrave called the "certain unity" of literary history. Tracing a historical course by spots of poetical time (rather than by unfolding expository sequence) entails a necessary fall from the grace of one great Mind into the local world of the poem, where contradiction – the ceaseless dialectic of "opposite and discordant qualities" – holds paramount sway.

The anthology pursues this dialectic in one other important respect. It takes a consciously antithetical point of view on the materials to be included. At the outset of this essay I mentioned the sharp difference between Wellek's synthetic view of Romanticism and various earlier views. The anthology reflects that differential in three principal ways. First, it includes a good deal of poetry – some of it, like Crabbe's, among the best writing of the period – that is not Romantic. Second, it gives a prominent place to work that was famous in its time but that later fell from sight. Third, it represents two key transitional moments of the Romantic period – the decades (roughly speaking) of the 1790s and the 1820s – more completely, and hence more problematically, than is done in narrative literary histories or anthologies of the period.

Synthetic historians tend to view their worlds in great sweeps. The Romantic period thus typically comes to us through a gradual "pre-Romantic" evolution mapped by now familiar signs (for instance, Gray, Collins, Chatterton, Macpherson, and perhaps Cowper). Nor do I mean at all to disparage such a view. But it *is* only a way of seeing things. One gets a very different vision from a tighter focus. At least as important so far as 1790s writers were concerned, for example, was the immediate impact of Sir William Jones's annotated translations of Persian poetry and the spectacular onset of the Della Cruscan movement. By foregrounding Jones's work and the Della Cruscans the *New Oxford Book of Romantic Period Verse* invites some alternative imaginings of our historical evidence and understandings.

Because a sense of historicality is so closely connected to causal models, early or precursive materials have always occupied the attention of critics. So Romanticism's relation to the late eighteenth century, if still inadequately treated, is a scene of deep scholarship compared with what we think about the 1820s. The anthology intervenes by printing a good deal of poetry that once occupied the center of cultural attention in the 1820s. These texts represent a small but serious effort toward a great need: the reconstruction of what was being written and read up to the passage of the first Reform Bill and the publication of Tennyson's 1832 *Poems*.

Situating the Romantic period and its literary works firmly within the latter perspective affords some startling views and insights. What do we think we see when we look at the 1820s and its cultural work in England? The years following the restoration of the thrones of Europe – a settlement orchestrated by England – have all but sunk from sight so far as English cultural consciousness is concerned. If remembered at all, they commonly define a dismal point of contrast with the earlier phases of triumphant Romanticism. At best we track a series of wounded beasts – the failures or madnesses of Darley, Beddoes, Clare. For the rest, critics simply shut the book of a Romanticism that seemed to translate itself into a commercialized nightmare: the new craze for Gift Books and Annuals like *Friendship's Offering, The Keepsake, Forget-Me-Not.* Literary history averts its gaze from this spectacle – there is scarcely a better word for the scene – because culture cannot easily capitalize its values. It seems an elegant dumpheap of factitious and overpriced trash – poor imitations of the life of the great Romantics.[16]

That aversion is a negative sign of a version of literary history – what Benjamin called the victor's version. It is the version that wants to distinguish sharply between documents of civilization – High Romanticism, so-called – and documents of barbarism – the gilded poetry and silver-fork novels of the 1820s and 1830s. But suppose one were to read the literature of the 1820s as a critical reflection on its Romantic inheritance. Writers like Hemans, Clare, Landon, Beddoes, Stoddart – to name a few representative figures – might tell a story of the death of the beauty that Romanticism created. Romantic nature is a cultural account of the biological order of things. The "meaning" it ascribes to this order is perpetual development and growth: in Wordsworth's classic formulation, "something evermore about to be." Such a vision translates "death" back into a phase or moment of a benevolent or splendid process of life.

The period of the 1820s presents a serious problem for (Romantic) literary history just because it appears to violate, in historical fact, this deep cultural myth of Romanticism. A Romantic agony begins when things of beauty do not appear joys forever – when no "abundant recompense" appears to balance the costs of Romantic commitments. Keats, Wordsworth's immediate inheritor, reveals and undergoes that agony. Of course he does so completely against his will, as it were. He wants nothing more than the joys of beauty and the realms of gold. What he keeps discovering, however, are pale kings and beautiful, merciless ladies: death that is deathless, true, but terrible for that very reason – death that is hardly endurable, and ranged with a beauty that must die not in a benevolent order of nature but in the gorgeous palaces of art, as *Lamia* shows.

In "The Fall of Hyperion" Keats announces this death in speciously heroic tones: "deathwards progressing / To no death was that visage." "Beyond that" shattered splendor with its pale vision of "the lily and the snow," Keats says simply, "I must not think." Beyond it lies the one story no Romantic poet wants to tell: the story of the death of art and culture. But the poets of the 1820s followed Keats (and Byron) to explore this "latest dream" dreamt on the cold hillsides of Romanticism. In Tennyson's 1832 book of *Poems* – and perhaps most memorably in works like "The Lady of Shalott" and "The Palace of Art" – this Romantic death appears to discover a new mode of expression, a form in which the death of art could itself be laid to rest. And at that point a corner had been turned. A Victorian corner.

III

I hope I shall not be misunderstood. *The Romantic Ideology* was read and criticized by some as a kind of debunking maneuver because of its antithetical readings of celebrated Romantic passages and works.[17] To the extent that such texts had been turned into idols of a Romantic cave, it might have appeared that I was trying to write them off the cultural scene. But the move was strictly a dialectical one – ultimately, an effort at a historical reimagining of Romanticism through an exposure of its concealed, sometimes even repressed, dialogical discourse. We do not debunk "Tintern Abbey" by sketching its sublimely egotistical projection of a sibling relationship; that relationship, cruel and benevolent at once, is one of the most powerful vehicles for the poem's structure of feelings.

Traditional critics have executed similar "debunkings" of Romanticism's celebrated works – most famously, I suppose, of Byron's "Fare Thee Well!" Nor is it entirely mistaken to argue, as Wordsworth and others would do, that Byron's poem to his wife is maudlin doggerel. Byron's poem is no less riven by contradictions than Wordsworth's, only in Byron's case the poem's cruelty is being carried by a deliberate *mask* of benevolence. Its doggerel, so-called, is merely the clearest stylistic signal of the poem's masquerade. Unlike Wordsworth, who pursues a style of sincerity and – in "Tintern Abbey" – comes (forward) to believe in his own benevolence toward his sister, Byron in "Fare Thee Well!" writes a rhetorical and quite *in*sincere poem. The work is self-conscious and duplicitous just where Wordsworth's poem is honest and unselfconscious. The ultimate (and untranscended) contradiction of Byron's poem is that its own awareness of contradiction does not entail an intellectual or moral *Aufhebung* – either for Byron as poet or for his readers. Byron's poem offers up to view – for those who have eyes to see and ears to hear – a vision of ultimate contradiction. The paradoxical result gives yet another turn to the screw of Romantic contradiction: Byron's Faustian discovery that truth is unredemptive. In Manfred's famous lament: "The Tree of Knowledge is not that of Life."[18]

ANNE MACK. Beauty as death, truth as insecure. You tell a bleak story.

JAY ROME. Perhaps it seems bleak because we so often take for truth what is actually Romantic hypothesis: that poetry, or art, will fill the void left by the previous hypothesis of Enlightenment. Romanticism is the battery of tests that the movement applied to its own ideological positions. Tennyson appears the sign of a new epoch because of the way he responded to the famous challenge put to him by his friend Trench: "Tennyson, we cannot live in art."

ANNE MACK. Well, he responded – for example in "The Palace of Art" – by arguing that beauty and deep feeling could not substitute for faith – any more than reason and enlightenment could. The Victorians are obsessed with the question of faith, religious as well as secular. Aesthetically absorbed, lacking either "honest doubt" or religious commitment, the Soul presiding in the Palace of Art is weighed and found wanting. Nonetheless, Tennyson's poem does not repudiate beauty and its palace:

> Yet pull not down my palace towers, that are
> So lightly, beautifully built.
> Perchance I may return with others there
> When I have purged my guilt.
>
> (293–296)[19]

That final play on the word "guilt" tells it all. The problem lies not in beauty and splendor as such but in the Soul's impurity. This poem stands exactly in the Keatsian tradition we glimpsed earlier – the line that passes into the "lightly, beautifully built" silver and gilded writing of the 1820s. If Tennyson turns a corner on Romanticism, it is a backward turning, an effort to recover a purified and "purged" ideal.

JAY ROME. True, but that program of correction transforms Romanticism into something entirely new. We see this change clearly, I think, at the end of "The Lady of Shalott" when Lancelot muses over the lady's dead body. The poem is famous as an allegory of the death of Romantic imagination. Paradoxically, however, nothing becomes this lady's life like the leaving it. Hers is an active death ("Singing in her song she died"), a deliberate move to terminate her ineffectually angelic life. Never had her social agency been more powerful than at the moment her corpse was carried into the heart of Camelot. "Knight and burgher, lord and dame" are terrified that a glory has passed from the earth. For his part, Lancelot reads the scene more calmly.

> He said, "She has a lovely face;
> God in his mercy lend her grace,
> The Lady of Shalott."

At their simplest – which is not their least important – level, the lines make an explicit plea for a grace beyond the reach of art. The prayer to God stands as an objective sign that this is a religious grace, something available through faith alone, not works. Also important is the logic (as it were) of Lancelot's thought. His prayer comes as if the lady's beauty were in need of God's mercy and grace. Her loveliness therefore suggests as well a kind of "fatal gift," the sign of something problematic lying at the heart of her poetical character.

ANNE MACK. And yet Tennyson's poem is not savage or tense like equivalent texts in Keats and Byron, or mordantly devalued like the poetry of Landon or Stoddart.

JAY ROME. The flat tone is unmistakable Tennyson – the sign of poetry affecting an absence of anxiety. The general populace reads the lady's face with fear, but Lancelot, the text's point of departure, remains undisturbed. Tennyson has unburdened his poem of the Romantic task of salvation. That task is returned to God. Beauty therefore emerges here as a device for clarifying vision. It makes no gestures toward an equivalent truth we might imagine it to symbolize. The poem is allegorical and decorative from the outset. As a result, the meaning of the poem, like the meaning of the lady's death, becomes, as it were, what you will. The poem is not imagined as a deep source from which we might draw life or faith. Romantic poems are organized in those ways, Tennyson's poem is different. Like the Lady of Shalott herself, it looks outward to its readers, without whom it cannot live or imagine living. It is, in short, a consciously social poem. It is Victorian.

The poem's ornamentality therefore marks its distance from a Romantic mode of address, where sincerity and personal feeling are paramount. Flaunting its artifice, Tennyson's poetry wears mortality on its face. Such annunciations of beauty, as Keats and Byron predicted, retreat from imaginations of transcendence. Beauty appears the sign of what is mortal. Gendered female, as in the poetry of Landon, such beauty and artifice come as figures of deceit and betrayal. Tennyson studied Landon and her immediate precursors, Keats and Byron, in order to reimagine those dangerous fatalities of beauty. But Tennyson takes his poetry's decorative forms to an extreme, paradoxically, in order to lower the temperature of the verse. The lady of Shalott's face is "lovely" and that is all. It has not launched a thousand ships or burnt the topless towers of Ilium. The citizens of Camelot are needlessly frightened. The poetry invites the reader to approach the poetry as Lancelot approaches the body of the lady: not struck with fear or wonder, but bearing a blessing that clarifies the situation by restoring its ethical and religious dimensions.

ANNE MACK. To me that placid surface is little more than a seductive deception. After all, this is *Lancelot* commenting on her beauty. If the death of this lady does not forecast the destruction of Camelot, that ruin appears in the depthless eyes of her beholder. The word "grace," in Lancelot's young mouth, is a sexist – indeed, a necrophiliac – word. Lancelot ultimately blasphemes with the word since his usage translates it into a purely formal and decorative meaning.

You're seduced by Lancelot and by Tennyson's beguiling surfaces, and you're even making us forget our real subject, the problem of periodization. When I cut through all this talk of Tennyson I find you arguing a position far removed from those dialogical modes of literary history you were celebrating a little while ago.

JAY ROME. Not so far removed. When I was talking about the poetry of the 1820s and the *New Oxford Book of Romantic Period Verse*, my thoughts inevitably went to Tennyson. His early work reflects and responds to the writing of the 1820s. The last two poems in the *New Oxford Book* will be "The Lady of Shalott" and "The Palace of Art."

ANNE MACK. Exactly. You end the collection with an editorial move that constructs a mastering (and worse still, a secret) historical narrative about Romanticism. So much for all that talk about a dialogical literary history.

JAY ROME. Where's the secret? I'm talking about it now, and it's explicitly present in the Introduction to the collection. It's not a *secret* simply because it's represented in a non-narrativized form. As I said before, we know how to read the grammar of anthologies.

ANNE MACK. Alright, let's call it an oblique rather than a secret history.

JAY ROME. Fine. Tell the truth but tell it slant.

ANNE MACK. Secret, oblique, slant – whatever. It's a master narrative, isn't it? You begin and end your collection in a certain way, like Yeats in his *Oxford Book of Modern Verse*. Those beginnings and endings constrain the material to particular historical meanings. When you stop your collection with those two Tennyson poems, you want us to imagine the end of Romanticism at that point, don't you? And you organize the anthology so that those two poems will come in with maximum effect in terms of the historical tale you're telling. "Obliquely," and so for maximum effect.

JAY ROME. Yes, that's true. But those two final poems have an authority of their own. They don't have to mean what I take them to mean. I might even change my mind about them. And didn't you just fling your different readings in my face a moment ago? Poems don't have to follow party lines.

Besides, you're discounting the formal inertia of the anthology, which is a collection of materials – in this case, evidence of what took place in the Romantic period. The evidence is organized to construct an argument for a certain narrative. But it's not a narrative itself. It's more like a building, or a picture.

ANNE MACK. And all sorts of evidence is left out.

JAY ROME. Of course, the book has its limits. What most attracts me to the anthology form – I speak from a literary historical point of view – is the *prima facie* character of those limits. "Heard melodies are sweet but those unheard / Are sweeter still." Isn't that always the case? An anthology is the very emblem of Derrida's "supplement of reading." It solicits revision, supplementation – it solicits your critique.

ANNE MACK. The devil can quote scripture to his own purpose.

JAY ROME. Who's the devil here, me or you? At any rate, you're the one playing the devil's advocate. If I'm the devil, it's you who take my part. I like spirits of negation. They're really just angels in dark clothes, aren't they?

ANNE MACK. You can't seriously want the negation or disproof of your own views.

JAY ROME. You're wrong, I really will settle for nothing less. Because I can't negate my views myself. I want to see the other side of my world. How did Tennyson put it:

> To follow knowledge like a sinking star,
> Beyond the utmost bounds of human thought.
> (31–32)

The second voyage of Ulysses, that's what I want. But I can't go by myself. So can you take me there? Do you know a way?

NOTES

1 Rene Wellek, "The Concept of Romanticism in Literary Scholarship," in *Concepts of Criticism* (New Haven: Yale University Press, 1963; originally printed in *Comparative Literature*, 1 [1949], 1–23, 147–172), 161.

2 For good surveys of these events see Jon Klancher, "English Romanticism and Cultural Production," in *The New Historicism*, ed. H. Aram Veeser (London: Routledge, 1989), 77–88; and Marjorie Levinson's two essays in *Rethinking Historicism*, "Introduction," and "Rethinking Historicism: Back to the Future" (Oxford: Basil Blackwell, 1989), 1–17, 18–63. For this essay I have adapted the title of Levinson's collection.

3 See, for example, M. H. Abrams. *Natural Supernaturalism* (New York: W. W. Norton, 1971); and Harold Bloom, *The Visionary Company* (Garden City: Doubleday, 1961).

4 Though the work of various recent critics might be instanced here, I cite particularly Peter W. Graham, *Don Juan and Regency England* (Charlottesville: University Press of Virginia, 1990), and the recent work of Peter Manning (see the essays on Byron collected in his *Reading Romantics. Texts and Contexts* (New York: Oxford University Press, 1990), especially "*Don Juan* and Byron's Imperceptiveness to the English Word," 115–144). Jerome Christensen has been writing superbly on Byron for several years, and his work is being gathered in that excellent study *Lord Byron's Strength: Romantic Writing and Commercial Society* (Baltimore: Johns Hopkins University Press, 1992). Susan Wolfson's studies of Byron are also important and relevant to the present discussion: see "'Their She Condition': Cross-Dressing and the Politics of Gender in *Don Juan*," *ELH*, 54 (1987), 595–617, and "'A Problem Few Dare Imitate': *Sardanapalus* and 'Effeminate Character,'" *ELH*, 58 (1991), 867–902. Some of my own recent work on Byron has run along similar lines (for example, "'My Brain is Feminine': Byron and the Poetry of Deception," in *Byron: Augustan and Romantic*, ed. Andrew Rutherford [Basingstoke: Macmillan, 1990], 26–51 – See also this volume, ch. 3; "Lord Byron's Twin Opposites of Truth," in *Towards a Literature of Knowledge* [Chicago: University of Chicago Press, 1989], 38–64; "Byron and The Truth in Masquerade,'" forthcoming in *Romantic Revisions*, ed. Tony Brinkley and Keith Hanley

[Cambridge: Cambridge University Press, 1992] See also this volume, ch. 4). Two key points of departure for recent feminist work in Romanticism are *Romanticism and Feminism*, ed. Anne K. Mellor (Bloomington: Indiana University Press, 1988), and Marlon Ross. *The Contours of Masculine Desire* (New York: Oxford University Press, 1989).

5 See my "The *Biographia Literaria* and the Contentions of English Romanticism," in *Coleridge's Biographia Literaria: Text and Meaning*, ed. Frederick Burwick (Columbus: Ohio State University Press, 1989), 233–254.

6 The most recent of these studies is in *The Textual Condition* (Princeton: Princeton University Press, 1991).

7 The first to suggest this critique was Marjorie Levinson, in a series of intense conversations and letter-exchanges shortly after the appearance of *The Romantic Ideology*. Her critique of Romantic studies continues, but her earliest lines of inquiry are set down in her essays in *Rethinking Historicism* (note 2). See also Clifford Siskin's *The Historicity of Romantic Discourse* (New York: Oxford University Press, 1988). Most recent to argue along these lines is Frances Ferguson in her critical review "On the Numbers of Romanticism," *ELH*, 58 (1991), 477.

8 This is the demand made by (among others) Michael Fischer in his early critique of *The Romantic Ideology* in *Blake: An Illustrated Quarterly*, 18 (1984–1985), 152–155.

9 Michael Taussig's approach to anthropology, set forth in a series of essays during the 1980s, offers another discipline's model of what I have in mind. The essays have just been collected as *The Nervous System* (London: Routledge, 1992).

10 See Charles Bernstein's collection of essays *Content's Dream. Essays 1975–1984* (Los Angeles: Sun & Moon Press, 1984); and Susan Howe's *My Emily Dickinson* (Berkeley: North Atlantic Books, 1985).

11 See two of Randall McLeod's published essays: "Unemending Shakespeare's Sonnet 111," *SEL*, 21 (1981), 75–96; "Unediting Shak-speare," *Sub-Stance*, 33/34 (1982), 26–55. Much of his most innovative work remains in typescript (such as "Information on Information"; "The bucke stoppeth here"; "Or Words to that dEffect").

12 Jeffrey Robinson, *The Current of Romantic Passion* (Madison: University of Wisconsin Press, 1991); Donald Ault, *Narrative Unbound: Re-visioning William Blake's The Four Zoas* (Barrytown: Station Hill Press, 1987).

13 A number of these have been published (often under transparent pseudonyms). The most recent (as well as most comprehensive) is "A Dialogue on Dialogue," published in the electronic journal *Postmodern Culture*, 2:1 (September, 1991).

14 *New History of French Literature*, ed. Dennis Hollier (Cambridge: Harvard University Press, 1989).

15 My edition here is *The Golden Treasury*, ed. Francis T. Palgrave, introd. William Tenney Brewster (New York: Macmillan, 1937).

16 One of the few recent critics to give any attention to the period is Virgil Nemoianu in his *The Taming of Romanticism: European Literature and the Age of Biedermeier* (Cambridge: Harvard University Press, 1984).

17 See James M. Kee, "Narrative Time and Participating Consciousness: A Heideggerian Supplement to *The Romantic Ideology,*" *Romanticism Past and Present*, 9 (Summer 1985), 51–63.

18 For a detailed exegesis of the poem along these lines see my "What Difference do the Circumstances of Publication Make to the Interpretation of a Literary Work?" in *Literary Pragmatics*, ed. Roger D. Sell (London: Routledge, 1991), 190–207; See also this volume, ch. 4.

19 All Tennyson citations are from *The Poems of Tennyson* (London: Longman, 1969).

CHAPTER 14

An interview with Jerome McGann

The following is a transcript of an interview between Jerome J. McGann (University of Virginia), Steven Earnshaw (University of Leicester), and Philip Shaw (University of Leicester). It was recorded at Warwick University, England, on 10 July 1992. Allusions in the interview to a paper relate to a talk earlier that same evening by Professor McGann entitled "Rethinking Romanticism."

PS: My first question refers to the work of Lacoue-Labarthe and Nancy in *The Literary Absolute*. I wondered how you saw your work in relation to the idea of Romantic literature producing its own critical reflection. Does Romanticism constantly demand critical perfection, and do you think that your work is a contribution to that demand?

JM: I'm not sure I agree with the premise that the literature constantly demands that perfection. There is an impulse in literary work / artistic work, generally, that is toward a certain kind of perfection, but it is not the kind of perfection, at least as I see it, that philosophers postulate, or should I say a philosopher like Plato postulates – which is one of the reasons why he tosses the poets out – because it's clear that poetry, insofar as it's imitation, cannot be a discourse of perfection, it has to be a discourse of imperfection. To my mind, poetical writing or imaginative writing, is imitation through-and-through, so it's always imperfect in a certain sense but, as in a recent book of mine [*The Textual Condition*], I try to point out there's another way of thinking about perfection where you'd say of Sister Theresa, or you'd say of Madonna, or you'd say of Michael Jordan, that they are perfect, and they *are* perfect in some sense. It's a highly inward sense, it's not a perceptual sense or theoretical sense. There's a further sense in which one would say of someone as ephemeral as Madonna, that the perfection probably would be very short-lived, its historicality is very short, that's clear. It's always clear in sports. Pindar for me is a very great poet because that is what he writes about, he is aware that his subjects are *that* human and *that* transient and so he tries to capture them at a moment of what he sees as perfection, but they're not transhistorical.

PS: So you wouldn't see Romanticism as a specific moment in the history of ideas? It raises the idea of imperfection and thus the need for perfection in a way that is unprecedented?

JM: Some Romantics – say, a theoretical writer like Coleridge, or a practical one like Wordsworth – see the presence of fragmentation and imperfection and use their work as a struggle against it. It is more-or-less heroic in that respect. It's also more-or-less self-deceiving in that respect, but not all Romantics do that. Byron certainly didn't. He is, it seems to me, a poet who woke up to realize that he had inherited ideas of perfection and that they were folly. So it's like trying to live on after the revolution has been destroyed – literally in this case – and how to live on without finally blowing your brains out. How do you now pursue culture knowing that culture is self-deceived, that it cannot be what you have been told or learned to believe it ought to be. His greatness for me is that he goes on. It's not an easy thing to do. Wordsworth lived under illusions, and he could not have carried out his grand project without agreeing basically to wipe out his self-critical intelligence. That's a limit to his work, but to say so is not a debunking. To say so is to *describe* his work.

PS: My second question is aligned to this idea of limits, and it's to do with your relation to poststructuralist thought. A lot of people, for example, suggest that Paul de Man's theory of rhetoric is self-circumscribing. Do you think that same criticism could apply to what you're doing with history?

JM: What you said of de Man I would not dissent from. What I do, what anyone does, is to have a project in mind that is more or less socially, collaboratively, imaginative. It does seem to me that Paul de Man's work was far more personally and subjectively imagined than I try to imagine my work. You can see it in his students. His students tend to be people who work along the lines that he believed in so passionately. If you knew my students you would know that in general this is not the way it is. I prefer to have students who think differently from me. People think of Marjorie Levinson, a student of mine, as an historicist critic. She's not, she's basically a psychoanalytic critic with a strong influence of Spinozistic and other philosophical thought. She's far more theoretically adept than I am. It was important for her to pass through, as it were, the tutelage and historical method that I drove down her throat. In any case, my work *is* circumscribed, but it differs from the kind of circumscription, as I see it, of de Man's work.

PS: I liked what you said at the end of the talk about being open to criticism and positively inviting it, which is, I think, something de Man didn't really do. Do you see your own project aligned in some way with what Derrida would call "responsibility for the other?"

JM: One of the earliest influences on me was de Man. I was educated at Yale. This is very early on. I went there in 1963. At that point de Man was a kind of underground figure. We passed around his essays on Hölderlin, his early stuff. There's a sense in which when I first read Bakhtin in 1975 it was a real problem for me because Bakhtin just overthrew my Yale education, and so at that point I was in a quite hostile relation to de Man, although, as a friend of mine used to say "You never wrote about it," and that is true. I was afraid of writing about him, taking his name in vain and all that. Now, as I look back on it, de Man seems to me to have been right about *aporias*. All those deconstructive moves on the text seem to me exactly the right thing to have made at that time. It's not unlike certain kinds of feminist deconstruction. The difference is, as I read de Man, he saw this in a highly Romantic or melancholy way, he saw this as failure. So when people criticized his writings he bristled, and defended the correctness of what he was doing, which seems to me a patent contradiction. Derrida is not like that, or has not been like that in his best works, which is why, to bring back de Man again, when the whole case of de Man came up and Derrida developed that series of articles in the *Critical Inquiry* exchanges, I was appalled at Derrida's performance there. I *do* understand that he wanted to defend his friend from what were clearly in certain cases the most mean-spirited kinds of attack. So many people were lying in wait to get him and they didn't need anything more than to have this kind of evidence of what they took to be the evil truth of his philosophical positions. But that didn't mean that Derrida had to become what he seemed to behold in the people that he talked with. He was incredibly contemptuous of his critics.

SE: How successful do you think your call for an engagement between the textual scholar and the hermeneutic critic has been?

JM: As I see the current scene, one of the liveliest areas of critical scholarship going on today is textual studies. Partly this is because, as I read it, the problematic of textuality came like thunder into that most sacred of areas, Shakespeare studies, focused on the two texts of *King Lear*, when it was shown that the whole tradition of delivering over Shakespeare's texts had been in several fairly important ways mistaken. The subject had to be rethought. It's not that you had to rethink the interpretation of Shakespeare, but you had to rethink the very textuality of Shakespeare in delivering it up. To my mind, the whole geography of criticism is really profoundly shaken, and this is beginning to happen in many areas, for example, in something as taken for granted as Emily Dickinson in our country and her sacred writing. Here the intervention of Franklin's facsimile edition about eight years ago has been decisive. It's clear that she has to be edited from the beginning – not just the poetry, but the letters. They're not what they appear to us to be. I think we're seeing similar kinds of dramatic events taking place for example in Hopkins. MacKenzie's OET [Oxford English Texts] edition stands in a radical contradiction to his facsimile edition. The Hopkins texts are not what we imagine them to be. In those two cases – they're interesting cases because they're both writers, especially Dickinson, who didn't write for print. When you don't write for print, what you're doing has a terminus in the activity you're engaged in right at that point.

SE: Is the kind of writing that is just for private use actually part of "the textual condition" you talk about, or is that only in operation when the writing enters the public domain?

JM: I used to think that there was such a thing as writing for private use, and obviously there is a difference between the way Byron writes for his massive public, or Tennyson, and the way Dickinson, or Hopkins write, in a much more restricted space. But they're all to my mind rhetorical spaces. Even if you are like, say, Dickinson, in many cases, writing to people who are dead. From the point of view of the writing, these people are still alive, you still have a conversation going on. But language is always coming through a Bakhtinian kind of dialectical scene, it's never private. Once more I'm going to come back to Dickinson because she interests me a lot. Until recently, people who wrote about Dickinson wrote about her as if she had no audience. There are clearly three different audiences in her work, at least, there may be more. She wrote for her family, and if you write poetry or whatever, you know that if you write a poem for your mother, or for your sister, now that's a certain kind of poem. Other people may read it, but that audience is determinative for that particular kind of writing. She wrote for her family, and she wrote for people in her small New England world, a certain kind of world, and that kind of environment can also be recovered analytically, and historically, and it *should* be recovered. Without recovering it you don't have the dialogical scene in which the writing is taking place. And then, at least at one other level, which is often named Master, which is often named God, which is often named Eternity, some other level of discourse that she's carrying on, perhaps with herself, perhaps with God, who knows what it is? But in any case it is not her family, it's not the town. It's another rhetorical order. Writing is always a conversation of some kind, dialogical as we say these days. It's essential that you explicate the scene of writing in this sense that we're talking about here, the environment where the conversation or intercourse takes place. For that means that you don't interpret in the way that comes to us through that highly patriarchal form of reading, which is hermeneutical interpretation of the word of God, where you have the Bible there, and the presumption is that there is a message in there with a meaning, which if you have enough grace – I guess that's what it all comes down to – you can arrive at a sense of it, but that meaning is there in a kind of transcendental and fundamental form. All the interpretations of course will vary over time, space and place, but the imagination is in the meaning – is there transcendentally. I don't think that we believe that, although I also don't think that our criticism is taking our own belief seriously – that reading, interpretation, is a conversation with a text that itself is what Keats called legendary, shot through with complicated, multiple, splintered, talk.

PS: Do you think it's possible to have a conversation with the non-human?

JM: Certainly, I believe that, in several senses. We talk with all sorts of non-human things, we certainly enter into conversations with our pets, with our plants. I think, for me, the world is alive in the way that John Cowper Powys believed.

SE: What distinguishes, in your view, literary knowledge from other types of knowledge? Does it, as you suggest in *Shall These Bones Live*, depend upon the "aesthetic experience," and if it does, how would you define the "aesthetic experience?"

JM: Scientific knowledge is committed to conceptualization. Its paradigm form for us is the replicatable experiment. That means that it's at once very abstract as a form of knowledge, and highly concrete as a form of replicated activity. Poetry in a certain sense is the opposite of this. To me, it has to be physical, poetry is – even if you don't speak it out loud – something that you get in your ears, your mouth, lips, and it's best, it seems to me, if you, as a teacher of poetry, get people to recite it, and physicalize the language. That's "the aesthetic" of poetry, literally physical or sensory, sensible. So knowledge in poetry is always coming through at the level of experience rather than at the level of concept. Insofar as concepts are in poetry they are there in highly concrete forms. Take something like *De rerum natura*, which happens to be a favourite poem of mine. Very abstract, a philosophical poem, full of ideas of various kinds, many of them "obsolete" ideas, but being carried in the poetry, although it's true, centuries ago, this was read the way we read Newton, or the way we read Einstein, as a scientific or a philosophical treatise, and now we no longer take it this way. Even then, the work was produced by a writer who clearly felt that the language was a total body experience, that knowledge took place in the entire organism. *That* to me is what distinguishes poetry from scientific knowledge or expository knowledge. It's language – total.

SE: Would you separate that experience, that experiential basis, from critical writing?

JM: It's very different, separate, and I thought you were going to say something like, "well, what's the difference between poetry and the conversation we're having right now?," which is basically what you are saying. The difference is that in poetry, the sensory elements are highly organized, decoratively organized, and the physical character of the language calls attention to itself. But we carry on our conversation here, our words just go away, we are so intent on transmitting messages or information that we don't pay a lot of attention to what we are saying. But in poetry, that's what it's all about, and you're constantly being brought back to an attention to the language as a thing itself. Fiction doesn't do that, which is why fiction locates a serious problem for me. I believe it's the case that when you read fiction (with certain exceptions – writers like Djuna Barnes, or fiction writers who are so poetical that the surface of their text calls attention to itself – but let's take a great fiction writer like Jane Austen or George Eliot), the language for the most part is a system that you are to pass through in order to get to the story that is being told. It's as if it were permeable. In poetry it's not, the surface of the poem is impermeable, it's resistant to you, it calls attention to its own rhetoric at the surface of it, but you go through the fictional surface in order to follow the story, unless you're a Joyce, or a modernist text, obviously you try to make poetical turning-points.

SE: So you're saying that the literary knowledge you get from fiction is different because the aesthetic experience is different?

JM: It has to be, it's certainly different for poetry, along the terms that I've described here. Clearly, other people may have different lines of thinking about this. By my commitment to an idea that poetry is language calling attention to itself, then immediately fiction proves itself a problem. As the novel in the Lukacsian sense rises you have the emergence of capitalism / bourgeois civilization. There are a lot of friends of mine on the left who make a great deal of this. It's inescapable that these two things have come together. What the meaning of it is, I'm not sure, and how one thinks about language in fiction as opposed to language in poetry I'm not sure. I think that Bakhtin had it backward, but I confess to you I don't know exactly how to think through the rest of this right now.

SE: How far are aesthetic responses shot-through with the ideology of the time? Is there a separate space for the aesthetic from the ideological?

JM: I don't think that anyone is able to escape false-consciousness. I mean, to me, ideology is, in one way or another, a state of misperception, false-consciousness, and to the degree that that's the case, it seems to me that no-one is ever able to get beyond that. As we sit here we're a part of it. In poetry, I know that the traditional view is that poetry like science in its highest and most ideal form, is imagined to be able to get beyond ideology. I don't believe that for a minute. It seems to me that science is clearly invested in political and cultural and social ends. It is in the service of certain kinds of authoritative powerful organizations and institutions. It's clear that poetry now, and literature in general, serves culture. To the degree that it serves culture, insofar as a culture is a system for maintaining certain kinds of social orders, it is ideological. I don't think these cultural services present a problem if you are aware that within hierarchies of dominant and indominant ideologies people are always shifting in and out. There's some sense in which one person may be more committed to, say, the service of the most dominant ideological state apparatuses, as opposed to somebody like Christina Rossetti, who wasn't. But in some sense we're all invested in different scales of ideological production, and I don't think that poetry is any different from that, or escapes any more.

SE: It takes me on to another point. You say that when we engage in critical activity it's always an ongoing dialectic between the present and the past, and that we should always "know thyself," know where we are at the present time. I've always had problems with this. How are we supposed to bare our ideological selves?

JM: We *can't* know ourselves, no-one can. This is an ideal that is put forward, which is unattainable. On the other hand, like ideals of any kind, it is there as a heuristic to organize, or help to organize, a pursuit of that kind of self-consciousness. Not that self-consciousness as itself, or in itself, is the sole end of life or the highest goal that one can perceive. Self-consciousness is a very important thing, but what about spontaneity? Without spontaneity you are dead. You must have that, that's another goal. You measure yourself by the authority of the goal of spontaneity as well. How to negotiate those things, well . . .

PS: Marjorie Levinson uses the model of transference and counter-transference in her introduction to *Rethinking Historicism*. I've always found that a very useful model for that past/present dialectic, and I wondered if you found that useful?

JM: No, I don't, Marjorie and I really part over Freudian structures. My distrust of Freudian structures is deep. I am very interested in more ancient ideas of dream and dream interpretation, I'm not hostile to the ideas of Freud. But Freudian models of the psyche, of dream, I resist them.

SE: As far as I can gather from my reading of your work, you do not allow theory any space separate from praxis, especially in *The Textual Condition*, your last work, where you say that "what is textually possible cannot be theoretically established," and you actually veer towards calling your approach "anti-theory." Do you think that theory and practice should always be coterminous, perhaps to the extent that no distinction can ever be made?

JM: Not necessarily coterminous but "dancing." You have to be trying to obtain that kind of self-consciousness that theory postulates. If you just *do* theory in the pursuit of that kind of self-consciousness you're constantly being called back. I am always called back by the authority of what people call "facticity" and the resistance that certain kinds of material realities or conditions raise up. I want the theoretical structures in fact to reveal them. So Blake is one of my great heroes. His idea of poetry was revelation: "If the doors of perception were cleansed, every thing would appear as it is, infinite." He literally saw poetry as something that just cleared away so he could see, as if knowledge were so impoverished that you had to begin at that most elemental level, because the impoverishment was an impoverishment of the body, so you turn the body inside out, you make the body reveal, just see. A theory doesn't just want to see, although "theoria" means "to see," it wants to see conceptually, which is a different thing. So, Kant and Blake, for me, are both theoretical – "seeing," as it were, imaginations. But the one is conceptually dominated and the other is aesthetically dominated. In a way, the whole world, in modernity's terms, is divided over the idea of whether you're committed to Kantianism or whether you're committed to Blakeanism.

PS: That's an interesting distinction. I'd've said Kant and Marx.

JM: Yes. Why didn't I say that? Probably because one of the most formative influences I know on my thinking has been religion. It's true that my family's religious life was always quite involved with social action, but the grounding was religion, and so my mind definitely tends to go in that direction. Marx for me is a conscious decision of choice, it's not instinctive, as it were.

SE: Do you see a collapse of literary studies into cultural studies, and if so, do you think it's desirable?

JM: [Laughing] I wonder what prompted that question? Does it show that I find that a problem?

SE: I always get the feeling that you have this real love of poetry which is at odds with a certain way that I see educational establishments in Britain going. It seems to me their desire is to do cultural studies. At the back of everything you write there appears to be this clinging to Blake, that ideal which seems to me doesn't have a space in the new way of looking at literature.

JM: I agree with that. I wouldn't have, maybe five or so years ago. But now I am not involved in cultural studies – it's not what I do – I'm interested in it, but it's definitely not what I do. I'm much more concerned about what used to be called "art" or "poetry," "imagination" perhaps you would call it. The world seems to be getting along very well with cultural studies as it always has. These things change from time to time, and some things I have more sympathy with than others, but art, especially in our day, seems to me to be in great peril, and it also seems to me to be a way of holding – and I *am* humanist in this sense – holding certain kinds of human ways of experiencing present and active. As I see our present cultural situation we're increasingly alienated from immediate experience. It's more and more wildly and complexly mediated. I do see that younger people seem to be able to maintain their aesthetic, as it were, more easily, than I can, in face of this. Young people especially seem to live in the world of simulacra, as if they were always in that vicinity. It's hard for me to live in that relation to simulacra.

SE: So do you find yourself fighting a rearguard action?

JM: I'm old-fashioned in the sense that I'm interested in textuality, I'm interested in editing, I'm interested in all sorts of memorial-type things.

SE: Yet you came up with the emergence of New Historicism, which is the latest thing, and here you are saying that you're old-fashioned. Do you just think New Historicism is an "old-fashioned topic"?

JM: To do historical studies well, you have to be trained and train yourself in certain kinds of skills that don't come very quickly. It's not that they're harder than other things, but they do take more time. Under the present institutional frame of reference that we live in, or the world that we live in as scholars, that kind of work is hard for a person to undertake, unless you want to take it in a kind of fast way – you are skilled and go after it. But really important scholarly work takes years for a person just to acquire the body of facticity that can be needed to work well. The institutions don't encourage you to do that. It's a difficult situation.

PS: You were talking earlier about "lived experience," I just wondered if it was possible to have a "lived" relationship with Postmodern culture, the idea of the simulacra, or whether or not in that sense that Baudrillard uses, the simulacra just overflowed everything – the map now covers the territory, there is no longer a distinction between the appearance and reality.

JM: We live in a world of simulacra, and whatever comfort one can take out of the fact that we know that this is the case – it may be an opening-up, an avenue for getting at a certain amount of human control over these things. I say that very skeptically because it does seem to me the case that what's happened in the United States over the past twelve or thirteen years has involved the implementation of a massive institutionally governed simulacra-driven presentation of culture to itself. Large portions of the intelligentsia are aware of it but it seems to have made no difference whatsoever. What has happened recalls for me one of my favourite passages of Byron, though I don't like to think of it as one of my favourite passages: "The Tree of Knowledge is not that of Life." That's a terrible idea for anyone engaged in intellectual life – to say it and to expect other people to believe it. Is that true? If that's true, it's a terrible truth.

PS: Well, Baudrillard would say you can't even say it's "true" anymore. *That's* the inflection.

JM: Once again you catch me in my old-fashionedness. We all speak in the language that we inherited, that we learned, and we have these conceptual forms that we have. I know there are other people, Baudrillard for one, whom I admire a great deal and read all the time, but who speak in a language that I have to reach for. It's not at all natural to me.

PS: Just to pick up on that quote you came out with earlier during your speech. You mentioned *Ulysses*, "to follow knowledge like a sinking star." I see you now as inhabiting "the voices that moan in the deep," to misquote Tennyson quite severely! Do you see yourself recovering dead voices?

JM: I do feel that what we don't know can be blessed, and probably *will* be blessed, in ways that we have no idea of, so you become committed to – and I certainly do see my own work in this way – to saving things, even though you have no sense what possible use they might have. It's like old people who have a house full of nick-nacks and they save them. Some of them will have associations, some of them will have, as it were, conscious meanings, but many of them will not, they are just there in some way that you don't understand.

PS: Felicia Hemans for example?

JM: That is the kind of writing she does, that is *exactly* the kind of writing she does. The simulacra poet of that period is Landon, and what her subject is, love, the great Romantic subject, and its illusions, told from a woman's point of view now which makes all the difference in the world. It's all very well to talk about it from a man's point of view but it makes a big difference when you pick up some subjects in a different frame of reference, a woman's frame.

SE: In *Social Values and Poetic Acts* you say that "'Meaning' in literary works is a function of the uses to which persons and social organizations put those works" [p. 125]. This seems to me to be firmly in the tradition of pragmatism. Do you see a great affinity between your work and pragmatism?

JM: Yes, clearly my work has strong affinities with the pragmatic tradition. (Europeans associated with what is called "Literary Pragmatics" have shown a good deal of interest in my work.) Dewey has been a strong influence on my thought – from the earliest time (1960 or so) that I thought self-consciously about the social function of art and imagination. But I don't think about pragmatism and its traditions in the way that, say, Dick Rorty does. My interests are more procedural than his, even more institutional and pedagogical (e.g., I spend a fair amount of time working on experimental classroom and curricular projects). I think that pragmatism as a philosophical pursuit is (to borrow your earlier term) a kind of anti-theory, or theory as practice. One of my principal "theoretical" projects right now is a hypermedia edition of the complete works of Dante Gabriel Rossetti. I see the edition itself as a theoretical act and intervention, a "statement" if you will about theory of textuality.

SE: In your article "A Dialogue on Dialogue" [*Postmodern Culture*, 2:1 (Sept. 1991)], one of the interlocutors claims that "our conversations" are grounded in "the pursuit of meaning, in hermeneutics and the desires of interpretation," rather than the pursuit of truth and power. What is the status of truth and power in your own work?

JM: "Power corrupts and absolute power corrupts absolutely." For better and for worse, that is for me an article of faith. My passion for poetry stems from my perception of it as an activity of loss. *Social Values and Poetic Acts* was originally titled *Buildings of Los(s)*, but the press drove me off that title by persuading me – I was stupid to agree – that no one would understand it – that readers might even think it was a book about architecture! Anyway, "Buildings of Los," that is what Blake understood poetry to be. For example, power enlisted as a machine for dismantling the structures of power – a house set against itself, and that therefore cannot stand; Emily Dickinson's religion, which eschews salvation (because salvation is part of an economic system of rewards and punishments, a system of power). And then there's "truth," if you will. Truth is for me inseparable ("ideally") from the decisions and acts that make up the drive toward the truth. Truth is therefore a kind of test of itself, or a test of the person who has made a commitment to it. The truth of the scientists and the philosophers is something else. Their Truths are all very well, in their ways, but they aren't "Troth." Except perhaps in the case of Socrates, who had finally to face Truth as Troth.

CHAPTER 15

Poetry, 1780–1832

AA, XX, and NN gather to talk.

AA. According to the official guides, our best view of the Romantic ranges extending across the great divide of 1800 will be found in 1798, or perhaps the immediately adjacent 1800: from that splendid overlook called *Lyrical Ballads*. It's a picturesque and (historically) important locale.

Equally arresting, however, is that more remote point known as *Songs of Innocence and of Experience* (1794). A favorite now of many, this vantage was scarcely known or frequented until the Pre-Raphaelites popularized it in their late-nineteenth-century aesthetic adventures.

Neither of these now famous spots of time[1] will lose its hold upon the imagination. We may start a long, an interesting, and a reasonably thorough exploration of Romanticism and its majestic adjacencies from both places, as many have already shown.

Traditional and favorite routes are, however, just that – traditional and favored. This particular world of the sublime and the beautiful is so extensive and complex that we may enter it, or move about its regions, in an endless variety of ways.

For instance, on the way to *Lyrical Ballads* we will inevitably skirt another spot that provides, in its fashion, an even more magnificent view of the territory. I mean the once-famous but now somewhat neglected outcropping called *Poems, chiefly in the Scottish dialect* (Kilmarnock, 1786). From the latter the way leads directly on to both Blake's *Songs* and Wordsworth and Coleridge's *Lyrical Ballads*. The route from Burns's 1786 *Poems* to *Lyrical Ballads* is well known if no longer so well frequented. But the rigs o' Burns run into the range of Blake. We trace this route very clearly by following certain of their shared territorial features: their critiques of moralized religion, their sympathy with the ideals of the French Revolution, and their commitment to what Blake called "exuberance" and "energy" (and Wordsworth, later, the "spontaneous overflow of powerful feelings").

Blake found his way by various paths, it is true, but one of them followed the trail of Burns. Indeed, Blake marked the route he took in one of his greatest early works, "The Tyger," although later travellers have failed to note the signs he left:

When the stars threw down their spears,
And water'd heaven with their tears:
Did he smile his work to see?
Did he who made the Lamb make thee?

Blake's starry spears of 1794 broke across the earlier sky of 1786 in another Satanic text, Burns's great "Address to the Deil." The second line of Blake's verse is an English translation of Burns's Scots:

Ae dreary, windy, winter night,
The stars shot down wi' sklentan light,
Wi' you, *mysel*, I gat a fright.

Blake's "smile" – like the high-spirited comedy of that associated text *The Marriage of Heaven and Hell* (1793) – is a memorial tribute to Burns, who also liked to treat his gods and demons with familiarity. Like Blake, he knew that all deities reside in the human breast, as the very next lines of his address to the "deil" show:

   Ayont the lough;
Ye, like a *rash-buss*, stood in sight,
   Wi' waving sugh.

The cudgel in my neive did shake,
Each bristl'd hair stood like a stake,
When wi' an eldritch, stoor *quaick*, *quaick*,
   Amang the springs,
Awa ye squatter'd like a *drake*,
   On whistling wings.

From Blake back to Burns; and from Burns on to Wordsworth, who learns to take spiritual instruction from the quotidian orders of nature out of texts like Burns's:

O'er rough and smooth she trips along,
And never looks behind;
And sings a solitary song
And whistles in the wind.
("Lucy Gray," 1800)

XX. Where did Keats take his lessons, from Burns or from Wordsworth?

Mortal, that thou may'st understand aright,
I humanize my sayings to thine ear,
Making comparisons of earthly things;
Or thou might'st better listen to the wind,

Whose language is to thee a barren noise,
Though it blows legend-laden through the trees.
("The Fall of Hyperion," written in 1819)

AA. From both and from neither. What we see here is a way of writing, a way of imagining the world, that was characteristic of Romanticism. The sensibility is broadly dispersed, translated, transmuted. A legend-laden[2] wind blows across the whole stretch of these everlasting hills. Although it has no beginning, we will not encounter it in the near-by range of the Augustans.

XX. I'm not so sure about that. James Macpherson's Ossianic texts often exhibit the same kind of weather. In the first of his *Fragments of Ancient Poetry* (1760), for instance, the warrior Shilric returns to his home in the Scottish highlands to discover that his beloved Vinvela has died in his absence. The fragment records a conversation between the parted lovers, but Macpherson's text makes it clear that we are not overhearing a human conversation, we are observing a sensibility conversant with legend-laden winds.

By the mossy fountain I will sit; on the top of the hill of winds. When mid-day is silent around, converse, O my love, with me! come on the wings of the gale! on the blast of the mountain, come! Let me hear thy voice, as thou passest, when mid-day is silent around. (I, ii)

The superstitions of Burns, the local tales memorialized by Wordsworth, the mythologies of Keats – all follow the same structural pattern we see here in Macpherson.

Note the date of this, 1760.

AA. And we can find similar things even earlier – for example, in the work of Gray and Collins from the 1740s and 1750s. The cultural fault lines along which the geography of Romanticism was formed will not be mapped on the grids of Cartesian geometries – what Blake called "the mill [of] Aristotle's Analytics." We need topological measures for discontinuous phenomena of these kinds, non-Euclidean mathematics of the type first pursued (for example, by Gauss and Bolyai) in – the Romantic Period itself! What we've been looking at here, in this view across the range that includes Burns, Blake, Wordsworth, Keats, and Ossian . . .

XX. . . . and they don't exhaust this landscape by any means.

AA. . . . no, of course not; but what we've been looking at is a kind of topological basin where sets of "attractors" (as the mathematicians say) hold dispersing phenomena in random patterns. Patterns, because the phenomena exhibit recursive forms (a few of which we have noticed); random, because the possibilities for other patternings are endless. We may come at these scenes and experiences from many directions. Patterning dissolves and other patterning appears; some of these patternings will recur in mutated forms, some will not. The locale is (like its own natural light) "incoherent"; but it is also a dynamic and self-integrated whole.

How do we get to know it, then? people sometimes ask. And I want to say, simply by looking at it. "If the doors of perception were cleansed . . ." – you know the rest. Even when we think we're following that great Romantic star, the imagination, we often close ourselves up and see only through the narrow chinks of our caverned brains. Take Blake and his *Songs* and "The Tyger," for instance. Turn your view away from Burns for a moment and observe the *Songs* from the vantage of children's literature, or against the background of that related and overlapping phenomenon, the tradition of emblematic writing. A whole new world of realities suddenly rises to your sight. And it is endlessly interesting, we could wander in this new world for a long time.

It is a world inhabited, for example, by that famous and highly influential family, the Taylors of Ongar. The highfalutin imaginations of Coleridge and Southey and Wordsworth shook their heads in melancholy dismay at what they saw as the failed and mad magnificence of Blake's writings. Jane Taylor had no such problems. Just as Blake incorporated (and thereby reinterpreted) Burns's "Address to the Deil" in "The Tyger," Jane Taylor (1783–1824) did the same to Blake's poem. She answered the famous theological questions of "The Tyger" with the augury of an innocence we have all but forgotten, so serious do we often get, so far do we wander from the pleasure principles laid down in the fields of childhood:

> Twinkle, twinkle, little star,
> How I wonder what you are!
> Up above the world so high,
> Like a diamond in the sky.
>
> When the blazing sun is gone,
> When he nothing shines upon,
> Then you show your little light,
> Twinkle, twinkle, all the night.
>
> ("The Star" [1806])

In effect, Taylor is reading Blake's "Tyger" through Blake's "Dream," another text recollected in Taylor's "Star." It is a crucial literary-historical move – whether we are passing through remote areas of our histories or through nearby (and perhaps academic) regions. When Blake added the *Songs of Experience* (in 1794) to the *Songs of Innocence* (1789), he established a critical model for Romantic dialectics[3] that would proliferate and endure. Taylor's poem is important because it reminds us that the dialectic is reversible, that the world of experience might be undone by entering it through Blake's "Lamb" or Taylor's "Star" or as it would later continue to be by works like Christina Rossetti's "Goblin Market" (1862). For this is a long and complex history that has been adopted by both parties to the dialectic.
XX. And as Blake said, the parties are and should be enemies. Wordsworthian recollection, the determinative model for Romantic memory, stands forever opposed to the primary energies celebrated by Burns and Blake . . .

AA. . . . and to the simplicities pursued by Taylor. It is crucial to be clear about the differential shining out in poems like "The Star" – a work that stands far closer, in ethos and history if not in time and style, to Burns's and Blake's poems and songs than to the secondary imaginations[4] of Wordsworth and Coleridge. Certain of Wordsworth's most splendid poems, so hateful to Blake, define the difference with great exactness. A guiding and protective star presides over the landscape of Wordsworth's "Michael" (1800), for instance, but the history that Wordsworth sees throws it into eclipse:

> The Cottage which was nam'd The Evening Star
> Is gone, the ploughshare has been through the ground
> On which it stood; great changes have been wrought
> In all the neighbourhood.

The cottage and its symbolic name have "slip[ped] in a moment out of life" into the care of a memorializing imagination ("To H. C. Six Years Old"). As in "The Solitary Reaper," Wordsworth accepts – triumphs in – the imaginative displacement of primary experience: "The music in my heart I bore / Long after it was heard no more." That displacement is unnatural to Burns, for example, whose song voice is inseparable from the voice of the girl known to Wordsworth only at two removes. So in Blake and Burns and Taylor, "the melancholy slackening" so characteristic of one strain of Romanticism does not (typically) "ensue" (*Prelude*, VI [1850]). Sorrow and happiness do not run in alternating currents, their relations are direct and immediate. All is "naive." The Wordsworthian model –

> We Poets in our youth begin in gladness;
> But thereof come i' th' end despondency and madness
> ("Resolution and Independence" [1807])

– is applied to this other Romantic strain only with difficulty because the logic of Wordsworth's "thereof" is refused. This happens because the dialectic of gladness and despondency, pleasure and pain, is not imagined as a conceptual relation but as an existential one. We see the situation clearly in much of Burns's work, not least of all in his masterpiece "Love and Liberty – A Cantata" (commonly called "The Jolly Beggars" [1799]).

> The Caird prevail'd—th' unblushing fair
> In his embraces sunk;
> Partly wi' LOVE o'ercome sae sair,
> And partly she was drunk:
> Sir VIOLINO with an air,
> That show'd a man o' spunk,
> Wish'd UNISON between the PAIR,
> An' made the bottle clunk
> To their health that night.

XX. Yet how difficult this resort to the wisdom of the body, even in an age self-devoted to Nature![5] Burns's lines expose the kinds of contradiction most writers could only engage through various forms of displacement. It violates decorum (social as well as literary) to make such a witty rhyme of the excessively correct (and English) "unblushing fair" ("unblushing"!) with the low dialect (and Scots) "sae sair," or to "pair" in this way all the other incongruities raised up by the passage. The inhuman treatment of women in traditional love poetry is here overthrown.

NN. Yes, but it is a reckless – ultimately a masculine – overthrowing, is it not? Splendid as Burns's love poetry is – including his more genteel love poems – he cannot deliver the complex truths exposed in the sentimental styles[6] developed (mainly) by women writers in the late eighteenth and early nineteenth centuries.

Ridiculed as "unsex'd females" by reactionaries like Gifford, Matthias, and Polwhele, writers like Hannah Cowley turned female experience in the male world to a test of that world's hidden truths. In Cowley's "Departed Youth" (1797), for example, we see the birth of a new Venus from the wreck of her 64-year-old body. The thefts of time are taken back in the poem's imperative to "Break the slim form that was adored / By him so loved, my wedded lord." The metaphysics of a Sternian sentimentality lead Cowley to exchange the body of her first nature – adorable, married, passive – for a *vita nuova*:

> But leave me, whilst all these you steal,
> The mind to taste, the nerve to feel.

As in the rest of the poem, Cowley here breaks the slim forms of her earliest language. As generous as Burns ("my wedded lord") and, if less vigorous, just as determined, her behavior preserves her inherited proprieties. "Departed Youth" invokes a whole series of favorite eighteenth-century terms and phrases from the lexicon of sensibility ("lively sense," "sentiment refined," "taste," "nerve," "feel") only to reembody them through a series of syntactic and lexical wordplays. If the poetic style is different, the poetic demand is exactly like the one Yeats would make famous, in the poetry of *his* old age, a century and more later.

Readers, especially twentieth-century readers, often miss what is happening in texts like these because they forget the conventions of a poetry written under the sign of what Shelley called "Intellectual Beauty." It is a sophisticated, an artificial sign – like that fanciful nature you two have been playing with in your conversation. But Romantic nature, as you know, is an allegorical construct of urbane minds. In the late eighteenth century, the allegory tended to assume picturesque forms because of the authority of sentimentalism. Cowley's verse and the entire Della Cruscan movement operate under that authority.

Although commonly understood to involve mental as opposed to sensuous phenomena, intellectual beauty is precisely the sign for a determination to undermine the body/soul distinction altogether. When Robert Merry ("Della Crusca") publishes his intention to quit poetry, Cowley ("Anna Matilda") writes to dissuade him:

> O! seize again thy golden quill,
> And with its point my bosom thrill;

The self-consciousness of such eroticism – it is nothing less than the Metaphysical verse of sentimentalism – is exactly the "point." Cowley calls for a "blended fire" of poetry and sexuality:

> The *one*, poetic language give,
> The *other* bid thy passion live;

Later Romantic writers become preoccupied with Paolo and Francesca, Launcelot and Guenevere, Tristan and Isolde, in order to explore what D. G. Rossetti would call "the difficult deeps of love." The kiss is the earliest figure of those deeps, and it focuses a great deal of Della Cruscan writing:

> The greatest bliss
> Is in a kiss—
> A kiss by love refin'd,
> When springs the soul
> Without controul,
> And blends the bliss with mind.
>
> (Charlotte Dacre ["Rosa Matilda"], "The Kiss")

The fact that we cannot tell whether it is the kiss or the soul that "blends the bliss with mind" underscores the radical confusions being sought in texts like these. They execute the drama that Mark Akenside called the "pleasures of imagination" (1744). Coleridge's measured "balance and reconciliation of opposite and discordant qualities" here "springs . . . [w]ithout controul" because Dacre's theory of imagination stands closer to a "Prolific" Blakean "Energy" than to Coleridge's more famous conceptual approach to the subject.

XX. Yes, and when Thomas Moore, in one of his many kissing lyrics, celebrates the same kind of "sweet abandonment" ("The Kiss" [1801]), he marks the close relation between eros and madness that Romanticism perceives and pursues. A great theme of Romantic culture, madness is the index of thwarted desire. Writers of the period fashion a poetry of madness in order to gain (paradoxically but precisely) the "controlless core" (Byron, *Don Juan*, I, st. 116) of imaginative abandonment. Demon lovers and desperate brains: both are familiar Romantic tropes, and while the one descends into the culture largely through the propagators of the ballad revival, the other is the offspring of those sentimentalist projects and writers you seem to favor.

In each case, a grammar of the fantastical is deployed in order to express what would be difficult or impossible to say otherwise. A pair of this period's early and influential writers, M. G. Lewis and Charlotte Smith, exemplify these two grammars very well, as we can see in this sonnet by Smith (1797):

Sonnet. On being Cautioned against Walking
on an Headland Overlooking the Sea, because
it was Frequented by a Lunatic

Is there a solitary wretch who hies
To the tall cliff, with starting pace or slow,
And, measuring, views with wild and hollow eyes
Its distance from the waves that chide below;
Who, as the sea-borne gale with frequent sighs
Chills his cold bed upon the mountain turf,
With hoarse, half-uttered lamentation, lies
Murmuring responses to the dashing surf?
In moody sadness, on the giddy brink,
I see him more with envy than with fear;
He has no *nice felicities* that shrink
From giant horrors; wildly wandering here,
He seems (uncursed with reason) not to know
The depth or the duration of his woe.

A machinery of transferred epithets, Smith's sonnet gradually measures a series of figural reflections between the seascape, the lunatic, and Smith herself. But even as these identifications culminate in the ambiguous grammar opening the sestet, Smith unfolds a glimpse of a far more wildered mental landscape. The self-consciousness of Smith's art – her "*nice felicities*" – produce the poem's final, disastrous revelation: that the delicate workings of the sonnet execute an awareness of the "giant horrors" one constructs by raising illusory (i.e., rational) defenses against them.

There is an imagination in Smith's sonnet at war with its cursed artifice and its limited, shrinking consciousness. Warned (reasonably) against a direct encounter with the lunatic, Smith goes to meet him in imagination because her own "moody sadness" – her feelings – possess a deeper knowledge than her defensive, civilized understanding. In 1812 Byron would make the drama of "Consciousness awaking to her woes" world-famous in the story of Childe Harold (Canto I, st. 92). This story, however, began to be told in the late eighteenth century's literature of sensibility, as Smith's sonnet shows. It is the story of the sleep of reason, its illusory dreams, and its "awaking" to that complex Romantic understanding that "Sorrow is knowledge" (*Manfred*, I, I).

A crucial feature of Smith's sonnet is its style of sincerity[7] – a style that would come to characterize so much Romantic poetry. The purpose of the style is to make the immediate experience of "the poet" the dramatic focus of the text – as if "the poet" were herself the poem's central subject, as if she were subject to the revelatory power of the poem she herself decides to write. Romantic melancholy is one affective consequence of the deployment of such a style: *mon coeur mis à nu*, and at one's own hand.

Much Romantic poetry will devote itself to a search for ways to defend itself against the dangerous self-divisions fostered by this style of sincerity. The most famous of these defenses was raised by Wordsworth, whose journeys into his *selva oscura* brought, his poetry argued, an "abundant recompense" for psychic wounding and suffered loss.

> For I have learned
> To look on nature, not as in the hour
> Of thoughtless youth; but hearing oftentimes
> The still, sad music of humanity,
> Nor harsh nor grating, though of ample power
> To chasten and subdue.
> ("Tintern Abbey" [1798])

That lesson would guide and trouble a great deal of subsequent poetry. Accepting – indeed, undergoing – such loss, Wordsworth discovered "That in this moment there is life and food / For future years," discovered (literally) a new spiritual life:

> a sense sublime
> Of something far more deeply interfused,
> Whose dwelling is the light of setting suns,
> And the round ocean and the living air,
> And the blue sky, and in the mind of man:
> ("Tintern Abbey")

Smith's sonnet does not romanticize her suffering in this way. For Smith, the recompense lies simply in the text's having broken through the curse and sleep of reason to discover the holiness of the heart's affections, however disordered. Indeed, the unstable character of feeling generated by her sonnet is the exact sign that a break-through has occurred.

AA. But Romanticism had other ways for exploring unknown worlds. The impersonal character of Blake's *Songs* would succeed to the age's greatest representation of psychic and social derangement in that epic of "the torments of love and jealousy," *The Four Zoas*. Madness in this work, however, appears an objective state of general spiritual existence rather than the subjective experience of a particular person. Consequently, the poem creates a textual environment where readers are thrown back wholly on their own resources. To read *The Four Zoas* is extremely disorienting because one must traverse the work with no guidance or protection – as if Dante were to have made his journey to hell without Virgil.

In the Romantic poetry of sincerity readers are spectators of the worlds and experiences that appear to be undergone by the poets. In this respect the Romantic poet serves at once as topic and guide for the reader, whose function is to observe and learn lessons of sympathy – to "overhear" the poetry, as J. S. Mill later said. Blake's poetry, by contrast, calls the reader to acts of final (self-)judgment. The great question posed by all of Blake's poetry is simple but devastating, how much reality can you bear to know? "If the doors of perception were cleansed, every thing would appear to man as it is, infinite" (*The Marriage of Heaven and Hell*, plate 14): but the world of the infinite will not be reconnoitered as if one were going a casual journey. It is a world of ultimate things, a world where one may expect only to be weighed and found wanting.

XX. Blake was interested in the poetry of Ossian and the ballad revival because such work appeared to deliver one into completely alien worlds: not the worlds of dreaming or the dreamer, but the worlds of dreams-as-such – those orders existing independently of the (un)conscious mechanisms that can sometimes establish contact with them.

Some of Coleridge's greatest poetry is essentially an argument that such ideal orders do in fact exist, "Kubla Khan" being the most famous and perhaps successful of these works. When he finally published the poem, Coleridge cased it in an elaborate prose framework that called attention to the dreamed character of the text and experience. Paradoxically, this personal rhetoric heightens the impersonal quality of the vision, as if the poetical text were the residue of a concrete world subsisting beyond mortal ken, a prelapsarian world where words rise up as things, a world occasionally glimpsed (perhaps in dream) by time- and space-bound creatures.

In "Kubla Khan" the act of dreaming is a trivial event when set beside the ideal world that appears to have suddenly and transiently arisen to view. It is as if the appearance were recorded to measure the distance between mortal dreamer and immortal dream. We observe the same kind of rhetoric in, for example, a poem like Byron's "Darkness." Beginning with a perfunctory gesture from the dreamer ("I had a dream, which was not all a dream"), the poem unfolds a detailed catalogue of Armageddon, which assumes an independent substantiality like Coleridge's vision of the world of Kubla Khan.

Byron's rhetorical procedure is put into relief when we set it beside the literary example that spurred him to his poem – Thomas Campbell's "Last Man." Although most of Campbell's poem is a first-person report of a dream of apocalypse, the dreamer is carefully defined at the outset as an imaginary "last man." Consequently, the fictional status of the poem is always clear. Coleridge and Byron, on the other hand, represent their texts through a rhetoric of immediacy. As a result, when their texts discard the psychological supports for their visionary representations, we appear to have entered worlds of dream rather than the dreaming experiences of particular persons.

The uncanny effect of Byron's poem is most disorienting not because the apocalypse we enter is a negative one, but because the otherworld of the text appears an independently authorized existence. As in the texts of the evangelists, the mediator of such an existence is not the focus of attention. (Because Byron was so famous, perhaps especially at the moment of this poem – 1816 – the subjection of dreamer to dream is all the more arresting.)

Keats's dream poetry is quite different, as one can see by looking at his great sonnet "A Dream, after Reading Dante's Episode of Paolo and Francesca" (1820):

> As Hermes once took to his feathers light,
>   When lulled Argus, baffled, swoon'd and slept,
> So on a Delphic reed, my idle spright
>   So play'd, so charm'd, so conquer'd, so bereft
> The dragon-world of all its hundred eyes;
>   And, seeing it asleep, so fled away—
> Not unto Ida with its snow-cold skies,
>   Nor unto Tempe, where Jove griev'd a day,
> But to that second circle of sad hell,
>   Where 'mid the gust, the world-wind, and the flaw
> Of rain and hail-stones, lovers need not tell
>   Their sorrows. Pale were the sweet lips I saw,
> Pale were the lips I kiss'd, and fair the form
> I floated with about that melancholy storm.

As in "The Fall of Hyperion," this poem gives not the dream as such but Keats's experience of entering the uncanny world of dream. The event is typically Keatsian, as one sees in early poems like "Sleep and Poetry" and "On First Looking Into Chapman's Homer." Although not literally a dream poem, the latter is, like "The Fall of Hyperion," the record of the discovery of the power of imaginative vision. The difference separating Keats's work, in this respect, from Blake's and Coleridge's and Byron's measures the close affinity of Keats to Wordsworth. Keats's dream poetry follows the form of, for example, the Arab-Quixote dream sequence detailed in the *Prelude* Book V – in this kind of work we behold the dreamer first; the dream itself is mediated as an experience of discovery.

In the Wordsworthian model, the discovery is then self-consciously meditated and read by the poet. In all such work the contrast with Byron's "Darkness" could not be more complete. As with *Manfred*, "Darkness" records a process of (as it were) *un*discovering the powers of the human mind. The epigraph to *Manfred* is telling: "There are more things in heaven and earth, Horatio, / Than are dreamt of in your philosophy." The special perversity of Byron's work would be picked up later by Poe, Baudelaire, and Nietzsche.

NN. Mediated or unmediated, Romantic dream poetry traces itself to the strange materials made available by late eighteenth-century philologists and ethnographers: ballad editors like Bishop Percy and Joseph Ritson, translators like Sir William Jones and Charles Wilkins. Jones's influential translations of Sanscrit originals are explicit testimonies to the reality of originary existences. The Vedic hymns reveal utterly strange worlds:

> Hail, self-existent, in celestial speech
> NARAYEN, from thy watry cradle, nam'd;
> Or VENAMELY may I sing unblam'd,
> With flow'ry braids that to thy sandals reach,
> Whose beauties, who can teach?
> ("A Hymn to Na'ra'yena" [1785])

The strangeness of these pieces of "celestial speech" measures something besides the distance between Orient and Occident. Indeed, the cultural differences between these two great worlds are not what drives Jones's interest in the Vedic hymns. On the contrary, the universalist eighteenth-century style of Jones's texts fashions a verse argument about secret congruences between East and West.

Through Jones's translations the Sanscrit texts reveal the vision of an originary and transcendent unity of being. The Vedic hymns are important for Jones's imperial intellect because they carry an "attestation strong, / That, loftier than thy [poetry's] sphere, th' Eternal Mind, / Unmov'd, unrival'd, undefil'd, / Reigns" ("Hymn to Su'rya" [1789]).

AA. Well, important as Jones was, Western writers found their favorite, unknown worlds much closer to home, in the folk literature of European culture. The poetry of the period is dominated by those sophisticated appropriations of original song and ballad materials, the literary ballads: texts like William Taylor's "Ellenore" (translated from an already sophisticated German text), Coleridge's "Rime of the Ancient Mariner" and "Christabel," Keats's "Belle Dame Sans Merci," Baillie's "Ghost of Fadon." Taylor's "Ellenore," for example, opens under a traumatic sign ("At break of day from frightful dreams / Upstarted Ellenore"), but the story means to deliver us over to strange realities all the more "frightful" just because they appear conscious and undreamt.

XX. Which is why the work of M. G. Lewis calls for special attention, as I said before. It not only represents a vigorous contemporary literary tradition, it was a tradition denounced by Wordsworth, who anticipated later criticism's retrospective view of the issues involved. When Wordsworth refers (in his 1800 Preface to *Lyrical Ballads*) to "frantic novels, sickly and stupid German Tragedies, and deluges of idle and extravagant stories in verse," he is reflecting on literary work of the 1790s that Lewis epitomized and fostered. No text illustrates better what Wordsworth disapproves of than *The Monk* (1796),[8] that wonderful "frantic novel" imbedded with several "extravagant stories in verse."

Wordsworth's phrase "idle and extravagant" points to what is most distinctive and peculiar about Lewis's work – its marriage of the comic and the ludicrous with the horrible and the terrifying. Rent by internal contradictions, the work appears to have little interest in bringing them under control – as if pure effect (and affect) were the sole resource and only plan of the writing. In this respect *The Monk*'s imbedded poems reflect the novel as a whole – and none more so than the famous ballad (much parodied, much imitated) "Alonzo the Brave and the Fair Imogine."

A tale of betrayed love, revenge, and damnation, the poem's most disturbing effects develop from the "idle and extravagant" way it handles its materials. When Alonzo returns from the dead to claim his false beloved at her wedding feast, he comes helmeted, his identity concealed. Faced with this strange wedding guest, Imogine barely manages to keep her composure:

At length spoke the bride, while she trembled—"I pray,
Sir Knight, that your helmet aside you would lay,
　And deign to partake of our chear."
The lady is silent: the stranger complies,
　His vizor he slowly unclosed:
Oh God! what a sight met Fair Imogine's eyes!
　What words can express her dismay and surprise,
When a skeleton's head was exposed!

All present then uttered a terrified shout:
　All turned with disgust from the scene.
The worms they crept in, and the worms they crept out,
And sported his eyes and his temples about,
　While the spectre addressed Imogine:

Although marked with the sign of comedy, the text's extreme civility ("partake of our chear," "dismay and surprise," "turned with disgust," "sported," and the like) is finally far more deeply disturbing than the poem's stock figural horrors. Lewis has introduced disorder into the most primitive levels of his work by upsetting the poem's aesthetic base. The text is anarchic – "idle and extravagant" – precisely because, as Wordsworth saw, it has made itself the primary instance of its im/moral subjects. A lord of misrule presides over this ballad – over the way the ballad materials are rhetorically managed. The poem exhibits a reckless and cosmopolitan savagery resembling nothing so much as the fiction of the Marquis de Sade.

AA. According to Wordsworth, these landscapes of savage places and demon lovers figure a natural world corrupted by men – specifically, by men (and poets) like Lewis and, later, Byron.

XX. But the devil's account is that the messiah fell and formed a heaven of what he stole from the abyss. According to this view of things, Lewis's work exhibits the eternal delight of its own idle and extravagant energies. How did Keats put it later – "might half slumbering on its own right arm" ("Sleep and Poetry")? Corruption and sin are problems according to the still sad music of humanity, not according to the mighty working of the universal order of things, the music of the spheres.

Henry Boyd's academic treatment of Dante is misguided, Blake says, because the critic brings ethical touchstones to Dante's work. But poetry for Blake is committed to the splendid struggles of Good and Evil. "The grandest Poetry is Immoral," according to Blake's view ("Annotations to Boyd's *Dante*"). And his further thought is also very much to the historical point. The Byronic and the Wordsworthian, the city and the country, the aristocrat and the bourgeois: "These two classes of men are always upon earth, & they should be enemies" (*The Marriage of Heaven and Hell*, plate 16).

NN. No doubt. But those two classes of men are not the only citizens of these worlds.

XX. True. Wordsworth and those who sympathized with his work – Coleridge and Hazlitt, for example – found as little to praise in the work of George Crabbe as in the work of Lewis, although Crabbe could hardly be seen as an idle or extravagant versifier. His representations of madness, for example, so detailed and methodical, empty themselves of all their Romantic possibilities. With "Peter Grimes" (1810) he writes a kind of case report of a deranged mind:

> "'All Days alike! for ever!' did they say,
> 'And unremitted Torments every Day.'—
> Yes, so they said:" but here he ceas'd and gaz'd
> On all around, affrighten'd and amaz'd . . .
> Then with an inward, broken voice he cried,
> "Again they come," and mutter'd as he died.

One has only to compare Grimes's imaginary visitations with those of Byron's Giaour. Both apparitions rise up from watery graves, but while Byron's hero lives in a charged erotic world – his despair is sublime and finally transcendent – Grimes has no access even to the negative dialectics of Romanticism. For Crabbe's work is a dismissal of eros, the world he sees and represents is survivalist at best. The grimmest reading of the culture of the period that we have, Crabbe's poetry is, for that very reason, an indispensable limiting case for criticism.

NN. But very much a special case. I was recollecting another differential. We customarily think of Byron's spectacular arrival on the cultural scene in 1812 as a turning point in the history of Romanticism . . .

XX. . . . as it surely was. His work distinctly sharpened the Romantic critique of culture. Byron's importance was to have (fore)seen that Romanticism itself would become a cultural norm. For this reason his work became the bar sinister across what he called the "wrong revolutionary poetical system" of Romanticism (letter to Murray, 15 September 1817).

The movement's systematic inertias deflected its revolutionary potential, turning the poets into schoolmasters, imagination into pedagogy. As Wordsworth, addressing Coleridge, declared:

Prophets of Nature, we to them will speak
A lasting inspiration, sanctified
By reason, blest by faith: what we have loved,
Others will love, and we will teach them how;
(*Prelude*, XIV)

The Byronic resistance to this potential in Romanticism recalls the exuberant independence of Burns and Blake. But later Romantics, paradigmatically Byron and Shelley, developed the sorrow that came with twenty and more years of dark knowledge:

But all the bubbles on an eddying flood
Fell into the same track at last, and were
Borne onward.
("The Triumph of Life" [1822])

NN. Byron's and Shelley's knowledge comes from deeper roots. Look at the cultural scene through Mrs. Barbauld's *Eighteen Hundred and Eleven* (1812), published the same year as Byron's *Childe Harold. A Romaunt.* As dark a vision as Byron's, Barbauld's poem imagines a world at war with itself.[9] The torments of contemporary civilization are not tares among the new spring wheat; they are a function of the presiding "Genius" of the European world in general:

There walks a Spirit o'er the peopled earth,
Secret his progress is, unknown his birth;
Moody and viewless as the changing wind,
No force arrests his foot, no chain can bind;

Seen from a contemporary vantage point, this is the spirit of what Mary Shelley would call "The New Prometheus," here imagined raising up "the human brute" from ignorance and darkness. Like Shelley's Frankenstein, Barbauld's Prometheus is a figure of severest contradiction – as one sees in the startling conjunction of "moody" with the Miltonic poeticism "viewless." A spirit of grandeur, beauty, and great power, he is a "destroyer and preserver" in a sense far more darkly imagined than Percy Shelley's West Wind. According to Barbauld, "arts, arms, and wealth destroy the fruits they bring."

Barbauld's is a root-and-branch critique of a systemic malaise. The most disturbing thought of all is that a demonic force can be traced as easily in the "arts" as in any other feature of civilization. The (Romantic) imagination that art is not among the ideologies is dismissed in Barbauld's text – as it was not in Byron's famous poem of the same year, and as it typically would not be in most Romantic texts.

Whereas Byron's despair held out a secret Romantic (i.e., personal) hope, Barbauld's final hope – the poem ends with a vision of freedom for

America – can only suggest an unnerving question: If spring comes, can winter be far behind?

Comparable to *Childe Harold. A Romaunt* in so many ways, Barbauld's poem differs from Byron's in one crucial respect – it genders the issues. The "capricious" Promethean Genius is gendered male; the knowledge of suffering, female. To note this is not to suggest the poem is arguing a moral equation of men with evil and women with good. It *is* to suggest, however, that a new way of seeing may emerge when an alienated imagination[10] comes to consciousness. The fact that Barbauld's poem – unlike Byron's – was denounced and then forgotten as soon as it appeared is telling, particularly given the respect and fame that Barbauld's work enjoyed. Barbauld's poem seemed grotesque and anomalous from a writer who had come to define the proprieties of the feminine imagination for almost fifty years.

In this respect her poem would prove a song before the dark sunrise of the poetry of the 1820s and 1830s. Literary history has all but forgotten this interregnum because its work is marked with the sign of a bourgeois Cain. With the emergence of Gift Books and literary Annuals as the dominant outlets for poetry, the arts appeared to have indeed destroyed their own best fruits and scattered the high altars of the imagination. It is a fast world dominated by a self-conscious trade in art and a studious pursuit of cultural fashion in every sense. In face of it twentieth-century readers learned to avert their eyes and await the coming of the reliable seriousness of Tennyson and Browning.

Two women – they both wrote for money, to support themselves and their families – preside over the poetry scene that developed with the deaths of Keats, Shelley, and Byron. One was Felicia Hemans, who would prove the most published English poet of the nineteenth century. The other was Laetitia Elizabeth Landon, the famous "L. E. L.," whose death in 1838 turned her life and career into one of the foundational cultural myths of the period.

In certain respects the two writers could not be more different: Hemans's work focuses on domestic issues and a Wordsworthian ideology of "the country," whereas Landon, distinctly an urban writer, explores the treacherous crosscurrents of love. Because each moves within a clearly defined female imagination of the world, however, their work independently establishes new possibilities for poetry.

XX. But what's so special about these two women? Literary historians have had no trouble characterizing the immediate aftermath of High Romanticism in relation to writers like Beddoes, Darley, Hood, and Clare.

AA. All interesting and important writers. But have they been read to deepen our understanding of Romanticism? Not even Clare has made much of a difference in this respect, although his work might easily have served. Neither his class position nor his madness has been taken seriously enough by critics or literary historians. Hemans and Landon are important because their feminized imaginations establish clear new differentials. Their work gives us a surer grasp of what was happening in those forgotten decades of the 1820s and 1830s.

Take Hemans for instance. The draining melancholy of her poetry carries special force exactly because of its domesticity. What is most unstable, most threatened, is what she most values – the child and its immediate world, the family unit (centered in the mother). Hemans's central myth represents a home where the father is (for various reasons) absent. This loss turns the home to a precarious scene dominated by the mother. As in Wordsworth, one of Hemans's most important precursors, the mother's protective and conserving imagination presides over a scene of loss (see "The Homes of England," for instance, or "The Graves of a Household"). But whereas Wordsworth's (male) myth of (feminine) nature licenses what he called a "strength in what remains behind," Hemans's is an imagination of disaster because (unlike Wordsworth's nature) Hemans's mothers are so conscious of their fragile quotidian state.

The disaster is clearly displayed in poems like "The Image in Lava" and "Casabianca." Theatrical by modernist conventions, these lyrics deploy Byronic extravagance as a vehicle for measuring social catastrophe and domestic loss. "The Image in Lava" studies the epic destruction of Pompeii in a bizarre silhouette of a mother cradling her child. The artist of the end of the world is here imagined not on a grand scale – as a Blakean "history painter" – but rather as a miniaturist. For Hemans, catastrophe is finally what Byron famously called "home desolation," and world-historical events are important only because they help to recall that fact.

> Babe! wert thou brightly slumbering
> Upon thy mother's breast,
> When suddenly the fiery tomb
> Shut round each gentle guest?

Hemans's poem is imagining a new burning babe and a new sacred heart. The events at Pompeii comprise a mere figure for the "impassioned grasp" that bonds child to mother. Burning in the fire of their relationship – setting their fires against "the cities of reknown / Wherein the mighty trust" – mother and child transcend the Pompeiian world. As Blake might have said, they "go to Eternal Death" (*Jerusalem*), which now reveals itself in and as the poem Hemans is writing, what she calls a "print upon the dust."

In "Casabianca," another poem of fiery immolation, Hemans emphasizes the psycho-political basis of destruction in "the cities of reknown." Explicitly set in a modern context (the Battle of the Nile, August 1798), the poem anatomizes the ideology of glory in the death of the thirteen-year-old "son of the admiral of the Orient," Commodore Casabianca. Standing to his duty in a secular fiery furnace, the boy is the central figure of a complex iconograph of the violence society exacts of itself as payment for its pursuit of power and glory. The sentimentalism of the scene is a feminizing textual move. The boy pleads for a word from his "unconscious" father that would release him from "the burning deck," but the language of the father is defined as a fearful symmetry of heroic silence and awful noise. The upshot is a poem of violent death brooded over by a beautiful but ineffectual angel of (maternal) love.

It is crucial to understand that Hemans's feminine imagination does not solve the problems it exposes. Her sentimentalism is revelatory. Readers cannot forget that "Casabianca" recollects one of Nelson's mythic victories over the French, and a turning point in the Napoleonic wars. But Hemans's poem deliberately forgets to remember that saint of English imperialism. Nelson and England's sea power supply the poem with its obscure and problematic scene.

Standing with the young Casabianca on the burning French flag-ship, Hemans puts the war and its champions in a better perspective: in worlds where power measures value, imaginative truth seeks to find itself in powerlessness. The young Casabianca's moral and emotional position, what the poem calls his "still, yet brave despair," defines the complete equivocalness of what he represents. That he stands as the *figura* of "Casabianca" – of Hemans's own poetry in general – is finally a central argument of the work.

Landon's writing devotes itself to similar pursuits, as a text like "Lines of Life" or her many poems for pictures show. "The Enchanted Island," for instance (after Francis Danby's painting of the same title), implodes upon its own "dream of surpassing beauty." Itself enchanted by that equivocal (and double-meaning) fantasy, Landon's poem initiates a severely antithetical reading of certain proverbial Romantic ideas, like "A thing of beauty is a joy for ever" and "Beauty is Truth, Truth Beauty." The truth that Landon repeatedly discovers in beauty – including the beauty of art – is death.

Keats of course had begun to make similar discoveries, but Landon's more intimate (female) knowledge of the institutions and machineries of beauty gave a special privilege to her work. Whereas Keats (like Byron) imagined a transcendent power coming from sorrow's knowledge, Landon's knowledge is like Eve's original (cursed) discovery of the cruel fantasy grounding the ideal of transcendent power.

Landon's imaginative authority rests in what she is able to fashion from her experience of passivity. The dynamic of love and courtship – Landon's great subject – supplies the (female) object of the enchanted (male) gaze with a special self-consciousness. The women in Landon's poems are shrewd observers of their spectacular society – cold spectators of a colder spectacle repeatedly masked in the warm colors of dissimulating love. In such a world the distinction between a woman and a thing of beauty is continually collapsing, as one sees in Landon's wonderful lines "Lady, thy face is very beautiful," where we are never sure if the text is addressing a mirror, a painting, or a woman.

A poet of *dis*enchantments, Landon works by putting the vagueries of imagination on full display:

Ay, gaze upon her rose-wreath'd hair,
And gaze upon her smile:
Seem as you drank the very air
Her breath perfumed the while:
("Revenge" [1829])

The enchanted i(s)land is equally under the spell of the assenting "Ay" and the gazing eye. The relation between the "Ay" and the eye is a recurrent preoccupation:

Ay, moralize,—is it not thus
We've mourn'd our hope and love?
Alas! there's tears for every eye,
A hawk for every dove.
("A Child Screening a Dove from a Hawk" [1825])

Here Landon muses on a painting by Thomas Stewardson, which is triangulated by two fearful eyes (dove, child) and one cold eye (hawk). Studying the aesthetics of the painter's moralizing and sympathetic eye, the poem succeeds through its ironic and self-conscious appropriation of the hawk's point of view.

The cruelty of the poem – not to be separated from its sentimental sympathies – anticipates the equally cruel drama displayed in "Revenge," which retraces Blake's "torments of love and jealousy":

But this is fitting punishment
To live and love in vain,—
O my wrung heart, be thou content,
And feed upon his pain.

In this world, love's "yes" is joined to the spectacular eye ("Ay, gaze . . .") and the coupling proves disastrous. Landon's speaker succeeds by entering fully into the terms of the relationship. Identifying with both her rival and her false lover, the speaker overgoes Keats's *voluptas* of pain by an act of incorporation. The poem thus inverts Keats's "Ode to Melancholy," a work Landon seems to be specifically recalling. Her speaker "feeds" not on a fantasy lady's "Peerless eyes" but on the "pain" masked by such a relationship. Landon's speaker becomes a "cloudy trophy" hung in the atrocity exhibition of her own poem.

Tennyson's early poetry is an effort to put a more benevolent construction on the hollow and mordant writing that filled his world. Although deeply influenced by Byron and Landon, he never even mentions the latter, and he struggles to exorcise his Byronic melancholy throughout his life. "The Palace of Art" comes forward under the famous injunction of Tennyson's early friend R. C. Trench: "we cannot live in art."

This thought locates what would become a key nexus of Victorian ideology – the preoccupation with social improvement and the commitment to the ameliorative power of public institutions and culture. Tennyson's poem imagines the "art" that "we cannot live in" – a specifically Romantic art – as unlivably self-critical, desperate, voluptuous. Arnold's normative critique of Romanticism, first defined in the preface to his 1853 *Poems*, is already articulated by the early Tennyson.

NN. Well, Baudelaire read Tennyson quite differently, as I recall – as the third in his dark triumvirate of Byron, Poe, Tennyson. Trench's remark carries a deeper critique of art and the worthwhileness of living in what Wordsworth called "the very world which is the world / Of all of us" (*Prelude*, XI). Baudelaire's work is written under that deeper, more atrocious sign: "Anywhere out of the world." He reads Tennyson as a kindred spirit.

Trench spoke to Tennyson as a well-fed wit of the bourgeois world that Baudelaire, like Byron and Poe before him, refused. Trench's distinction between art and the world poses a practical decision and assumes the absolute value of a quotidian life in society. Tennyson is a thoroughly Victorian writer partly because his life's work unfolds under the challenge laid down by his friend. Everywhere assuming the validity of that thought, Tennyson's work puts it to the test of his poetic imagination:

That he who will not defend Truth may be compelled to Defend a Lie,
that he may be snared & caught & taken (Blake, *Milton*, plate 8)

Because Tennyson (like the Lady of Shalott) is an artist and not (like Trench) a knight or burgher, his work comes to its Baudelairean positions by agreeing to defend the untruths of his corporeal friend Trench.

XX. So Tennyson is just another late Romantic.

NN. Not at all – anymore than Baudelaire is a late Romantic. Of course Tennyson and Baudelaire don't abandon the inheritance of Romanticism: one traces many connections to their immediate forebears, as one does in Browning, or Arnold. Tennyson is Victorian because the dominant context for his work is social and institutional. In the Romantics the context is subjective and interpersonal.

Even when Tennyson writes a poem of self-exploration and expression – *In Memoriam*, for example – the work is organized to move beyond the personal: the poem is, after all, framed on one end by an address to Queen Victoria and on the other by a celebration of the marriage of Tennyson's sister. Byron's *Don Juan* is every bit as socially conscious as *In Memoriam*, but its egotistical sublimity is overwhelming. The contrast with Tennyson couldn't be sharper.

AA. Yes, and the development of that paradigm Victorian form – the dramatic monologue[11] – helps to define the differences. Putting a frame around its subjects, the monologue drops the appearance of a mediating consciousness. Byron's "dramatic monologues" – poems like *The Lament of Tasso* and *The Prophecy of Dante* – are clear vehicles of self-expression. "Ulysses" (1832) and *Pauline* (1833) are not, partly because they could not be: unlike Tennyson and Browning, Byron's "dramatic monologues" come from an author already famous as a poetic ventriloquist.

XX. Perhaps Tennyson and Browning are just more guarded and circumspect in their dramatic monologues – as if the formulas of Romanticism, and especially late Romanticism, bore too much reality for Byron's shocking public displays. That, at any rate, appears to be what Clare believed, as his late acts of Byronic imitation show. That they are "madhouse" poems – poems of an incarcerated self – defines the point of such work exactly. As his work began to be culturally appropriated, Clare's madhouses began to frame his work – the way his class status was used to frame his other work.

In this sense the Northampton madhouse should be seen as the formal equivalent of the Victorian dramatic monologue. Northampton allows readers to turn Clare into a social and cultural subject even in his own writings. The event is quintessentially Victorian. It even defines the High Victorian way with Romantic writing in general: culture over anarchy, the triumph of art as sweetness and light.

AA. Is that a Victorian or a Romantic way? The cult of the primitive and uneducated genius, the ethnographic reading of art – are these not preoccupations of the "Romantic period"?

XX. The history of cultural forms appears always to move in opposite directions, doesn't it?

NOTES

1 A key Romantic concept, formulated by Wordsworth in his *Prelude* project. Wordsworth's idea is that experience yields certain sacred moments that preserve a restorative power through one's later life. Such moments often come without one's realizing their importance at the time of their occurrence. Memory clarifies their significance. These moments testify to the invisible but permanent presence of a benevolent Spirit in the universe. See *Prelude* (1850) Book II, 208–286.

2 Keats here touches on the strong ethno-mythological impulse apparent throughout Romantic art. The ballad revival fed into Romantic primitivism; early cultural documents were recovered and imitated because they were read as "legend-laden." Romantic art made one of its objects the recovery of unconscious, innocent, and naive powers.

3 Blake's diad "Innocence" and "Experience" is a version of the dialectic more famously set out in Schiller's "On Naive and Sentimental Poetry" (1795–1796), and in Wordsworth's distinction between the "spontaneous overflow of powerful feelings" and "emotion recollected in tranquillity" ("Preface," *Lyrical Ballads* [1800]). According to these two (subsequently normative) views, contemporary poetry – that is, Romantic poetry – "takes its origin from" the "sentimental" or "recollective" element – from the self-consciousness that permits a modern poet to recreate "in the mind" "an

emotion, similar to" the original "naive" and "spontaneous . . . feelings." That *self-consciousness*, later denominated "Romantic irony" (in Germany) and secondary imagination (by Coleridge, *Biographia Literaria* [1817]), is the critical term which for these thinkers generates the reciprocal concepts of the "naive," the "spontaneous," and the "primary imagination."

4 No idea is more fundamental to Romantic art than the idea of "imagination." On the other hand, no idea is more protean. In general, Romantic imagination designates the power – usually associated with a poetical sensibility – to perceive non-ordinary reality, or the non-ordinary aspects of the everyday world; and to create and project to others one's perception of such things.

5 Many Romantic writers – not all – gave a special privilege to the idea of nature. Wordsworthian Romanticism tends to a kind of pantheism. Nature was generally regarded as a kind of spiritual resort, a refuge from the conflicts and divisions of life in society.

6 Other than the ballad revival of the eighteenth century, no pre-Romantic movement was more important for Romanticism than sentimentalism. The aesthetics of sentimentalism are defined early in Mark Akenside's *Pleasures of Imagination* (1744). The Della Cruscan movement of the 1780s and 1790s provided the crucial immediate stimulus for the development of Romantic forms of the sentimental.

7 Although Romantic art tends to represent itself as spontaneous and unstudied, these qualities are aesthetic effects of rhetorical strategies. Two key devices are (1) a detailed presentation of a concrete immediate context for the poetical text (epitomized in the famous subtitle of Wordsworth's "Tintern Abbey"); (2) the construction of a poetic revery, as if the reader were "overhearing" the poet musing – in several senses – aloud.

8 This book signals the importance of "the Gothic," and in particular the Gothic novel, for Romantic writers. "Tales of Terror" and "Tales of Wonder" appear throughout the period and they testify to Romanticism's preoccupation with conditions of social and psychological dislocation, on the one hand, and with mythic and primitive materials on the other.

9 Barbauld's poem is a late reflection on the dominant political event of the Romantic age – the French Revolution and its aftermath, the Napoleonic wars.

10 Romanticism feeds off various experiences of alienation and is preoccupied with marginal writers and localized sensibilities. The idea is that alienation (as well as various congruent forms of experience, like historical backwardness) give privileged insight precisely by standing apart from normal experience. In this context, women's writing of the period possesses a singular importance.

11 Although formal equivalents of this mode can be found throughout the Romantic period, the subgenre is distinctly Victorian. Paradoxically, its Romantic foreshadowing appears not so much in poems like *The Lament of Tasso* as in "The Solitary Reaper" or *Childe Harold* or any other highly subjective Romantic work. In Romantic writing, the "monologue" is a "dramatic" presentation of the poet in *propria persona*.

CHAPTER 16

Byron and Romanticism, a dialogue (Jerome McGann and the editor, James Soderholm)

JS: I'm struck by your insistence on "objectivity" regarding your essays on Byron. Is this objectivity as in "20–20 hindsight" or objectivity as a rhetorical pose: the mask of Kantian disinterestedness? Or have you another, perhaps more Byronic slant on the meaning of this objectivity? It's odd to see an historicist and post-Nietzschean using the anathematized "O" word. Kindly explain.

JJM: Positivist and Postmodernist takes on the idea of "objectivity" have always fed on each other, it seems to me. My references to my objectivity are therefore partly mischievous and rhetorical. Philosophers – I'm not one – would probably call my views "critical realism." Just because I wrote those essays doesn't mean I can't look at them in a critical way. Nor is that option simply a function of a temporal gap. Surely we all strive for a critical view of what we do or think, even in the immediacy of these events. But then no one ever escapes an horizon of "subjective" interests and purposes – to make an ideal of such an escape is ludicrous. So there I am, like yourself, looking "objectively" at my essays and at my immediate reflections on those essays. The look is full of purposes and interests many of which, no doubt, I must be quite unaware of. My unawareness is as much an "objective" condition, even to me, as my awareness. That I might have a limited view of my situation is certain. But everyone's views are thus limited. Self-reflection is no more liable to subjective limits than any kind of thought or perception.

JS: What are some of these purposes and interests – the ones you are aware of? Why collect these particular essays at this particular moment in your life? Your "General analytic and historical introduction" sheds light on these purposes, but perhaps you also have a word or two to say. Is the very attempt to shape and publish this collection an attempt at self-criticism?

JJM: I grow to realize that my least self-critical impulse is this passion for self-criticism. Being right, in either sense of that word, seems deplorable to me – a feeling that itself must be deplorable in ways I have difficulty realizing. (Some of the farthest right thinking I know, by the way, now comes from the left.)

But to answer your question: no, I haven't collected these essays as "an attempt at self-criticism." I take such "attempts" as a given of any thinking at all. My conscious purpose was more polemical. I was thinking of the Cultural Studies legacies that came with the "return to history." A backwash of these currents has begun to be noticed – a relative neglect of the minute particulars of literary works as they are literary and aesthetic. The New Critical origins of much of my work, which has been noticed and sometimes attacked during our New Historicist years, may perhaps gain a new salience at this moment. I just saw a revival of Stoppard's *The Real Thing*, and was struck by the relevance of one of its key moments: an extended apology for language "as such" by the playwright character.

And Byron is central to what I have in mind (as he has been, along with his avatar Wilde, so central to what Stoppard has done). Because while Byron has always been a kind of magical being, his writing – his prose and his poetry – remains relatively neglected – when compared, say, with the kind of attention that Wordsworth's or Keats's writings continue to draw from academics. My own New Critical history suggests how and why these currents run as they do. Thematics remains a preoccupation of academic criticism when it tries to engage "the literary." But Byron's importance as a writer, – like Wilde's, like Stoppard's – is a function of his writings' style, the way his work realizes thinking as a total body experience – ultimately, as a kind of intercourse. Reading him we arrive at another definition of the human: "Man," a new Aristotle might say, "is a languaged animal."

JS: But clearly not all men – and women – are 'languaged' equally. Some are happily enmired in the thickness of language, while others try to make the medium as invisible as possible. How do you now see, for example, the difference between Byron and Wordsworth when it comes to the issue of style and medium? And Shelley?

JJM: There is a key Wordsworthian experience that is very different from the equivalent key experiences of Byron and Shelley. It is intensely personal and quasi-mystical. He speaks of being "laid asleep in body [to] become a living soul," and of a moment when "the light of sense goes out but with a flash" that reveals "the invisible world." This encounter validates the entire Wordsworthian ethos. It is the pledge – really, the lived experience – of a supernatural and ultimately a benevolent ground to human existence. It is a truth that, once awakened in the mind, never perishes. What so moves us in Wordsworth's writing, I think, is our recognition of this experience as a kind of catastrophic need in Wordsworth. His famous "sincerity" is a style for laying bare that needful heart.

The Wordsworthian drama is thus largely a psychic one, an engagement between the soul and God. It yields as it were naturally to every kind of depth analysis, most pertinently for us to analyses through (sympathetic) Freudian and (deconstructive) Marxist mythologies.

In Byron's and Shelley's cases, however, the poetical scene is very different. Laying depth-psychological models on their work is a pretty thankless task. The results always seem either ludicrous or banal. Marxist or cultural-historical studies of their work are much more successful, however, because the analytic of disillusion is focused on public rather than private worlds.

Tracking Wordsworth's poetry will inevitably take you back to the mysteries of God and divinely constituted worlds, where human beings work out their salvation in fear and trembling. Tracking Byron's and Shelley's verse always ends in the complexities of mortally ordered worlds, where God and the gods are, like the pursuits of science, natural forms of human desire and imagination.

JS: I'm reminded of one of your favorite distinctions in Blake – between forms of worship and poetic tales, and the idea that illusion (false consciousness? bad faith?) converts the former into the latter. But I take it Byron's poetic tales never were forms of worship, and that's what first and finally distinguishes him from Wordsworth and all the "vatic" poets.

JJM: I'm not sure I understand you or what you're driving at. Blake's idea is that every human experience begins as an imaginative realization of existence, and that the primal conditions of such realizations are "poetic" and assume the vehicular forms of "poetic tales." "Forms of worship" are ritual moral derivations from those primal conditions of experience – forms drawn out of the primal forms. For Blake – I think – it would be a contradiction in terms to worship a poetic tale. Worship is reserved for God. Poetic tales are revelations.

JS: It may be a contradiction, but isn't that contradiction at the heart of most dogma and hypocrisy – and Byron's "cant"?

JJM: Oh I see what you mean: not Blake's CHOOSING forms of worship from poetic tales, but TURNING forms of worship into poetic tales. Blake would have been dismantled by such an idea. But it does seem to me a very Byronic idea, and even a kind of map for understanding the Shelleyan/Byronic critique of first-generation English Romanticism. Beyond that, the idea involves a more general critique of art and poetry turned to the service of culture and the culture industries: for instance, the institutionalizing of various forms of Romanticism from Wordsworth's psychomachia to Byron's defiant "Born for opposition."

JS: Can or should Byron's oppositional stances (poses?) be institutionalized? Isn't being "Born for opposition" also a resistance to all forms of worship, including the worship of (the idea of) Romanticism? I suppose I'm also asking you to reflect on the meaning of writing essays on Byron and essaying a Byronic, oppositional life.

JJM: It's an interesting problem you point to, in the context of a modernist ethos that sets such a value on revisionist art and thought. The problem has cleaved all cultural practices for at least 200 years. And the problem registers in an especially acute way for educators and scholars, whose office is preservative, even conservative (in the strictest sense of the term). For us, the sin against the light is surely this: to fail the language(s) given to us, to neglect or debase them. Pedants are as apt for this sin as journalists. So there is good writing (which is not fine writing) and good speaking (for which we have few public models): to care for these things has always been to stand in opposition. Beyond that we have the model of Socrates:

the unexamined life is not worth living. Both of these ancient touchstones acquire for me a fresh value through our modern sense of a "thick history," of a present rich with contradiction and difference, of many pasts and many futures. We cultivate ourselves and our world by cultivating this inheritance of difference. Byron is surely the very emblem of a "home" difference – not a resident alien but an alien resident. For scholars and educators, I can hardly imagine a better model in a world as administered as ours is – where even difference is administered and becomes what Byron grieved to see himself become, partly at his own making: "a name," a word.

JS: The idea of failing the language given to us and being bad custodians of culture reminds me of Alexander Pope and the "uncreating word" that voids Creation by delivering us into the evil of Dullness. Of late, you lament the "administered world" and its impoverishing of the imagination. How does a writer or critic cultivate the "inheritance of difference" in a world so bent on institutional sameness, including the sameness one begins to expect from certain prestigious presses? How has your own work, particularly in the essays preceding this dialogue, augured Byron's "radical" difference and his resistance to becoming merely a name?

JJM: I've no idea how to answer those two questions. To the first I'm inclined to quote Shelley: "each to himself must be the oracle." To the second, I can't say that my work has been useful or not – how could I know this? But your questions put me in mind of something I might comment on in regard to Byron's " 'radical' difference and . . . resistance."

First of all, we want to remember that Byron and Shelley – and Blake too for that matter – were figures of failure. Los(s) is the central Power in Blake; Byron's heroic emblem is a Promethean Isolato who makes a victory of his own death; and Shelley is, as he regularly tells us himself, an ineffectual angel. When you are in "opposition," it seems clear enough, you are at best a secondary force, at worst invisible and insignificant. "History" is written by the winners, as we know. It is true, however, that figures like Byron brought a mode of creative doubt, as it were, to the event of "victory." And they wrote this doubt at large, as it were, as a public prophecy and not simply as a psychical condition. This move made it possible to begin writing histories that would be multiple and self-contradictory. In a dialectic of winners and losers, the Byronic imagination foresees the perpetual return of the repressed.

This myth, Byron's foundational imagination, captured the Euro-American aesthetic and intellectual scene for over a hundred years. In the twentieth century it would mutate from a dialectical to a fractal model – Bakhtin's heteroglossia being the best-known literary version of this mutation. We don't have history, we have histories, an n-dimensional field of events precisely defined by the idea, the necessity, of loss at every point.

So it won't do, in my judgment, to try to read Byron as a hero of opposition, or as a hero at all. His emblem is exactly his first "Byronic Hero," the Giaour – a brutal renegade who admits he would have killed the only person he loved if she had betrayed him as she betrayed her legal master. *The Giaour* tells a story of "'radical' difference and . . . resistance" and the poem itself remains a "lost" and failed masterpiece of the period. It is precisely not a poem to point a moral or adorn another tale. The great closing couplet of *The Corsair* sums the matter with exquisite precision:

> He left a Corsair's name to other times,
> Linked with one virtue, and a thousand crimes.

In the story of the poem, the one virtue is his sinful love. In the history of culture, that virtue translates as Byron's immoderate art – at once shocking, brilliant, and consciously debased.[1] All his poetry is like those famous, or infamous, early tales: a network of contradictions whose function is to create the Baudelairean reader.

JS: I think I'm following you, but to make sure, tell me how you read and teach the following lines from *Don Juan*; it's the shipwreck scene from Canto II where the survivors must resort to cannibalism. Byron's luckless tutor Pedrillo is about to be consumed.

> He died as born, a Catholic in faith,
>   Like most in the belief in which they're bred,
> At first a little crucifix he kiss'd,
> And then held out his jugular and wrist.

I suppose my question is this: how can we keep these lines from becoming dull? By having students recite them? By not explaining away Byron's desire to shock and debase? That is, by not turning his cantos into canticles?

JJM: Dull?! Have you known readers who found these lines dull? This would amaze me. The lines, as well as the whole notorious passage they locate, might fairly be called "offensive," "shocking," "debased," even "immoral" – I think they've been so characterized from the beginning. And since I regard all readings of poetry as correct – that is to say, as representing some kind of proper (OR improper) reaction, some reflection of human thought and feeling – then these critical readings tell an important set of truths about the passage. I wouldn't want to – not that I could – cancel or trash these readings. What I would want to do is put on display as many readings as possible, as many as one knows of or can imagine. And then try to explain how and why readers might come to these various readings.

Recitation necessarily comes into any interrogation of a poetical text. Recitation is the *sine qua non* of all interpretation, its mortal ground as it were. This passage, for instance, is remarkable for its metrical precision, which it fairly flaunts. A good deal of the effect is secured because of this assiduous correctness of form, which "imitates," in a wonderfully outrageous way, the ritual of the scene. The blasphemy – Pedrillo enacting his *imitatio Christi* – is lightly carried, is barely perceivable and all the more shocking for that deftness. Here we see Byron's splendid artistic gifts in full play – which is, I think, exactly why certain (moral) readers find the passage so horrid. The passage enacts the privilege Byron gives to "poetic tales" over "forms of worship."

This brief commentary, needless to say, barely touches the richness of the passage, which goes to the core of the shipwreck scene in its last series of breathtaking exposures of the frailties of human beings. Imagine David or Ingres painting *The Wreck of the Medusa*: that would be a picture something like what Byron gives us here.

JS: I have read the lines from *DJ* and have had students read them and, yes, I have seen the students have rather dull reactions. It takes a great deal to shock or offend students who have been fed MTV and Nirvana and Marilyn Manson. If truly "nothing is sacred," then the witty transmogrifying of forms of worship into poetic tales loses its energy and, well, *sprezzatura*. Tell me more about how and why you countenance "improper readings" as "correct." Is "lethargy" an improper response, or is that in another category? And I wonder if Byron's forms of irony are too subtle – yes, even in the lines quoted above – for many readers today, for whom irony is a jackhammer.

JJM: What you describe isn't reading, is it?! It's a refusal to read. And I confess that when I say that "all readings are correct," I don't have in mind – haven't had in mind – the refusal of reading as a type of reading.

But now that you raise the issue it seems quite important, doesn't it. The refusal is a "reading" of "literature" as prima facie "dull." Whose problem is that anyway? I'm reminded of Frank O'Hara's splendid (Byronic) comment on the matter in his manifesto "Personism":

> But how can you really care if anybody gets it, or gets what it means, or if it improves them? Improves them for what? For death? Why hurry them along? Too many poets [printer's devil: and professors] act like a middle-aged mother trying to get her kids to eat too much cooked meat, and potatoes with drippings (tears). I don't give a damn whether they eat or not. Forced feeding leads to excessive thinness (effete). Nobody should experience anything they don't need to, if they don't need poetry, bully for them, I like the movies too.[2]

JS: Verbum sat . . . But for better or for worse, for richer, for poorer, we are in the business of serving up poetry for students, many of whom don't give a damn whether they eat or not, or even if we really care about making them eat. This problem – and I think it is one – could and perhaps should take us far afield, but let me try to pull the subject back to Byronic resistance and the Baudelairean reader (who rears his head in several of your essays). You often claim that Byron anticipates Baudelaire in imagining such a reader, a reader who becomes the image of the cannily deceptive author. But I'm struck in our present discussion just how much training, education, patience, good will, and even a certain – pardon me – sincerity is required to participate in this contract. Our "resistant" students are leagues away from such an understanding – call it ironic connoisseurship – and presumably we must teach them to develop the taste by which to enjoy, or even construe, Byron's poetry. Like Pedrillo, we must open a vein to repast them. But if they don't want any part of the literary covenant – even when that covenant is deliriously funny, sexy, and sweetly irreverent – what then must we do? Tell them to wait for the movie to come out?

JJM: First of all this: I don't claim that Byron anticipates Baudelaire. I simply say – it is a complex fact – that Baudelaire took some of his most important ideas from his meditations on Byron, whose work he admired and clearly saw himself as continuing.

Second, I still think O'Hara's comment is all that needs to be said. But let me gloss his remark in this way. If we have any "duty" towards resistant students, it is to give as good a performance as we can of the art and poetry we love. O'Hara's comment, and the whole of the "Personism" essay, is a model of such a loving performance. It goes without saying that we have at our disposal many kinds of performative options – good scholarship being not the least of them.

JS: What do you consider bad scholarship?

JJM: The whole raft of things that my critical reviewers have found lacking in my work.

JS: Push that raft toward me.

JJM: Criticism, like charity, begins at home. Do you want me to itemize some of my horrid gaffes and blunders? The grotesque failures of proofing in several of my earlier books? The many, many times, in the Byron edition, when I cut corners in my editorial notes – because it was clear, having at last learned what scholarly editing entailed, I began to realize the true impossibility of the task I had blithely, and ignorantly, undertaken. The transcription errors.

Bad scholarship includes that kind of thing. Worse still is silence on such matters, or pretending that something is the case when you know it isn't exactly so. Worst of all is losing clarity of mind: about the difference between scholarship and journalism; about the modesty scholars need before the works they inherit and pass on; about thoroughness and honesty as "the bound and outward circumference" of the scholar's imagination.

JS: I'm intrigued by your distinction between scholarship and journalism. How do you mark the differences between the two? Do you think a lot of scholars have been teased into the journalistic mode because they are simply tired of the "fit audience, though few" or are there other reasons for scholarship deliquescing into journalism?

JJM: It's not a question of "scholarship deliquescing into journalism," as if one were a good thing and the other bad. Many scholars ought to turn their work into journalistic venues, or work in those venues in more or less regular ways. Scholars are after all teachers too and their pedagogy shouldn't be bound in the classroom. What I refer to is a peculiar hybrid nourished by publishing demands laid upon young scholars by the profession. Scholarly work is expected that can't be done without years of experienced research. So corners get cut, and the moves are concealed in a jargonized, often pseudo-theoretical discourse. The result is a kind of intramural journalism, an easy-to-read handling of the novelties or commonplaces of the immediate cultural and professional scene.

Work of this kind is difficult not to produce given the constraints of the profession. It has, as we know, laid us open to various philistine attacks and injured our cultural authority.

But lamentations are so dreary, so ineffectual. The only thing to do is work against that grain as best one can.

JS: Actually, what I mean by "deliquescing" is precisely that hybrid. But this raises another question: is the difference between journalism and scholarship akin to – even parallel to – the distinction between "the news" and "news that stays news"? I wonder how criticism – ANY criticism – can hope to stay news. Perhaps Byron intuited this when he opens his masterpiece by rejecting the heroes vended to him by the gazettes and selects instead his old friend, Don Juan, a figure who has admirable staying-power. Was this Byron's way of working against the grain – i.e., being oppositional by being radically traditional?

JJM: The news that stays news is poetry – that was Pound's point, wasn't it? As opposed to temporizing texts. And yes, most of what we call "criticism" is temporizing, of this place and time. Like eighteenth-century sermons – a genre, I've been told, that dominated the print of that period – "criticism" has been general over our Ireland. And that's fine, though we who write it should be under no illusion about its place and function.

Our scholarly vocation is to pass on the news that stays news. It is such a privilege! Being the retainers of Don Juan.

JS: It's true that criticism has snowed all over our Ireland (mad Byron hurt us into criticism?). But do you think critics might take a few more chances in evolving forms of "temporizing" that engage the primary texts in more fecund, extramural ways? Your early book on Swinburne, for example, a work that tilled new ground but was perhaps too "literary" and experimental to become influential, has remained a fallow possibility. You applaud Susan Howe's book on Emily Dickinson.[3] And, since Sontag was largely right in *Against Interpretation*,[4] why have most critics resisted taking more chances with their work? We are allowed to "get personal" now, but that seems to be an etiolated form of, for example, Pater's Impressionism.

JJM: Yes, what a critical gain if we had more imaginative critical activity. But we do have some splendid writing along those lines. Nearly all of Charles Bernstein's critical work, for instance, or Steve McCaffery's. Of course they're poets, like Susan Howe. But then what of Jeffrey Skoblow – his remarkable book on Morris, *Paradise Regained*, and his even more brilliant book that appeared only last year – a study of Burns and Scots poetry. And Randall McLeod has been writing the most innovative

Renaissance and textual criticism for more than two decades. Just four years ago Jena Osman and Juliana Spaar edited that double issue of *Chain* (Vol. 3 Parts 1 and 2 [Spring/Fall, 1996]) devoted to imaginative forms of criticism. So we do have enterprising work – mostly by young people, not by older scholars like McLeod (for some a figure of legend, for others an outrage and scandal).

McLeod is a particularly interesting figure because his scholarly credentials are unassailable. He is one of the most learned and broadly read scholars alive today. His passion for exactitude is nearly as rare as his critical originality. McLeod's and Skoblow's astonishing flights are grounded in the thoroughgoing rigor of their work. Imaginative criticism and scholarship, then, by all means – but demanding and exigent as well.[5]

The recent biographical forays by various professors are something else entirely, of course.

JS: It's odd that biographical treatment of Byron is an imperative (as your teacher Cecil Lang long ago argued) and yet to put one's *own* biography forth as an equal imperative seems wrongheaded. Have we in some sense looped back to the beginning of this conversation and the idea of objectivity? There's something of a puzzle here, for Byron is also known as a great "objective" writer on one level, and yet deeply autobiographical on another. What follows from this paradox for his critics? Is your own objectivity somehow a "reflection" (or is that the wrong word) of Byron's? And is there some connection between irony and objectivity?

JJM: Well, James, surely there's "biography" and biography. A scholar's or critic's biography might be quite interesting, but next to Byron or Dickinson or Colette? "Be real" as the youngsters say. Certain figures – those three are simply obvious ones – seem great Stars in all senses of that word. Their force fields are immense and they are part of the map of the universe, at once elements in it and powers that help to organize it.

That's rhapsodic and perhaps unhelpful here. But your comment reminds me of the still-neglected study of the relation of biography to works of art and to culture and history. In our recent scholarly "return to history," the "biographical element" remains largely, as we say, "untheorized." Psychoanalytic models continue to dominate, and these are models – despite the efforts of writers from Marcuse to Foucault and beyond – that make a hash of "history."

Here's a thought experiment out of Trotsky's *History of the Russian Revolution*, where he included a chapter that asked the question: "Would the Revolution Have Taken Place Without Lenin?" That it's an impossible question is exactly what makes it interesting. It's a question that forces Trotsky to reconsider the premises of his narrative. And his answer – a very weak one – locates one of the greatest moments in his remarkable work.

"What Would the Romantic Movement Be Without Byron?" Without Mary Robinson? Without Laetitia Elizabeth Landon?

JS: Rather than "get real" let me get ideal. That means getting Shelleyan. For when you speak of what History would be like without Great Men – or Ignored but Great Women – I think of Shelley's *Defence of Poetry* and his wondering about what our civilization would be like had Homer, Dante, Shakespeare, and Milton not lived. Since he saw the genius of *Don Juan* he might have added Byron. And certainly he had high hopes – in every sense – for *Prometheus Unbound*. As you say, this is rhapsodic stuff. And now I wonder (this is becoming rather wonderful) how far you believe in the Great Man theory – the Star-struck theory – of History (and Literary History)? Your rhetoric suggests you do, but then you also seem to believe, as the remarkable Shelley also did, that authors are both the creators and creatures of their age. Have we all sufficiently "theorized" how Byron weighs into this question?

JJM: If I understand what "the Great Man/Woman Theory" is, I'm sure I don't "believe in" it. What does seem to me important, perhaps especially in this "return to history" we are part of, is that we should think in terms of histories that "were actually filled with living [people], not by protocols, state papers, controversies and abstractions." That's (more or less) Carlyle praising Walter Scott's historicism. And Carlyle was writing in this way as part of his critique of Enlightenment history, a fact we do well to remember since our "New Historicism" emerged from that ferociously enlightened period we now call "Theory." Much in our new Cultural and Historical Studies remains highly theoretical and "enlightened." But history is a field of desire – a theater of cruelty even, pleasure and pain. When I spoke above about "theorizing Byron" I spoke ironically, of course. But not insincerely. History without a sure relation to the engines of desire is not just boring, it is unenlightened. And your reference to Shelley couldn't be more apt.

JS: What do you mean by "ferociously enlightened"? In what sense is or was that true? Or am I once again not registering an ironic tone?

JJM: Let's say "self-ironical." "Theory" brought remarkable liberations to literary studies and in the midst of those times one scarcely saw the costs involved, much less counted them. Now they're only too apparent. I'm not speaking here of the crisis in general education – deeply troubling but not a subject for this conversation. I'm thinking of the scholarly difficulty inherent in any posture of critical distance. One can't practice any critical investigation without standing back to observe matters coolly – even severely. But then one can't pretend to authoritative understanding unless one adopts what Rossetti called "an inner standing point." The paradox locates one of criticism's regular difficulties. Another has been captured in that line from Burns: "To see ourselves as others see us." Students of human studies, we often speak and think an alien and even ludicrous discourse – at least so it may reasonably appear. We're not talking about quantum mechanics after all. Byron's critique of Wordsworth and Coleridge in *Don Juan* was vulgar and probably unfair too. But it was also (a) witty and (b) true. Not theoretically true of course, as we see in the historical aftermath, when many people decided they understood and liked what Wordsworth and Coleridge were saying. So then not Wordsworth and Coleridge needed "explaining" but Byron!

"I wish he would explain his explanation": the comic point of that splendid passage in *Don Juan* seems once again very clear and current. Not for Coleridge and Wordsworth – they have outsoared the shadow of our night. For us.

JS: Let me dwell for a moment on "self-irony." In *Flaubert's Parrot*, Julian Barnes describes Irony as: "Either the devil's mark or the snorkel of sanity." What I love about Byron is how his irony demolishes this either/or by giving us both diabolism and lucidity in equal measures and often with bracing simultaneity. Then it's just a matter of whether the temporizing glossers (critics) can catch a ride on his mind and desire, or whether we succumb to the sort of canting routines and ludicrous habits that Byron loved to burlesque. But before I get carried away, let me have your response to Barnes's witty, witting disjunction.

JJM: But surely you're right, it's not an either/or, it's a both/and. The best (and worst) thing about the devil is that's he's supremely sane – getting tossed out of heaven can really clear your head I think. And the best (and worst) thing about God or the gods is that they're completely crazy, as that wonderful film put it. Look at all the god-haunted creatures – St. Theresa, St. John of the Cross, Bataille, Byron himself for that matter. Wordsworth loving to see the look of an unfeeling fortress. All of this is crazy, as Mephistopheles tells Faust. One of the signal marks of a "Modern" consciousness – a consciousness like Mozart's, Goethe's, Byron's, and all their successors from Delacroix through Poe, Baudelaire, Nietzsche, and beyond – is the ways they transform that either/or into both/and. Blake called it "The Marriage of Heaven and Hell."

JS: In what ways can criticism attend [to] this marriage? After all, not just anyone can get tossed out of heaven.

JJM: Yes, I think we have all finally been thrown out. Modernity, "the world turned upside down," the Fall of the Angels. It's a general condition, though some are still unaware that this remarkable event has occurred. But the persons I just mentioned – lots of others might be added to the list – have been important because they registered this moment with such acuity. And in the event we have discovered the Nova Scientia called Pataphysics, the Science of Exceptions. Byron is of course an exquisite instance of the pataphysical – his work and his life as well. Pataphysics comes to set a measure to all the normative sciences. Its elementary formula is "a equals a if and only if a does not equal a." Norms are based on a rationale of the mysterious, a "ratio" imposed on reality in order to make it usable in certain determinate ways. Exceptions make up the field of normative derivations – just as, to return to a Romantic and scholarly frame of reference, Schiller's concept of the naive is derived from the energetic field of sentimentality.

JS: So Byron's being "born for opposition" is also one of these exceptions? But if the field is made up of exceptions, then the "rationale of the mysterious" (nice title for a book!) also accounts for Wordsworth's writing "exceptional" sonnets in favor of capital punishment. In this new register, what ISN'T exceptional? There must be degrees of the pataphysical, no? Is there some analogy here to submitting to Conrad's "destructive element" – the one in which modernism found baptism?

JJM: Your Conrad reference is so very apt. These days I think in terms of what Rossetti called the "inner standing point" as a necessity of art. It's the precise analogue (and forecast) of what Conrad was speaking about. In a Modern situation art occupies an inner standing point with respect to both its subjects and its materials. Its moral authority comes from the explicit character of its social "complicities," so to say – whatever point of view it takes. Even were it to take that peculiar modernist (and neo-classical) standpoint of "disinterestedness," the horizon of Modernity would force out the pataphysical revelation: that disinterestedness represents and executes a certain ideological position. And Wordsworth is yet another fine instance of an art that moves us by its losses and failures, by its involvement in the "destructive element," an involvement all the more rich because of its unwilling participation. Blake and Byron, in that respect, are "more Modern" than Wordsworth. But because the whole ethos is ruled by a Science of Exceptions, all forms of artistic expression become more or less consciously pataphysical.

JS: Just as Byron had more Rousseau than St. Augustine in him, so he must have had more (nascent) French absurdism in him. And I take it the parodic element is the prolifically destructive one, no? But I need a clarifying example of what you've been presenting: to under-stand this inner standing. Something generously nonsensical where the law of non-contradiction pirouettes.

JJM: For Byron, yes, parody – including self-parody – is pivotal. For Wordsworth I should say "cant" – Byron's word – is the "prolifically destructive" element. Cant, for example, about the famous "abundant recompense" that issues from "loss." This representation is cant. Byron's registration of this kind of falseness was as acute as it was defensively unfair, however. For the truth is that Wordsworth's cant is the (self-)destructive element that generates the heartbreaking (self-)revelations of his heartbreaking verse, which is a kind of perpetual machine of suffering and loss fueled by Wordsworth's cherished moral illusions. "Abundant recompense" is a "cherished madness of [Wordsworth's] heart." To read that fearful myth as "truth" is to learn nothing from it. With Wordsworth, alas, the possibility of generous nonsense seems to have stopped with that magical and charming neglected masterpiece "The Idiot Boy." But of course it's absurd to say "alas" here, given that river of *lacrymae rerum* that issued from his pen. It is one of the rivers of (our) life. Shelley revealed something important about the river when he insisted upon its benevolent transformation in

Prometheus Unbound – I'm thinking not only of the incomparable "My soul is an enchanted boat" but of the later moment when Earth translates the figure of Death into a mother calling to her child, "Leave me not again" (III, 3, 107). That event is the exact equivalent of the moment in *The Marriage of Heaven and Hell* when the angel's tormented vision of "hell" is imaginatively translated into a Garden of Eden.

JS: The lucid Lucifer must be, then, both Ironist and Parodist. Do you recall what Dr. Johnson said after having cited Satan's [in]famous line about "the mind is its own place"? He observed, with specific gravitas, "Yes, but we must remember that Satan is a liar." And Byron, by his own admission, was a "devil of a mannerist" when he wrote *Manfred* and nearly cribbed Satan's lines. Would you say that modernism as we've been discussing it occurred when readers first began taking Satan as NOT lying. Blake must have believed that Milton himself was the first such reader. Byron's mock-epic submits to the Satanic element with gusto and a certain Enlightenment hope. Hence,

> Man fell with apples, and with apples rose.

Is there a more efficient, brilliant example of "ratio" than this? Has "the Fall" – and its downward spiral – ever been more happily reversed and parodied, a deformation transformed through sheer ingenuity, as Byron's mind skiffs like an enchanted soul?

JJM: There's another ancient tradition that holds Satan to be the most rigorous kind of truth-teller – like Mephistopheles. His rigor indeed is what traps unwary mortals, who generally have much less control over their wills. Satan *chose* to disobey. It is this other tradition that Byron's Cain invokes and exploits. Byron makes Lucifer the Last (Enlightenment) Man, which is to say that he makes him a figure of the High Romantic. *Manfred* is another type of work altogether – an outrageously parodic (and self-parodic) text and the clear forecast of *Don Juan*'s miscegenated parodies. *Manfred*'s legacy is comic, sentimental, Bakhtinian: Joyce or J. C. Powys, for instance; *Cain*'s is critical, reflective, Derridean: Pound, Riding, Perec.

JS: I'm reminded of lines you often cite and critically gloss, from Byron's "[Epistle to Augusta]," written about the time he was hatching *Manfred*.

> The fault was mine—nor do I seek to screen
>   My errors with defensive paradox—
> I have been cunning in mine overthrow
> The careful pilot of my proper woe.

Is Byron being, at long last, a rigorous truth-teller, or is self-parody "screening" his errors even as he rather proudly confesses them? So many "exceptional" nuances to sift through. But is there a trap in these lines?

And for whom, precisely, are they meant? What – hypocritical? – readers do they imagine?

JJM: Poems always lie in wait to trap unwary readers, don't you think? Or unwary writers of poems. They leave no one safe. And so that lovely text of Byron's. Is it truth-telling "at long last"? Yes it is, it stretches itself back over those Years of Fame and lays Lord Byron out for an autopsy, like the corpse of Greece he himself anatomized in *The Giaour*. Is Byron "screening his errors"? Yes, of course, for the confession is an apology and even a kind of justification. Its hypocrisy comes clear as soon as we isolate the model and convention of what is written there: it's that most self-deceived and hypocritical of all rhetorics, the Christian confession of one's sin before God. Byron wrote *Manfred* to begin his astonishing effort to unmask and exorcise that fearful anti-human rhetoric, which raises such a barrier against self-clarity. And then later, in the ludic "Forgiveness-Curse" sequence in *Childe Harold* Canto IV, he left that rhetoric in utter shambles.

JS: Do you also consider the following stanza to raze that rhetoric, or to be facetious about it, which amounts to the same thing? The narrator is describing the education of Don Juan in Canto I.

> Sermons he read, and lectures he endured,
> And homilies, and lives of all the saints;
> To Jerome and to Chrysostom inured,
> He did not take such studies for restraints;
> But how faith is acquired, and then insured,
> So well not one of the aforesaid paints
> As Saint Augustine in his fine Confessions,
> Which make the reader envy his transgressions.

Is there yet another odd self-justification nested in these lines, even as Byron "clarifies" himself to himself (and to others?) by looking into the glass of irony? At some level, did Byron want his English readers, even those whom he had wounded, to "envy his transgressions"? But is this finally Byron's trap, or the trap of all beguiling rhetorics?

JJM: What a passage you've chosen, one of the most cryptic in the poem. The clear irrelevance of this to the character Juan is the reader's signal that Byron is here seriously *en masque* – talking about himself, and, of course, as you say, about and to the reader. Always the reader. And I certainly agree with your suggestion that he is reflecting BEFORE HIS READERS on the textual intercourse that has been going on since at least 1812, when he woke and found himself famous.

The passage is a mare's nest. What is this "faith" being spoken of here, what is this absence of "restraints," what is the relation of these things? The reference to St. Augustine's *Confessions*, and to readerly "envy," is too close to the Byronic reading scene to miss. The text is certainly another of those "mad, bad, and dangerous to know" moments. I don't know what it all "means" but I do know that it is a classic example of calling the reader to thought and judgment. Surely its only "meaning" is like Ahab's doubloon (Ahab, the direct linear descendant of the Byronic Hero). Or I think as well of Demogorgon's way of talking and of Asia's realization that "Each to himself must be the oracle" of their prophetic import.

JS: I take it that Byron is looking back to St. Augustine through Rousseau yet without citing the "apostle of affliction" who really did make his sins appear enchanting. The lives of the saints become "Studies In Faith" rather than in Prohibition, and as such they are insurance policies against the sort of temptation that St. A., despite himself, could not avoid: the temptation to confess himself, in writing, AS A VISIBLE, LEGIBLE TRANSGRESSION. Rousseau happily fell prey to the same urge, and Byron, who could hardly resist being what Starobinski calls "the cynosure of all eyes," turns the world into his confessor, and thus violates his own privacy. This is both autotelic and autoerotic: the poet/oracle at once center and circumference. The performance must have given Byron exquisite pleasure.

JJM: Yes he's certainly thinking of Rousseau – Byron was fascinated by the comparisons his contemporaries drew between himself and the apostle of affliction, and of course he explicitly summoned the comparisons in *Childe Harold*, Canto III. For critical review, however – we want to remember that. Is there any doubt that he passed a terrible judgment on himself in that canto – turning as he does on his chief *figurae*: Napoleon, the Byronic Hero, Rousseau. "The performance must have given Byron exquisite pleasure": indeed, and that is just what horrifies him. Never was his bleeding heart more effectively trailed across its double mirror, the mirror of art and the bloody landscape of Europe in which he reflects upon his heart and his art. From Rousseau's *Confessions* through Waterloo, Byron conjures a vision of the Pleasures of the Imagination. It is his first explicit and comprehensive – and of course political – critique of Romanticism, the whole of it now viewed as a kind of Satanic School with himself as the furthest fallen angel. And when he is able, a few years later, to observe the Coda of that pitiful tragedy, the Congress of Vienna and the European Settlement, the conclusion is so wretched he can only raise that self-defense of his ludic cynicism, so touching and so fragile.

JS: Sometimes that liberally bleeding heart is awfully hard to follow, as in the following, stanza 84 of *CHP III*.

> What deep wounds ever closed without a scar?
>   The heart's bleed longest, but heal to wear
> That which disfigures it; and they who war
>   With their own hopes, and have been vanquish'd, bear
> Silence, but not submission: in his lair
>   Fix'd Passion holds his breath, until the hour
> Which shall atone for years; none need despair:
>   It came, it cometh, and will come,—the power
>   To punish or forgive, in one we shall be slower.

"The heart's bleed"? "bear / Silence"? And that penultimate line is so, well, BAD (as poetry). The whole stanza seems to be an encoded message: a hall of encryptions. What a tremendous relief to have "Clear, placid Leman!" stretch out before us in the next stanza, in contrast to the deeply "troubled waters" of the stanza above.

JJM: I guess I don't understand your first two questions – about the heart's wounds bleeding longest, or about the hopeless having to bear the silence their hopelessness has chosen. But that the stanza is encrypted, yes. Its coded immediate subject – the unnamed Lady Byron and all those he saw as supporting her public campaign – is exceedingly difficult for Byron to treat honestly. That's why, every time he does (before 1819), the poetry turns tormented, as it does here. And the issue goes to the heart of what we've just been talking about here: hypocrisy, cant, self-deception. How can he justify himself when he knows his own guilt, how expose the hypocrisy of his attackers? So he works by encryption, or what he will later see as "the truth in masquerade."

But on the second issue, the "BAD . . . poetry." I wonder why you think it bad, I don't at all. Indeed, the stanza seems to me quintessentially Romantic and Byronic. Romantic, first, because the stanza rides on a rhetoric of sincerity. Byronic, second, for the reasons we've just been discussing. The stanza illustrates "the spoiler's art" as well as any I know in Byron – the art, that is to say, of forcing recalcitrant material to submit to his willfulness. Byron comes to his language posing Humpty Dumpty's famous question: "Who is to be master?" His treatment of the Spenserian stanza in *Childe Harold's Pilgrimage* is simply breathtaking for me, and this stanza is no exception. He succeeds exactly because he is completely aware of "the irregularity of [his] design" on the stanza. Its spoliation is the emblem he raises for the human spirit against "history, tradition, and the facts." Later, in *Don Juan*, he will reflect on this untrammeled Romanticism and call himself "a devil of a mannerist" in deploying it. Spoiling one's language inheritance to save its human spirit – Wordsworth's very program in another dialect and register, of course – will come under Byron's critical judgment, as do all things for him.

One final word about this stanza you quote. Look at that remarkable last couplet and ask yourself: in WHICH one? And what precisely does Byron mean by "slower"? Or consider that image of an inexorable fatality in the penultimate line. Byron flaunts his own power in all his writing but, as this stanza intimates, the act involves a bold temptation of Fate. Byron summons the "power" of Fate knowing full well that he cannot exempt himself from its authority should his fearful prayer be answered.

JS: If so, then perhaps this summoning is Byron's "amor fati," an idea and ideal that seems to operate in several registers: for example, the piloting of the stanza towards technical spoliation. Is that somehow a reflection of his malaise or productive of it? Or is this like trying to pull apart the dancer and the dance?

JJM: It's not his malaise, the stanza reflects a general condition of culture. "Byron" is its representative figure in this case, as "Byronism" is one of its strains. Nor is the condition adequately represented as a "malaise," any more than (say) Wordsworth's famous language "reforms" are adequately characterized as such. Those reforms doomed, for example, whole ranges of important poetical work to a long period of cultural invisibility and exile. Here Crabbe is the exemplary case, an artist of immense skill and power. But he speaks an alien tongue to our Romantically trained ears. And so do a number of important women writers who have recently swum into our ken. Byron's "malaise" is a prophetic diagnosis of his own culture and its Romanticism. That's why it still speaks to us so directly.

JS: I think – I hope – what also speaks to us directly is the opposite of this malaise: what I would call Byron's "gay science" or his "joyful wisdom." I refer again to those lovely apples.

> Man fell with apples, and with apples rose,
>   If this be true, for we must deem the mode
> In which Sir Isaac Newton could disclose
>   Through the then unpaved stars the turnpike road,
> A thing to counterbalance human woes;
>   For ever since immortal man hath glowed
> With all kinds of mechanics, and full soon
> Steam-engines will conduct him to the Moon.
>
> And wherefore this exordium?—Why, just now,
>   In taking up this paltry sheet of paper,
> My bosom underwent a glorious glow,
>   And my internal Spirit cut a caper:
> And though so much inferior, as I know,
>   To those who, by the dint of glass and vapour,
> Discover stars, and sail in the wind's eye,
> I wish to do as much by Poesy.

A more delightful, self-delighting dialectic of gravity and levity, of gravitation and levitation, is hard to imagine. It's Byron Unbound, no?

JJM: Indeed, as Shelley thought:

> These are the spells by which to reassume
> An empire o'er the disentangled Doom.

NOTES

1 Cf. McGann, *Byron and Wordsworth* (Nottingham: The Byron Foundation, 1998). By "consciously debased" I mean what Madame de Staël meant when she described Goethe's art in the first part of *Faust* in the same terms. Her explication of Goethe had a signal impact on Byron's view of his own writing, and specifically on *Manfred*.

2 Frank O'Hara, "Personism. A Manifesto," in *The Collected Works of Frank O'Hara*, ed. Donald Allen (New York: Alfred A. Knopf, 1959), 498.
3 Susan Howe, *My Emily Dickinson* (Berkeley: North Atlantic, 1985).
4 Susan Sontag, *Against Interpretation* (New York: Dell Publishing Co., Inc., 1964).
5 Randall McLeod, "Editing Shakespeare," *Sub-Stance*, 33–34 (1982), 26–55; Random Clod, "Information on Information," *TEXT 5* (1989), 239–283; Random Cloud, "Fiatflux," in *Crisis in Editing: Texts of the English Renaissance*. ed. Randall MC Leod (New York: AMS Press, 1992), 61–157. Charles Bernstein, *Content's Dream* (Los Angeles: Sun & Moon Press, 1986); *My Way. Speeches and Poems* (Chicago: University of Chicago Press, 1999); Susan Howe, *The Birth-Mark. Unsettling the Wilderness in American Literary History* (Hanover and London: Wesleyan University Press, 1993). Steve McCaffery, *North of Intention. Critical Writings 1973–1986* (New York: Roof Books, 1986); Steve McCaffery and B. P. Nichol, *Rational Geomancy. The Kids of the Book Machine. The Collected Research Reports of the Toronto Research Group 1973–1982*, ed. Steve McCaffery (Vancouver: Talon Books, 1992). Jeffrey Skoblow, *Paradise Dislocated* (Charlottesville: University Press of Virginia, 1993) and *Dooble Tongue. Scots, Burns, and Contradiction* (Newark: University of Delaware Press, 2001).

Subject index

Authors index

CAMBRIDGE STUDIES IN ROMANTICISM

GENERAL EDITORS

MARILYN BUTLER, *University of Oxford*
JAMES CHANDLER, *University of Chicago*

1. *Romantic Correspondence: Women, Politics and the Fiction of Letters*
MARY A. FAVRET

2. *British Romantic Writers and the East: Anxieties of Empire*
NIGEL LEASK

3. *Edmund Burke's Aesthetic Ideology*
Language, Gender and Political Economy in Revolution
TOM FURNISS

4. *Poetry as an Occupation and an Art in Britain, 1760–1830*
PETER MURPHY

5. *In the Theatre of Romanticism: Coleridge, Nationalism, Women*
JULIE A. CARLSON

6. *Keats, Narrative and Audience*
ANDREW BENNETT

7. *Romance and Revolution: Shelley and the Politics of a Genre*
DAVID DUFF

8. *Literature, Education, and Romanticism*
Reading as Social Practice, 1780–1832
ALAN RICHARDSON

9. *Women Writing about Money: Women's Fiction in England, 1790–1820*
EDWARD COPELAND

10. *Shelley and the Revolution in Taste: The Body and the Natural World*
TIMOTHY MORTON

11. *William Cobbett: The Politics of Style*
LEONORA NATTRASS

12. *The Rise of Supernatural Fiction, 1762–1800*
E. J. CLERY

13. *Women Travel Writers and the Language of Aesthetics, 1716–1818*
ELIZABETH A. BOHLS

14. *Napoleon and English Romanticism*
SIMON BAINBRIDGE

15. *Romantic Vagrancy: Wordsworth and the Simulation of Freedom*
CELESTE LANGAN

16. *Wordsworth and the Geologists*
JOHN WYATT

17. *Wordsworth's Pope: A Study in Literary Historiography*
ROBERT J. GRIFFIN

18. *The Politics of Sensibility: Race, Gender and Commerce in the Sentimental Novel*
MARKMAN ELLIS

19. *Reading Daughters' Fictions, 1709–1834*
Novels and Society from Manley to Edgeworth
CAROLINE GONDA

20. *Romantic Identities: Varieties of Subjectivity, 1774–1830*
ANDREA K. HENDERSON

21. *Print Politics*
The Press and Radical Opposition in Early Nineteenth-Century England
KEVIN GILMARTIN

22. *Reinventing Allegory*
THERESA M. KELLEY

23. *British Satire and the Politics of Style, 1789–1832*
GARY DYER

24. *The Romantic Reformation: Religious Politics in English Literature, 1789–1824*
ROBERT M. RYAN

25. *De Quincey's Romanticism: Canonical Minority and the Forms of Transmission*
MARGARET RUSSETT

26. *Coleridge on Dreaming: Romanticism, Dreams and the Medical Imagination*
JENNIFER FORD

27. *Romantic Imperialism: Universal Empire and the Culture of Modernity*
SAREE MAKDISI

28. *Ideology and Utopia in the Poetry of William Blake*
NICHOLAS M. WILLIAMS

29. *Sexual Politics and the Romantic Author*
SONIA HOFKOSH

30. *Lyric and Labour in the Romantic Tradition*
ANNE JANOWITZ

31. *Poetry and Politics in the Cockney School: Keats, Shelley, Hunt and their Circle*
JEFFREY N. COX

32. *Rousseau, Robespierre and English Romanticism*
GREGORY DART

33. *Contesting the Gothic: Fiction, Genre and Cultural Conflict, 1764–1832*
JAMES WATT

34. *Romanticism, Aesthetics, and Nationalism*
DAVID ARAM KAISER

35. *Romantic Poets and the Culture of Posterity*
ANDREW BENNETT

36. *The Crisis of Literature in the 1790s: Print Culture and the Public Sphere*
PAUL KEEN

37. *Romantic Atheism: Poetry and Freethought, 1780–1830*
MARTIN PRIESTMAN

38. *Romanticism and Slave Narratives: Transatlantic Testimonies*
HELEN THOMAS

39. *Imagination Under Pressure, 1789–1832: Aesthetics, Politics, and Utility*
JOHN WHALE

40. *Romanticism and the Gothic*
Genre, Reception, and Canon Formation, 1790–1820
MICHAEL GAMER

41. *Romanticism and the Human Sciences*
Poetry, Population, and the Discourse of the Species
MAUREEN N. MCLANE

42. *The Poetics of Spice: Romantic Consumerism and the Exotic*
TIMOTHY MORTON

43. *British Fiction and the Production of Social Order, 1740–1830*
MIRANDA J. BURGESS

44. *Women Writers and the English Nation in the 1790s*
ANGELA KEANE

45. *Literary Magazines and British Romanticism*
MARK PARKER

46. *Women, Nationalism and the Romantic Stage*
Theatre and Politics in Britain, 1780–1800
BETSY BOLTON

47. *British Romanticism and the Science of the Mind*
ALAN RICHARDSON

48. *The Anti-Jacobin Novel: British Conservatism and the French Revolution*
M. O. GRENBY

49. *Romantic Austen: Sexual Politics and the Literary Canon*
CLARA TUITE

50. *Byron and Romanticism*
JEROME MCGANN ED. JAMES SODERHOLM